FRONTLINE
PRESS LTD.

Banana Republic Revisited

75 Years of Madness, Mayhem & Minigolf in

MYRTLE BEACH

Will Moredock

Frontline Press, Ltd. / Charleston, S.C.

Jacket photos: Jack Thompson
Cover Design & Technical Assistance: Maryam Naderi
Interior Design: Julie Burnett & Maryam Naderi

Moredock, Will.
    Banana republic Revisited: 75 Years of Madness, Mayhem & Minigolf in
Myrtle Beach / by Will Moredock.
    p.cm.
    Includes bibliographical references and index.
    ISBN 978-0-9723829-2-2
    Library of Congress Control Number: 2015906792

    1. Myrtle Beach (S.C.)   I. Title.

10 percent of all sales of this book go to the
Jack Thompson Photographic Trust

To Jimmy Chandler

1949 - 2010

May his work continue

More Praise for *Banana Republic*

"Moredock manages the lurid story in a conversational style that makes for captivating reading."

John Grooms, *Creative Loafing*

"Moredock is nothing if not entertaining. He is also a thorough researcher and sentimentalist, all of which come together to make his book, *Banana Republic: A Year in the Heart of Myrtle Beach,* a complex and touching memoir."

M.L. van Valkenbugh, *Charleston City Paper*

"What a clever writer is Will Moredock.
"There you are, pleasantly reading about nude dancers, drugs, tattoo artists, body piercing, poker machine casinos and the high life. Then, you realize that for some 100 pages you've been reading about urban planning and zoning. You have been seduced."

Terry Calhoun, *The State Port Pilot*

"It remains my firm assessment that Will Moredock came to Myrtle Beach and Horry County with the general intent of trashing the community, trashing Burroughs & Chapin Co. and denigrating many other aspects of life here."

Pat Dowling, Burroughs & Chapin Co.

That California get-rich-quick disease of my youth
spread like wildfire; and it produced a civilization
which has destroyed the simplicity and repose of life,
its poetry, its soft romantic dreams and visions, and
replaced them with the money fever, sordid ideals,
vulgar ambitions. . . and the sleep which does not
refresh. It has created a thousand useless luxuries
and turned them into necessities and satisfied. . .
nothing. It has dethroned God and set up a shekel in
his place. Oh, the dreams of our youth, how beautiful
they are. And how perishable.

— Mark Twain

Know ye the land where the cypress and myrtle
Are emblems of deeds that are done in their clime?
Where the rage of the vulture, the love of the turtle,
Now melt into sorrow, now madden to crime?. . .

— George Gordon, Lord Byron

Be careful what you wish for — you just might get it.

— Proverb

Contents

Introduction –
Myrtle Beach, Ten Years Later

There is magic in Myrtle Beach. Millions of people feel it. They come to this golden stretch of Carolina sand each year to get a piece of it. With their dollars and their sheer numbers they have transformed this once remote southern backwater into one of the top tourist destinations in America.

The word I most associate with Myrtle Beach is youth. It is the place where people of a certain age come to feel young again, to relive a moment that slipped away long before. It is the place where spring-breakers, bikers, honeymooners, and young runaways come to create their own moments and memories, which they will carry for the rest of their lives. Youth is the essence of Myrtle Beach. It is the city that never grows old. It cannot age because it is constantly being reborn. Bulldozers are always at the ready, standing by to sweep away some house, hotel or store that has outlived its usefulness, that has become dowdy or unfashionable. In its place will rise something gleaming and modern, something with little context or tradition, something immediate and momentary, like all of Myrtle Beach.

Myrtle Beach is always changing, always churning. This is what makes it such a magnet to über-capitalists, to the young and the transient, and so appalling to so many others. And yet, for all the physical change, little seems to change in terms of attitudes and values. Myrtle Beach has been described as South Carolina on steroids. Horry is one of the most Republican counties in the United States. There is deep suspicion here of environmental regulation, cultural diversity, of democracy itself.

For all of Myrtle Beach's modern architecture and modern problems, it seems curiously trapped in the past, in its own adolescence. And like any adolescent, it is constantly fretting about its image, trying to create its identity.

On the one hand, it wants to be an international tourist destination; on the other, it fights to remain a small town with Southern Baptist ways and traditions. Only two decades ago did the town get around to legalizing Sunday alcohol sales. And in the last year a local big-box store yanked all copies of atheist author Christopher Hitchens's international bestseller, *God Is Not Great*, off the shelves within an hour of a customer's complaining and threatening to organize a boycott.

In the spring of 2013, hackles went up along the Grand Strand as TLC Network premiered a reality show called "Welcome to Myrtle Manor," which followed the conflicts, crises and bad behavior of an extended family of local fools, who operated a trailer park, hair salon and hot dog business, amid bickering, brawling, drinking and courting. The show was roundly condemned by TV critics for being tasteless and stupid and by local residents for being phony and misrepresenting Myrtle Beach. All charges were true.

Myrtle Beach remains an enigma to itself as much as to the world. The eternal adolescent is strangely jaded and cynical. It frets and fusses and snarls at its critics, but the sun is always over its shoulder, the waves break and sparkle on its beaches and being there lets me feel young and adventurous and innocent again. That's what keeps me and millions like me coming back.

Frontline Press released *Banana Republic: A Year in the Heart of Myrtle Beach* in October 2003. *Banana Republic* was my report on one year in this fabled city – 1999. Ten years later, with Myrtle Beach celebrating its seventy-fifth birthday, I thought it was time to bring out my book again with an updated introduction, examining some of the issues of the last decade.

In about four hundred pages, *Banana Republic* presented an unprecedented historical, political and social profile of the town, along with the corporate shenanigans which kept its politics fractious and its growth frenetic and uncontrolled. To write this book, I moved to downtown Myrtle Beach in 1999 and spent three years researching. The book sold well and got generally good reviews everywhere but in the offices of the Burroughs & Chapin Co., which created the town and still dominated its politics and growth in 1999. In an op-ed column in the Myrtle Beach *Sun News*, then-

B&C spokesman Pat Dowling wrote, in January 2004, "It is my assessment that Will Moredock came to Myrtle Beach and Horry County with the general intent of trashing the community, trashing Burroughs & Chapin Co. and denigrating many other aspects of life here."

As with so many of his assessments, Pat Dowling was wrong. I did not come to Myrtle Beach in 1999 with the intent of trashing anything, but that did not stop me from using his gratuitous comment in marketing my book.

Sun News columnist Bob Bestler devoted a couple of nice columns to *Banana Republic* and there were several other favorable mentions there. But local broadcast media seemed to take the position that it was their responsibility to protect the public from bad news. I had no luck getting air time on local radio talk shows. One television station scheduled me for an interview, then called at the last minute, saying they had a conflict and would have to reschedule. Of course, they never called back and never returned my calls. Another station kept putting me off, but requested a copy of my book every time I called. I sent them three or four copies over several weeks before they informed me that the book had been out too long to be newsworthy.

In the years following publication of *Banana Republic*, the nation has seen a dramatic economic downturn; Myrtle Beach and the Burroughs & Chapin Co. are no exceptions. B&C has fallen on hard times, in part because of the recession, in part because CEO Doug Wendel backed some bad development projects. The company has greatly reduced staff and has moved its corporate headquarters out of the prestigious Founders Centre on Oak Street and into a former real estate sales office in the Grande Dunes development. Along the way, Wendel and his sidekick Pat Dowling were both replaced. B&C stuck with its new CEO less than two years before bringing in James W. Apple, in 2010. Observers are trying to divine B&C's new corporate strategy. Early in 2013, the company sold ten thousand acres of inland real estate, land it had held for decades and, it was assumed, would ultimately develop. A few weeks later it plunked down $43 million to purchase Barefoot Landing, the huge North Myrtle Beach shopping and entertainment center, which competes directly with its own Broadway at the Beach complex.

Myrtle Beach was hit hard by the Great Recession. When American families lose their paychecks, one thing they discover they can live without is a long-distance vacation, or even a long weekend at the beach. Those who did come to Myrtle Beach scaled down their visits, spending more time in their hotel rooms, eating take-out pizza and ramen noodles, watching DVDs and playing video games.

Golf is huge in Myrtle Beach and it was suffering even before the economic downturn. South Carolina has approximately three hundred and sixty golf courses. A third of those courses are along the Grand Strand; fifty-one percent of traveling golfers in S.C. tee up in the Myrtle Beach area.

In 2004, Grand Strand golf courses saw more than four million paid rounds. They have not reached that number since. Green fees are down and twenty courses closed between 2005 and 2007. Paid rounds have increased somewhat from the depth of the recession, but they have been flat for the years 2010 through 2012, according to Myrtle Beach Golf Holiday, the local marketing conglomerate.

One thing that perennially holds back Myrtle Beach tourism is the lack of direct and dependable air service from points north. Myrtle Beach-based Direct Air became the latest local carrier to leave the market when it abruptly stopped flying and filed for bankruptcy in March 2012. This was particularly hard on the local golf industry, which depends on air service to bring many of its players to the area. As I wrote in *Banana Republic*, ". . . sixty-four percent of Grand Strand golfers were from out of state. . . a fact not lost on anyone who has stood in baggage claim at Myrtle Beach International Airport and watched the golf bags glide down the conveyor."

But Myrtle Beach is nothing if not resilient. It has weathered hurricanes, bad press and economic downturns for decades and always comes back stronger, if not necessarily wiser. Tourist numbers were down 7.5 percent between 2007 and 2009, with tourists spending less per capita than they had before the recession. By the spring of 2013, the recovery was complete, according to the State Department of Parks, Recreation and Tourism; Myrtle Beach was once again setting tourism records.

Likewise, the recession took its toll on the Grand Strand's phenomenal growth. Nearly 12,000 residential building permits were issued in Horry County in 2005. That number collapsed with the recession and by 2011 (the last year for which numbers are available) they were still languishing at 1,491. By spring 2013, single-family home sales had rebounded. *The Sun News* reported that closings for single-family homes along the strand in May stood at 473, just twenty-seven fewer than in May 2006, and 126 fewer than closed in September 2005, the highest monthly closings ever. But even in the face of this good news, Myrtle Beach had the nation's eighth-highest foreclosure rate among metropolitan areas, according to RealtyTrac.

When I moved to Myrtle Beach in 1999, the skyline along the beautiful Strand was pierced by numerous construction cranes erecting new and ever-higher towers to accommodate the rising tide of tourists. Construction cranes along the beach were as much a part of the local scenery as the single-engine airplanes which flew up and down the coast with banners advertising seafood buffets and two-for-one T-shirt deals. But with the recession the cranes had vanished from the Strand.

By March 2013, construction was on the rebound. *The Sun News* reported that the Grand Strand would soon get its first new beachfront hotel in four years, a fourteen-story tower on South Ocean Boulevard. There were also plans for a new marina on the north end of the Strand and the first new fishing pier in decades. Myrtle Beach was back!

Standing in the 900 block of Ocean Boulevard on a chilly morning in March 2013, the evidence of change was all around. Most stunning was the disappearance of the famed Pavilion Amusement Park, an institution and a legend since 1948. The Burroughs & Chapin Co. had built and nurtured the park for over half a century, alternately threatening to close it down for more lucrative development and to keep it open as an act of philanthropy.

In 1998, Doug Wendel told *The New York Times*, "If we were not the magnanimous, loving, caring company that we are, we would abandon [the Pavilion]." In 2013, the eleven acres of empty Ocean Boulevard property stood as a weedy reminder of B&C's magnanimous, loving, caring nature. To see that huge, empty, dark lot on a summer evening, when all around it is lights and noise and life, is like gazing into a hole in the fabric of the universe. A large zipline, with six parallel six-hundred-foot lines, now occupies the eastern end of the lot, adjacent to the Kings Highway, but it is no substitute for the great summer carnival which occupied the spot for more than fifty years.

The Pavilion Amusement Park was dismantled after the 2006 season with plans on the drawing board for a huge, upscale condo and retail complex that would transform Ocean Boulevard. Then the housing bubble burst, taking much of the economy with it. Weeds were growing along much of Ocean Boulevard in early 2013, evidence of others who had miscalculated. They got the land cleared, only to see their capital vanish. There were now weeds and parking lots where Mother Fletcher's club, where Bon Villa, Pier View and other seedy oceanfront motels had stood a few years before. Bali Bay, a five-story oceanfront condominium complex, was ninety percent complete in 2009, when capital dried up and the developer shut it down. In 2013, it stood with weeds and chain-link fence around its footings, an eyesore in the heart of the tourist district. On the bright side, there has been a small burst of private residential development along South Ocean Boulevard for the first time in decades. But these are not the cozy cottages that lined the boulevard so many years ago. These are houses, sitting atop tall flood pilings, and the prices start at $300,000.

In 1999, Myrtle Beach was looking to jump-start its declining downtown business district, and at the top of its to-do list was a new boardwalk. The debate over downtown redevelopment was long and contentious, but in May 2010 the Myrtle Beach Boardwalk & Promenade opened to great fanfare and has received rave reviews ever since. The 1.2-mile boardwalk cost $6.4 million, and was immediately ranked by *National Geographic* magazine as the number three boardwalk in the nation, behind Atlantic City and Coney Island. In June 2013, *USA Today* ranked Myrtle Beach's boardwalk food number fifteen in the nation.

The crown jewel on the new boardwalk is the SkyWheel. Standing 187 feet high, it is the tallest Ferris wheel in the eastern United States, has forty-two enclosed gondolas, and is illuminated by a million LED lights. It goes nicely with the new Slingshot Bungee attraction directly across Ocean Boulevard.

City manager Tom Leath told *The Sun News* that the SkyWheel is "big enough to be an iconic feature for the city." So was the Ocean Forest Hotel and the Pavilion, but each was demolished to make way for something more mundane and profitable. It will be interesting to see how long the SkyWheel lasts.

Horry remains one of the fastest growing counties in the nation. The 2010 census recorded 269,291 souls, a thirty-seven percent increase over the 2000 count. Such stunning growth brought predictable pains. The massive road-building projects described in *Banana Republic* were becoming inadequate by 2013. Now planners were pushing ahead with the next generation of asphalt, but they encountered the usual problems. Taxpayers wanted roads, but they didn't want to pay for them; and there were always the environmental concerns. Development has ravaged the fragile ecosystem of the southeastern coast for decades and rarely has development been more brutal than in Horry County. The county is run largely by and for developers and the Republican establishment is there to do their bidding. At a GOP candidates' debate in March 2013, the mention of local environmental activist Nancy Cave drew boos and snorts.

Likewise, the building boom to accommodate all the new residents produced a lot of shoddy housing, and rental and sales scams. In 2005, at the height of the housing boom, bartenders and taxi drivers were flipping houses. There was an average wait of eighty-five days on the market for the sale of single family homes and eleven days for condos, according to *The Sun News*. In a state noted for its low standards of consumer protection, the state legislature lowered those standards in 2005, by reducing from thirteen years to eight a home builder's liability for shoddy work.

The Burroughs & Chapin Co. has faced multiple claims of mold in their new, high-end Marina Inn condos at Grande Dunes. They are hardly alone. The courts have seen much litigation over condos and construction practices in the past decade.

LegalMatch.com offers a local website that promises to help locate "Myrtle Beach Construction Dispute Lawyers." "Because of the large cost in time and money involved, litigation in Myrtle Beach, South Carolina, is considered a last resort," the site says. "However, in rare cases, it does become necessary."

Golf provides a vivid example of the cycles and excesses of Myrtle Beach development. In *Banana Republic*, I told the story of Myrtle Beach golf from the first course − Pine Lakes, in 1930 − to the turn of the century, when Myrtle Beach crossed that prestigious threshold of one hundred courses. At that time many of the courses were being built not to meet a demand for golf, but to sell real estate. The prestige of living on a golf course can still fetch top dollar for a home site and can still cloud buyers' minds with images of a fairway in their backyard.

The result was inevitable. Between 2005 and 2007, the saturated Grand Strand golf market shrank from approximately one hundred and twenty courses back to a hundred. Lawyers got rich as homeowners filled the courts with suits against developers. Home builders rushed in, slicing off pieces of closed golf courses to feed the housing boom. Of course, the housing boom subsequently went bust, but much of the litigation continues today.

One of the strangest stories I reported in *Banana Republic* was the great Air Force base land grab. In the early 1990s, the Defense Department started shutting down unneeded military bases around the country. One of them was Myrtle Beach Air Force Base, in operation since the early days of World War II.

With the closure of the base, many players jumped into the game to get a piece of more than four thousand acres of choice real estate in the middle of the Grand Strand. One of them was a young hustler named Robert Blackburn, president of Timberland Properties, Inc. Blackburn had the plan to develop a world-class theme park called Isle of America, replete with a luxury hotel, golf villas, twenty-seven holes of golf, an amphitheater, and jobs for some twenty-five hundred. He had the backing of Governor Carroll Campbell and other state wheelers and dealers.

Blackburn appeared to be a thirty-five-year-old magician, a promoter with a silver tongue, a golden Rolodex and the ability to make anything happen. He certainly had the ability to lure local investors into his dream with their retirement savings and pensions. He dropped big names of potential partners, including Michael Jackson and a billionaire Saudi oil prince.

Deadlines passed and no construction was begun on Isle of America. Finally, it became obvious that the emperor had no clothes – at least Robert Blackburn had no money and no one was coming forward to bail him out. TPI declared bankruptcy in 1997, after Blackburn and his corporate cronies had spent two years living like princes off their small investors. Dozens of local people lost $2.5 million on Blackburn's fantasy, but no one went to jail or was even charged with any misbehavior. It was just business as usual in South Carolina.

The silver lining behind the Isle of America fantasy was what has come about in its place over the last decade and a half. Had Isle of America been born, there would have been no space for a major expansion of Myrtle Beach International Airport and Horry-Georgetown Technical College, no space for the International Technology and Aerospace Park and, most impressively, I think, for The Market Common, a dazzling new urban village of shopping and affordable housing that city leaders had been trying to get off the ground since the 1990s.

Curiously, someone else came forward in the last decade to build a new mega theme park in Myrtle Beach. It was called Hard Rock Park, located on some fifty-five acres in Fantasy Harbour, between U.S. 501 and the Intracoastal Waterway. Fantasy Harbour itself was a complex of failed country music, ice skating and other theaters which blossomed briefly in the 1990s. The huge Hard Rock entertainment complex contained five – count 'em, *five!* – roller coasters, all with a pop music theme, as the brand would imply. There were numerous other rides and shows, of course, and plans for an enormous Hard Rock Hotel.

Unlike Isle of America, this $400 million boondoggle was built and opened for business in the spring of 2008, just in time for the great housing bubble collapse. In that regard, it was an echo of the legendary Ocean Forest Hotel. Billed as the grandest hotel between Atlantic City and Miami Beach, the Ocean Forest opened in Myrtle Beach on February 21, 1930, four months after the stock market collapse. The magnificent hotel went into receivership and passed through a series of owners until it was destroyed in a dynamite implosion in 1974.

According to *The Sun News,* Hard Rock Park was the dream of Dick Rosen, the former CEO of Myrtle Beach-based electronic parts maker AVXCorp. Rosen brought on board major international real estate developers and speculators, creating Myrtle Property Owners to execute the plan. There was a wildly optimistic prospectus showing gross earnings in that first year of nearly $62 million. That would mean bringing more than three million people a year through their gates – or nearly nine thousand people a day, every day of the year, even in fall and winter!

The Burroughs & Chapin Co. had long before done a feasibility study and determined that a year-round theme park would not work in Myrtle Beach, but these hustlers apparently never heard of it, or didn't care.

Hard Rock Park opened in April 2008 and it was immediately

clear that the park was not making its numbers. The fall was precipitous and breathtaking. At the end of the summer the $400 million park closed its gates and sought bankruptcy protection. A group of investors snatched it up for $25 million, rebranded it Freestyle Music Park and reopened for the summer of 2009. It was all for naught. Freestyle closed after one season and the park has sat silent and empty for four years. Several parties have shown passing interest in the property, but at mid-2013 no one had moved on it.

That has not stopped the litigation. According to *The Sun News*, Myrtle Property Owners said in court filings that Rosen Investments and the theme park developers "consistently and egregiously misrepresented financial and other details of the theme park project as well as its overall likelihood of success.... The inaccuracy of Rosen's representations was something that was known to South Carolina local residents such as Rosen, but not to claimants, who did not live in South Carolina."

Myrtle Beach never goes long without a major public dispute. As I documented in *Banana Republic*, that dispute in 1999 was Burroughs & Chapin's monstrous multicounty business park, by which it screwed Horry County Schools out of millions of dollars in revenue and Horry County and Myrtle Beach councils were totally complicit. The business park battle divided the county, its leaders and institutions, and the schools are still suffering the consequences.

In 2013, the public fracas involves the Myrtle Beach Area Chamber of Commerce, which is accused of being involved in a pay-to-play scheme, paying off politicians to support a local option sales tax. The IRS and the FBI investigated the political donations, but no charges have been filed.

The scandal has resonances from the past. Shortly after I started researching *Banana Republic* in 1999, word hit the street that federal investigators were in town asking questions about certain politicians and business people. Some of my sources assumed that I was one of those feds and dropped me cold.

More sad than scandalous is the recent news from Atlantic Beach. In *Banana Republic*, I wrote about the history and ongoing tragedy of this tiny, historically black beach town, surrounded on three sides by North Myrtle Beach. In 1999, Atlantic Beach was wrestling with the same issues black municipalities all over the country were facing: crime, corruption, declining population, lack of resources to maintain basic services.

In May 2013, Mayor Retha Pierce, aged sixty-three, was booked into jail on a charge of third-degree assault and battery against a town council member. It was only Pierce's latest run-in with the law. As *The Sun News* reported, she had faced a number of charges over the years, including driving under the influence, resisting arrest, trespassing and hit-and-run. Most of the charges were eventually dropped, but they were part of a bigger pattern of misconduct involving town officials, ranging from bribery to election fraud to various felonies and misdemeanors, dating back many years. Some suggested that the state might mercifully put the town out of its misery by revoking its charter.

After the Pierce arrest, *The Sun News* editorialized, "We've written so many times about the leadership woes of Atlantic Beach over the years that frankly it's becoming hard to get worked up about the latest indiscretion by Pierce or her compatriots in town. We imagine readers are becoming just as tired.... We've said it before – and we'll no doubt say it again – but there seems little prospect of the town fixing its own problems. Outside help is sorely needed."

Atlantic Beach, once a symbol of black pride, has sadly become an embarrassment to all associated with it. It represents one more chapter in Horry County's sorry history of race relations, which still plays out in public policy and private behavior.

Horry County is a mere eight percent black in a state that is approximately thirty percent black. Retirees tilt the demographic heavily to the older end of the spectrum, while the service economy attracts a blue-collar workforce. In short, Horry is the perfect breeding ground for Republicans, and they dominate its politics and culture. In 2008, John McCain carried the county with sixty-two percent of the vote; in 2012, Mitt Romney took sixty-four percent.

Despite all denials, Republicanism and racism walk hand in hand through Horry County, as they do throughout the South. After the 2008 presidential election, a source told me, there was something close to fury among local white residents. Some of them greeted one another – even strangers – with racist denunciations of Barack Obama. Shortly after the election, GOP state Rep. Alan Clemmons, of Myrtle Beach, addressed a gathering of Republicans, denouncing the "busloads of voters" who came to the polls in the day before the election to cast absentee ballots. Clemmons didn't have to say who was on those buses. To the consternation of white politicians, black churches have been using their vehicles to get their members to the polls for generations. African Americans call this practice "souls to the polls." But among certain whites, the phrase "busloads of voters" — like "welfare queen" — has become code for black.

Shortly after his remarks, Clemmons introduced a voter ID bill at the State House in Columbia, with the not-so-subtle purpose of reducing the number of voters on buses. Voter ID eventually passed the House, but it was largely de-fanged by the Senate before it reached the Governor's desk.

With the 2010 census, South Carolina gained a seventh congressional seat for the first time since 1930. No one was surprised when the GOP legislature drew up the new district centered on Horry County. And no one was surprised when a raft of Republican candidates declared for the seat, because the winner of the GOP primary was going to be the first representative from the new district.

That candidate was Tom Rice, a local real estate lawyer who only two years before had been elected chairman of Horry County Council. As county council chairman, he was regarded as moderate and pragmatic, but as a congressional candidate in a crowded GOP field, he made a hard right turn, established his credentials with local tea party groups, took the Republican nomination in a runoff and won the general election against a little known Democrat, with fifty-five percent of the vote.

Tom Rice materialized on the political scene in 2008, with the creation of a grassroots movement of Myrtle Beach residents aimed at taming the two monstrous motorcycle rallies that descended on the city each year. In *Banana Republic*, I described in some detail the siege of the Harley Davidson Rally and the Atlantic Beach Memorial Day Bike Festival.

The ten-day Harley event started in mid-May and was followed almost immediately by the four-day Memorial Day Bike Festival. The two rallies together drew over half a million bikers and their wives, girlfriends, families, groupies, camp-followers and hangers-on. The bikers and their friends were a rowdy lot and their sheer numbers clogged the roads and streets for the better part of a month. The sound of motorcycles reverberated through the city, night and day, without interruption. Locals would go for weeks without a good night's sleep. A number of bikers were killed in accidents every year. Many Grand Strand residents with time and means simply left the area each May to avoid the mayhem, violence and noise. While some bars and strip clubs did a land office business during the biker rallies, many restaurants, golf courses and family amusements lost money as regular tourists stayed away in droves.

Criticism of the bike rallies took on a distinctly racial tone. The Atlantic Beach Memorial Day Bike Festival was composed of young

African Americans on sport bikes. Their rowdy behavior drew most of the anger and venom from local residents. A number of restaurants and motels along the Strand started closing over the Memorial Day Weekend, rather than deal with the Memorial Day bikers.

In 2003, a group of black bikers, along with the South Carolina chapter of the National Association for the Advancement of Colored People, sued the City of Myrtle Beach and a number of local and national franchise restaurants for discrimination. Three years later, the NAACP triumphed in every federal discrimination suit it brought against businesses and the City of Myrtle Beach. The Myrtle Beach police department was required to use the same traffic patterns to control biker traffic on Ocean Boulevard during the Harley-Davidson Rally and the Memorial Day Festival.

The 2008 bike rallies were unusually rowdy and on the last day of the Memorial Day Festival, a Coastal Carolina University student was shot and killed downtown in a dispute over a parking space. As it turned out, the dispute and killing did not involve any bikers, but coming as it did, with nerves raw and patience exhausted, it provided the catalyst that residents had been waiting for.

Within days, angry citizens descended on a city council meeting to demand action against the bike rallies. Their organization was called Take Back May and their leader was Tom Rice. Myrtle Beach City Council voted to raise property taxes to pay for anti-rally efforts. Over the next year, the council passed a number of ordinances aimed at making the Myrtle Beach experience as unpleasant as possible for motorcyclists. These included laws against loitering in downtown parking lots, new restrictions on muffler noise, restrictions on vendors in the city limits and − most onerous and most controversial − an ordinance requiring all motorcycle riders to wear helmets.

The City was dragged into court over the new rules and most of them − including the helmet law − were eventually struck down. Along the way, the City spent hundreds of thousands of dollars in litigation in addition to the hundreds of thousands it had spent fighting the NAACP suits a few years before.

While Myrtle Beach lost the legal battles, the Harley riders got the message that they were no longer wanted and they have largely stayed away in recent years. As the 2013 Harley event approached, a number of local merchants made special effort to lure as many bikers as possible into the city and into their businesses. Numbers for the Harley rally have been slowly returning in the last four years, but they are far from what they were in 2008. One effect is that recent Harley rallies have been quieter, tamer, and less troublesome for police and residents. No bikers were killed in the 2013 Harley-Davidson Rally for the first time anyone can remember.

The Atlantic Beach Memorial Day Festival is another matter. Numbers remain high; behavior remains rowdy and deadly. Six bikers were killed in Horry County over the Memorial Day Weekend, half of the traffic fatalities for the entire state. Five of those fatalities were inside the Myrtle Beach city limits.

According to *The Sun New,* Myrtle Beach police arrested a twenty-seven-year-old Georgia woman for shaking "her bare bottom" while riding on the back of a motorcycle. The driver of the motorcycle, also from Georgia, was charged with "racing the motorcycle's engine unnecessarily for the woman to shake her butt," the newspaper reported. What *The Sun News* scribe witnessed was an amusement called "bouncing," which I described on page 116 of *Banana Republic*: "A woman riding behind the driver must lean forward and put her arms around the man's waist, thrusting her butt up in a provocative manner. . . . Drivers would race their engines while holding the brake, causing their bikes to shimmy from end to end. Their women's upturned butts would bounce like jelly, as men closed in with their cameras."

The campaign to drive the bikers away – at least the Harley-Davidson riders – proved divisive. While the average Myrtle Beach resident wanted to be able to sleep and use his roads and streets in safety, a loud and angry minority of people in the hospitality business decried the lost revenue. They called themselves BOOST – Business Owners Organized to Save Tourism – and their leader and spokesman was former mayor Mark McBride, who made himself the subject of much of *Banana Republic*.

I described McBride as a demagogue of preternatural instincts, a shrewd, manipulative office seeker, a disastrous office holder. Since then I have come to see him in a larger context. McBride is an American archetype, a man of limited skills or education (a degree in hotel and restaurant management from the University of South Carolina), but infinite ambition, who seeks to make his way in the world through politics. In McBride's case, he had endured several failed restaurant ventures and a brief fling at real estate before he was elected mayor in 1997, at age thirty-three. He was an instinctive populist and opportunist, always making himself the spokesman for the angry and resentful. He built his early career intoning piously against Gay Pride events in Myrtle Beach, against the Atlantic Beach Memorial Day Bike Festival, against the influence of the Burroughs & Chapin Co. It was not surprising to see that he had hooked up with BOOST by 2010.

As a candidate, McBride was tall, handsome, and articulate. His manner of speech was measured and moderate. He seemed like a breath of fresh air in a city hall full of good old boys. But as mayor, he proved to be uncompromising, sanctimonious, and devious.

And he scored points with his right-wing Christian base by defending "traditional values." Here is what he told *The Sun News* about gays and lesbians: "We are going to set our community standards. We don't want this garbage on the Boulevard. . . I don't believe that kind of activity should take place in a family entertainment area. What you do privately is your own business, but I don't want to end up seeing transvestites and drag queens and people being led around on leashes in dog collars. . . I don't want to be a gay basher. But I'm not carrying their flag."

McBride proposed an illegal and unenforceable ordinance to keep the Atlantic Beach Memorial Day Bike Festival out of town. He called for using the National Guard to control black bikers. It won him scorn and scolding from city council members and editors of *The Sun News*, but his base loved it.

At the same time McBride was preaching morality to the city and trying to enforce it with the National Guard, he was using the city credit card for family vacations and keeping city travel money for personal use. When *The Sun News* brought this fact to light, he was forced to pay arrears – interest-free. And there were other financial irregularities as well as abuse of his city cell phone privileges.

His relationships with council members and city staff were so contentious and abusive that council had to pass rules to control the mayor's behavior. But even this did not prevent Mark McBride and Councilman Wayne Gray from famously coming to blows in 1999.

McBride won reelection in 2001, running against Wayne Gray. The victory seemed to confirm in his mind that he was a man of destiny. The next year, when centenarian Strom Thurmond retired from the U.S. Senate, McBride joined a host of Republican candidates vying to replace him. He was vastly overspent, overwhelmed and over his head, taking only two percent of the vote in the GOP primary. Lindsay Graham went on to take the nomination and the Senate seat.

Two years later McBride was in the GOP primary to succeed Senator Fritz Hollings and he did no better than before, gaining two percent of the vote. Jim DeMint won the nomination and went to the Senate.

By 2005, Myrtle Beach voters had had enough of the mayor's bad behavior and overweening ambition. They put him out in favor of businessman and sports promoter John Rhodes.

But McBride had not tasted enough defeat. In 2008, he did not have the $10,158 filing fee for another U.S. Senate race, so he tried to get 10,000 signatures, which would put him on the ballot to challenge Graham in the Republican primary. He made it an ugly campaign against Hispanics and immigration reform, but he failed to gain the necessary signatures and Graham won easy reelection.

During that campaign *The Sun News* editorialized: "The important question about McBride. . .is whether he could actually be a senator. The gentleman, shall we say, is mercurial. During his terms as mayor, he often evinced a short attention span and was on the losing end of a goodly number of 6-1 City Council votes."

McBride lost a comeback attempt against John Rhodes in 2009. Along with his political defeats he had two more restaurant failures and his wife left him. He has struggled to keep his hand in politics, but his career seems to be over. The last I heard, he was waiting tables at a high-end restaurant in North Myrtle Beach.

My last encounter with McBride was on election night 2005, in the Myrtle Beach council chamber, where the votes were being counted and McBride watched his political career come crashing down. Our relationship was never warm and after *Banana Republic* was published in 2003, his dislike of me could only have deepened. I did not approach him in the crowd that evening; I had no idea what to say. But in that moment – surely one of the most painful of his life – he walked over, shook my hand and wished me well. It was a moment of grace and humanity in the worst of circumstances. That's the way I wish to remember Mark McBride.

I will also mention "Kevin," the bright and spirited waif I met on the Boulevard in the summer of '99. Kevin's mother was an alcoholic who spent her evenings in local dives while her twelve-year-old son spent his days and nights hanging out on the Boulevard, getting in trouble with the law and eventually getting kicked out of school. The Department of Social Services took him into custody, placing him first in a supervised home for boys in Conway, then in another home near Columbia. His mother abandoned him without notice and moved to Florida. I tried to keep in touch with Kevin by phone for some weeks after he was taken away, until a DSS caseworker ordered me to have no further contact with him.

In preparing this book, I was able to find Kevin online. He is living in the upper Midwest, where he has had a couple of minor run-ins with the law – not surprising for someone of his background. We communicated briefly through Facebook in August 2013. In his initial Facebook message to me he wrote: "My life has turned from a crap chute of young and dumb, into a most successful and happy present. I have a girlfriend of 71/2 years, that I love and cherish dearly. We have a beautiful little girl together... along with her daughter from a previous relationship..."

There was more in a phone conversation that followed. Kevin appears to be healing himself with love and a small, quiet town far from the madness of Myrtle Beach. He is a testimony to the power of the human spirit to rebuild a broken life.

Finally, I would like to say a few words about environmental lawyer Jimmy Chandler. I interviewed Chandler a couple of times when I was researching *Banana Republic* in 1999 and 2000. He was warm and low-key, deeply knowledgeable about the law and passionate about the environment.

For nearly three decades he waged a David-vs.-Goliath battle against huge corporations and developers, winning more than his share of the battles. In 1991, he forced a large paper mill to reduce the level of dioxin it discharged into the Sampit River, outside Georgetown. In 2000, he used the law to shut down a massive hazardous waste landfill on the shores of Lake Marion. He transformed coastal dredging regulations and won many other victories through his tiny nonprofit, the S.C. Environmental Law Project.

Jimmy Chandler died of cancer in 2010. He was sixty years old and left a sterling legacy of service and friendship.

The State newspaper of Columbia wrote this: "Since the early 1980s, the unflappable Chandler had been the face of environmental law in South Carolina's Lowcountry and a leading advocate of protecting the marshes, beaches, rivers and lakes that define the Palmetto State."

Chandler could have made vastly more money playing the other side, lobbying and litigating on behalf of polluters and despoilers, but he chose to stand on the side of reason, community and the Earth. He represented the best in all of us. That is why I dedicate this book to him.

A Winter Night by the Sea

Myrtle Beach still haunts my memory. Not the Myrtle Beach of high-rise hotels and theme restaurants and crawling, honking traffic. No, the Myrtle Beach that returns in my dreams is a little town on the dunes, where modest frame houses with broad front porches lined up along Ocean Boulevard, where the small hotels were owned and operated by long-time residents or by retired couples from Long Island or Schenectady. This is the Myrtle Beach I remember, the place where my family came for summer vacations in the 1950s, the place where I first glimpsed the ocean, tasted cotton candy and rode a Ferris wheel. Years later I cruised the Boulevard and checked out the clubs with buddies from the University of Georgia.

The Myrtle Beach of my memory bears little resemblance to the sprawling, multi-billion dollar resort that drew thirteen million people in 1998. I am a witness to that little town of sand and coquina streets, of bungalows that were cooled by electric fans and the ocean breeze sweeping through open windows and screened porches, where dolphins danced just beyond the breakers and my family caught blue crabs in the tidal creeks and walked back to our rented house to boil them up on the kitchen stove. There isn't much left of that town except the name – and the memories.

After college, I went for years without finding my way back to Myrtle Beach, but wherever I lived, it was never far from mind or conversation. There was always someone who was going there or who had just come back. Myrtle Beach has a way of making news – often with a major storm, sometimes with murders and scandals and, in 1974, with the demolition of the grand old Ocean Forest Hotel. Whenever I returned to my old playground for a weekend, I was amazed and not altogether charmed at how it had changed, like seeing a bratty niece or nephew after several years. No amount of snapshots or postcards could prepare me for the physical and spiritual transformation this child of my youth had undergone.

By the late 1980s I was back in South Carolina, writing for an afternoon newspaper in Columbia. A friend suggested we drive to Myrtle Beach to spend a long January weekend overlooking the surf. Winter rates were incredibly low, she told me, and if we didn't mind the wintry blast, we could walk the broad silver beach as if it were our private estate. The notion struck me as thoroughly unnatural – like celebrating Christmas in July. But heathens that we were, we headed east on a Friday afternoon. For a little over thirty dollars a night we had a spacious ocean-front efficiency and a quiet, relaxing weekend.

So began my long fascination with Myrtle Beach in winter. I have returned for at least one weekend – sometimes two or three – every winter since, and the images are always startling. From a sunlit city of dreams and pleasures, Myrtle Beach in winter becomes a place of haunting stillness. I have seen icicles hanging from the roller coaster at the Pavilion Amusement Park. I have seen newspapers blowing down Ocean Boulevard like tumbleweeds in a Western ghost town. I have seen the empty shops and dark hotel lobbies staring out at the gray January like tombstones.

From occasional winter sojourns, it was a small step to spending New Year's Eve in Myrtle Beach. On the last day of 1998, I checked out some of the party options at local clubs and settled for an inexpensive soiree at a beachfront dive called Bummz. There I toasted in the New Year – my third in Myrtle Beach – with a pleasant group of educators from upstate New York who were dreading their return to the Albany tundra. I slept late the next day, then rose to spend the afternoon by the window of my motel room, pondering the ocean and the last year of the millennium.

The ocean is mysterious and awe-inspiring in any season. Sociobiologist Edward O. Wilson has written that human beings have a primordial yearning to live where we can look out over water and open spaces from a high, secure perch. Looking out to sea from my perch on the second floor of the Roxanne Hotel, I could hardly argue. Primordial yearning had turned Myrtle Beach into an international tourist destination. I had recently read Lena Lancek's and Gideon Bosker's book, *The Beach: The History of Paradise on Earth*. In it they argued that the beach has always stirred mankind's boldest passions and imaginings. Armies have clashed on the beaches of the world. Empires have been won and lost there. Religions have been born by the water's edge; great art and great loves have been inspired by the meeting of land and sea.

I spent a couple of hours, on the second day of 1999, driving U.S. 17 – Kings Highway, as the locals call it – from Pawleys Island in the south to the North Carolina border, that golden stretch of sand called the Grand Strand. On the north end of the Strand lay the unincorporated fishing village of Little River; below that, North Myrtle Beach; then Atlantic Beach; ritzy Briarcliffe Acres; Myrtle Beach, Surfside Beach and unincorporated Garden City Beach, before the Strand drifted out of Horry and into Georgetown County. Wherever I looked, the land was being scraped bare for new housing, new retail space, new roads. Along a single mile of oceanfront in Myrtle Beach stood three construction cranes, teasing new high-rise hotels out of the sand. Other cranes were at work in North Myrtle Beach and Surfside. Where U.S. 501 crosses the Intracoastal Waterway, the land was being stripped to make way for a Home Depot and a Wal-Mart SuperCenter. North of Myrtle Beach, at U.S. 17, great concrete pillars marched across the landscape; in another year they would carry on their shoulders the Conway Bypass.

On my little self-guided tour, I passed NASCAR SpeedPark, the IMAX and Palace Theater, Ripley's Aquarium, Carolina Opry and House of Blues. There were new theme restaurants: Planet Hollywood, Hard Rock Café, NASCAR Café, All-Star Café. There was Broadway at the Beach, a new 250-acre shopping and entertainment venue and its older rival, Barefoot Landing, with 110 shops and 15 restaurants. Just across the Intracoastal Waterway on U.S. 501 were Waccamaw Factory Shoppes and Myrtle Beach Factory Stores, two of the reasons Horry County posted $5.5 billion in retail sales in 1998.

Yet in the midst of this glitz and corporate virility the city has managed to maintain some of the flavor of cotton candy and chili dogs. On Ocean Boulevard, the T-shirt shops, pizza stands and Pavilion Amusement Park and Arcade were quaint reminders of the way things used to be. Most of the older hotels along the Boulevard were still locally owned (even if some of those locals were from India) and showed a passion for tropical imagery and suburban conformity. On a short stretch of Ocean Boulevard South, the Tropical Oasis stood a block below the Tropical Winds, which was adjacent to the Tropical Seas, which was across from the Sea Oats, which was a block above the Sea Crest, which was a block below the Palm Crest. For the traveler who still didn't get it, there were also the Palms, Royal Palms, Palms Inn and Sea Palms, to say nothing of Sea Banks, Sea Gypsy, Sea Island, Sea Witch, Sea Horn, Sea Hawk, Sea Side, Sea Dip, Sea Coast, Sea Park, Sea Cove, Sea Mist, Mystic Sea, By the Sea, South Seas, Sea Sand, Golden Sands, Silver Sands, Ocean Sands, Coral Sands, Holiday Sands, Bermuda Sands, Atlantic Sands, Sand Bucket, Sand Castle, Sand Dollar, Sandy Beach, Coral Beach . . . and so it went.

Myrtle Beach has always been proud of its "family" image. In the 1950s, the little family-owned motels and restaurants, the quiet sandy streets and the Pavilion Amusement Park all lent themselves to a comfortable Ozzie-and-Harriet atmosphere. But if the fifties was the Ozzie-and-Harriet decade, it was also the decade of James Dean, Elvis and Brando. Likewise, Myrtle Beach had its "outlaw" side. Young people along the Strand were experimenting with soulful new sounds and a lusty new dance step called the shag, challenging the code of race relations and sexual propriety. Myrtle Beach Air Force Base kept local beer consumption and testosterone levels sky-high. You could get drunk, get laid and get tattooed, all in one stop, at a couple of notorious roadhouses along the south end of the Strand.

Myrtle Beach forty years ago was as complex and as paradoxical as human nature. It was a refuge in the heart of the Bible Belt, where people could "relax" for a weekend. The city preserved its "family values" atmosphere while keeping a slightly naughty reputation. If many restaurants chose not to serve alcohol and innkeepers made sure the couples checking in were actually married, their decisions were personal. The roadhouses were always there for those who wanted something more.

In 1999 many people wanted to see things as they had been in 1960. Powerful corporate and public forces sought to "clean up" Myrtle Beach, sought to Disney-fy it, some said. You could see those forces at work in the recent demolition of the 31-unit Harts Villa on Ocean Boulevard – a 76-unit condominium tower would soon stand in its place. You could see it in the proliferation of Florida palm trees among the local condos and shopping malls, hundreds of miles from their natural habitat. Despite the pleasure it has brought to countless millions of people over the years, there were some who thought Myrtle Beach should be more like Miami Beach, more like Orlando, more like Hilton Head. They spoke of family values and described a safe, tidy, well-ordered corporate fun factory, where undesirable people and products were kept out, where the city gates were guarded against unwanted elements.

The culture wars that were wracking the nation in 1999 were splitting Myrtle Beach and the communities of the Grand Strand. Americans have always battled over values, and a county that had tripled in population in twenty-five years was going to experience growing pains. But there were those who said the Grand Strand was not just changing too fast, but also growing too fast – too much sprawl, too much traffic, too many people. The questions for Myrtle Beach were daunting: How could a tourist town be a comfortable home to those who lived there year 'round? Could traditional Southern, Protestant values survive in a town that sought to be an international business and entertainment destination? Could a community of conservative retirees and business people bring themselves to demand more regulation of developers and "trash" culture? Could a city of immigrants now pull up the bridge and say, "Enough!" to those waiting at the gate?

The little beach town I remember still had some tatters of her small-town past − you could see it in her downtown church spires, in her civic clubs and social service organizations − but she was shedding them quickly. It seems the small town girl got drunk at her first sorority party and wanted to impress everyone with her pedigree. She called herself an international resort and the Golf Capital of the World. She boasted shamelessly, dropping gaudy names and numbers to describe her tourism and population growth and, without blushing, compared herself to Las Vegas and Orlando. Was she really Cinderella? Or was she Evita?

These were some of the questions I was tossing around that Saturday night, January 2, 1999, as I sat on the stool at Michael's Bar & Grill, sipping a Budweiser and watching the Orange Bowl. In balmy Miami, the University of Florida was beating poor Syracuse like a drum. Outside, a winter storm whipped palm trees along Ocean Boulevard and lashed rain against the front windows of the tavern.

Leaving Syracuse to its fate, I drove to my hotel through streets that looked like something out of a Dashiell Hammett novel. Back in my room at the Roxanne, I watched the rain blow against the glass beachfront door, as I pulled a notebook from my travel bag and started writing.

There is a picture that has become a Myrtle Beach icon, hanging like an old family portrait, in living rooms and offices about the town. It is the July 8, 1961 cover of the *Saturday Evening Post,* featuring the lounge of the local Dunes Golf and Beach Club, where two dozen middle-aged men sit around tables, laughing, drinking, playing cards. A single black, liveried waiter serves drinks. Like the South Carolina of a century before, this 1961 world was about to be swept away by forces these small-town arrivistes could neither control nor comprehend.

What was emerging in its place was not clear and not altogether pretty. Yet, for all of its problems − the tackiness, crime, traffic and all the rest − Myrtle Beach is still the place where millions choose to visit each year, the place where thousands more come to retire, to work, to stake their claims, to follow their dreams. And that night I sensed that I would soon become one of them.

Inventing Myrtle Beach:
Dreamers, Builders and Hucksters

If Myrtle Beach is the child of the earth and the sea, as some of its more lyrical promoters claim, then Franklin G. Burroughs is its godfather. More than a century after his death, the vision of that stern patriarch is still invoked by developers of this sandy northeast corner of South Carolina. According to family legend, Burroughs in his last years stood on the empty, windswept beach and told one of his daughters, "I may not live to see it and you may not, but some day this whole strand will be a resort."

Who knows? Perhaps he did say it. Burroughs was a savvy businessman, who knew of Coney Island, Atlantic City and other urban beach resorts of the late nineteenth century. And he owned miles of pristine beach bordering some of the most desolate, uninhabited land on the continent. Still, in a town of hype, hucksterism and ceaseless promotion, the story has the tinny *plink* of a marketing spiel, something you would expect to find in a real estate brochure.

Between Winyah Bay, South Carolina, and Cape Fear, North Carolina, the forces of nature conspired against generations of dreamers. The rising and falling of ancient oceans deposited deep layers of sand and clay, unsuitable to large-scale agriculture. When the oceans rose to their present level at the end of the last ice age, they defined a perfect crescent of sandy beach, unbroken by any river, from Winyah Bay to Cape Fear. With no harbor or deep-water access, the ninety-mile arc of sand remained barren of any major settlement; behind the beaches the thin soil supported only isolated yeoman farms. On the Cape Fear, Wilmington became an important Southern port of entry; on Winyah Bay, Georgetown became the world's leading exporter of rice and the second wealthiest county in the United States. Between the two lay a wasteland of forest, swamp and dunes.

Yet the region was not without appeal. A good man with a knife and gun would never want for food. The forest teemed with deer and bear, turkeys and raccoons. The black waters of the Pee Dee and Waccamaw rivers offered fish, turtles and alligators; and, of course, there was the ocean, with its abundance for the taking. Early settlers were amazed at the depth and richness of the forest. Ancient stands of giant cypress lined the riverbanks. Behind the shore, enormous pines, cedars and live oaks stood gnarled by years of ceaseless Atlantic wind, sculpted into forests of huge, haunting bonsai. There were also water oaks, willow oaks and scrub oaks, a variety of hollies, including the hearty yaupon, with its translucent red berries, several species of magnolia and, of course, the wax myrtle (*Myrica cerifera*), which grows so abundantly along the sandy coast. But the land offered little in the way of marketable crops or commodities.

The region was divided early between the colonies of North Carolina and South Carolina. Otherwise, history virtually passed it by. The county carved out on the South Carolina side of the line was named Horry (pronounced OH-REE, equal emphasis on each syllable) in honor of Peter Horry, an officer and aide to General Francis Marion. The county seat was named Conway, in memory of another local Revolutionary War hero. Ironically, hardly a shot was fired on Horry County soil throughout the Revolution. The same was true in the Civil War. While Wilmington, Georgetown, Charleston, Beaufort, Savannah and Jacksonville all fell to Union troops, Horry County emerged unscathed and virtually unnoticed. There was simply nothing there to fight over. The county's geographic and economic isolation was its most distinguishing feature; its self-reliant folk came to refer to their home as the "Independent Republic of Horry."

This was the world Franklin Burroughs came home to in 1865. A native of Martin County, North Carolina, Burroughs came to Conway in 1856, served in the Confederate Army and spent the last months of the war in a Union prison camp near Chicago. Back in Conway, the little town on the Waccamaw River, Burroughs wasted no time in getting on with his life. Throughout the county, rough-and-ready entrepreneurs began to exploit the region's great resource: timber and naval stores. In the Waccamaw backwaters stood cypress trees 600 years old and twelve feet in diameter. East of the river were longleaf pines 100 feet tall. The forest rang with saws and axes against ancient wood; great rafts of logs floated down the Pee Dee and Waccamaw rivers to Georgetown. Stills boiled down pine resin to make turpentine and pitch for industrial and maritime use.

In 1866, Franklin Burroughs entered into two important unions. One was his marriage to Adeline Cooper, which produced five children. The other was his partnership with Benjamin G. Collins, which produced the Burroughs & Collins Company. Thirty-two years old, Burroughs was on his way to being the wealthiest man in the vast Horry County forest.

His new company ran steamboats up and down the black waters of the Waccamaw and his commissary stores served the sawmill camps and towns that sprang up along the river. But his true interest was timber. He owned mills and stills and produced huge quantities of lumber and turpentine. While most of his competitors simply bought timber rights, cleared the land and moved on, Burroughs took the longer view. In the depressed post-Civil War economy, land was cheap and Burroughs bought it up at begging prices – sometimes as little as a dollar an acre. In the last decades of the nineteenth century, his company amassed an empire of some 100,000 acres, including miles of empty, windswept beach.

The first railroad came to Horry County in 1887, connecting Conway to Wilmington. Its possibilities were not lost on Burroughs. The line provided passenger service and better means of getting his products out of the remote wilderness than floating them down the Waccamaw River. Burroughs began building his own railroad from Conway, across the swamps and backwaters, to an outlet on the coast. He died in 1897, not living to see the task complete. Sons Frank and Donald took over the company and oversaw the completion of the railroad, in 1900, and the laying out of streets around the terminus. The little lumber camp was called New Town, to distinguish it from the "old town" of Conway.

The Burroughs and Collins families dissolved their partnership in 1900; the Burroughs descendants kept most of the land and the company name, as well as the railroad. That fourteen-mile stretch of track would soon yield unexpected dividends and confirm Franklin Burroughs' uncanny prescience.

For years, inland residents had traveled by foot, horseback and mule wagon to reach the sandy shore, where they spent hot summer days camping, picnicking and fishing. Now, with a rail line running directly from Conway to the beach, the trip was faster and safer than ever. There were no passenger cars in those early days. Travelers rode flatcars back and forth to the beach and did not seem to mind that sparks from the locomotive burned their skin and clothes. The lure of the beach overcame all trepidation.

In time, the company answered the demand for passenger cars and met the market for accommodations by building the Seaside Inn, a rambling, three-story, gabled hotel with a broad front porch running the full length of the building. The Seaside Inn lacked indoor plumbing or electricity, but there were other amenities, including changing rooms, a boardwalk down to the beach and an open pavilion where musicians performed on summer nights and couples danced in the evening breeze. In the town's first marketing ploy, the Burroughs family changed the name from New Town to Myrtle Beach, recognizing the local wax myrtle shrub.

The first dirt road – a circuitous southern route – connected Conway to the resort in 1914. Mile-long traffic jams were decades away, but the automobile had reached the shore. The family sold oceanfront lots in their new resort for $25; to lure quality development, they threw in an extra lot free to anyone who would agree to build a house worth $500 or more. It was the first "Buy-1-Get-1-Free" offer in a town that would become famous for them. Ocean Boulevard was laid out parallel to the beach, just behind the first dune line. Streets intersecting Ocean Boulevard from the west reflected the town's lack of history, heroes or culture; they were named simply 1st Avenue, 2nd Avenue, 3rd Avenue, etc. To ensure public beach access, these streets were extended across Ocean Boulevard, to the dune line; these access "alleys" were eventually deeded by the company to the city.

The Burroughs family possessed enormous assets but lacked capital. They found a fountain of cash in Simeon Brooks Chapin, a wealthy financier with offices in Chicago and New York. In 1912, an intermediary introduced Chapin to the Burroughs brothers. Out of this meeting grew a partnership called Myrtle Beach Farms Company, whose role was to develop a family resort along the Horry County shore. By the late 1920s, cottages extended a mile north and south of the Seaside Inn and the year-round population of the town was 200. Even so, the electric company in Conway cut off the power to Myrtle Beach after Labor Day. Among summer cottage owners, the joke was, "Last one out, turn off the lights." In the Roaring Twenties, the Woodside brothers, a wealthy textile and banking family from Greenville, South Carolina, came to Myrtle Beach and built the legendary Ocean Forest Hotel and the area's first golf course.

The 1930s saw the opening of the Intracoastal Waterway by the U.S. Army Corps of Engineers. The great ditch ran two and a half miles behind the oceanfront, cutting the town off from the mainland. Myrtle Beach would forever be an island, but the Waterway helped drain the area – once known as Withers Swamp – making the town healthier and more desirable for development. The decade brought all the tangible signs of progress: telephone service, a weekly newspaper, a high school, municipal incorporation.

Even in those early days, Myrtle Beach had begun to show some of the schizophrenia which, seventy years later, would drive it to distraction. On the one hand, it was just a small Southern town – like thousands of small Southern towns – where segregation was strictly enforced, where Catholics and Jews were largely invisible, where Protestant notions of predestination reinforced rigid class lines and determined almost everyone's roles and attitudes.

On the other hand, it was . . . *the beach*, a place of passion and mystery, a land where laws and limitations seemed to vanish, where love and wealth and power lay within a person's grasp. Generations of developers, promoters and hucksters have discovered the power of the ocean to make people take leave of their senses. They are still tirelessly at work and Myrtle Beach is the proof of their success.

Over the years, thousands of Carolinians have come to build their cottages and castles along the strand, betting their fortunes and their happiness that the next time Neptune goes bowling, he will not hurl one of his storms down on their little corner of the world. But every generation or two there comes a leveling, a mighty reckoning. For pious and vaguely superstitious Southern folk, there seems to be a message in all this – that mortals have ventured too close to the abyss, have tempted the fates beyond endurance. But when the skies clear and the debris is hauled away, the dreamers are back with their bulldozers, their concrete and timbers. They will be ready for the next storm. The secret, they know, is deeper foundations and stronger prayer.

The Ocean Forest Hotel provided the grandest example of beach folly. In the late 1920s, the Woodside brothers built the stunning white tower north of Myrtle Beach, on land they purchased from Myrtle Beach Farms. Ten floors high, with a ballroom, Italian marble floors and crystal chandeliers from Czechoslovakia, the Ocean Forest shimmered above the vast, empty beach like some spectral castle sprung from the mystic Carolina sand. It was the greatest hotel between Atlantic City and Miami Beach. In the booming decade of the Twenties, it was planned as the perfect golf and beach layover on the long, slow train rides between Florida and points north.

But its timing was disastrous. The grand opening took place on February 21, 1930, five months after the stock market collapse. No amount of champagne and caviar could disguise the nightmare engulfing the nation that day. As the economy contracted, so did the dreams and fortunes of the hotel's millionaire guest list. The Ocean Forest went into receivership and passed through a series of owners until it was imploded in a dynamite demolition in 1974. It lived less than half a century.

The grand hotel is forever swathed in myth and irony. Built as a retreat for the rich and famous, its construction required the work of hundreds of laborers and artisans from Northern cities. They returned home with stories of the fabulous Carolina beaches, inexpensive and less than half the distance to Florida. Myrtle Beach was a resort where even a glazier or a mason could aspire to bring his family. These working-class dreams got a boost in 1934, when the 312-acre Myrtle Beach State Park opened on U.S. 17, south of the town. The park offered a great pavilion, public swimming and showers, as well as campgrounds. In 1946, Colonel Elliott White Springs, the flamboyant head of Springs Cotton Mills, purchased thirty-four acres adjacent to the state park, as a recreation site for employees of his upstate textile mills. He built inexpensive housing, more campgrounds and a fabulous fishing pier. The two parks helped to permanently cast Myrtle Beach as a blue-collar resort.

During the Great Depression, Myrtle Beach became an escape from the national trauma, a refuge for drifters and dreamers, eccentrics and outcasts. Its geographic isolation and littoral whimsy made it a natural hideaway, a place of new beginnings and new identities. Through those perilous times the Burroughs family's vision and benevolence guided the town. Their company donated land for churches and the town's first jail, on Oak Street. To provide more retail services, Simeon Chapin created the Chapin Company in 1927. Located on Main Street, Chapin's store sold groceries, clothes, household goods, furniture, hardware, fuel oil and gasoline to generations of Myrtle Beach residents. He later created a foundation, which supported churches and charities and established Chapin Memorial Library in 1949.

The post-World War II economy brought unprecedented prosperity and mobility, as family cars and vacations became part of the American way of life. In 1948, a direct, paved highway – U.S. 501 – was opened between Conway and the beach. It was a fourteen-mile drive through pristine swamp and forest, where deer and bears were frequently seen. That same year, Myrtle Beach Farms Co. built a large arcade adjacent to its beachfront pavilion and Earl Husted brought his traveling carnival rides and parked them permanently across Ocean Boulevard from the pavilion. Husted didn't offer much – a merry-go-round, a Ferris wheel, a few kiddie rides – but he provided the nucleus of what generations of Southerners have come to know as the Pavilion Amusement Park. Around the arcade and amusement park appeared bars and restaurants, gift shops and more arcades. Some of them – Peach's Corner, the Bowery, the Ocean Front Bar & Grille and the Gay Dolphin Gift Cove – are still operating after half a century. Those few blocks of Ocean Boulevard – from 7th Avenue North to 11th Avenue North – are the historic heart of Myrtle Beach.

For millions of people, mention of the Pavilion or the Boulevard conjures the magic of whirling, flashing lights, the smell of cotton candy and the sound of the carousel. For others, it's the memory of that first beer, the first evening cruising on the Boulevard, the first tryst on the beach with the Pavilion lights in the distance. And always – in a million private reveries, stretching back over more than a half century of war and peace, of confusion and transformation – Myrtle Beach is the memory of a warm summer night, full of stars and youth and hope.

Myrtle Beach Grows Up

By the time I discovered Myrtle Beach as a child of the 1950s, many others had begun to take notice, as well. The post-war boom had transformed the Horry County shore and given it a new name. In 1957, the state legislature officially designated the beach between Waccamaw Neck and the North Carolina border as the Grand Strand. Garden City Beach and Surfside Beach arose south of Myrtle Beach; to the north were Briarcliffe Acres, Windy Hill Beach, Crescent Beach, Atlantic Beach, Ocean Drive Beach and Cherry Grove Beach. But the franchise name – the town that was winning fame throughout the Carolinas and beyond – was Myrtle Beach.

All these towns nearly vanished on the morning of October 15, 1954, when Hurricane Hazel, a Category 4 storm with 150 mile-per-hour winds and a sixteen-foot tidal surge, roared ashore. South Carolina took a $281-million hit that day, with the heaviest damage occurring on the north end of the Strand, where the eye of the storm crossed the coast. Cherry Grove, Windy Hill and Crescent Beach lost over 1,000 houses. The front row was reduced to mounds of rubble, with twisted plumbing jutting from the sand. Long stretches of Ocean Boulevard were washed away.

What was disaster to some was urban renewal to others. On the day after the storm, a leading citizen of the town told his son, "This will be the salvation of Myrtle Beach." Indeed, the old town of cottages, boarding houses and ten- and twenty-room, family-run hotels was largely consigned to memories and photo albums. In its place grew a new town of larger, more ambitious hotels, better constructed, with more amenities and more appeal.

Growing up in Myrtle Beach in the 1950s and 1960s, Anton Poster felt the sense of expectation community leaders expressed about their town. "Everybody was waiting for the time to come when Myrtle Beach would become a resort," he recalled. "I had it drilled into my head that this was going to be a resort. . . . They were waiting for that *pop*" – he snapped his fingers – "and we would be a resort and we would be rich."

In 1968, low-cost flood insurance became available through the National Flood Insurance Act. With private investment insured by the federal government, out-of-state money poured into the Grand Strand. National chains bought up old hotels, demolished them, and built oceanfront high-rises. The long-anticipated *pop* resounded across the region with the condo boom of the early 1970s. Myrtle Beach was on its way to the major league of American resorts. And it was totally unprepared.

Horry County did not even have a county council or an administrator until 1977. Like most Southern governments, the county and its municipalities prided themselves on low taxes, cheap labor and lack of regulation; they didn't talk much about poor schools, marginal infrastructure and public service. Stormwater had always been a problem in the flat coastal environment. But with ever more land being covered with concrete and asphalt, ever more rainwater was being channeled through the region's 180 stormwater pipes onto the fabled white beaches. And the roads, built to serve a little beach town of bungalows and boarding houses, were overwhelmed by the flood of automobiles that descended each summer on the Grand Strand.

In 1974, that grand old lady of the beach, the Ocean Forest Hotel, went down in a dynamite implosion. The debris was trucked off to fill a marsh for future development and residents near the hotel were soon signing petitions and marching down to City Hall to protest the condos that were planned for the site. Myrtle Beach was growing up.

The explosive growth of the 1970s changed more than the Myrtle Beach skyline. It changed the way people thought of themselves, their neighbors and the earth beneath their feet. A few complained that the Grand Strand was losing its charm, its innocence, its natural beauty. But they seemed eccentric and irrelevant in the face of economic forces sweeping the region.

In 1967, a group of wheeler-dealers pooled their resources to take advantage of two of the region's greatest attractions – its golf courses and its mild winters. The product of their labor was Myrtle Beach Golf Holiday, a consortium of hotels and golf courses which presented themselves in "golf packages" tailored to different tastes and budgets, designed to make planning a golf excursion as simple as placing one phone call. The enterprise succeeded beyond all expectations. From twelve courses sprinkled around the Grand Strand in 1967, the number exploded to 100 by 1999, making Myrtle Beach the self-styled "Golf Capital of the World."

Business, like golf, recognizes no season and the two passions blend like scotch and water. With this in mind, business leaders determined to make their town a trade and convention mecca. The Myrtle Beach Convention Center opened in 1967, expanded in 1976 and again in 1994, to its present 175,000 square feet. In 1998 it booked some 457 events, bringing 650,000 people to the area.

In 1988 Calvin Gilmore brought his 2,200-seat Carolina Opry Theater to the Grand Strand. Carolina Opry featured country music and the kind of wholesome, down-home entertainment that filled tour buses and put Branson, Missouri, on the map. His success inspired imitators; within a few years there were over a dozen theaters along the Strand, most of them featuring country music.

Miniature golf – always popular on the Strand – mushroomed in the   1990s. Cashing in on the Southern love of racing, amusement park owners built go-cart tracks, with their two-cycle buggies dressed up as NASCAR and Formula I racers. Next came the water parks, offering great sliding boards, fountains, sprays and pools; and theme restaurants, led by Hard Rock Café and Planet Hollywood. In 1987, a development group called Carolina Sands created Barefoot Landing, a megacomplex of shopping, dining and entertainment built around a freshwater lake in North Myrtle Beach. By the mid-1990s, it was possible to spend a fun-filled week at Myrtle Beach and never even see the ocean.

The man responsible for making the world aware of these wonders was Ashby Ward. A former television news anchor and PR director for the South Carolina Technical College System, Ward started his broadcast career at a television station in nearby Florence, where he was "Captain Ashby," dressing in a silver space suit and hosting an afternoon kiddie-and-cartoon program. In 1974, he became president and CEO of the Myrtle Beach Area Chamber of Commerce, building it into a juggernaut of commerce and promotion. With an annual budget of $7.5 million, more than 2,200 members and sixty employees working out of four Grand Strand offices, the MBA Chamber of Commerce in 1999 was the second largest chamber in the Southeast. Every day it handled between 2,000 and 3,000 inquiries and mailed out one ton of information to potential visitors around the world.

Throughout these years of transformation, Myrtle Beach Farms Company maintained a benign posture toward its namesake and progeny. Most of the company's energies were directed toward managing its agricultural interests, including its tobacco allotments in one of the largest tobacco-growing counties in the nation. It did little direct development, choosing to sell land for others to develop. The great exception was Myrtle Square Mall, on U.S. 17. Opened in 1977, it was the first mall in the region and was universally received as a blessing from the city's corporate benefactor.

Perhaps it is the comfort people feel with round numbers or perhaps 1990 truly was a watershed year for Myrtle Beach. Whatever the reason, that was the year many longtime residents say things finally came unhinged in their quiet Southern beach town.

On September 22, 1989, Hurricane Hugo slammed the coast just above Charleston and cut a $10 billion swath through the Carolinas. The Grand Stand was shut down for months and the price tag for Hugo ran to the hundreds of millions. The relative damage did not equal that of Hurricane Hazel, but the shock and sense of vulnerability did. As Myrtle Beach dug out of the debris in the last weeks of the 1980s, many residents knew that they were leaving something behind. Old hotels and houses were bulldozed away. New and bigger towers rose from the dunes. History turned a page.

In 1990, the area reached a milestone when the U.S. Census Bureau created the Myrtle Beach Metropolitan Statistical Area, a major marketing and development tool. The Myrtle Beach MSA encompassed all of Horry County and included 144,053 residents.

Also in 1990, Myrtle Beach's old corporate benefactor reached a milestone of its own. For generations, Myrtle Beach Farms Company had remained little more than a spectator to the region's transforming development. But that was about to change. The Burroughs and Chapin families consolidated the old Myrtle Beach Farms Company and the Burroughs & Collins Company to create the Burroughs & Chapin Company, Inc. Company CEO Egerton Burroughs went looking for new blood and new vision to lead the company. He found his man in 49-year-old Douglas P. Wendel, a Maryland transplant who had come to the area in the 1970s and held several public administrative posts.

Wendel took the helm in 1993 and embarked on a program of corporate social engineering that would forever change Myrtle Beach and the Grand Strand. By 1997, the Burroughs & Chapin Company (B&C) had its own water park, Myrtle Waves, and NASCAR Speedpark and NASCAR Café, officially licensed by the racing organization. Most impressively, B&C created Broadway at the Beach, a $250 million-dollar shopping, dining and entertainment complex to rival Barefoot Landing. Located on U.S. 17 Bypass, Broadway at the Beach sprawled across 350 acres that, only a few years earlier, had grown corn, beans and tomatoes for Myrtle Beach Farms. Broadway at the Beach opened in 1995 and instantly became the state's premiere tourist attraction, offering theaters, restaurants, nightclubs and more than ninety specialty shops. It soon drew more than ten million visitors a year and received the South Carolina Governors' Cup, the state's top tourism award, in 1996.

Broadway at the Beach represented a new chapter in the life of the old family company. Under Doug Wendel's guidance, there was no room for corporate paternalism or sentimentality. The new Burroughs & Chapin would be an aggressive developer of new properties and attractions, but also an aggressive player on the public stage, shaping the political and cultural climate to meet corporate ends.

In 1997, B&C announced plans for Lakeshore Village, a cluster of ten to twelve hotels around Broadway at the Beach, as well as South Beach Resort and the $1.5 billion Grande Dunes development. A year later the company unveiled plans for its 1.3 million-square-foot Mall of South Carolina on U.S. 501. In January 1999, B&C announced that it would develop four new strip malls around the Grand Strand, with a combined 785,000 square feet of retail space. All of these developments flew in the face of the city and county's twenty-year land use plan to reduce urban sprawl and traffic.

Myrtle Beach's daily newspaper, *The Sun News*, had a research firm conduct focus groups to plumb the public attitude toward the company and its behavior. Every one of the more than fifty participants had heard of Burroughs & Chapin and had an opinion about the company. The paper reported: " . . . the consensus was that the company is an opportunistic, short-sighted profiteer. Burroughs & Chapin and, to a lesser extent, International Paper are synonymous with overdevelopment of the Grand Strand."

Letters to the editor of *The Sun News* voiced public hostility toward the giant developer. A typical letter from a Georgetown resident ran in January 1999: "I saw a poster one day that showed a wide spectrum of animals running from a bulldozer and a paving machine that left a field of concrete in their path. It's sad that if B&C saw it, I'm sure they would have absolutely no comprehension of its significance."

By some counts, Horry was the second fastest-growing county in the United States in the late 1990s. The U.S. Census Bureau reported that Horry County's 3.1 percent population increase for 1998 ranked it 168th in the nation. But an industry research group took a more jarring perspective. U.S. Housing Markets ranked Horry County between No. 1, Naples, Florida, and No. 3, Las Vegas, Nevada, in number of residential housing permits issued per thousand residents.

Across the Intracoastal Waterway and miles inland the impact of development was felt in towns like Aynor, Longs and Conway. Twelve miles from the nearest dune, the little town of Loris grew by forty-nine percent between 1990 and 1997. Under development just west of the Waterway was Carolina Forest, an eleven-thousand-acre city that International Paper Co. carved out of the coastal pine forest. When Carolina Forest is complete in 2020, its seventeen square miles will hold thirty-seven subdivisions, five million square feet of commercial space, up to ten golf courses and sixty thousand new residents.

Demographic chaos had come to this tradition-bound, homogeneous little world. Longtime residents – some of whose families had been in the region more than 200 years – found the flood of new residents threatening to more than just their peace and quiet. One of them told me – with only slight exaggeration – that thirty years before, there had been mo karaoke re Eskimos in Horry County than Catholics or Jews. By 1999, Our Lady Star of the Sea Catholic Church had the largest sanctuary on the Grand Strand and was the largest Catholic church in South Carolina. And there were two synagogues and a Jewish day school in Myrtle Beach.

Dominated by tourism workers and retirees, the new population was largely composed of rootless and short-term residents. Thousands of them arrived each year, thinking they had found their little piece of Paradise. Now they stepped out their front doors in the morning to see rows of apartments going up across the street. They went to sleep at night with the lights from a theme restaurant twinkling through their bedroom windows.

The fastest growing segment of the population was retirees, who lived and socialized in their own communities and cliques. One of every four Horry County residents in 1997 was fifty-five or older. On the other end of the spectrum were young people – often very young, often with children of their own – drawn to the low-paying service and retail economy. Between the affluent retirees and the young service workers lay a relatively small middle-income and middle-age group. In this polarized world there was little interest in daycare or education. Retirees wielded their well-organized influence to demand a dispropor-tionate share of public resources for health and emergency medical care.

Children of transient, low-income service workers were raised with-out extended families and critical social services. "Arcades and amuse-ment parks are used as baby sitters," said Dr. Linda George, a Duke University sociologist who has studied retirement communities. "Kids are very knowledgeable of miniature golf, but what else do they know?" She predicted, "The longer the town goes in this direction, the less likely it will be to draw more middle class, professional and corporate types."

Horry County's boom undermined all values and relationships. As the population swelled from 144,000 in 1990 to 175,000 in 1998, real estate values exploded. With reassessment in 1998, the estimated mar-ket value of Horry County real property increased from $8.7 billion in 1990 to $15.6 billion in 1999.

Change in real estate values sparked change in other values. In earlier times, local politics had been a mix of civic and business inter-ests, headed by the tourism industry. In the 1990s, real estate and devel-opment had come to dominate local elective and advisory boards; county government became a swamp of corruption, favoritism and influence. Council members appointed friends and associates to the planning, zoning and appeals boards and were repeatedly caught in questionable business relationships.

Residents have long suspected developers bent the rules and the rule-makers to their will. In another report on their focus group research, *The Sun News* wrote that "residents said they believe that local politicians cater to special interests; don't consider the general popula-tion in their decision making; govern only to get re-elected; are incom-petent and corrupt; and centralize power in the hands of a few." Elected officials are "generally seen as incompetent, ineffective, unsophisticat-ed, unethical and opportunistic. Business and the wealthy are seen as controlling forces," *The Sun News* wrote. "Residents . . . feel elected officials go against their wishes to cater to business." Sixty percent of residents felt local officials cared more about tourist dollars than they did about the peace of mind of their own constituents. Forty-seven percent felt that the effects of tourism had been mostly negative, due to the strain it placed on roads and government services.

The 1990s saw a parade of scandals, indictments and resignations in county government. By 1998, county council meetings were frequently punctuated by screams, threats and innuendo. In an effort to bring civility to council proceedings, the county hired a "team building" consultant to attend the annual council retreat and help members work through some of their differences. The effort was a notable failure.

The evidence of unplanned, uncontrolled growth was everywhere along the Strand – in the sprawling suburbs and crawling traffic and crowded schools; in the churned-up earth where new houses, malls, roads and golf courses would soon take root. The Myrtle Beach Area Chamber of Commerce liked to boast of the region's 2,000-plus restaurants. Of course, 2,000 restaurants meant 2,000 flashing, blinking roadside attractions, offering All-U-Can-Eat seafood buffets, breakfast buffets, Chinese buffets, pizza buffets, Mexican fiestas, barbecue, pancakes, steaks, hamburgers, "World Famous Hot Dogs," early-bird specials, golfers specials, catch-of-the day specials, as well as happy hours, *karaoke*, two-for-one margaritas, three-dollar pitchers and the "sexiest waitresses in town." And there were the miniature golf courses, punctuated by smoking volcanoes, pirate ships, dragons, jungle animals, dinosaurs, helicopters, airplanes, explosions and waterfalls. Perhaps most disquieting were the beachwear stores, with their pastel neon signs and facades and their tall windows displaying truncated female mannequins in skimpy bikinis and acres of Myrtle Beach souvenir T-shirts, towels, shot glasses, boxer shorts and hermit crabs. Along U.S. 501 – the front door of Myrtle Beach – strip clubs competed for the traveler's eye with strip malls, Triple-X video shops, fireworks warehouses, fast food franchises, convenience stores, branch banks, video casinos, used car lots and mobile home factory outlets. And everywhere – everywhere – the billboards lined up behind one another, promoting everything from massage parlors to churches.

By 1999, the Grand Strand had become the poster child for coastal development run amok. Along the Southern seaboard, anxious residents called for more zoning and regulation, lest their towns become the next Myrtle Beach. A municipal candidate in one North Carolina town won election on the slogan, "Don't have Emerald Isle turn into another Myrtle Beach." When residents of Holden Beach, North Carolina, organized to control development along the entrance to their town, one declared, "This is the first thing people see when they go into Holden Beach, and we don't want this looking like Myrtle Beach, selling all that garbage. . . ."

An Ocean Isle, North Carolina, official got in another jab: "We don't want a Myrtle Beach atmosphere." When residents of Sullivan's Island, South Carolina, called for more zoning in their upscale community, they cited Myrtle Beach as the fate they wished to avoid.

A letter to the editor of *The Sun News* expressed the rising sense of alarm: "You don't see that Myrtle Beach has turned into 'Tackyland.' Please don't call it a family beach because it is not! This has been allowed to happen in pursuit of the almighty dollar. It's time to get your heads out of the sand dunes!"

Chamber of Commerce president Ashby Ward dismissed all fears: "Almost none of us could afford to live here without the tourism economy," he said. "A natural assumption on the part of some local people is that they're ignored, but basically it's the only economy we have right now."

Some of the criticism came from a most surprising source. The development of Myrtle Beach "is comparable to strip mining – the same irreversible conversion of a landscape into money, the same brutal indifference to the intricate, sustaining systems of biological life, to the past and to the future." That was the judgment of Franklin G. Burroughs Jr., great-grandson and namesake of the man who started it all in the 1890s. An award-winning essayist and Harvard-educated English professor at Bowdoin College, Burroughs was raised in Conway and has published two elegiac books – *The River Home* and *Billy Watson's Croker Sack* – about the people and the natural history of Horry County. Writing in the magazine Preservation, Burroughs continued, " . . . suppose . . . some dreadful miscalculation landed you in Myrtle Beach. If you bought this magazine and are reading this article, you will not be happy there, not unless you suffer from some sort of bipolar, postmodern affective disorder – perhaps a malignant hypertrophy of the ironic impulse."

Doug Wendel would have nothing to do with this surly negativism: "Development has never been embraced as a good thing, because people are selfish and they don't like change," the CEO explained. "This area has come of age, it has been discovered and people are going to continue coming here. Burroughs & Chapin will continue to do projects and provide opportunities for new people to come in."

They Called It
Mayberry-at-the-Beach

The three sentinels stand over downtown Myrtle Beach, as they do in thousands of small Southern towns – the spires of the First Baptist, First Methodist and First Presbyterian churches. Surrounding the Pavilion Amusement Park and built on land donated by the Burroughs family, the churches keep watch over the traditions and morals of a town that many feel has already lost its way. On Sunday mornings, their bells and carillons summon the faithful to worship, even as sinners sleep off their hangovers and debauches in thousands of hotel rooms and the city judge runs an assortment of drunks, brawlers and disturbers of the peace through his court with stiff fines and a rap of the gavel. God frowns on such miscreants, and so do the good people of Myrtle Beach.

Take away the beach and the canyon of oceanfront hotels, take away the strip clubs and the golf courses, the roller coasters and the 2,000 restaurants, and Myrtle Beach is essentially a medium-sized Southern town – "Mayberry-at-the Beach," as some have called it – a town of neighbors, of Christians, of cultural and political conservatives. People join the Rotary Club and the Lions Club because they think they can make a difference. They follow the high school teams with religious zeal and hold barbecues to support the rescue squad and high school bands.

In January 1999, Myrtle Beach firefighters raised money to buy seven-year-old David Barr a new bicycle and send him to Walt Disney World and the Children's Burn Camp, after he was pulled from a house fire. That same month a freighter jettisoned fuel oil at sea and marine birds started washing ashore, covered with the black slime. Hundreds of people volunteered time and materials in a vain attempt to rescue and rehabilitate the stricken creatures. Also in January, area residents dedicated the Peace Wall at Chapin Park. The wall was covered it with 4,000 ceramic tiles, hand-painted by children, reflecting their visions of peace. It is a veritable garden of colors and images depicting flowers and peace symbols, children and birds, crosses and Stars of David.

After Hurricane Mitch killed nearly 10,000 people in Central America late in 1998, local residents raised $50,000 to send eighty tons of flour, rice, beans and cooking oil to survivors in Honduras. Senators Ernest Hollings and Strom Thurmond arranged Air Force equipment and personnel to transport the food from Charleston. "It's physically representative of the generosity of the Grand Strand," said Howard Barnard, director of lay ministries at First Presbyterian Church.

Letters to the editor of *The Sun News* provided a window into the soul of the community. The impending Senate trial of President Bill Clinton was on the mind of a lot of readers early in 1999, and the judgment was clearly against the President *and* his long-suffering wife. A typical letter urged the Senate to boycott the President's upcoming State of the Union address. "Lies and partisanship are the watchwords of the Democrats in Congress," thundered another.

Letters to the editor allowed true believers to expound on sin and salvation, cite biblical chapter and verse and split theological hairs. Writers did not hesitate to speak for the Almighty on any number of subjects. Mark Sims of Loris consigned Gordon Dew of Myrtle Beach to damnation because Dew, in his own letter, had challenged biblical authority.

As in small towns anywhere, there were plenty of cranks and crackpots, if the letters were any indication: "The first of the four horsemen of the apocalypse has been riding for the past two decades 'as a conqueror bent on conquest.' (Revelation 6:2) A much-acclaimed spiritual leader is busily trying to form a one-world religion under his leadership. . . . Neither our religious nor our spiritual leaders are warning our people of these upcoming tragedies of world war, world famine and world pestilence, so that they will not be caught totally by surprise."

Other letters offered a host of right wing conspiracy theories concerning one-world government and things that go bump in the night. One correspondent cited the death of some orange trees on the coast of Georgia as "proof" that the planet is actually cooling, and that global warming is a hoax. Another writer stated that there was no energy crisis and claimed knowledge of a secret government file proving there was a 10,000-year petroleum reserve. Letters routinely denounced "liberals," "liberal Democrats" and "the liberal media," as well as the Kennedys, Jesse Jackson, the American Civil Liberties Union and the National Association for the Advancement of Colored People.

There were also the gentler letters, the ones thanking police officers, firefighters, emergency medical personnel, friends and neighbors for their support in crisis and mourning: "On December 17 at Briarcliffe

Mall, I was taken with a diabetic seizure," wrote George and Jan DuBois of North Myrtle Beach. "My husband and I want to thank the Lake Arrowhead Rescue and Medics, the employee of Radio Shack, the mall security, the gracious woman who ran for orange juice, the offer of candy, the gentleman who aided my husband in holding me and all the very concerned people."

Archie Elliott of Myrtle Beach wrote: "If all police officers and the public in general were as kind-hearted and good people as Officer Robert Rhodes, this world would be a better place to live in for all concerns [sic]."

Under Myrtle Beach's three great steeples, Main Street intersects Broadway, a quiet stretch of neat low-rise buildings that look like a Norman Rockwell portrait of small town America, circa 1960. Along with City Hall, in 1999 there were an Army-Navy store, a couple of loan offices and three small print shops, two florist shops, several little restaurants, a dry cleaner, a tax and accounting service, a small engine repair shop and the little Piggly Wiggly grocery store. Several stores contained shrines to one or more of the Southern Trinity: Jesus, Elvis and Robert E. Lee.

On Oak Street, a few blocks from Broadway and Main, stood the Law Enforcement Center and, across the street from the center, the giant engine driving this $5 billion tourist machine – the Myrtle Beach Area Chamber of Commerce. Just inside the modern, glass and brick building, lay the seven-foot-wide MBA Chamber of Commerce logo – a hollow doughnut of a sun set above stylized blue waves – cast in terrazzo in the lobby floor. Beside it, a small brass plaque with the message: "This Visitor's Lobby Is Sponsored by The Generous Contribution of The Burroughs & Chapin Co. Inc." At the foot of the circular stair stood a small sculpture, cast in glass and bronze, portraying Franklin G. Burroughs and Simeon B. Chapin, two men who never met, but whose legacy dominated this town like twin Caesars. The inscription: "A Vision From the Beginning. They Shared the Dream of A Seaside Resort on A Beautiful But Barren Shore."

In a town with a historic inferiority complex, Chamber of Commerce president Ashby Ward was the perfect antidote – part therapist, part cheerleader, part economic advisor. From Wilmington,

North Carolina, to Georgetown, Charleston, Beaufort and Savannah, the Southern seaboard is a string of gracious old cities, full of history, culture, grand houses and public buildings. Hilton Head is not as old, but the international resort bears the seal of genuine wealth and power. Myrtle Beach, by contrast, has always been the "Redneck Riviera" – a town of T-shirts, draft beer and foot-long hot dogs. But Ashby Ward offered a new vision. Myrtle Beach had a destiny, he told his parishioners. It would be to tourism what San Francisco was to the Gold Rush, what Houston was to the oil boom. He never missed a chance to boast of its astounding growth and rising stature. And in the process of transforming Myrtle Beach, he transformed himself.

Myrtle Beach was probably the only city in the nation where the local Chamber of Commerce chief was quoted in the media almost as much as the weatherman. When a government agency or trade group released tourism data, when airlines adjusted their schedules, when gas prices rose or fell, *The Sun News* was on the phone to find out what Ashby Ward made of it. And he never disappointed. His rosy and erudite pronouncements were part of the cultural landscape. Such a presence was he that *Sun News* columnist Bob Bestler poked gentle fun at him and reported Ashby Ward sightings at public events. While staff members referred to him and addressed him in almost whispered obsequiousness as "Mr. Ward," in some Grand Strand circles he was – like Elvis and Roseanne – a one-name celebrity. When economic news broke, people wanted to know: "What does Ashby think? What did Ashby say?"

To reach millions of potential visitors each year, the MBA Chamber of Commerce had a Web site and distributed a number of publications. Its most ponderous medium was the *Myrtle Beach Area Vacation Guide: Where to Stay and Play*, an eight-by-ten-inch, 360-page glossy book, with thousands of repetitive photographs of people enjoying the hotels, restaurants and golf courses of the Grand Strand. The Chamber printed 400,000 of these hefty tomes each year and handed them out free of charge in their four offices.

The Chamber was quick to get on the Web, advertising its site in fifty states, plus Canada, the United Kingdom and Germany. At www.myrtlebeachlive.com one could find an astounding compilation of data, some of it useful, some of it just plain bragging. For instance, Myrtle Beach was ranked the number one beach destination by motorcoach carriers and tour operators in the United States. *Byways* magazine, a publication of the National Motorcoach Network, said Myrtle Beach was the second most highly preferred destination in the

United States and U-Haul International listed Myrtle Beach as a "Top 50 Growth City." *American Demographics* ranked Myrtle Beach as the second fastest-growing metro area in both projected annual population and projected employment from 1995 to 2005.

There were stats enough to keep a baseball junky happy through the long winter months. The MBA Chamber had demographic statistics, geographic statistics, economic statistics, even climate statistics: there were, on average, 215 sunny days in Myrtle Beach each year, 150 overcast days and 42 frost days. The average air temperature was 64 degrees; average water temperature, 66 degrees. The Web site listed distances from every major American and Canadian city east of New Orleans (845 miles) and south of Ottawa (967 miles).

Among visitors to the Strand in 1997, fifty-nine percent were professional; seventeen percent blue-collar; nine percent retired. Approximately thirty-one percent were in the $60,000-plus income range and nine percent in the $20,000-or-less group. There were statistics on the age of visitors, their length of stay, their origin, their preferred activities and the type of visitor party. Families remained the largest group, representing forty-three percent.

If there was a worm in Ashby Ward's apple, it was crime. In the early 1990s, a series of tourist murders in Florida made international headlines and cost that state untold millions in tourism dollars. Some said it is only a matter of time before something like that happened on the Grand Strand. Horry County had the highest crime rate in South Carolina in 1998, eighty percent above the statewide average. A large portion of that crime was committed by the 13 million visitors who came to the Grand Strand each year, as Ward was always eager to point out. It was a distinction that would matter only to a chamber of commerce chief. "You can't compare a tourism destination with a typical community," Ward said in 1997. "A community like ours can never be the place it would like to be because all the visitors skew the crime rate."

Horry County was such a magnet for criminals that *The Sun News* periodically ran photos of wanted felons from far corners of the country, with the notice that they were suspected to be in the area. On January 1, 1999, the FBI announced the arrest of Eric John Neal, wanted in connection with bank robberies in Arizona and North Carolina. He had been living in North Myrtle Beach for a year.

Police said criminals on the lam came to the Grand Strand because their out-of-state license plates did not draw a second glance in this tourist mecca. Perhaps they were right, but I suspect the town's growing reputation as a wide-open, anything-goes environment was an irresistible draw to those who lived on the edge of the law. People come here, after all, to play, to relax, to drop their inhibitions for a few days. For many, the next step is a trip to the booking room at the Law Enforcement Center.

There is something else about this town that drives people over the edge. People come here – both tourists and residents – in search of something they have lost or something they never had. They come to get rich or to find happiness. They come after divorces and bankruptcies, they come with their estranged wives and girlfriends, hoping that somehow the magic of this town will heal everything, will make them whole and happy and prosperous. They come here as they would go to Lourdes or Fatima, seeking a miracle. In time they discover there are no miracles, but there is plenty of booze and drugs and places to get in trouble. And so the blue lights flash and the sirens wail through the Myrtle Beach nights; the "police blotter" in *The Sun News* lists fights and brawls, stabbings and shootings, domestic violence out of all proportion to the city's population.

Drugs were a plague along the Grand Strand in 1999, and the public relations aspect of the disease was as critical as dealing with the fact itself. Myrtle Beach never invested in a drug dog. Some claimed that having a dog would draw attention to the city's ugly problem, though Myrtle Beach Police Chief Warren Gall flatly denied such motivation. "Of course, there are drugs in Myrtle Beach," Gall told me. "There are drugs in every American city." During a few days in January, Myrtle Beach police seized thirty grams of powder cocaine and arrested three suspects, one from Miami. Horry County narcotics officers intercepted a package from Miami containing 400 doses of the designer drug Ecstasy, popular in local dance clubs.

In the tenderloin district around the Pavilion, crime was endemic, much of it driven by drugs. In August of 1998, Terry McElroy was murdered in Room 319 of the Castaways Motel, a notorious Boulevard flophouse. McElroy was popular and widely known on the Boulevard. The 34-year-old Canadian had arrived in Myrtle Beach a few months before, drawn by the town's reputation and bright lights. He had worked in several beachwear stores and – according to some who knew him – he moved drugs on the Strip. Police charged his two roommates with the murder.

Most Boulevard crime was less dramatic – robberies and burglaries to buy drugs. The early hours of January 2, 1999, saw robberies at two Boulevard flophouses. Within days, another man was robbed in the Bon Villa Motel and a woman was slashed at the Castaways in a domestic dispute. It was just a quiet winter week on the Boulevard.

Boulevard of Dreams,
Boulevard of Tears

On a warm January day in the second week of 1999, I stood on Ocean Boulevard at 9th Avenue North, gazing across the street at the Pavilion Amusement Park. With the first breath of spring, it would roar to life once more. Hundreds of thousands of lights would flash and blink; music would pour from the old German band organ; engines would whirl and spin and toss squealing, gleeful revelers through the muggy summer nights, creating memories to last a lifetime. But now it hibernated in the gentle Carolina winter, waiting. . . waiting. . .

I closed my eyes and tried to picture this place as it must have looked a century ago, without the funk and litter and hip-hop music pounding from cars and pickup trucks, tried to picture women in bustle skirts and men in straw boaters strolling over the dunes. This is where it all began, with the Seaside Inn standing where the Log Flume now runs, with a string and brass band thumping out dance tunes under a small pavilion. Everything that is Myrtle Beach — the millions of tourists who come here each year, the billions of dollars in commerce and development, the fun and the filth, the greed and the glory — all started on this spot.

For me, this place is as historic as any battlefield. This is sacred ground. What happened here changed and brightened millions of lives. Yet there was no marker, no monument to remember that past. Indeed, there was no historic marker anywhere in the City of Myrtle Beach. Nothing has a chance to become historic; the bulldozers move too fast. Myrtle Beach exists only in the moment. What is here today will be swept away tomorrow, like the litter each night on Ocean Boulevard. A moment of pleasure and then — irrelevance. A historic marker on this corner would look as out of place as a Ferris wheel in front of Independence Hall.

Whatever else it is, Myrtle Beach is intense and immediate. It leaves emotions and impressions, rather than a visual narrative. There was certainly nothing memorable in the mundane commercial architecture, the look-alike hotels and bars. I can barely picture Sloppy Joe's, the legendary restaurant and bingo parlor that once stood on this corner. It was open around the clock, through all seasons, and they made a hell of a cheeseburger. What I remember are the smells of chili and grease and the warm feeling of sitting with friends over a beer. There was a sign behind the counter: "We Doze, But We Never Close." Well, Sloppy Joe's was closed now and Ripley's Believe it or Not! Museum stood on the site.

In 1987, Ripley's set out to remodel its façade. The plan called for cracked and shattered walls, creating the effect of an air raid or an earthquake. The design was meant to be a visual grabber for an audience to view the collection of shrunken heads, six-legged cows and other oddities from around the world. The Community Appearance Board reviewed the plan and pronounced it good. "I thought the whole thing was done quite tastefully, and was rather interesting and appropriate for the area," a board member told *The Sun News*. "One side has a crack down it, a window has been split and it looks like a lot of jagged bricks on top."

Indeed, it did. Ripley's was perhaps the most distinctive piece of architecture in Myrtle Beach in 1999. That the project was deemed "appropriate for the area" said a good deal about the area.

The blocks immediately around the Pavilion were a clutter of low-rise commercial structures, housing seedy motels, bars, arcades, beachwear and T-shirt shops, all punctuated by flashing lights and garish signs. Season close-out signs were still hanging in the beachwear windows in January: "SAVINGS UP TO 85%!!!"; "T-SHIRTS – BUY 1, GET 1 FREE"; "SELLING OUT FOR '98–EVERYTHING MUST GO!" Mannequins stood nude in the windows, awaiting spring fashions. In some Boulevard flophouses, such as the Tides and the Castaways, the front entrance doubled as a convenience store, where the desk clerk could rent rooms and sell guests a six-pack to drink on the verandah.

To those who knew a tourist resort as an antiseptic, corporate-crafted experience, Myrtle Beach could be a shock. There were no green spaces on the Boulevard in 1999, no benches, no sidewalk cafés, no Mousekateers with brooms and dustpans, sweeping up every cigarette butt. Even in January, the Boulevard was filthy. There were curbside garbage cans every twenty paces, but why use them? This was Myrtle Beach, after all. People came here to escape their jobs, parents, spouses, responsibilities. In Myrtle Beach, garbage cans are a symbol of repression.

Many tourists are surprised to discover they are in a real town. Disney's corporate fun factory has so insinuated itself into our public psyche that visitors find it hard to understand that Myrtle Beach is a workaday town, replete with children, schools and churches. Residents like to sleep at night. They want to have access to their roads and public places. They don't like going out in the morning to find beer cans on their lawns and drunks sleeping in their carports. To maintain order, Myrtle Beach maintains one of the largest police forces for a town of its size in the nation – 167 positions in 1999, to serve 25,000 residents – and the cops have a reputation for toughness. The thousands who spend a night in the Myrtle Beach jail each year can attest to that.

Another error that has ruined many a vacation is to think this is New Orleans. It may feel like a wide-open town, but make no mistake – this is Baptist country. State law forbids the consumption of alcohol on public property. The Myrtle Beach jail serves breakfast to countless tourists who mistake Ocean Boulevard for Bourbon Street. *Laissez les bon temps roulez*! does not play here.

Nevertheless, lawlessness is a part of Myrtle Beach culture. It starts on the Boulevard, where a spot check of thirty beachwear and souvenir shops revealed that eleven had no current business licenses; and it extends to the outermost corners of the county, where developers run roughshod over zoning and environmental regulations.

On the Boulevard that January day, drugs were bought and sold and used almost as casually as cigarettes. Marijuana smoke wafted from alleys and shop doors, along with the pulsing, pounding sound of techno-pop and hip-hop music. Nitrous oxide cylinders lay in the gutter, along with cigarette butts, food wrappers and pizza crusts. Boys with spiked, multicolored hair wore baby pacifiers on chains around their necks to protect their teeth from the grinding induced by an Ecstasy high. Drug paraphernalia had been outlawed in Boulevard shops for years, but it still made news when authorities conducted a sting and busted a shop owner. Police found a pharmacopia of drugs on kids when they made routine arrests for other violations. The Myrtle Beach Police Department reported 424 juvenile arrests in 1999.

In a town that has been called the T-shirt Capital of the World, City Hall fought a twenty-year war against "obscene" T's, including the ones that featuring Dr. Condom, the happy prophylactic; the ones that scream "Eat Me!"; the ones that conceal male and female genitalia in obscure line drawings.

In July 1988, Myrtle Beach police arrested twenty-eight Boulevard

T-shirt vendors. Mayor Bob Grissom said he couldn't "see what type sick person it would take to wear those T-shirts." Before it was over, the American Civil Liberties Union was called in, a review committee was established to determine what T-shirts violated community standards, and the city was written up in The *Washington Post* and *The Atlanta Constitution*. "The controversy may be one sign of the social pains in this increasingly urban area . . . as it tries to decide what kind of city it wants to be when it finishes growing up," the *Post* reported.

The paper quoted Jacob Garon, one of the merchants who was arrested: "The people who have lived down here for years are fighting it," he said. "Maybe it looks obscene to them, but it doesn't look obscene to the tourists."

In 1996, city council specifically defined and outlawed what it found to be obscene in the corporate limits of Myrtle Beach. The ordinance was almost as titillating as anything a T-shirt vendor could print. It prohibited selling or wearing "any depiction or description . . . of any sexual intercourse; masturbation; sadomasochistic abuse; sexual penetration with an inanimate object; sodomy; bestiality; uncovered genitals, buttocks or female breast; defecation or urination; covered genitals in an obvious state of sexual stimulation or arousal; or the fondling or other erotic touching of genitals, the pubic region, buttocks or female breasts."

With that perfectly clear, Boulevard T-shirt vendors were reduced to peddling tamer material. Today, the T-shirt trade celebrates Myrtle Beach and Southern culture, as well as such hedonistic and working class ideals as Fords, Chevrolets, spring break, biker rallies, drugs ("Why Go To High School When You Can Go To School High?"), alcohol ("One Tequila, Two Tequila, Three Tequila, Floor!"), misogyny ("Treat Me Like the Bitch That I Am"), alcohol *and* misogyny ("15 Reasons Why A Beer Is Better Than A Woman"). But no breasts, buttocks or pubic regions.

T-shirt vendors posed another problem for the city's image: many were accomplished con artists. Their scam involved finding some poor sucker who could be pressured into buying a customized T-shirt with various decals ironed onto it. There would be little discussion of price – especially the cost of the wax paper used to separate the iron from the decal or the "fluffing charge" imposed when the merchant shook the T-shirt after applying each decal. When the job was done, the shopkeeper presented the stunned vacationer with his new shirt and an itemized bill for as much as $100. If the customer balked, the merchant reached for the phone and threatened to call the police. It was a well-rehearsed, widely practiced scam, as attested by the numerous complaints to tourism and city officials. In 1995, city council required that T-shirt vendors present a written cost estimate to the buyer before any custom work was done. The ordinance specifically outlawed the threat of arrest to force a customer to make a purchase.

Another image problem for this very image-conscious town was body piercing. Piercing brought out the seamy side in both the piercers and the pierced. To promote their services, Boulevard piercers plastered Polaroid snapshots of their happy customers across the windows of their shops. Passers-by could see fat, hairy guys pointing proudly to the rings in their nipples; or teenage girls with tongues flopped out to show off their new stainless steel studs; or thrusting their pelvises to display rings in their navels.

Young shills stood outside the piercing pagodas, hawking and spitting, puffing on cigarettes and daring tourists to come in and "feel the steel." The shills had felt the steel many times. Their ears, lips, tongues and noses were perforated with rings and studs. One young Boulevard denizen had at least seventeen pieces of metal sticking out of his head. Another had a horizontal bar sticking through the flesh between his eyes, giving him a Cyclops effect. As I walked past him, he beckoned me toward the door of a piercing parlor. "Hey, dude, wanna get pierced? I can get you a deal." He shifted his weight from foot to foot, puffing on his Camel Light. There were multiple rings through his ears and one through his lip.

"Maybe next time." Then I asked, "Why do you get pieced?"

He grinned broadly, showing a mouth of yellow, rotting teeth. "Fashion!" he said.

The fashion had seized the younger generation. Some piercers did as many as a dozen jobs an hour, sending hundreds of kids back home to mom and dad, after a weekend in Myrtle Beach, with jewelry dangling from body parts where none had been when they left home. City Attorney Joe Wettlin grew tired of taking calls from outraged parents, threatening to sue the city. In 1996, city council required anyone being pierced to be eighteen years of age or have the consent of a parent or guardian. Like other Boulevard ordinances, this one was tough to enforce. Piercing continued to flourish, attracting bad publicity to the town and a seedy crowd to the Boulevard.

Piercers charged, not for the hole they put in your body, but for the ring or stud they put in the hole. Hand-scrawled signs listed prices for various piercings, along with daily "Specials," like the menu board in a truck diner.

Navel – $18.99
Eyebrow – $18.99
Tongue – $23.99
Nipple – $23.99
Ear – $18.99

"Numbing Available Upon Request"

The numbing agent used by most piercers was Lidocaine. First aid kits were also available as part of the package from some piercers.

Cosmetic piercing of body parts, other than ear lobes, was new in South Carolina – so new that there were no laws regulating it in 1999, no standards of training or hygiene. In this age of AIDS, anybody could set up a piercing parlor in a garage or the front window of a beachwear shop – and many did. Some piercers did not have access to running water or a restroom. Because piercing was considered naughty and nonconformist, it naturally came to Myrtle Beach first. Blondies was said to be the first shop to offer it. By 1999, there were dozens of piercing shops along the Boulevard and dozens more in other locations on the Grand Strand. Nobody knew how many, because there was no bureaucracy to oversee them.

Everywhere, signs advertised "Professional Body Piercing," yet I saw no body piercing diplomas from body piercing universities. The primary requisite for the body piercing profession – like the oldest profession itself – seemed to be a burning desire to practice. Claims of professionalism were meant not just to allay health fears; they were a cry for respectability from this seedy, renegade class of entrepreneurs. Most piercers said they would welcome some regulation of their industry, if it would weed out the more nefarious operators, yet they seemed incapable of regulating themselves. Operators' personal appearances reinforced their image of nonconformity. Male piercers tended to be unshaven and unkempt. The women often dressed like streetwalkers.

Nate Fogel worked in one of the four Pit Bull Piercing stands. His card read, "Don't Get Stuck By A Prick – Get Pierced By A Pro." He had multiple piercings himself, long stringy hair, baggy flannel and denim clothes and looked as if he slept on the street. I wouldn't let him change the oil in my car, let alone stick needles through me. I brought this up with him. Wouldn't he look more professional if he cut his hair? I asked. Or wore a white lab coat? Or washed his clothes?

"I think people judge us by what we do, not how we look," he offered smugly.

Nate turned to piercing after years of building prefab log cabins, he told me. He found Myrtle Beach through word of mouth and came to town in December 1998.

Brandy McKinnon, 19, was a piercer at another Pit Bull location a few blocks away. She had pierced in Atlanta, arrived in town the week before and landed a job within days. She came to Myrtle Beach to "get away from life's mistakes," she told me – specifically, her boyfriend.

Angie Baird, 23, had a similar story. On the lam from her husband, she was an experienced piercer who recently arrived in Myrtle Beach. Much pierced and tattooed herself, the lovely, raven-haired young woman was working at Boulevard Beachwear when I met her. She had been piercing since she was sixteen, she told me. Like Brandy McKinnon, she believed that women make the best piercers, because they are patient and gentle. She talked to her customers as she prepped and disinfected the site, she said, taking them through the procedure. She would tell them to take a deep breath, then to let it out. As the customer exhaled, she quickly pushed the needle through. "It's all flow," she said. "I always try to go with the breath."

Tommy and Jackie Michaels did their piercing at a stand called Dr. Pierce in the front window at Bargain Beachwear. They pierced dozens of people a day and were observed by hundreds more. Tommy was from Israel, Jackie from the Jewish community of Mexico City. They had a ten-year-old son, Sammy. It was their dream to some day have a Dr. Pierce in every mall in America, like Hair Cuttery, with universal standards for sanitation. "One name that families and parents trust, no rip-offs, no infections," Tommy Michaels said. "I believe I have been put here for this."

Max Alon was manager of Ocean Wear. Another Israeli, Alon was surly, cynical and wary from the scrutiny of press and authorities over the piercing issue. He said I was trying to "trash" his business "like all the rest of them always do." Actually, his shop was one of the cleanest in the area, but Alon said he wanted to get out of the piercing business. "It attracts shit people," he said. He was one of the few piercers on the Boulevard who was not pierced.

Another was Rich Russell. He had been pierced, but now, at age thirty, had allowed the holes to close. "I guess I outgrew it," he said. Russell was the manager of Can-Am Gifts, a Boulevard shop that has pierced as many as 120 people a day. Located in the back of the shop, his piercing room was as spotless as a hospital facility.

Russell told me he doesn't do "the really weird shit." In Russell's vernacular, the "weird shit" refers to two specific procedures. The "Prince Albert" is the piercing and placing of a ring through the tip of the penis. The "hood" is the piercing and placing of a ring through the labium, just below the clitoris. Most piercing is purely cosmetic; it visually enhances sex appeal. But some piercings are said to enhance the sex act itself. A ring through the nipple – male or female – will increase sensitivity. A stud through the tongue will stimulate a woman during oral sex. A ring through the penis produces the same effect in more conventional conjugations. As for the ring through the labium, several piercers told me that after women get the "hood," they often take up jogging for the stimulation it gives them.

Josh Woolbright was one piercer who did the "weird shit." Woolbright ran Kugi's, a hole-in-the-wall shop between the Boulevard and the boardwalk and he did a couple of genital piercings a week, he said. Requests for that specialty were particularly strong during the annual Harley-Davidson Rally.

But all that was about to come to an end. In October 1998, Myrtle Beach city council passed an ordinance to ban body piercing on the Boulevard. A group of piercers had gone to federal court and won a delay, but time was running out on their injunction. On April 17, 1999, body piercing would become illegal, creating another underground industry, another law for Boulevard merchants to ignore or evade.

In the mid-1990s, a film student named Lisa Bazadona spent four Boulevard summers painting temporary tattoos to pay her way through college. Drawing from that experience, she wrote a screenplay for her senior thesis project at the State University of New York. Her professor, independent filmmaker Robert Siegel, was so taken with the script that he optioned it, put together a production company for the project and spent 28 days shooting on the streets of Myrtle Beach in the autumn of 1998.

Called *Swimming*, the film featured a talented, largely unknown young cast, including Lauren Ambrose and Jennifer Dundas Lowe. As described in the director's synopsis, the coming-of-age story focused on "the sun and flesh world of Myrtle Beach where contact is often skin deep and relationships even less so [sic]. . . ." The young restaurant workers, body piercers and T-shirt peddlers talk their way in and out of painful relationships – including a lesbian infatuation – in what reads like Ingmar-Bergman-on-the-Beach. (The film was released to a very short run and mixed reviews in the summer of 2002.)

The world of lonely and desperate young people Bazadona discovered was very much in evidence in 1999. Mostly male and mostly white, they came from every Southern state and throughout the Midwest, usually arriving in the spring and summer, when there was work to be found and they could sleep comfortably outside. They dressed in the baggy, shapeless garb of skateboard outlaws or the sagging, beltless pants of "jailhouse chic." Their T-shirts promoted cigarettes and liquor they weren't old enough to buy. Some had tipped and tinted hair; others, greasy locks and ponytails. They wore sport caps with the bill flipped down on the back of the neck or toboggan caps pulled down over their ears. Around their necks were chains of gold and hemp. Cigarettes were universal; sharing and lighting them together was part of the camaraderie of the Boulevard. And all were pierced: rings through their noses, ears, eyebrows, nipples and navels; studs through their tongues. They collected around the entrances of the body piercing bazaars, showing off their holes and hardware. They shucked and jived, shouted and cursed, laughed and slouched with one hand thrust deep into their baggy pockets, another lifting a cigarette to their lips. They growled malevolently at any perceived challenge, punctuated each inarticulate utterance with a stream of "Fuck . . . Fuck . . . Muthafucker!" They hawked and spat, flipped their cigarette butts into the street and lit more.

Some were obviously striving for effect, like the burly young punk with shaved head and two pit bulls lunging on the end of chains as he walked menacingly down the sidewalk. And the guy with the metallic green hair, a spiked leather collar on his neck and the T-shirt that read, "SEXUALIS PATHOLOGEA – Dead Girls Don't Say No." And the couple, the guy smoking a cigarette and leading his girl down the Boulevard with a chain though the ring in her navel, as she licked an ice cream cone.

It was as stylized as *West Side Story*, except these young punks had no gangs they could belong to. And for the most part, they had no jobs, no cars, no families, no place to live. But they had the Boulevard and – for a few hours each day – some companionship as they bantered and whistled at the girls and set up their next drug scores. They were almost celebrities in their belligerent nonconformity, returning year after year, thousands of them living on the streets, sleeping on the beaches, turning tricks, panhandling, fighting, crying, begging, going hungry, going to jail. Like millions of others, they came here because they heard Myrtle Beach held some balm, some elixir that would give them hope and happiness. Most of them would only have their hearts broken one more time. Some would go berserk and we would read about them in the newspaper after a night of mayhem or tragedy. Others would grow more jaded and cynical; a few would even grow up.

South Carolina Rolls the Dice

On January 12, 1999, Jim Hodges stood on the south portico of the State House to take the oath of office as governor. With thousands of other groundlings, I watched what looked like a Gilbert and Sullivan pageant. Two hours in the cold were rewarded by the oath of office and the new governor's boilerplate inaugural address. The only thing I remember from the leaden speech was the thumping affirmation: "The Hodges Administration will be a pro-business administration." As if there were ever a doubt.

It was an anticlimax to one of the most remarkable campaigns in recent state history. The former representative from Lancaster County had come out of nowhere to challenge Republican incumbent David Beasley for the Governor's Office, while first-string Democrats were happy to watch him march to his slaughter. But a funny thing happened on the way to the election. Beasley proved to be one of the most inept politicians in memory and, in handing the election to Hodges, he reversed more than a decade of GOP ascendance in the Palmetto State.

Beasley was the none-too-bright son of a wealthy Darlington banking family. As a Clemson University baseball player and member of the General Assembly, he was famed as a hell-raiser and a skirt chaser. (Gary Hart's *femme fatale* Donna Rice was one of his arm trophies.) By the late 1980s, the young senator could see which way the wind was blowing. He not only took the mantle of Christian fundamentalism; he took a bride and began siring a clutch of little Beasleys. In 1992, he switched from the Democratic Party to the GOP, positioning himself for the big prize. He won the nod from popular Republican Governor Carroll Campbell, along with the party nomination to succeed Campbell and, at age 37, Beasley rode into office on the Republican tidal wave of 1994. Then everything went wrong.

In the year before the 1996 elections, a couple of Washington pundits happened to drop the name of South Carolina's telegenic young governor as a potential running mate on the national GOP ticket – if not in '96, then perhaps in 2000. With the memory of Dan Quayle fresh on everyone's mind, anything seemed possible. They were heady times for young Beasley. He must have thought he heard Destiny whisper his name. As it turned out, she was only whistling "Dixie."

Before he could be taken seriously as a national candidate, Beasley had to slay a dragon in his own house. Since 1962, the Confederate flag had flown above the State House dome, just below the Palmetto State and the United States flags. For many white Southerners, the Stars and Bars stood for their heritage and the courage of their Confederate ancestors. But to African Americans, it was a vivid, ubiquitous symbol of racism and they had lots of memories and photographs of men with white robes and Confederate flags to make their argument. Republican legislators sabotaged all attempts to compromise the flag off the dome in the early 1990s. Beasley courted the white "heritage" groups in his 1994 campaign, promising to protect the flag against all transgressors, but he now had his eyes on a bigger prize. In 1996, Beasley announced that he had been shown – through prayer and Bible reading – that the Confederate flag should come down. The governor's conversion was short-lived, however. He took a beating from fellow Republicans and was roundly denounced in conservative circles throughout the state. He accepted his lumps and dropped the issue. But the heritage groups felt personally betrayed and swore vengeance.

Beasley had shot himself in the foot; even so, he might have limped to an easy re-election. But he wanted to make a bold gesture to solidify his Christian right base. In his State of the State address in January 1998, he came out against video gambling, declaring it a "cancer" and saying it undermined the value of hard work and preyed on working-class families. In the process, he made blood enemies of the state's $2.5 billion dollar video poker industry. The video gambling moguls – men like Fred Collins, Henry Ingram, Alan Schafer and Jimmy McDonald – retaliated by pouring millions of dollars into state Democratic coffers. Some of them spent hundreds of thousands more on personal campaigns denouncing Beasley in newspaper, billboard, radio and television ads. It was all part of the most expensive statewide campaign South Carolina had ever seen.

Candidate Hodges was happy to take the gambling money. As a state representative in the early 1990s, he had decried video gambling and called for a ban. But now, in the heat of the gubernatorial campaign, he saw the error in his ways. Video poker should not be banned without a referendum, he declared, and if he were elected, he would let the people pass judgment on the game in a direct vote. As for the Confederate flag, he promised he would stay out of the controversy.

So it happened that David Beasley handed the election to the Democrats by alienating one of his most important constituencies – working class whites. It was the working class people of South Carolina – black and white – who poured their wealth and their dreams into video poker machines, hoping to change their luck, to change their lives, to beat the odds of flipping hamburgers or processing poultry in this backward, minimum-wage state. It was working class whites, by and large, who were most vocal, violent and vehement in their support of the Confederate flag. And it is to the eternal shame of South Carolina that so many of her people saw no deliverance beyond the liquid crystal images dancing on the video screen; felt no pride beyond a scrap of cloth representing a corrupt nation which died more than a century before.

On the day Hodges took the oath of office in Columbia, South Carolina became the province and possession of the video poker industry. In a state where gambling did not legally exist, some 7,000 businesses – nearly one in every three retail businesses in South Carolina – offered video poker. That was more gambling venues than any other state, including Nevada, New Jersey or Mississippi. There were 36,000 gambling machines in the state, or about one for every 1,100 residents. As David Plotz wrote in *Harper's Magazine*, "Video poker is South Carolina's white noise, so pervasive that you stop noticing its ugliness."

Nowhere was video poker more pervasive or ugly than in Horry County, where history and culture offered fertile ground. The legendary card games at the old Ocean Forest Hotel drew high-stakes players from all over the East Coast and Myrtle Beach once boasted a horse track and a dog track on Kings Highway. The famous *Saturday Evening Post* illustration of the lounge at the Dunes Club shows the good old boys sitting around poker tables, their cards, chips and money plainly in view.

On Inauguration Day 1999, there were some 3,300 video poker machines in Horry County – or three per square mile, one for every forty-six residents – generating more than $350 million in annual revenue for the video poker industry. Along with video poker grew the corollary industry of pawn, loan and check-cashing shops, sometimes operating out of the same buildings. From one end of the Strand to the other, the garish signs and flashing lights beckoned travelers into video casinos – or "video malls," as the industry dubbed them. But video gambling was not limited to casinos. In bars, restaurants, service stations, convenience stores and laundromats, the liquid crystal screens stood lined against the walls, seducing with their promise of electronic jackpots. The dead-enders, the down-and-outers would sit for hours, for days, pushing their dollars into the machines, pushing the buttons, watching the cards flip up on the screens, while the stubble grew on their faces and their fingertips turned yellow from nicotine.

With video gambling firmly entrenched and market-tested on shore, could casino boats be far behind? In November 1998, *Victori Casino* dropped anchor in Little River, the picturesque fishing village just below the North Carolina border. The 100-foot purple-and-white catamaran offered six-hour excursions beyond U.S. territorial waters, where state laws against gambling did not apply. Instead of video poker machines, the *Victori Casino* offered Las Vegas-style gambling, replete with slot machines, roulette wheels, blackjack tables and croupiers.

Little River was immediately divided, especially when two more gambling boats announced they were coming to town. "Three gambling boats in Little River is ridiculous. Not one person in my neighborhood is for it," local resident Maggie Weldon told *The Sun News*. "If I could get out, I would."

At Little River United Methodist Church, the Reverend Paul Wood and his followers collected 875 signatures on a petition asking the General Assembly to crack down on the gambling epidemic. Their orders came from the *United Methodist Church Book of Discipline*: "Gambling is a menace to society, deadly to the best interests of moral, social, economic and spiritual life, and destructive of good government. As an Act of faith and concern, Christians should abstain from Gambling and should strive to minister to those victimized by the practice . . . "

Local businesses along the Little River waterfront organized a lobbying group to secure legislative protection for casino boats. Motel owner Jim Hans said his occupancy rate rose from fifteen percent to more than seventy percent during the off-season. "I'd rather fill my motel with golfers and casino patrons on Memorial Day weekend than bikers," Hans said. "The clientele is completely different [from video poker players]. They're snowbirds and blue hairs, no blue collars hocking their tools for cash to play." The Little River Chamber of Commerce endorsed the casino boats and Ashby Ward offered membership in the MBA Chamber.

Feeding the gambling craze in Horry County were millions of tourists and day-trippers from North Carolina. A quarter-mile from the state line, Little River was said to be the most saturated gambling environment in South Carolina. "Little Reno," as the unincorporated town of 5,000 was called, was home to sixteen video poker casinos, a total of 584 gambling machines in 124 locations.

Almost lost in the frenzy and the anger over gambling was the memory of Rodney Graham. On February 23, 1998, the body of the twenty-two-year-old Excalibur Security guard was found on the floor of State Line Casino in Little River. He had been shot, execution-style; a large sum of money had been taken from the casino. It took law enforcement agencies until December 1998 to charge Christopher Costa and Lou Bezer with the murder. Both were former Excalibur employees; Costa was already on parole for stealing money from State Line gambling machines.

As the General Assembly opened for business in January, Republicans tried to make hay out of the gambling debate, but found themselves as conflicted as the rest of the state. Their first order of business, they announced, would be a ban on casino boats. "I have made it a top legislative priority," House Speaker David Wilkins said. The casino boat bill would move "at warp speed" through the House, he announced.

Though new to South Carolina, the casino boat owners clearly understood how the game was played. Documents from the State Ethics Commission showed that, in the first quarter of 1999, *Victori Casino* owner Dewayne Williams spent $145,000 on lobbyists in Columbia. Williams got his money's worth. The bill to ban casino boats sailed through the Republican-controlled House in near record time but died a slow and painful death in the Democratic-controlled Senate.

As the Senate debate wore on, thousands of South Carolinians received an unsigned postcard with this message:

> Fact: South's [sic] Carolina's largest industry, tourism, is facing a crisis. Last year, S.C.'s tourism industry suffered the biggest

decrease in history. Mississippi's casino tourist attractions are taking away more and more of our state's tourism dollars.

It was a bold exposé, indeed. Only problem was, it was all wrong. "It's as wrong as it can be," a state tourism official in Columbia told *The Sun News*, citing facts and figures to show that 1998 had set records for tourism in the state. "So the postcard is a bald-faced lie."

The casino boat debate seemed to bring out the worst in everyone. In mid-January, Senator Robert Ford of Charleston went on a fact-finding mission to the Grand Strand. He emerged after a week of intensive research to disclose his results: "I counted forty-seven escort services in the phone book," the bombastic Democrat announced. "I called seven of them and spent some time with those folks. Over four or five days, I had an occasion to frequent some of the nude nightclubs where the women weren't just topless, they were completely naked, with lap dances and massages and the whole nine yards."

Legislative efforts to preserve the Grand Strand's family image were a waste of time, Ford said, because that image "is based on a lie that Myrtle Beach is a family beach."

"There's more sin in Myrtle Beach entertainment than anywhere else in South Carolina," Ford said on another occasion. "Men from all over the world go to Myrtle Beach to have a good time. If they want to maintain a family beach atmosphere, casino boats are the least of their worries." Ford accused Burroughs & Chapin of driving the anti-casino boat campaign. "They want to control everything," he said.

The forces of righteousness were apoplectic. "Oh, my God!" was Representative Tracy Edge's terse comment. Senator Dick Elliott of North Myrtle Beach took the floor of the Senate to defend the honor of his county from Ford's scurrilous remarks. Myrtle Beach is a family beach, he declared, "and by golly, any way we can, we're going to keep it that way!"

Ford remained defiant in his indictment of Myrtle Beach: "It's the sin capital of South Carolina. Nobody should get mad about that. It is."

Despite Senator Ford's rhetoric, gambling boats represented only a tiny portion of the gambling in Horry County. The real action was in the 3,300 liquid crystal screens, said to be the source of a wave of crime and bankruptcies in the county.

One thing for sure: Pong never generated such controversy.

Pong, the first video game, came out in the mid-1970s. Invented by Norman Bushnell, Pong used a liquid crystal screen to display a white ball, which two players tried to volley past one another, as in Ping-Pong. More novel than challenging, Pong was soon followed by Pac-Man, Space Invaders, Galaga, Donkey Kong and hundreds of other liquid crystal thrills. By the early 1980s, video games were conquering the world, but they were doing it two bits at a time. The challenge for video game manufacturers was to get people to drop five dollar bills, ten dollar bills, whole paychecks into a machine. Video poker was as inevitable as telephone sex and a hell of a lot more lucrative.

Under the state constitution of 1895, gambling was illegal in South Carolina. Because it officially did not exist, there were almost no laws to govern it, no commission to oversee it, no restrictions by age or background on who could own machines or play them, no regulations on the payout rate of the machines, and only a minuscule tax on gambling revenues. South Carolina was the Wild West of gambling and nowhere more than in Horry County. And some powerful interests wanted to keep it that way.

"At rock bottom, South Carolina has a gambling problem because it can't decide whether it's a puritanical state or a libertarian one." So wrote David Plotz in a brilliant exposition of South Carolina's video gambling crisis in *Harper's Magazine*. "The interior of the state is severe, religious and conservative, but coastal Carolina is high-spirited and honky-tonk. The state beverage is milk, but the state university mascot is a gamecock."

Puritanical South Carolina "abjured a lottery and rejected Vegas mogul Steve Wynn's 1994 proposal to build six dockside casinos," Plotz wrote. "Meanwhile, libertarian South Carolina embraced video poker, a form of wagering that seemed innocent, mild-mannered, and hardly to be gambling at all."

Video poker came to South Carolina as a byproduct of the juke box and vending machine industry. Fred Collins was one of many small businessmen who made his living in this marginal service sector. In the mid-1970s, Collins introduced the first video gambling machine into South Carolina in the form of a "kit" that could be added to the Pong game. A decade later, when the stand-alone poker machines were developed, Collins and some 400 other jukebox and vending route operators started putting them in businesses around the state, splitting profits with the business owners.

The problem for these entrepreneurs was that South Carolina law forbade "games of chance." To get around this legalistic hurdle required some equally legalistic legerdemain: poker, it was reasoned, was no different from pinball and pinball rewards good play with free games. "Suppose it costs twenty-five cents to play a game of pinball or poker," Plotz wrote. "Well, then each skillfully won free game must be worth twenty-five cents. And if each game is worth twenty-five cents, surely you ought to be able to collect a quarter for it. And if you collect a quarter for one free game, surely you should be able to collect 4,000 quarters for drawing a royal flush."

To nail down this legal argument, state Senator Jack Lindsay – the Senate's budget wizard and legal finagler – quietly inserted a tiny amendment into the 1,000-page 1986 budget bill, striking the words "or property" from a law banning any game from distributing "money or property to a player." Lindsay was acting at the behest of his friend Alan Schafer, who owned a huge roadside attraction called South of the Border. (It is worth noting that this constituent service occurred shortly after Schafer was released from federal prison, following his involvement in fixing Democratic primary elections in Marlboro County. And at the time of his death in 1991, Lindsay was facing indictment in the epic Operation Lost Trust investigation of State House corruption.)

The little words "or property" went unnoticed until 1988, when the state arrested a convenience store operator, charging him with paying out hundreds of thousands of dollars to video poker players. When the case went to court, industry lawyers argued that in dropping the word "or property" from the law, the General Assembly clearly intended the machines to distribute credit slips, which could then be redeemed for cash. The state Supreme Court upheld this reading of the law in 1991.

Wrote Plotz: "Without a debate, without an open vote, without a public referendum, South Carolina had legalized gambling."

With its new "legal" standing, video poker metastasized into every crevice and corner of the state. As one critic observed: "There is not a place in South Carolina where there could be a machine and there isn't one." Vending operators competed feverishly to get their machines into new businesses. Some would provide taverns with tables, chairs, beer coolers and other hardware to win the video poker concession.

As video gambling's profile rose, so did opposition, mostly from Christian Republicans. Opponents managed to pass some laws limiting poker. One was a $125 daily cap on winnings, designed to ensure that video poker was played for low stakes. To forestall video casinos, another law set a limit of five poker machines per location. Responding to public criticism, the poker industry agreed to a county-by-county referendum and, in 1994, twelve counties voted poker out. (Horry voted 24,800 to14,473 to keep it.) Not happy with that result, the poker industry went to court and had the referendum thrown out.

As for the $125-a-day cap, poker operators simply ignored it, advertising jackpots in the thousands of dollars. They circumvented the law through long division. Jackpots of more than $125 were paid off in daily $125 installments. "The industry said it would just be low-stakes gambling – $125," a leading critic complained. "But these people were criminals. They never obeyed the law. They decided they were going to engage in high-stakes illegal gambling until someone stopped them and no one did."

Nothing demonstrated the industry's determination and shrewdness more than its dodge of the five-machines-per-premises limit. It didn't take the operators long to parse the language of the law to its simplest and most improbable meaning. The State Department of Revenue ruled that a "premises" must have fire walls, a business license, a power meter and an attendant. That's all. And with those specs, any operator could pack as many "premises" as could be fit into a building.

The first "video mall" – the industry never called them casinos – was built in Columbia in 1995. Hundreds of these casinos – divided into warrens, each containing five video poker machines – sprang up across the state, clustering along the North Carolina and Georgia state lines, where they enticed thousands of people a day to cross the line and play. By 1999, nearly fifty percent of the state's poker machines were in casinos.

To anybody who has never seen one, it is hard to impart the sense of sheer weirdness of these casino monstrosities. What the operators sought was to offer a taste of the elegant and the exotic to a class of people who had never known either. Typically, these chambers of the surreal were dimly lit, mirrored mazes with floral print carpets and an endless tape of soft rock music in the background. The larger ones offered concrete sculptures, huge plastic palm trees and other ersatz flora, large gilt-framed reproductions of nineteenth century romantic landscapes and still lifes, mounted hunting trophies, fountains and waterfalls running over cast concrete stones. To keep their customers from wandering off, most casinos offered "free food" to their players. This typically consisted of a stainless steel buffet pan of hot dogs beside a buffet pan of potato chips.

Walking through the place, the visitor would pass among the

cubicles – or "premises," to be quite legalistic – each containing five video machines, blinking and flashing in the semi-darkness. At most of those machines sat bleary-eyed losers, staring into the screens, burning through packs of cigarettes, hoping, hoping, always hoping. That's what these people did, mostly. These gloomy environs were the refuge and the trap of working class hicks, louts and the elderly. In the entrance to each cubicle sat a $6.50-an-hour attendant, chewing gum, reading a newspaper, yakking on a cell phone, anything to pass the hours and fulfill the letter of the law that each "premises" must be attended.

Plotz wrote: "I have gambled in Vegas casinos, Indian casinos, Mississippi dockside casinos, bingo parlors, horse tracks and dog tracks, but if there is a gambling house one-tenth as depressing as a South Carolina video parlor, I have not seen it." Sad to think, but these gloomy, bizarre precincts, full of false scenery, false music and false hope, may have been South Carolina's most original contribution to Western civilization.

Unlike Las Vegas casinos and Indian casinos, South Carolina's video gambling casinos offered no high-paying jobs. They didn't even generate heavy construction jobs; most were created by renovating existing buildings. And unlike the upscale gambling meccas of Atlantic City, Las Vegas and Indian reservations, South Carolina gambling brought very little new money into a community or the state. The huge majority of gamblers were local people and the huge majority of those could ill afford the luxury of losing. And therein lay the crisis: Las Vegas and Atlantic City sent their problem gamblers back home to some place far away to drink and divorce, to steal and embezzle, to file bankruptcy and commit suicide. In South Carolina, all the social problems of gambling stayed right here. Video poker "is the crack cocaine of gambling, gambling at its most addictive and virulent, producing few economic benefits and high social costs," Plotz wrote.

A statewide clinical survey of video gamblers found the rate of compulsive gambling was twice as high in South Carolina as in Las Vegas. An experienced player could punch more than a dozen hands of video poker per minute. No form of gambling was faster. For that reason, psychologists said, no form of gambling was more addictive. And no form of gambling was more ubiquitous. In South Carolina, a compulsive gambler could hardly go out of his house without encountering a poker machine.

As the epidemic spread, stories appeared in the media and day-to-day conversation of people who had lost their homes, their savings, their family fortunes to video poker. A local businesswoman told me she was in the process of having one of her salesmen charged with larceny. She said she had started missing checks, then whole deposits before she called in professional help to find out where the money was going. Confronted with the evidence of his thefts, the salesman confessed that he had been playing the machines for six months; he had lost everything and was reduced to moving in with his parents.

In one horrific incident, a 28-year-old sergeant named Gail Baker crossed the river from Hunter Army Air Field near Savannah, Georgia, to gamble at one of the casinos clustered around the head of the U.S. 17 bridge. It was a hot August day in 1997, and Baker left her ten-day-old daughter in the car with the windows closed. When she returned more than seven hours later, the infant was dead.

Around the state the number of Gamblers Anonymous chapters had tripled since 1994. In Horry County, there were at least three. I talked to "Chuck," a retired New Jersey public school teacher and car salesman living in a neat, inland mobile home park with his second wife. Chuck told me he had gambled in Reno and Atlantic City for years and "it never bothered me." In 1990, he and his wife came to Myrtle Beach and he encountered video gambling in the form of Cherry Masters, an early video gambling device. "It started out as a harmless little thing," he said. He could gamble on Cherry Masters for pennies a game. "I could play all day for $20." Then the new generation of machines called Pot-O-Gold rolled into town, and the price of poker skyrocketed. The minimum play cost twenty-five cents and a player could bet as many dollars as he wanted on a hand. And the machines were everywhere – "every filling station, everywhere you step out the door," Chuck said.

"It got to the point that the only thing I thought about was gambling and how to get enough money to gamble that day," he said. His wife would leave for work at 7:00 a.m. and he would be at the machines by 7:15. "To me, my job was playing those machines eight hours a day."

"Most gamblers lose all sense of reality," Chuck told me. People will take a forty percent loan from a video casino operator and think nothing of it. He once saw an elderly woman collapse from hunger and fatigue after thirty-six straight hours at one machine. As she was taken away, she cried not to let anybody touch "her" machine.

"It's so easy. Just push the button – BAM! Push the button – BAM! No waiting, no putting in quarters one at a time or pulling the arm, no waiting for coins to drop out. Just pure action," Chuck said. "Completely hypnotic."

In 1993, when Chuck was in the hospital for heart surgery, bounced check notices started landing in the mailbox. This was the first his wife knew of his problem. He had cleaned out their savings account and cooked the books to keep her in the dark. When he returned home, she gave him the phone number for Gamblers Anonymous and ordered him to start attending – "or else." He promised he would – but he lied.

"People who gamble are habitual liars," said his wife, listening in on our conversation.

Chuck kept taking out loans. He sold his pickup truck and wiped out his wife's savings. When he was at the 1997 Super Bowl in New Orleans, his wife intercepted the mail from the bank and the finance company. That's when "it all hit the fan," Chuck said. His wife delivered the ultimatum: get help or she would leave. Again she gave him the number for Gamblers Anonymous. This time he used it and started attending meetings three times a week. His wife enrolled in GamAnon, a program for spouses of addicted gamblers.

With Gamblers Anonymous, Chuck had gotten a grip on his life. When I talked to him, he had not placed a bet in more than two years and he was leader of the Gamblers Anonymous group in Conway. He had no checkbook or credit cards; his wife handled all the household finances, including his pension and Social Security checks.

Like Alcoholics Anonymous, Gamblers Anonymous is a twelve-step program of spiritual and psychological enlightenment and mutual support. But there is a difference between the gambler and the drunk, as Chuck reminded me. "You can't spot a gambler, but you can spot a drunk. The drunk is falling down. You can smell it on his breath. But who's going to help a gambler?"

"If there was ever a case for government restriction of gambling, South Carolina is it," Plotz wrote. But two months into the legislative session, the Republican-controlled House and the Democratic-controlled Senate were in bitter deadlock on video gambling. Without legislative action, the industry would pass another year – unregulated and virtually untaxed. Emboldened by its defeat of Governor David Beasley and by the most expensive lobbying campaign in state history – at least a million dollars over the last twelve months – video poker was as arrogant and sassy as ever.

The Great Air Force
Base Land Grab

In 1940, Myrtle Beach opened a small municipal airport in the pine barrens south of town. In barely a year, America was at war. The Army Air Corps commandeered the airstrip, using it as a training base. The government seized thousands of acres of empty pine forest west of the Intracoastal Waterway to serve as a bombing and gunnery range. With peace, the air base was deactivated and returned to the City of Myrtle Beach. But that "long twilight struggle" – known less poetically as the Cold War – had just begun.

In 1954, city officials offered to donate the Myrtle Beach Municipal Airport to the Air Force if it would reactivate the base. The offer was accepted, but the deal nearly fell apart when the Air Force announced it planned to buy twenty-four acres of beachfront for recreational use – and the facilities would be racially integrated, in keeping with military policy. When local officials and the white public howled, the Air Force backed down. In those fearful times, national defense trumped all other considerations. Myrtle Beach Air Force Base became part of the Tactical Air Command and home of the 354th Tactical Fighter Wing. Over the next four decades, thousands of young airmen were dispatched to make Myrtle Beach safe for democracy. Many enjoyed their tour so much they retired here and made Horry County their home.

My awareness of the Air Force presence on the Grand Strand began on a mid-summer afternoon in the late 1950s. Playing in the surf, I was stunned by the sound of three F-100 Super Sabre jet fighters screaming down the beach in formation, a few hundred feet overhead. I clasped my hands over my ears and looked around to see hundreds of others doing the same. It may have been the "sound of freedom," as Jack Webb used to say, but to the uninitiated it was a near-traumatic experience. For my family and me the trauma lasted only a week each summer, but for locals there was no escape. Sonic booms and ground-hugging fly-bys might happen any hour of day or night.

On December 16, 1957, a fighter crashed into the woods a couple of miles from the base, killing the pilot. The plane might have fallen as easily on downtown Myrtle Beach. Some people probably thought the price of freedom was pretty high, but a local payroll of 3,400 military and 650 civilian personnel took some of the sting out of it.

By the late 1980s, the Cold War was winding down. The country's massive military establishment needed to be trimmed and Myrtle Beach Air Force Base was high on the "white elephant" list. A bipartisan commission was appointed to select military bases for closure. On April 12, 1991, Secretary of Defense Dick Cheney dropped the ax on Myrtle Beach.

The base land reverted to the city, which suddenly was faced with some mind-boggling questions. Here – in the middle of the Grand Strand – were 4,000 acres of undeveloped real estate. Who would control it? Who would develop it? What would they build?

It took two years from the time of the announced closure until the Air Force actually vacated the premises. In the meantime, a curious mix of players was queuing up to get a slice of the action. The Air Force Base Redevelopment Authority was created to promote and officiate the land rush. A company was brought in to renovate, rent and manage the 777 base housing units. Advocates for the homeless and deaf came forward to demand some of the housing for their clients. Horry County School District wanted land for new buildings. The county and city took a slice for parks and recreation. Horry-Georgetown Technical College got land and buildings for an extension campus. Myrtle Beach International Airport got 1,244 acres for future expansion. Most important, the state-owned utility, Santee Cooper, was awarded 1,555 acres in a land swap with the Air Force. That's when things started to get fast and loose.

There were in Horry County a smooth-talking 35-year-old real estate salesman named Robert Blackburn and his friend and attorney Eugene Lawrimore. Blackburn, Lawrimore and some other local operators were full of big plans. They wanted to create a grand amusement park called Isle of America on 1,000 acres of base land. The $500 million project would be built by the same company that created Walt Disney World's EPCOT Center and would be managed by Knott's Berry Farm of Buena Park, California, which operates some of the largest theme parks in the country. Isle of America would include several hundred upscale homes, 3,200 hotel rooms, 200,000 square feet of retail space and twenty-seven holes of championship golf.

Yet for all their extravagant talk, Blackburn and Lawrimore possessed neither the proverbial pot nor the window. What they did have were friends in high places. Two of them were Governor Carroll Campbell and Campbell's longtime crony and fixer, Dick Greer. On September 24, 1993, Campbell's office ordered Santee Cooper to give first right of refusal on 1,000 acres of base land to Timberland Properties, Inc., Blackburn's real estate company, rather than put the property out for bids.

TPI nearly lost the option because it could not come up with money for the purchase. That problem was solved at the last minute when Lawrimore put in a call to Greer, who put in a call to a real estate developer friend, who came through with a $4 million loan. For his trouble, Greer received a $70,000 finder's fee. (Greer was later indicted in the Operation Lost Trust federal investigation into state government corruption and pleaded guilty to possession of cocaine.)

TPI's contract with Santee Cooper set a deadline to begin and finish construction of Isle of America. If the developer failed to meet its obligation, Santee Cooper would buy back the land at the original sale price. Blackburn pledged that a construction bond would be issued to cover all costs. "It guarantees the project will come in on time and at a fixed price," he told *The Sun News*, "It's an absolute guarantee."

Governor Campbell repeatedly assured investors and the public that the state would "do its due diligence" in checking TPI's financial bona fides. With 1,000 acres of land in hand and with the imprimatur of the governor and the state utility on their project, TPI officials started writing checks and signing up investors. A Methodist minister-cum-real estate salesman named Hart Rist was one of their leading shills.

From the beginning, the Isle of America project had its skeptics, including Burroughs & Chapin CEO Doug Wendel. "We simply don't have the year-round population figures or the year-round tourism figures to carry a theme park," he told *The Sun News*.

City councilman Mark McBride was also doubtful. "We (city council) asked to see a construction bond for two years," he said. "They're offering to do it now, but they haven't done it yet. Who knows? Maybe they can still do this. But I would have shut up a long time ago if I saw that something was actually going to happen."

Indeed, pinning down TPI on deadlines and financing for the giant development proved problematic. Santee Cooper was especially anxious and sought to have TPI officers identify the investors and lenders who were going to swing this $500 million deal. TPI stalled and obfuscated; they hinted vaguely that Japanese bankers, a billionaire Saudi prince and even entertainer Michael Jackson might be silent backers. The Sun News reported that three of the major partners and investors TPI claimed to have on board were, in fact, not committed. Phone calls from local investors and state officials to TPI were not returned. The company applied for, and received, a ninety-day extension on its construction deadline. Then, on February 14, 1997, the house of cards collapsed. TPI defaulted on its contract by not starting construction on the theme park. The company was granted a ninety-day "cure" period to begin construction, but it failed once again. Santee Cooper bought back the base land and Isle of America was dead. On June 17, 1997, TPI declared bankruptcy, claiming assets of $28,000 against debts of more than $7.3 million.

In the acrimony and investigations that followed, it turned out that more than 130 small investors lost some $5 million in the TPI collapse, as well as local businesses which were owed money. Yet even as the company was going down the tubes, Blackburn and other TPI officials continued to pay themselves $200,000 salaries. Lawrimore received $427,000 in legal fees and the company spent another $167,000 on travel, meals and entertainment. And there were other irregularities. It seems that TPI failed to register the stock it sold to about 100 investors. Furthermore, Blackburn used the base land as collateral for an $850,000 loan – a mortgage which Santee Cooper was forced to pay off with taxpayers' money when the land was returned to the public utility.

"How did we allow public trust land to be parceled out and then returned, mortgaged?" thundered a state senator. It was, of course, a rhetorical question.

When the smoke and dust had cleared, there were no criminal charges; nobody went to jail. Many newcomers expressed shock at the audacity of the TPI scam, but long-time residents barely raised an eyebrow. This is how we've done business for 300 years.

The TPI boondoggle tied up the Air Force Base land for four years and cost Santee Cooper much face and even more money. Now it had to start over in finding someone to buy and develop the land. This time it opened the sale to the public, placing a request for bids in the *Wall Street Journal* and other national publications. The minimum bid would be $20 million, with all bids submitted by November 11, 1998. When bids were sorted and appraised, only three were accepted. One was from a New Jersey-based developer, an offer that was ultimately refused because the developer wanted conditions on the sale, which Santee Cooper would not grant.

The second was from none other than Burroughs & Chapin. The

B&C "bid" was actually an offer of a land swap, mind-boggling in complexity and breathtaking in audacity. It proposed building a Strom Thurmond Federal Trade Center, creating an industrial park at Myrtle Beach International Airport, and privatizing the county-owned airport by leasing it to a company of B&C's choosing. What the B&C proposal did not include was any cash for the land.

B&C's "bid" was dead on arrival at Santee Cooper. The utility needed cash to pay off TPI liens on the base property. On January 25, 1999, the state utility announced it had found a buyer for the land – and the decision was a shocker. The company chosen to develop the crown jewel of Grand Strand real estate was WBLC of Jacksonville, North Carolina, an enigmatic limited liability corporation with a four-letter name and unknown assets. WBLC was headed by a car sales-man/orthodontist named Ledyard Ross, who made his fortune giving automobile loans to high-risk buyers at interest rates approaching 30 percent, and a diamond salesman named Ed Burrell. Outside of Santee Cooper corporate offices, nobody had ever heard of the outfit or the mysterious men who ran it.

"I have no idea who they are," Councilman Wayne Gray told *The Sun News*.

"Their names haven't been mentioned around City Hall," planning director Jack Walker said. "I don't have a clue who they are."

Even Ashby Ward was nonplussed. "I was very surprised," he said. "I didn't even know those guys were in the running."

"Those guys" only added to the consternation by refusing to discuss their plans for the property. "I don't want to sound smart," Ross said, "but I really can't comment on it until the deal is final."

Bob Bestler had a typically acerbic observation: "Can we only hope they don't turn it into the world's largest Used-Car-Lot-By-the-Sea?
. . . We don't need a TPI all over again – but that may be what we're looking at."

In less than three years, WBLC – operating under a new name – was in bankruptcy. Myrtle Beach didn't get a Used-Car-Lot-By-the-Sea. It got another TPI.

Race and Memory in Horry County

On February 18, 1999, South African Archbishop and Nobel Peace Prize Laureate Desmond Tutu spoke at Coastal Carolina University, in Conway, as part of the school's Black History Month observance. In his soft, lilting voice, Tutu told his audience there was only one way to heal his bleeding country after the end of apartheid. A Truth and Reconciliation Commission was appointed to hear the stories of the victims, to record the tales of murder, torture and terror, and to make them a part of South Africa's history that could never be denied.

"We knew . . . that to not deal with the past is to victimize the victims a second time around," the archbishop said.

Local activist Michael Burgess would understand perfectly. After the City of Myrtle Beach bought the old Rivoli Theater in 1999, the Cultural Arts Council was charged with preparing a history of the building. The committee responsible for writing that history could not bring itself to admit – or to believe – that the theater had once been segregated, with blacks forced to sit in the balcony. As a CAC member, Burgess confronted this revisionist history and ran into a wall of opposition. "They are used to black people being on committees for reasons of aesthetics, because we make them look balanced and fair," Burgess told me, "but when one of us says something that challenges their view, they find ways to keep us in the margins." There were heated discussions over the way the official history would handle the balcony and the issue of segregation. Burgess held his ground and pushed through a statement that acknowledged the balcony of the Rivoli theater was once used to segregate blacks.

"We cannot heal without admitting that people have been hurt," Burgess said. Indeed, much of the anger and confusion over race in America – and in Horry County – stems from the denial that great crimes have been committed.

Racism is the elephant in America's living room – everyone steps around it, politely pretending it isn't there, even as it dominates the thoughts, the habits, the lives of everyone in its presence. The laws of chattel slavery and racial segregation were abolished generations ago, yet old ways of thinking still live in the interstices of our society. In the long catalogue of crimes against blacks, the stealing of their land is rarely mentioned.

Following World War II, developers began to eye the Southeastern coast and dream of the possibilities. Before they could bring in the bulldozers, they had to get title to the land. Hundreds of thousands of acres of isolated, subtropical coast belonged to African Americans, who had lived there, passing the land down through their families for generations. Ownership was collective – heirs property, it was called – and it passed without benefit of written will. The custom flew in the face of Anglo-Saxon common law, making property owners vulnerable and, ultimately, victims.

Developers sent their lawyers to meet with members of the family that owned a desirable tract. An offer would be made to one of them for his portion of the land. When that family member took the money and signed over his portion, the developers moved in for the kill. With title to a portion of the property, they could then go before a judge and argue that the property could not be divided "without prejudice to the tenants in common." The judge would "remedy" the dispute with an order to sell the entire tract at a courthouse partition sale. The family that had owned the property for generations would have no recourse and likely no legal counsel or money to bid on their own land. "Heirs property is a huge problem," Thomas Goldstein, a Charleston attorney who has fought for black property owners, told *The Sun News*. "Much of the development at Pawleys Island is legally stolen property."

In the 1980s, partition sales were such a lucrative business in the Waccamaw Neck, Goldstein said, "Many companies would specifically request their attorneys to check county records to locate and obtain small interests of heirs property for purposes of bringing partition sales." Untold thousands of acres of Southern coast have been seized at pennies on the dollar. Those acres have been converted into billions of dollars in development.

Developers then poured salt into ancient wounds by calling their new golf courses, condominium and retirement communities "plantations." The allure of that word and its connotations seems irresistible to white developers and their customers. Today, thousands of these pretentiously titled "plantations" dot the Carolinas and Georgia coast. Around the Grand Strand lie Carolina Waterway Plantation, Plantation Pointe, Plantation Resort, Plantation Apartments, Kingston Plantation, Brunswick Plantation & Golf Resort, River Oaks Plantation Club, Pawleys Plantation Golf & Country Club, Ocean Creek Plantation, Plantation Harbor, Conway Plantation, Deerfeld Plantation, Cimeron Plantation – and the list goes on. Staffing all of these "plantations" requires many housekeepers, groundskeepers, dishwashers and other slightly-above-minimum-wage workers, often bussed in from miles away to labor on land their ancestors once owned.

There is more ugly history in the covenants of restriction that were included in most residential property sales in the South before 1964. Myrtle Beach Farms – the corporate precursor of Burroughs & Chapin Co. – was hardly alone, just more prolific, in its issuance of deeds with this clause from 1927: "The property hereby conveyed shall not be sold, devised, mortgaged or donated to any person of the negro race nor to any corporation whose stock is controlled by members of said race, nor shall members of said race be permitted to rent, lease or reside on said property without the joint consent of a majority of the bona fide adult residents of Myrtle Beach and upon such terms as may be by them jointly agreed upon."

By 1941, Myrtle Beach Farms' exclusionary policy had expanded: "Neither this property nor any part thereof, nor any interest therein shall ever be sold, leased or conveyed to anyone other than a person of the caucasian race, or to a corporation owned and conducted by persons of the caucasian race."

For the MBA Chamber of Commerce, development is the elixir that cures all ills. But for African Americans, the more things change, the more they remain the same. Of course, there is no hint of racial animosity from the giant Myrtle Beach promotion machine. In fact, there is little hint that black people even exist. The Grand Strand maintains a solid front in the official image it projects – the image of a community that is conservative, family-friendly and white, white, *white*. While the MBA Chamber of Commerce does advertise in black magazines and professional journals, its most visible piece of promotion is the *Myrtle Beach Area Vacation Guide*. The Chamber prints more than 400,000 copies of this tract each year – a bestseller by almost any publishing standard – and distributes it on CD-ROM.

The 1999 edition of the *Vacation Guide* contained 360 glossy pages, featuring thousands of photographs of tens of thousands of white people having the time of their lives at the beaches, swimming pools and restaurants of the Grand Strand. Leafing through the *Vacation Guide*, I counted eight black faces – some of them recessed almost to the point of invisibility – in various crowd shots.

Something similar happened with the two leased access cable channels that promote local restaurants and other amusements. Beach TV (Channel 45) ran through the litany of tourist spots. With the exception of entertainers and service personnel, blacks were virtually invisible. Yet the TV cameras carried viewers back to the kitchens of leading Grand Strand restaurants to show smiling black faces and black hands preparing the food. In one especially egregious spot for The Filling Station, the camera showed a stout, middle-aged black man bussing a table, while the voice-over said, "Meet Isaac, the best busboy on the beach." Grand Strand Video Magazine (Channel 33) took a similar no-show attitude toward minorities. The 1961 *Saturday Evening Post* illustration of the Dunes Club lounge still largely defined the role of blacks in Myrtle Beach in 1999.

Blacks were also invisible in the scores of brochures that filled the lobbies of restaurants and hotels up and down the Strand. With the exception of the brochure for Burroughs & Chapin's Pavilion Amusement Park, I did not find a single black face among the hundreds of gleeful, well-scrubbed folk pictured enjoying local accommodations. These brochures were designed by individual businesses, so there was no central policy-making body responsible for their content. But you do not have to be Oliver Stone to suspect there was some collusion – however subtle and informal – to remove minorities from the public face of Myrtle Beach. As with the Chamber of Commerce's *Vacation Guide* and other publications, any random pointing and clicking of a camera around the Grand Strand would surely capture more African Americans than these brochures and magazines revealed. It's hard to imagine any industry – with the possible exceptions of country music and stock car racing – that would so ignore African Americans in their advertising and marketing efforts.

If the face of Myrtle Beach recreation is white, the business face is even whiter. *The Sun News* each Sunday runs a feature called Business

Pulse, which recognizes new hires, promotions and accomplishments with a photograph and couple of lines of copy. Of the hundreds of business people featured in Business Pulse in 1999, only eight were black.

The Sunday edition of *The Sun News* also offers Real Estate Plus, a thick supplement featuring scores of real estate sales people and the hundreds of millions of dollars worth of property they sell each year. In 1999, no black realtors were pictured in the supplement. In all the Real Estate Plus ads, in the hundreds of pictures of people enjoying the good life on the beaches, golf courses and patios of the Grand Strand, blacks appeared in only two. (The Federal Housing Administration and The Sun News used African Americans in public service and promotional ads in Real Estate Plus.)

Horry County's sad history of racial enmity does not need to be traced to its ancient origins, but a few low points might be instructive. Under the state constitution of 1895, blacks were disenfranchised and segregated from white society through a host of "Jim Crow" laws. Under the new regime, a "deadline" was drawn across northern Horry County, between the towns of Loris and Aynor, to keep blacks out of the western portion of the county. Any black who did not already live west of the line was not allowed to cross. In 1905, a railroad construction crew camped near the deadline was fired upon and a man was killed.

Under segregation, blacks were not allowed on the beach and had to be off Ocean Boulevard after sundown, unless dressed in the white uniform of a domestic or hotel worker. In Myrtle Beach, blacks were forced to live on the Hill, a close-knit neighborhood that thrived for generations, nearly a mile from the surf. With several liquor stills and cabarets, grocery stores and restaurants, the Hill must have once looked like something out of *Porgy and Bess*. The neighborhood sported names like Tin Top Alley and Racepath. Hog Lot Ditch ran through the heart of the community, flooding homes and yards with every heavy rain. Now officially called the Booker T. Washington Neighborhood, the Hill is still there, still poor and black, filled with crime and drugs, a wound that won't heal.

The violence and ignorance endemic to the poor, rural coastal plain provided a fertile breeding ground for the Ku Klux Klan. Since the 1920s, the Klan has staged daylight marches and midnight rides through Conway, Myrtle Beach and other towns. In the early 1960s, the Klan burned a thirty-foot cross at the Ocean Forest Hotel to protest black housekeepers staying overnight on the property. There were cross-burnings and marches in the 1970s to protest school desegregation.

In the Klan resurgence of the early 1950s, there were an estimated 5,000 members in Horry and neighboring Columbus County, North Carolina. Local law enforcement officers openly supported the Klan, as did much of the white population. In 1950, a rural Horry County house was dynamited and three people were killed. Nothing was ever proved, but it was assumed to be an act of Klan terror.

In the most audacious act of Klan violence, the hooded brethren rode out of North Carolina on a sultry August night in 1950. They sped down U.S. 501 to Myrtle Beach in a motorcade of twenty-seven cars and pickup trucks, most of them with South Carolina license plates. They were heading for the Hill and a nightclub called the Whispering Pines, run by a larger-than-life character named Charlie Fitzgerald. Some said Fitzgerald came out of Louisiana, where he must have learned a thing or two about life in the French Quarter. Others said he ran gambling, bootleg liquor and prostitution – including some white girls – out of his notorious cabaret. What is known for sure is that Fitzgerald cut a broad swath when he walked downtown with his women on his arms and a revolver on his hip. He made obeisance to no one and that upset a lot of the white folk. The Klan was coming to town that August night to teach Charlie Fitzgerald a lesson.

They headed down Canal Street with horns blaring and circled the block several times before stopping in front of the Whispering Pines. There was a shoot-out. Hundreds of bullets were fired through Fitzgerald's club, terrorizing everyone inside. Fitzgerald and some of his friends returned fire, holding off more than sixty Klansmen until they kicked down the doors and stormed in. Fitzgerald and about thirty patrons were whipped and beaten. The fire fight and beatings took place a few hundred yards from the Myrtle Beach Police Department, yet no one in blue made an effort to intervene.

Fitzgerald was gagged, bound, thrown into the trunk of a car and hauled out to a nearby swamp. There, in the headlights of the cars, he found himself in a circle of hooded, robed men. They stretched him over a fender and bullwhipped him until his clothes, then his skin and flesh were shredded. Finally, one of the men pulled out a pocket knife and cut off his ears. They left him on the logging road, alive – but just barely. While recovering from the attack, Fitzgerald was arrested for distributing pornography and served several years in state prison. He never recovered his health from the physical and psychological terror of that night.

During the shoot-out, one of the Klansmen – 42-year-old James Daniel Johnson – took a .38 caliber bullet in the back. His cronies hauled him to the hospital in Conway, but he died en route. On removing his Klan robe, hospital personnel were shocked to find a uniform underneath. Johnson was a member of the Conway Police Department. Twelve men – including the Grand Dragon of the S.C. Klan – were arrested in connection with the raid, but the all-white Horry County grand jury refused to indict and the charges were dropped. No one was ever punished for the crime.

After half a century, the Charlie Fitzgerald incident still resonated with many older people in the black community, but most were loath to discuss it with whites. Hence, it is almost totally lost to the memory of white people in Myrtle Beach. Charlie Fitzgerald's widow was still alive in 1999, still making her home on the Hill a few blocks from where her husband's club once stood. "I know that thing you want to talk about," she told me in our two-minute interview. "I don't talk about that with nobody." I suspect that she meant "nobody white."

With the passage of civil rights legislation in the 1960s, African Americans could ride a roller coaster and buy a hot dog on Ocean Boulevard. County schools were integrated in the late 1960s and early 1970s. But blacks held little political and even less economic power. There were constant and bitter reminders that blacks were still second class citizens. One of those reminders came in May 1980. When Liza Carolina, an elderly black woman of the Longs community, suffered a heart attack, her son tried to rush her to the hospital in Myrtle Beach. A highway patrolman stopped and arrested him for reckless driving, leaving his stricken mother at the scene, where she died.

In August 1989, generations of simmering resentment boiled over in a most peculiar way. It started when Conway High School football coach Chuck Jordan replaced his black quarterback with a white quarterback. In response, thirty black players walked off the team and – with their parents – took their complaint to officials of the National Association for the Advancement of Colored People. Bill Gibson, chairman of the NAACP's national board, said the boycott was "only the runny nose of a patient who has a major virus, and maybe pneumonia."

Taking an angrier tone was the Reverend H.H. Singleton, president of the Conway chapter of the NAACP and a teacher at Conway

Middle School. Singleton said Jordan's decision showed "callous and racial intolerance that seems to have bordered on racial bigotry."

What started out as a coach's personnel decision came to divide the school, the town, the county. More than sixty white parents pulled their children out of Singleton's science classes. White and black teachers did not talk to one another. On September 6, 1989, Horry County Schools Superintendent John Dawsey suspended Singleton from his teaching job, saying he had become a disruption to the school. On November 18 – after four days of hearings and seven hours of deliberations – the all-white school board voted 5-1 to fire Singleton. More than 1,200 protesters took to the streets of Conway, led by NAACP national executive director Benjamin Hooks. Black parents pulled their children out of Conway schools to protest. In 1991, a federal judge reinstated Singleton to his job with back pay; in 1999 he remained an outspoken and courageous leader of the black community.

The racial power balance in Horry County would seem to be improving. There were African Americans on the county council, the Myrtle Beach and Conway city councils, the county board of education. But there were still private "segregation academies," and blacks remain shut out of most high-paying jobs, and victims of disproportionate poverty and crime. The social fabric bears the scars of history. The remnants of segregation remain.

In Horry County's long history of racial strife, it is encouraging to remember that from this bloody little corner of the world a man like Ernest Finney could rise. Finney was a young Conway lawyer in 1955, when he attended his first convention of the South Carolina Bar at the Ocean Forest Hotel. But he was not there as a member; he was not even allowed to join the all-white organization. He was moonlighting as a waiter. Over the next years, Finney defended hundreds of people arrested in civil rights demonstrations and became one of the first blacks elected to the General Assembly in the twentieth century. On February 24, 1999, the 69-year-old crusader announced his retirement as Chief Justice of the South Carolina Supreme Court. "He bled for his people," said a longtime friend. "God bless, he used his brilliant legal mind to free some of them."

It was a small but inspiring victory. Yet some battles must be fought over and over again.

Black Pearl on the Grand Strand

By 1999, the most dramatic vestige of segregation in Horry County was Atlantic Beach. In the 1930s, a laudromat owner named George Tyson bought a small tract north of Myrtle Beach from white owners. Tyson dreamed of a black-owned beach, where domestic servants and laborers could party and spread a blanket on the sand. When Tyson ran into financial troubles, he organized a group of black doctors and educators from around the Carolinas. They formed the Atlantic Beach Company and bought Tyson's land.

The Black Pearl, as it was called, flourished through the 1940s and 1950s. Blacks from across the eastern United States vacationed here. On summer weekends, farm workers came from local tobacco fields by the truckload. Buses brought clubs and church congregations. And, of course, it was the playground of domestics who worked in area hotels and homes. Thursday was "Maid's Day," when white employers released their workers early for a holiday. That is how I first came to know Atlantic Beach. When my family vacationed here in 1959, my mother talked our maid into coming along, promising her a day in Atlantic Beach. Taking her there and picking her up on that July day was an adventure and – for my mother – a thoroughly unnerving experience. Driving through the little town, we were completely cut off from "our" world, completely surrounded by "the other." We had never seen so many black people – hundreds of them on the streets, in the hotels, a thousand or more on the little beachfront. Everywhere, music poured from clubs and houses as people danced and celebrated. We'd found a little Caribbean village in the heart of this redneck Baptist kingdom.

Music is an important part of the Atlantic Beach story. Before integration, black entertainers playing the Ocean Forest ballroom or the many white beach clubs were barred from white hotels. After performing before an all-white crowd, they headed to Atlantic Beach – often followed by white revelers – where they put on late-night shows at the Cotton Club, the Black Magic

Club, the Hawk's Nest or one of the other legendary cabarets. Count Basie, Ray Charles, Billie Holliday, James Brown, the Drifters, Martha and the Vandellas, the Tams, Bo Diddly and Otis Redding all left memories in Atlantic Beach which linger like a melody on a summer breeze.

Atlantic Beach was incorporated in 1966 and elected its first mayor and council. Two years later, when the towns of Windy Hill Beach, Crescent Beach, Ocean Drive Beach and Cherry Grove Beach consolidated to form North Myrtle Beach, Atlantic Beach chose not to join. The decision was a result of generations of hostility and distrust. As Mayor Joe Montgomery told *The Sun News* in 1987, "This is a gold mine. But we want to maintain our heritage and our identity and we want a certain amount of control. We want to learn from mistakes that were made in other places, like Hilton Head."

Atlantic Beach certainly had no reason to trust its neighbors. White property owners used to run ropes into the water on either side of the town with signs warning blacks to stay off their beach. "Even the ocean is segregated," residents used to say. Ocean Boulevard still bears the scars of that segregation. Running eight miles from one end of North Myrtle Beach to the other, it stops abruptly at the city limits of Atlantic Beach. Fences and hedges cross the path of the road, as visually and spiritually ugly as the Berlin Wall. In recent years, planners have tried to open Ocean Boulevard to help move traffic along the beachfront, but Atlantic Beach officials refuse. They will not open the gate to forces they say would destroy their culture and their community. In a world where black neighborhoods have always been split by freeways and railroads, this is one arena where they have control.

When Jim Crow was banished, black tourists found more comfort and variety in the hundreds of white-owned hotels and restaurants nearby. The Black Pearl went into decline. In the midst of this multi-billion-dollar phenomenon called the Grand Strand, Atlantic Beach looks like something out of the Third World. A drive through Atlantic Beach in 1999 was sobering. The streets were eerily quiet. There were no high-rises, no neon-studded emporiums. Signs were hand-painted and badly spelled. Half the lots were undeveloped; the other half contained boarded-up cottages, mobile homes, dilapidated juke joints and motels. On the oceanfront were cinder block walls of old beach clubs that lost their roofs in Hurricane Hugo. I once saw a rooster scratching in the sand near one of those old shells. The graffiti-covered ruins stood stark against the sea and sky, reminding passers of some mythic past, full of pride and hope and music.

In 1999, the Black Pearl was one of the smallest, poorest towns in South Carolina. Its 475 residents had a per capita income under $7,000. Its 98.5 acres and 450 yards of beachfront were surrounded on three sides by North Myrtle Beach. The largest business in the town was Crazy Horse Saloon, a white-owned strip club on Kings Highway. Such is the price of pride.

There have been at least four efforts over the years to revitalize Atlantic Beach with public grants and private investment. They were all stillborn, victims of history and memory. Residents have an innate suspicion of outsiders – especially *white* outsiders – waving money and making promises. A redevelopment effort in 1989 had the backing of the Governor's Office, a $250,000 planning grant and involvement of a major Columbia developer. But the plan called for condemnation of property to assemble a tract large enough for a high-rise hotel. Residents reacted instinctively. "This is just a way that folks are being set up so people can steal their land," a property owner said at a stormy council meeting. "I just can't see any other motive but to steal land from the people of Atlantic Beach." Town council killed the plan.

Said an elderly resident: "This Atlantic Beach was a God-given piece of land for poor, poor black people and God is not going to let this land be misused. At some point, something is going to happen to make this place worthwhile. Just not these high-rise buildings."

When one of the state's leading law firms offered the town pro bono assistance, they were spurned for an alleged conflict of interest. "This is the first time we've been called crooks when trying to do pro bono work," said an angry attorney in the firm.

Atlantic Beach had other problems endemic to blighted black neighborhoods everywhere. The Black Pearl was a cesspool of drugs and crime, corruption and mismanagement. Shots rang through the nights and arson was epidemic in abandoned buildings. Several police officers on the six-man force were convicted of bribery and other crimes; there were two mass police walkouts.

Officers were not allowed to arrest loiterers in front of a local honky-tonk owned by a town council member. In a similar incident, Mayor Joe Montgomery fired the town's building inspector before the inspector could officially recommend condemning the mayor's decrepit liquor store. Then the mayor and the chief of police were convicted of bribery and conspiracy for taking payoffs from the manager of the local strip club. Having the town manager arrested for drunk driving in 1998 contributed to the image of a town out of control.

For lack of revenue, Atlantic Beach cut back garbage pickup to once a week in 1994, and nearly had to turn off its streetlights. The town limped along for several years in the mid-1990s without a formal budget. A December 1998 audit by a local accounting firm found fifteen problems in the town's accounting system, dealing with collections and deposits, budgeting, documentation and employee records. In July 1998, Atlantic Beach reached its nadir with the murder of town clerk Al Scott in the office of the hotel where he worked.

In the early weeks of 1999, Atlantic Beach was embarked on another attempted renaissance. With the backing of Litus Properties, the town created the Black Pearl Land Company to carry out a $300 million development plan. "The majority of the property owners are seventy-five years old now," said John Skeeters, a council member and chairman of the new company. "It's to their advantage now to sell or lease." The town received a $500,000 state grant to plant palm trees, put in a fountain, sidewalks, gutters and drainage. The project was completed in April, for the annual Atlantic Beach Memorial Day Bike Festival.

In 1980, John Skeeters and three other residents were brainstorming ways to bring business to town. The idea they struck upon was to send invitations to black motorcycle clubs from New York to Texas, inviting them to a rally at Atlantic Beach over Memorial Day Weekend. The Carolina Knight Riders motorcycle club hosted the event and in its first years it was little more than a cookout at the Knight Riders clubhouse on S.C. 90. As the event grew in popularity, so did the numbers attending the annual rally – from a few thousand to 10,000, then 20,000, then 30,000. Girlfriends, camp followers and hangers-on came to outnumber the bikers as the fame of the four-day party spread. The four blocks of Atlantic Beach could no longer contain the burgeoning festival, as it spilled over into North Myrtle Beach, then Myrtle Beach. Beyond its sheer numbers was the issue of behavior. These black, urban revelers partied in a style that clashed sharply with the white, conservative culture of the Grand Strand.

The Memorial Day Bike Festival reached a watershed in 1995, when an estimated 60,000 bikers and friends descended on the Strand, creating historic traffic jams; shocking locals with rude and threatening behavior, public urination, defecation and sex acts; leaving the roads and streets buried under tons of garbage. Letters of outrage from vacationers and locals ran in *The Sun News*; some visitors said they would not come back. Businesses on U.S. 17 suffered because neither employees nor customers could reach them through miles of traffic gridlock. Myrtle Beach Police Chief Sam Killman said, "When you sit in traffic two to three hours, this is not the quality of life we are seeking. . . . I have significant concerns about the public's safety within this city and county. We made more than 2,000 charges in a four-day period. That's over 500 a day. That tells me we're not getting voluntary compliance of our laws."

The Memorial Day Bike Festival gave white antagonists a material grievance and it gave city councilman Mark McBride an issue. Following the 1997 festival, McBride proposed the city hold a referendum to ban the Memorial Day Bike Festival from Myrtle Beach. The notion of placing cops at the city limits and turning back bikers was illegal and slightly crazed. But the gambit got the first-term councilman noticed in a mayoral election year.

Two years later McBride was mayor, but he was obviously hungry for more. With Memorial Day three months away, he called on Governor Hodges to send the National Guard to maintain order during the event. He had the backing of the local tourism and hospitality lobby. However, he did not have the support of the Governor, the other three Grand Strand mayors or his own council. All agreed that having the National Guard on patrol was not the image the Grand Strand needed to project. "He doesn't believe the use of National Guard troops is appropriate at this point for that purpose," the Governor's spokeswoman said on February 11.

When someone suggested that the Guard might be deployed without military uniforms, Atlantic Beach Mayor Irene Armstrong snapped, "I don't care if they're in their PJs. People are going to know they're the Guard."

Rites of Spring

Like a rain forest, the Boulevard is a living environment, home to annual cycles of migration and renewal, its colors and fauna changing with the seasons. The rowdy, feral youth who shout and grunt along the sidewalks in January are joined by the spring break crowd from scores of colleges and universities. They, in turn, are followed by high schoolers, trying to pass for twenty-one, trying to be cool and smart, strutting, crowing, drinking, vomiting, getting arrested. The month of May brings two enormous motorcycle festivals each year, with the Boulevard transformed into a 100-decibel carnival of flesh, chrome and leather. June through August, families dominate the Boulevard – at least during the daylight hours – playing at the Pavilion and the arcades, continuing a tradition of half a century.

The Boulevard is many things to many visitors, but for the young, it is the mating ground and battleground in the great imperative of life. From March through September, the parade of vehicles begins before sundown and continues deep into the morning hours, as young men in their longbed pickup trucks, some carrying lawn chairs and sofas with leering, laughing, beer-swilling boys from small towns throughout the Carolinas, drawn by the sun, by the sea, by the knowledge that there will be thousands of young women from small towns throughout the Carolinas, in their tank tops and shorts, with their pierced navels and tattooed shoulders, their curiosity and passion for life – and this being Myrtle Beach and Myrtle Beach being magic – then maybe, just maybe, they'll get lucky.

The Boulevard is a study in automotive decadence, but in the eternal game, fuel efficiency counts for nothing. These machines run on testosterone. Pickup trucks are sexual totems, the visible measure of a young man's status and potency, big and noisy as a bull moose, bright and flashy as a firefly. They boom with woofers and tweeters, roar with glass-packed mufflers, glow with neon pipes underneath and road lights on top, roll on giant mud tires and bounce on hydraulic shocks. They sport Confederate and Harley-Davidson insignia, "No Fear" decals and bumper stickers that warn, "If Your Heart's Not In Dixie, Then Get Your Ass Out." Ultimately, of course, size trumps all technology and design, a fact celebrated on hundreds of Big Johnson T-shirts in Boulevard shops.

The monster that transcends all others in this priapic parade is the High Mobility Multipurpose Wheeled Vehicle – the Humvee or Hummer. Developed by the U.S. Army as an upsized version of the plucky little Jeep, this 6,800-pound monster with the 160-horsepower diesel V-8 engine was made famous during Operation Desert Storm. Now anybody with $90,000 to spend on personal transportation and an indifference to 13-mile-per-gallon fuel efficiency can join Arnold Schwartzenegger, Al Unser, Ted Turner, Coolio, Andre Agassi and others with a strong need to make an impression. On the Boulevard, where impressions are everything, the Hummer is the undisputed champion of the cruising machines.

The many hotel verandahs overlooking the Boulevard give this Baptist town a strangely Latin feel. Barely-dressed men and women spend the summer nights dancing and cavorting, drinking and teasing anyone on the street who strikes their libidinous fancy.

Through the spring and summer nights Myrtle Beach police ride herd on this frenzy, using powerful Crown Victoria cruisers, Avalanche mountain bikes, two-seat propane "golf" carts and foot patrols. Despite their best efforts – and thousands of arrests each season – crime is a way of life on the Boulevard. Each year brings at least one murder and numerous assaults, rapes and robberies within hailing distance of the Pavilion Amusement Park. A sense of danger is part of the Boulevard's allure and it is enhanced by vendors who display in their windows a bewildering array of exotic swords, sabres, stilettos, butterfly knives, brass knuckles, spiked knuckles and blade knuckles, clubs and blackjacks, ninja-chucks, whips, chains and handcuffs. The best selection of these implements of mayhem is at the Red Hot Shoppe, along with a full complement of fetish gear in rubber, leather and chain. The female mannequins in the Red Hot Shoppe windows are dressed for action.

Across 7th Avenue North from the Red Hot Shoppe stands the Sea Palms Motel, owned and operated by three generations of the Rabun and Mitchell families. Kyle and Karon Mitchell are children of Myrtle Beach. They met in front of the Electric Circus Arcade in the summer of 1978. When I met them in 1999, they were in their late thirties, living in a house a block from the Red Hot Shoppe, with two sons in their early teens. They had weathered Hurricane Hugo together, worked night and day, year in and year out, and expanded the family's original one motel into a cluster of five small motels under the Sea Palms name. And they had seen the Boulevard transformed by the music and hedonism of a younger generation.

Pointing to the frenzied crowd of youth cruising late one night, Karon told me, "When we were those kids' age, our parents knew where we were going when we went out and when we were coming home. These kids' parents don't know what they are doing or where they are except that they're *in Myrtle Beach*."

Kyle and Karon Mitchell protected their own sons from the temptations of the Boulevard with strong family bonds and deep Baptist faith. But they could not escape it. The Boulevard was their bread and butter, so they had made their peace with it and learned to live with it. On summer nights, Karon sat in the parking lot of her motel, surrounded by friends, family, hotel guests, telling stories about hurricanes she had witnessed, about shell collecting, about the changes she had seen in Myrtle Beach. She would shout to SUVs and pickup trucks on the Boulevard: "Hey, slow down! Turn down that music!"

Spring breakers and high schoolers were welcome at the Sea Palms, but Karon Mitchell ran a tight ship. She once grounded a young man for a night for misbehaving – and he actually stayed in his room! On another occasion, a young guest came to her with a problem. The girl's tongue had become infected after it was pierced and studded. Karon put on rubber gloves, went into the girl's mouth, removed the stud and called her mother in North Carolina to come and pick her up. Kyle once used a pair of pliers to cut a ring out of a boy's navel after it became infected. It's all part of life on the Boulevard for the Mitchells and becomes grist for Karon's future seasons of storytelling.

The Boulevard is the river of life that sustains the oceanfront of Myrtle Beach. In the winter, it is virtually dry, a quiet, empty canyon behind the beachfront high-rises. In the summer it comes to life, surging over its banks with rowdy, randy, desperate youth. When it is running high, the Boulevard is a torrent of hope and joy, loss and despair, roiling, bounding, carrying the dreams and memories of generations on its crest. It is an essence, a life force that animates this town, gives it character and vibrancy. It has been here almost as long as there has been a Myrtle Beach – long before Broadway at the Beach, Barefoot Landing, Fantasy Harbour and other corporate amusements – and it will be here long after they are gone.

In 1959, *Time* magazine dispatched a scribe to Fort Lauderdale, Florida, to report on a new phenomenon called spring break. For several years, college students throughout the eastern United States had been descending on the south Florida town in March and April for a youthful bacchanal. The correspondent described a scene of rowdiness, vandalism and mass intoxication. "It's not that we drink so much," a Notre Dame senior explained. "It's just that we drink all the time."

Concluding that no real harm was done, *Time* reported, "The townspeople regard the invasion with edgy amusement; student watching has become a local sport."

The writer closed by asking a coed why she made the migration to Fort Lauderdale. "This," said the young woman, whose identity is lost to history, but whose ear seems keenly cocked to the voice of her generation, "is where the boys are."

A thousand miles away, at Michigan State University, novelist Glendon Swarthout knew a great title when he heard one. A forty-one-year-old lecturer in literature, he had built his reputation on children's books and Western novels, including *The Shootist* and *They Came to Cordura*, his gripping 1957 novel of the Mexican Revolution. Swarthout had witnessed the annual migration from the northern end of the circuit and had considerable anecdotal material to draw on.

The horny-handed Western writer was somewhat out of his element in treating the lives and loves of his hip young characters on the make in Fort Lauderdale; and the fact that he chose a coed as the narrator of his sand-and-sun epic was a literary reach well beyond his grasp. Yet Swarthout became the first to show on a national scale what countless others would demonstrate in years to come: it's almost impossible to lose money selling spring break.

Random House released *Where the Boys Are* in January 1960. The 239-page novel was a light, genuinely funny read. The story is told in the voice of Merritt Andrews, a bright, curious, slightly ditzy freshman coed from an unnamed Midwestern university who comes to Fort Lauderdale to see what all the excitement is about. She describes the scene in her patented teenspeak: "You've seen those movie travelogues of the beaches on the Pribiloff Islands up by Alaska where the seals tool in once a year from the Bay of Fundy or some place to pair off. . . . The Beach at Lauderdale has a similar function."

The novel met mixed reviews and sold 22,000 copies before peaking in March 1960. Not a seismic literary event by any measure, but *Where the Boys Are* did offer something any promoter – or movie producer – would find irresistible: a well-defined and affluent market, i.e., America's college population.

A movie was inevitable. MGM Studios went on a crash production schedule and in November 1960 the film was on the silver screen. Starring Delores Hart, Yvette Mimieux, Paula Prentiss and other largely forgotten players, the celluloid rendition of *Where the Boys Are* bore little resemblance to the linotype version. But it filled movie theaters through the long winter and sparked a thunderous migration the next spring.

That annual spring break exodus has spread to hundreds of locales over the past four decades, the Grand Strand being only one of them.

Spring break on the Grand Strand always peaks on Easter weekend, a most unholy event in this most conservative of Southern towns. Outside law enforcement agencies come in to help police the streets; the jails fill up with bedraggled young men from hundreds of miles around.

Before the early 1990s, the Easter debauch was centered in North Myrtle Beach. In 1987, I was in North Myrtle to do a newspaper story on the annual bash and was taken aback by the full-throttle hedonism of it all. The moment provided an early warning that there was a generation gap between me and the people I liked to think I was one of. On a college campus, there are legal and cultural restraints on behavior. In a beach town on spring break, there was nothing to mask the drunken, profane, inarticulate, self-absorbed nihilism everywhere around me. Was this the way my parents' generation viewed mine? Maybe I was just turning into an old fart, but I wasn't the only one.

Over the years, the spring break crowd at North Myrtle Beach grew in numbers and rowdiness, lured and intoxicated by a veritable fantasy land of beer company promotions, including bands, bikini contests and free T-shirts. There was even a thirty-foot ski slope and the Coors Silver Bullet jet, which buzzed the beach and performed aerial acrobatics. In 1990, an estimated 100,000 kids hit town. Authorities cited beer cans filled with sand and thrown through windows, public sex and urination, widespread underage drinking and huge amounts of garbage on the streets and beach. A police officer was hit in the head with a beer bottle.

"They even urinate, defecate and have sex in my storage room," a shop owner told *The Sun News*. "They're a drunken bunch of animals. They are not human."

In 1991, North Myrtle Beach pulled in the welcome mat. Authorities kicked out the beer promoters with their ski slopes and bikini contests. Drinking on the beach was banned. Extra law enforcement was brought in to hold the line. Spring breakers cried foul and said they were taking they party elsewhere. North Myrtle Beach has been relatively free of spring break mischief in recent years – certainly quieter than Myrtle Beach, where the streets stay noisy and littered and the jails full each spring.

By mid-March of my Myrtle Beach year, the first wave of college students was rolling into town. Signs went up on gas pumps, telling customers to pay before pumping. Other signs warned that shoplifters or anyone caught walking a restaurant check would be "prosecuted to the fullest extent of the law." Convenience stores cleared the center of their floors to erect five-foot-high display stacks of beer. Beachwear shops were stocked with beer bongs and T-shirts celebrating the glories of inebriation. Several hotels suffered heavy vandalism and made mass expulsions of spring break students.

Myrtle Beach is still rather blustery in mid-March. But DNA will find a way. If the beach was too cold for these undergraduate Pribiloff seals, the Boulevard was just right. Here the kids could strut their stuff, automotive and anatomical. As the weather warmed through March, more anatomy came into view and the automotive show grew longer and louder. The cruising started each day before noon – trucks, cars, SUVs, motorcycles – and by early evening, the traffic was backed up bumper-to-bumper, for ten blocks north and south of the Pavilion.

From sidewalks and verandahs, guys called to convertibles full of squealing, giggling girls, who bumped and ground together in little choreographed lap dances as they sang along in harmony with Janet Jackson on the stereo. Guys complimented girls' clothes, butts, tits; girls complimented guys' cars, accompanied by guttural squeals. Boys with video cameras prowled the sidewalks, challenging the girls – "Hey, baby, smile for the camera!" – who would smile and wave and sway their hips. Bolder Lotharios crowded around cars full of friendly babes, conducting two-minute courtships, exchanging names and phone numbers. The lucky ones would get a kiss, a grope, a flash of nipple. "Titty flashing" was well rehearsed and discreet because cops were everywhere, walking up and down the rows of traffic, shining their lights in the cars, ordering kids to turn down their stereos, arresting anyone who did not immediately comply, anyone who leaned too far out of a moving vehicle, anyone who got caught off the sidewalks after a warning. And woe unto the kid who got caught drinking in a moving vehicle. His car was stopped as cops converged from all directions. Everyone was ordered out and ID-ed. Offenders were handcuffed and left on the sidewalk, grinning stupidly in their baggy pants and open shirts, while their libations were poured out on the street.

The influx of undergraduates added a new demographic to the Boulevard. Girls in black dance dresses and black fuck-me pumps, girls in black leather pants and black platform pumps, girls in black hot pants and black go-go boots cut a dangerous swath down the sidewalks on their way to the dance clubs – Mother Fletcher's and Freaky Tiki on the Boulevard and Xanadu on U.S. 17. The clubs were dark, dank, wretched caverns that reeked of stale beer and cigarette smoke; with strobe lights, lasers and mirror balls and closed circuit television above the dance floors and multiple bars to keep everyone thoroughly quenched. One club kept bottles of beer iced down in galvanized aluminum livestock troughs. The music was techno and hip-hop and ear-splitting. Crowds stood hip-to-thigh around the dance floors, pushing, squeezing, groping, teasing. Marquees outside the clubs promised dollar draft beer and two-dollar mixed drinks. There were college nights and ladies nights; wet T-shirt contests, wet & wild contests, bikini contests, boxer shorts contests, fine hiney contests, sweet buns contests and booty shaking contests.

Radio stations broadcast live feeds from the dance floors, with frenetic DJs promoting contests and drink specials, along with the "bikini babes," and the Freaky Tiki Love Shack. Drunken club-goers were invited to howl their names and other personal data over the airwaves.

. . . We give it to you a little harder every single week night at 10:30, and then we give it to you harder when you come down to the Freaki Tiki on Freaky Thursday. . . . You gotta come down here and join the party. You know what, man? Ladies night! This is the best night of the week, because we're gonna to be slam-jam packed full of people and beautiful women, right? That's right! Beautiful women all over the place and looking *real* good! . . . I tell you what! We got a men's bikini contest with $200 on the line! That's right! Cash! Money! . . . Definitely a party you don't want to miss. Everybody's gonna get some cheap drinks, man! Dollar a draft and wine, all night long tonight! Plus, it's ladies night! It's a neighteen-and-up party. . . . Xanadu! Saturday night live! . . . We'll be here till three o'clock this morning, so come on down to the Freaky Tiki, where the party never ends. . . . From now on, the whole weekend's just one big ride, baby.

I saw a T-shirt in the local shops that might have made a fitting souvenir for hundreds young visitors: "Come on Vacation, Leave on Probation – Spring Break 1999."

Easter weekend, 1999: Cars, trucks and SUVs lined up, bumper-to-bumper, for thirty blocks on Ocean Boulevard. Troopers from the Highway Patrol were in town to help control traffic. Myrtle Beach cops and troopers walked up and down the Boulevard, flashing their lights in the cars, ordering people to buckle up and to turn down their stereos.

I was on the Boulevard, note pad in hand, when I came upon the crucifixion. Unlike the original Crucifixion, this one took place on a Saturday and drew very mixed reviews. At 7:00 p.m., Dick Button became the star of the sixth annual Crucifixion re-enactment, presented by Living Faith Church and featuring a cross, crown of thorns and copious amounts of stage blood. Traffic stopped dead still on the Boulevard. Families, couples, drunks, tourists, spring breakers – all stared in stunned disbelief at the writhing, bloody man being "nailed" to the cross before them. A man grabbed his wife's arm and said, "Let's get out of here." At the nearby Florentine Hotel, fraternity boys jeered. Others gasped and sobbed. Members of the Living Faith congregation passed out tracts with the message: "Truth: Jesus is alive. Tragedy: To never experience what Easter really means. Triumph: Your destiny in life through His resurrection power."

I watched the spectacle for about ten minutes, then moved on, choosing to take my chances with the publicans and the sinners – and there were plenty of them on the Boulevard that night. I spent the evening taking in the magic of a spring night, the smell of pizza and beer on the air, the sound of arcade games and the Pavilion carousel. On the boardwalk, I watched waves lapping at the shore as seagulls nestled in the sand.

At midnight, Easter morning began. Two hours later, daylight saving time kicked in. The throngs along Ocean Boulevard took no notice of either. The Pavilion turned out the lights at midnight and many of the shops did, too. The bars and dance clubs kept right on rocking. At 3:30 a.m. (DST) the Boulevard and connecting streets were choked with vehicles and pedestrians. Police watched the hedonistic frenzy from curbside and walked down the middle of the street, barking orders.

At 4:00 a.m., officers moved in and barricaded Ocean Boulevard at 8th and 9th avenues north, directing traffic out to Kings Highway. Workers descended on the sidewalks, tarmac and outdoor café around the Pavilion bandstand, sweeping and hosing the pavement. Others set folding chairs in front of the stage as young men assembled and tested sound equipment.

Weary cops warned stragglers off the Boulevard: "Cruisin's over. Time to find your hotel room," one of them growled at passing 4x4s. "Cruisin's over."

Seagulls nestled in the sand in the chilly predawn hours.

Final preparations were completed when Easter lilies were placed on each of the café tables; then chairs were placed on the bandstand. By 5:30, all was ready. At 5:45, the first arrivals started taking their seats, facing east, across the bandstand, toward the sea, awaiting the sunrise.

The sun came up gray and pink through the Atlantic fog. Seagulls rose from the sand in ones and twos and threes as dawn crept inland. Several hundred faithful arrived in casual dress, filling the seats as Christian pop music oozed from the sound system. One couple arrived with their pet corgies on leashes; others brought dachshunds and a Great Dane. The elevated Pavilion concourse filled with worshippers, as did all the walkways and tarmac around the bandstand.

Four members of the Myrtle Beach Ministerial Association led the service. The orange sun was rising from the ocean mist at 7:00, when the faithful sang the first hymn – "Christ the Lord Is Risen Today." What followed was an hour of bathed-in-the-blood song and sermon that only the truest believers could sit through without wincing.

The community sunrise service was one of several held up and down the Grand Strand that morning. It represented a side of Myrtle Beach rarely heard, except to raise its voice in damnation and disapproval. But if strip clubs, video gambling and motorcycle rallies have changed the landscape of the Strand, the true believers had not given up the fight. And in this bitter test of faith vs. commerce, they had found themselves a leader. He was there among them that chilly morning, as he should have been, down close to the bandstand with his wife Laura and their two children. The Reverend Dr. Wayne Miller, pastor of Cathedral Baptist Church, singled him out and introduced him to the congregation as a "hero of the faith." Mayor Mark McBride seemed not the least embarrassed by the accolade, but accepted it with a gracious dip of his head. It was just the right gesture from this modest yet handsome young man who seemed so favored by Destiny.

Mayberry Gets A New Mayor

To millions of people, Mayberry is not some mythical place spun from the mind of Andy Griffith. It is their town, their neighbors, their way of life. It is everything that is right with America and everything that is most threatened by modernism and mass culture. Of course, the heart of Mayberry is its people – honest, hard-working, no-non-sense folk, who know right from wrong, who aren't afraid to speak up for their values and their stake in the community, people like Kyle and Karon Mitchell and A.V. "Ducy" Blake, Jr.

All three had lived their whole lives in Myrtle Beach. All three had owned and operated Boulevard businesses. For the Mitchells, that meant their Sea Palms Motel. Blake's family owned the little Blake Motel and the once-legendary Electric Circus Arcade, in the heart of the Boulevard amusement district. The Electric Circus had been closed for several years in 1999, in part because Blake was tired of dealing with the rough young crowd that had taken over the Boulevard. The huge building stood fallow, but Blake and his wife ran the parking lot behind the building and kept it full at five dollars a car for six months of the year.

Blake didn't like what he saw when he looked around his home-town. "This was the most magic place in the world," he told me. "It was unique. You couldn't have duplicated it for any amount of money." But something went terribly wrong. He pointed to the drugs and the crime that had become endemic in Myrtle Beach. He pointed to the political machinations of Burroughs & Chapin. "There's enough here for everybody – always has been," he said. "I never thought I'd live to see one company try to take it all for themselves."

But if you really want to get Ducy Blake started, just mention the Atlantic Beach Memorial Day Bike Festival, the annual rally that brings hundreds of thousands of young African Americans to the Grand Strand each May. "They have Atlantic Beach. They have their own towns they can trash and tear up," Blake fumed. "They don't have to come here. Nobody asked them to come here. They're just trashy, uncivilized people."

The Mitchells were also harsh critics of the Memorial Day Bike Festival and usually spent long nights standing guard at the front of their hotel when the black bikers were in town. "Have you seen the way their women dress and the way they behave?" Karon Mitchell asked me. "I'm sorry, but that's just plain indecent. It's not right for them to subject all of us to their behavior. I have two young boys. I don't want them exposed to that.

"This is a *family* beach. This is a *family* town."

Karon Mitchell has other causes. In 1996, she made statewide headlines when she staged a one-woman protest in front of a Boulevard beachwear shop that was selling T-shirts she considered inappropriate. Realizing he was overmatched, the shop owner dumped the offending merchandise. Mitchell did not hesitate to go down to City Hall to share her opinions with council or staff on a range of issues. She even made an ill-fated run for city council in 1995.

Karon Mitchell's ideas of decency and morality, responsibility and community were shared by thousands of her fellow citizens in Myrtle Beach and Horry County. Most importantly, they are shared by her friend and fellow Baptist, Mark McBride. As a city councilman, McBride made himself the spokesman for the Mitchells, the Blakes and many other angry citizens. In 1997, they responded by making him their mayor.

Mark Struthers McBride had come a long way since those days in 1986, when he seemed to be struggling to find his place in the world. In that year he returned to his hometown with a degree in hotel and restaurant management from the University of South Carolina. He had recently married and opened a small ice cream shop, but he was restless and looking for something else.

City Manager Tom Leath said he first met the future mayor when McBride made an appointment out of the blue to come to Leath's office for some career counseling. "Probably about two years before he ran for council, he came to see me and wanted to talk about what he should do with the rest of his life," Leath told me. "He was sort of kicking around going to law school. . . . I'm a lawyer and . . . so he came to see me about whether I thought that was a good idea." Leath suspected McBride's mission had as much to do with politics as career advice. Whatever McBride's motivation, he chose against law school – to Leath's everlasting sorrow. McBride says he does not remember that meeting.

In 1991, McBride made his first foray into elective politics, with an uninspired and unsuccessful bid for Myrtle Beach city council. It was during that campaign that he first introduced himself to Larry Bragg.

A Savannah native, Bragg came to Myrtle Beach when he was stationed at the air force base in the early 1960s. On leaving the military he got into real estate and eventually came to lead Bragg & Edge Realty Company. Submerging himself in community service, he won numerous professional and civic awards, ran unsuccessfully for city council and managed political campaigns for others. In 1984 he joined the Community Appearance Board and rose to the chairmanship.

A couple of months after his defeat, McBride called Bragg and asked him to meet for lunch. "He told me he really wanted to run again and had heard about me . . . and would I agree to run him?" Bragg recalled during an interview in his office. "I didn't give an answer then 'cause I really didn't know. From what I saw about him, he had a passion, wanting to serve. He obviously looked good. So I didn't discount him."

Indeed, Mark McBride appeared to be the perfect candidate. Articulate and composed, he stood over six feet tall, trim, with dark, wavy hair and features that have been called Hollywood handsome. He had an attractive young wife and an infant son.

Bragg came along at a critical moment for McBride. The young politician was out of the ice cream business and "between jobs," as Bragg recalled. "So I thought, well, maybe he would be good in a career in real estate. So I brought him here and helped him get his [real estate] license." He joined Bragg's Community Appearance Board to get some exposure and experience. Throughout the period, the two men worked together daily and Bragg felt like he knew his young associate well. This was not to say that McBride was a gifted real estate salesman. In fact, one of the few things the two men still agreed on is that McBride's real estate career was an experiment that failed.

"The real estate career didn't last long," Bragg said. "Some people are cut out for it and some aren't." McBride's problem, according to Bragg, was "expecting instant gratification. It's very, very, very hard work. . . . He became very frustrated, I think, that it didn't just take off immediately. . . . We mutually agreed that real estate was not his cup of tea." McBride left real estate to launch his next doomed venture – Mark's Delivery – in 1994.

But, politically, McBride's star was rising. He ran for city council again in 1993 and Bragg agreed to manage his campaign. "Not many people knew him," Bragg said. "We crafted the campaign from the standpoint of a new face, new voice, at least having a seat at the table; recognizing and respecting your elders, but having a seat at the table. And it worked. And he went on city council in November of '93."

On city council McBride made himself known as a populist maverick with a flair for the dramatic. An instinctive politician, he understood people's hot buttons and was not afraid to push them. He once brought a bong and other drug paraphernalia he had purchased on the Boulevard to a council meeting to demonstrate the illegal activities going on there. When Burroughs & Chapin threatened to close the Pavilion in 1996, he called on the council to pass an ordinance prohibiting the company's move. Council members pointed out that they had no such authority, but the populist rhetoric played well and gained McBride valuable press.

In May 1997, the Atlantic Beach Memorial Day Bike Festival drew some 100,000 black bikers, whose behavior outraged many Grand Strand residents. Councilman McBride called for a referendum to ban future motorcycle rallies. His proposal was designed to generate maximum divisiveness. It would allow residents to vote separately on whether to keep or to ban each bike festival – the white Harley-Davidson rally and black Memorial Day event. Of course, it was all staged for the gallery. Such a ban would have been illegal and unenforceable, but with anger at black bikers running high, it was a perfectly timed pitch.

McBride got another boost in February 1997 when word hit the streets that a gay and lesbian club would soon move into the old Rivoli Theater, less than a block from the Pavilion. This was a red flag in the face of Christian conservatives and McBride did not let the opportunity pass.

"We're going to set our community standards. We don't want this garbage on the Boulevard," the young councilman told *The Sun News*. "If that involves lingerie bars, questionable bars, we have a lot of cleaning up to do."

Given the chance to soften his remarks, McBride dug in his heals several days later. "What I said, I meant. I don't believe that kind of activity should take place in a family entertainment area. What you do privately is your own business, but I don't want to end up seeing transvestites and drag queens and people being led around on leashes in dog collars. I don't condemn them. I don't want to be a gay-basher. But I'm not carrying their flag."

McBride's timing was as propitious as his target. In the tradition-bound state of South Carolina, where Strom Thurmond was elected to the U.S. Senate on a segregationist platform in 1954 and had not been retired, where the Confederate flag still flew above the State House, homosexuality was viewed as the nemesis of all things Southern and Christian.

In May 1996, Greenville County Council adopted a resolution declaring homosexuality incompatible with community standards. The decision prompted organizers of the Olympic torch run to Atlanta to shelter the flame in a van as it passed through the county. In 1997, GOP leaders in Charleston County forced the local Republican prosecutor, David Schwacke, out of the closet by publicly accusing him of downloading gay pornography and soliciting gay sex on his office computer. In the Columbia suburb of Irmo, a high school principal canceled a free school concert by the Indigo Girls after parents complained that the rock singers, Amy Ray and Emily Saliers, were lesbians. A Republican candidate for state agriculture commissioner in 1998 vowed to protect the family farm from the "homosexual movement."

In a story about the state's simmering homophobia, *The New York Times* described "the pervasiveness of fundamentalist Christianity, which interprets scriptural warnings against homosexuality as God-given truth; the ties between religious conservatives and the state's surging Republican Party . . . the South's history of institutionalized bigotry, and the state's resistance to cultural change, racial and otherwise."

In this atmosphere, McBride could see which way the wind was blowing and set his sail.

State and local gay rights activists denounced McBride, catapulting the councilman from the split to the top of the front page. "There is a large majority of gays and lesbians who will not keep quiet," said local activist Linda Robertson. "I am appalled that a city council member can be so uneducated and prejudiced in today's society."

McBride's stock was on the rise.

At a raucous city council meeting in March 1997, some 300 gay and lesbian activists came out to denounce McBride and call for equal rights. Quoting from Scripture, a handful of conservatives denounced the activists. McBride defended himself, saying he was no gay-basher, but adding, "We need to promote activities that speak of family values, a wholesome, healthy and clean atmosphere and giving tourists what they expect when they visit Myrtle Beach. To encourage and perpetuate this non-traditional family behavior is contrary to the city's best interests."

The temperature rose when gay activists asked for an ordinance prohibiting discrimination based on sexual orientation. McBride opposed it. "They are human beings and they are citizens and that's all the protection they need," McBride told *The Sun News*. "I don't think their group is a protected group."

Organizers of the S.C. Gay & Lesbian Pride Festival struck back, announcing they would hold their annual event in Myrtle Beach in 1998. As many as 10,000 activists would answer the summons to the Grand Strand, organizers promised. "After some of the things that transpired, the gay and lesbian community started bonding," Linda Robertson told the press. " . . .It's not a reaction to McBride, but he has unknowingly helped to bring this community together." The MBA Chamber of Commerce and several city council members quickly welcomed the event. "They have as much right to be here as anybody else," Councilwoman Rachel Broadhurst said. "If they go properly and get their permits, I don't see why they wouldn't be welcome." McBride was not available for comment, but the city would hear plenty from him soon enough.

By this time McBride was out of real estate and running a fast-food delivery business called Mark's Delivery. Nevertheless, he and Larry Bragg had remained close. In 1996, Bragg was elected as a delegate to the Democratic National Convention in Chicago and – depending on who is telling the tale – either Bragg invited McBride to join him or McBride asked if he could come along.

"Mark had never been . . . to a national political convention," Bragg said. Though McBride was acting more and more like a Republican on the nonpartisan city council, Bragg – then chairman of the Horry County Democratic Party – agreed to take the neophyte along for a civics lesson. "I thought, well, maybe I could expose him to different aspects of the political system," Bragg recalled. "So he asked to go and, you know, he's very charming."

Even the collapse of his food delivery business that same month did not stop McBride from taking a week off for politics and, for Larry Bragg, it was a good thing he did. While they were together in their Chicago hotel room, Bragg suffered a stroke. It was McBride who called 911 and possibly saved his friend's life. Today Bragg still runs his real estate business, still attends to his municipal and civic duties, but he is a shadow of his former robust self, moving about slumped heavily on an orthopedic cane.

Bragg was recovering from his stroke in January 1997 when he flew to Washington for the second Clinton Inauguration. Once again, McBride asked to come along (or Bragg invited him) and drove to Washington to join his friend for the festivities. Riding back to Myrtle Beach together in McBride's pickup truck, the two had a lot of time to talk.

"He had always joked around about wanting to run for mayor or run for Congress," Bragg said. "And I told him . . . he needed to learn patience, because when he was on council, he sort of enjoyed the role of being the burr under the saddle, which is fine for a lone council person. Even though you can't garner leadership, it still brings another perspective to the table. . . . . But being young, a lot of times young people are impatient. And it seems to be almost a psychological thing, once a person is elected to city council, I don't know if it happens that night at midnight, or the next day or whatever, then the next logical thinking is mayor.

"So we were driving back from the inauguration and he talked and talked and talked about running for mayor," Bragg said. "He wanted me to run him for mayor. Finally, I told him 'yes' just so he would pull over and let me go to the bathroom and get me a Pepsi-Cola. . . . It almost became a game. I said, 'I'm dying of thirst. I need to take a pill, you know, I need a Pepsi-Cola. . . . I've really gotta go to the bathroom.' [McBride said] 'No, no, not gonna stop.' I'd say, 'We just passed a rest area.' 'No, no, not gonna stop.'

"So, I don't know, after about 200 miles from Washington, I said, 'All right, fine.' So he pulled over at a rest area – I think it was Burger King. It had a Coke machine."

For the rest of the trip McBride continued to badger his friend about managing his campaign for mayor – "Remember, you promised."

And Bragg answered, "'No, no, Mark, it's not time. You really need to run for [council]. . . .' At least he didn't pull over and throw me out of the truck." Needless to say, McBride's memory of that trip differs from Bragg's.

Bragg thought the issue was closed, but a few weeks later he heard the buzz that McBride was going to run for mayor and Bragg was going to manage him. Bragg tried again to reason with his young friend, "but it went in one ear and out the other."

In fact, McBride got the message loud and clear. He went out and hired Marion Foxworth and Cameron Viebrock to manage his campaign.

As the November election neared, candidates for mayor and city council began to preen and identify their issues. While others addressed such pressing but decidedly unsexy matters as stormwater control, downtown redevelopment and protecting residential areas from commercial encroachment, McBride went straight for the red meat issues of morality and law and order. "Public safety issues are some of the things we need to look at differently," he said in an August 1997 interview with *The Sun News*. It was a strange turn for the candidate who had built his early reputation on the rhetoric of controlled growth.

On the September 20 filing date, McBride joined Councilman Harry Charles in challenging twelve-year incumbent Mayor Robert Grissom. He continued to sound the family-values theme and said he would use the mayor's bully pulpit to bring the public discussion back to the issues people cared about: "Fifteen years ago in Myrtle Beach, we didn't have a proliferation of adult entertainment, we didn't have video gambling, we didn't have Sunday liquor sales. . . . The reality is, we are a conservative part of the country. We're losing everything we stood for. I think residents are asking us to do something."

The mayoral campaign turned nasty when McBride distributed leaflets that distorted Charles' voting record. Charles responded in a candidates' forum, saying McBride was "stupid and ignorant. If Mark McBride possesses one ounce of decency, he would get up and tell you this is a distortion of fact."

In that forum, McBride reiterated an earlier pledge to ask for the National Guard to control the Memorial Day Bike Festival. Grissom and Charles said the Guard should not be used for civil law enforcement.

Standing side by side, the three candidates made a startling contrast. Harry Charles, at 75, trim, with a thick shock of white hair, was a retired Air Force Colonel who had flown bombing missions over Germany. He had been adjutant attorney and practiced as a civilian attorney after his retirement from the Air Force. He had served eight years on city council. Bob Grissom was a 76-year-old World War II veteran, ready-mix concrete executive, twelve-year mayor, twelve-year county treasurer, wheeler-dealer and lifelong politician. McBride stood nearly a head taller than both men, who were old enough to be his grandfathers. He had a degree in hotel and restaurant management from the University of South Carolina, one term on city council and a record of failed business ventures.

But what McBride lacked in experience, he made up in visual and emotional appeal. He did not hesitate to use his wife, Laura, and their children, Struthers, 7, and Millson, 5, as props. At the time of the election, McBride worked in his wife's telecommunications business.

On Election Day, November 4, 1997, incumbent Bob Grissom received 1,806 votes to McBride's 1,452; Harry Charles was eliminated with 1,082 votes. A runoff was scheduled for November 18.

The incumbent and the young challenger had a televised debate, as Charles threw his support to Grissom. The campaign grew ugly, but McBride's tactics drew the most criticism. An ad appeared in *The Sun News*, listing prominent McBride supporters. Yet three of the people on the list quickly spoke up to say they had not given permission for their names to be used. "Your name's all you've got," said one local artist who found her name used in vain. "If you don't want your name used, it should be honored."

Then, on the day before the runoff, another political ad appeared in *The Sun News*. Placed by a mysterious Committee for Equal Access to Local Government, the full-page ad featured a cartoon figure of Bob Grissom being manipulated by puppet master Doug Wendel. The text of the ad charged that, under Grissom, the city had raised taxes five mills to pay for landscaping for B&C's Broadway at the Beach development. The ad also overstated the amount of money from a tax rebate that went to Broadway at the Beach projects and the amount of hospitality tax revenues that went to B&C projects. There was no time for the Grissom campaign to respond.

"That's the kind of thing that could easily sway 100 votes," Coastal Carolina University political scientist Jack Riley told *The Sun News* a week later. One hundred votes would have been enough. The day after the ad ran, Myrtle Beach voters went to the polls again and this time they elected Mark Struthers McBride by forty-two votes − 2,228 to 2,186. After hearing the results announced at the Law Enforcement Center, where the votes were counted, McBride blinked back tears. "This is for my mother, who passed away last May," he said.

In the days following the runoff, *The Sun News* did something it should have done earlier; it checked out the source of the mysterious political ad. Reporters had no trouble tracking it down to Marion Foxworth, McBride's campaign manager, and Harold Worley, the North Myrtle Beach hotelier and former state legislator. The Committee for Equal Access to Local Government was formed on November 14, the day it paid $1,100 in cash to place the ad. However, the committee did not file its state-required organization papers until November 19 – the day after the runoff election. A committee member who helped pay for the ad delivered a package containing the text and the cartoon to *The Sun News*. She later told reporters she did not know the contents of the package. McBride maintained he had seen the cartoon, but had not authorized it to be used in any political advertising.

Mike Todd, the artist who drew the cartoon, later challenged McBride's claim of innocence. "I was hired by McBride," Todd told *The Sun News*. "It is not true that he had nothing to do with [the cartoon]." Furthermore, Todd said, McBride's wife had personally delivered photographs to his house to be used in creating the cartoon. Laura McBride vehemently denied delivering materials to Todd.

The State Ethics Commission reviewed the matter, saying there was a violation of the law in paying for the ad in cash; however, no action was taken. The votes were certified and McBride was declared the winner. A philosophical Bob Grissom said, "It's all over now. People who use those tactics to win elections pay for it eventually. I don't want to make an issue of it." Eight months later, Grissom was dead of a heart attack.

McBride's friendship with Larry Bragg was permanently ruptured by the mayoral campaign of 1997. Like a number of McBride's former political and business associates, Bragg ended up feeling betrayed in their relationship. But Mark McBride had already moved on. A young man in a hurry had no time for regret or remorse.

Fire at City Hall

In the early years of his council career – before he discovered black motorcyclists and gays – Mark McBride's favorite rhetorical target had been the Burroughs & Chapin Co. That campaign reached its apex in the political cartoon that ran in *The Sun News* the day before the runoff election. "The rules have just changed," McBride announced immediately after his victory. "Everybody is going to be treated fairly. It doesn't matter if it's the beachwear store or Burroughs & Chapin or the guy who owns the guitar shop."

Now, with the election behind them, it was clear to the company and particularly to the new mayor that further animosity would be unproductive. McBride took the opportunity to say that he would work with B&C: "I'm not here to run Burroughs & Chapin out of town. I just don't think we negotiate real well with the company," he told *The Sun News*. "You just can't keep changing the rules for special people." For its part, B&C said it looked forward to working with McBride, though it characterized the anti-Grissom ad as "vile and despicable."

Whatever the political differences between the mayor-elect and the development company, it soon became clear they shared similar tastes in entertainment. With the Gay & Lesbian Pride Festival scheduled for spring of 1998, it was announced that the Village People, a 1970s pop group, had been signed to perform an outdoor concert at Broadway at the Beach. The concert was backed by Broadway at the Beach clubs and merchants, who ponied up a $50,000 deposit to land the group.

Best known for their 1970s disco hits "Macho Man" and "YMCA," the openly gay performers wore flashy "macho" costumes, and were a longtime favorite in the gay community. There was alarm at B&C headquarters. The company's Broadway at the Beach complex was a temple of family values. B&C asked its tenants to drop their association with the Gay & Lesbian Pride Festival and cancel the concert.

In a December 1, 1997, advertisement in *The Sun News*, B&C stated their case: "Our company abides by the laws governing fair and equal treatment of all individuals. However, as a private company, we have not, nor do we intend to be forced or intimidated into supporting organized activities that we believe endanger the historic values of our nation and the cornerstone truths on which they are based."

B&C's tenants didn't give a damn about the landlord's "historic values" and "cornerstone truths." When they refused to cancel the Village People concert, Burroughs & Chapin got tough. In a December 4 notice the company stated tersely: "We have decided that it is not in the best interests of Broadway at the Beach to have any special events during April 30-May 3, 1998, which can be misinterpreted as an endorsement of the Gay and Lesbian Pride March to be held during the same period."

There was almost universal shock at the company's high-handed action. Said Eric Anzalone, a member of the Village People: "It's been a while since we had a cancellation. We've never had anything like this happen." Pride Festival organizers denounced B&C's "egregious action."

Tony Snell, told *The Sun News*, "Really, they're not helping themselves or anybody. After this, what is next? Will they prohibit music by openly gay and lesbian artists like Elton John and k.d. lang? Will they ask individuals their sexual orientation before entering Broadway at the Beach?"

B&C's action was questioned editorially by *The Sun News* and columnist Bob Bestler blistered the corporate mandarins: "The cynic would say the company sees an opportunity to endear itself to the population of Myrtle Beach by touting 'family values' at the expense of gays. The strategy helped elect a mayor, didn't it?. . .

"Nothing, I think, shows the nastiness of Burroughs & Chapin's position more clearly than its opposition to the Village People. This is homophobia at its worst.

"As a group, the Village People has become an American icon. In the summer of 1996, at the Olympic Games in Atlanta, two Village People songs – 'YMCA' and 'Macho Man' – were played about as often as the national anthem."

The Village People concert was moved to the House of Blues in North Myrtle Beach, as Horry County polarized over the approaching Pride Festival. A group of Baptist ministers said they would organize a boycott of any restaurant or business that promoted the festival. "I'm totally against the festival," said the Reverend Ray Cribb of South Conway Baptist Church. "It goes against the Bible and I'm going to do anything I need to do to let folks know I'm against it. If they want to live that way, fine. But don't shove it down my throat."

Tensions rose as the new mayor was sworn in on January 6, 1998. "I don't promote or endorse that lifestyle," McBride said. "They're asking for special rights for a preference that is against traditional family values." In a February council meeting, the mayor was odd man out in a 6-1 vote to close the streets on May 2 for the Gay Pride Parade. "For sixty years this community has promoted itself as a family beach with family values," McBride told a chamber of angry gay activists and business people. "I believe we're opening our door to all the other groups across the country, like the skinheads and all these Black Panthers, if we allow this group. We'll become the soapbox for all these groups."

"Tonight you have insulted my family, Mayor McBride," said organizer Patrick Evans. "I have family values and I question if you know what they are."

McBride further demonstrated his political savvy by naming labor unions, along with skinheads and the KKK, among the "undesirable" elements that would storm the streets once the Gay Pride Festival opened the gates. Local postal workers picketed to protest McBride's remark and the state AFL-CIO said it would ask labor groups affiliated with it – as many as thirteen million people – to boycott Myrtle Beach as long as the city appeared to discriminate against any group. An alarmed Ashby Ward said, "We've had groups threaten before to call a boycott. But this is probably the largest of these kinds of threats. . . . I think it is misdirected." Ward reminded AFL-CIO members that McBride was alone among council members in voting to bar the event.

But McBride was not alone among citizens. On March 17, 130 angry Christians came out to the council meeting, unannounced, with signs and placards, denouncing the Gay Pride Festival. "We are here to stand in support of the Mayor of Myrtle Beach, who in recent days and months has come under tremendous attack and pressure by special interest groups and our local media," said the Reverend Cribb. "Mayor McBride has made a tremendous stance for decency and traditional family values."

"Mr. McBride, I commend you, sir, for standing up for the people of Myrtle Beach and what God stands for," said a Surfside Beach supporter.

And a woman from Conway added her hosannas: "Jesus loves each person here tonight, but he does not love the sin. Rebellion is just as bad as the immoral acts of homosexuality. I support Mayor Mark McBride and I hope that we will grow as a Christian community."

There were allusions to Hitler in the stormy session council members defended themselves angrily and piously. Asked after the meeting if he had known the group was coming, McBride said, "No, I didn't orchestrate this." Many were skeptical.

The Sun News ran pages of letters to the editor, pro and con, some from as far away as Iowa, Ontario, Texas, Florida, New Jersey and West Virginia. McBride's supporters seemed to envision a vast conspiracy of greedy merchants, liberal media and godless sodomites bent on destroying "traditional family values" and the very Republic itself. Many letter writers purported to be Bible scholars, quoting at length from the books of Leviticus and Romans.

"In the eyes of the Lord Jesus Christ, son of God, your lifestyle is a sin," a North Myrtle Beach man warned gays. "If homosexuals and lesbians do not change their loathsome, disgusting, sickening, nasty, repugnant, dirty and immoral lifestyle, they're going to bust hell wide open."

Wrote another: "I would like to congratulate our mayor for his stance on homosexuality. He, to me, is a majority of one. When this happens and is over and the people see for themselves how these people conduct themselves, there will be more outcry than when the black bikers came and went. . . . "

From Little River came this letter: "I support Mayor McBride's position and would go even further. Do away with all group displays and street parades. To hell with business greed! It's time some consideration be shown to our neighborhoods and residents. . . ."

On Sunday, April 26, 1998, more than 1,000 people gathered at a local stadium for the Citizens for Traditional Family Values Rally. With a huge American flag as backdrop, gospel singers, ministers, GOP leaders and wannabes – including the lieutenant governor – were on hand to dish up a heaping helping of that old-time religion. The event also featured Michael Johnston, a "recovered" homosexual, host and producer of a weekly radio program in Newport News, Virginia, dedicated to monitoring the "homosexual movement" in America. And, of course, the day would not be complete without Mayor Mark McBride.

"Some people find it strange that a rally like this is necessary," McBride told the faithful that day. "Why should we come together to celebrate the traditional? The answer is simple. It is time for the people of good will to remind each other that they are not alone and that things like family, moral certainty and the character of our society have been taken for granted for too long. So that now those who do not value the wholesome find it easy to encroach upon the very fiber of what we believe."

McBride was applauded throughout his address and was echoed by other speakers during the three-hour event. "I agree with Mayor Mark McBride," said Van Jenrette III, an ambitious GOP flunky. "The community has to set its standards. The question is, 'Who defines what is deviant behavior?' It is not up to those people who are deviant to define it for you."

"If we had more people who happened to be elected officials like Mark McBride, America would be a better place. . . . " Lt. Governor Bob Peeler said. "A country without God is a country without a future. But first, we have to be the mothers and fathers, husbands and wives God would like us to be."

At the end of the rally, Sunni Crowley of Myrtle Beach told *The Sun News*, "I think it's about time people of this community took back their community. I think [McBride] is swimming upstream and a lot of people don't like that. But I think he's headed in the right direction."

McBride's homophobic rhetoric got nationwide attention, including a front-page story in *The New York Times*, in which he said, "What we've built ourselves on over the last sixty years is the traditional family base. People don't come here to be subjugated to all the progressiveness, all the sophistication, all the enlightenment of big-city life." Lester Maddox couldn't have said it better. While the local chamber of commerce and the state tourism board spent millions of dollars to promote the Grand Strand as a friendly, modern resort, the young mayor was confirming its old sobriquet: the Redneck Riviera.

As news of homophobia in Myrtle Beach spread, pledges of support poured in from around the nation. Yet fewer than 8,000 people turned out for the much-ballyhooed festival and parade. Some 120 gay and lesbian couples exchanged vows in a ceremony at Myrtle Beach State Park, while a couple of miles away, 150 Christians gathered at First Baptist Church to study biblical strategies for ministering to homosexuals. Mayor McBride sent his wife and two children out of town for the weekend.

The festival provided the first test of Mark McBride's leadership. His next test was thundering down the road in the form of the Harley-Davidson and Memorial Day bike rallies. He wouldn't pass them any better than he did the Gay Pride Festival. But there would be two lasting impressions of the Mayor to come out of his homophobic belligerence. One was *The New York Times* story about homophobia in South Carolina.

The other was the gun permit.

In June – weeks after the Gay Pride Festival – McBride revealed that he had worn a bulletproof vest at the Traditional Family Values Rally. He had received threats during the Gay Pride controversy, he said. On June 17, a strange and "mentally unstable" man had come into City Hall asking to see him. In a council workshop McBride announced that he had recently received a concealed weapon permit and undergone training. Now the mayor needed City Manager Tom Leath to give him permission to keep a gun in his desk at City Hall. Council members were unsympathetic, and asked Leath to draft a resolution against bringing concealed weapons into City Hall without approval from council. "We just don't need that image of a pistol-packing mayor," Councilwoman Rachel Broadhurst said. "I think we have a responsibility to set an example and having a gun in City Hall is not the example we want."

Almost from the day Mark McBride was sworn in as mayor, city government had become a battleground. Snipes and barbs between McBride and the six-member council became more personal and frequent as the petulant mayor questioned his colleagues' motives and they questioned his integrity. McBride routinely came up on the short end of 6-1 votes.

On March 19, 1998, came the "water glass incident." In the midst of a heated workshop discussion with Councilman Chuck Martino, McBride's water goblet was broken. "I put my glass down and left the room to use the bathroom," the mayor later explained to *The Sun News*. "It must have been a defective stem." Others present said it looked like he slammed it down on the table.

Later in that meeting McBride told his colleagues, "I was informed by city attorney that a council member had inquired how to remove the mayor. We just don't need that. There is someone who is feeding this and stirring this," he said. He had heard from "four different sources" that there was a coup in the works to oust him, he said.

Martino explained that a citizen had requested information on how to remove the mayor and he had passed the request on to Attorney Wettlin. "I asked Joe [Wettlin], I told Mark about it and then I told the other members of the council," Martino said. "It wasn't a secret. It's not a conspiracy."

"There's just some pettiness that has to be put aside and some jockeying for position that isn't in the best interest of the city," McBride said. "We need to rise above it."

"I think, Mark, that's very nice," Councilwoman Judy Rodman told him, "but I've got to be honest with you, I've never been so subjected to slaps in the face as I was Tuesday," she said, referring to the 130 demonstrators who showed up at the March 17 council meeting. "What happened Tuesday night was orchestrated."

"I did not orchestrate the meeting," McBride said. Martino, Rodman and other council members doubted his sincerity.

"We're saying, when you and your cohorts set this up, that's not right," Broadhurst scolded.

Councilman Wayne Gray said, "I'm finding some inconsistencies with you, Mayor." He said he thought the Tuesday night demonstration was just another McBride attempt to embarrass the council and the staff.

"Me or anybody around me didn't orchestrate it," the embattled mayor repeated. "The people at the meeting, that's public sentiment."

"Maybe you have lost so much credibility that I can't believe you," Broadhurst said.

What the new mayor lacked in credibility he compensated for in his mastery of Robert's Rules of Order, using procedural maneuvers and jargon to thwart the council. One citizen told him during the public comment portion of a meeting, "If you would adhere to the Constitution as strictly as you do to Robert's Rules of Order, you would have no problems."

In the all-too-typical council meeting of March 25, 1998, Rachel Broadhurst tried to bring up a motion to reconsider the use of accommodations tax money. McBride blocked her motion, saying it was inappropriate and he could allow only a motion to rescind the appropriations.

"I don't think we want to rescind the money," Broadhurst said.

"The only motion I believe is proper for me to accept is a motion to rescind the money for groups that haven't received the money," McBride said.

City Attorney Joe Wettlin told council they could overrule the mayor's opinion with a two-thirds vote of council.

"If the only alternative we have is to overrule the decision," Broadhurst said, "I'll make a motion to overrule the chair's decision."

"We have a motion for appellation of the chair," McBride said without explanation. The motion to overrule died for lack of a second, so Broadhurst made a motion to amend the agenda to clarify the appropriation of accommodations tax money.

"The chair rules he cannot accept that motion," McBride said. "It's the chair's opinion. Then again, if council doesn't agree with the chair's ruling, you have the right to appeal through appellation of the chair."

Council members did not know how to bypass McBride's "appellation of the chair" ruling, and the mayor won the point. At the end of the meeting, Broadhurst brought the subject up again. "I chose not to continue to discuss appealing your decisions, because I didn't want to give the media another circus to report. I don't agree with the ruling. I'd very much like to, at our next workshop, have an expert talk to us about Robert's Rules of Order."

At the April 10, 1998, council meeting, rules and procedures were on the agenda again. "I never found a rule called 'appellation' in Robert's Rules of Order and neither has anyone else I know of," Attorney Wettlin told the council. In keeping with state municipal law, Wettlin had prepared a six-page set of rules to replace the 106-page Robert's Rules of Order. Council was discussing the new rules that night.

"Frankly, I think this is a waste of time," McBride said. "I think we ought to move on with the business of the city . . . and quit this pettiness."

"I couldn't agree more," Broadhurst said. "That is why this is so important. It eliminates high-stress, strung-out feelings because we have to argue a point of order."

"So if you can't understand Robert's Rules of Order, you make your own rules?" McBride asked.

Apparently so. Wettlin's Rules of Order were adopted on a 4-3 vote at a May 26 council meeting.

Things down at City Hall only got worse. McBride had campaigned on a platform of firing city manager Tom Leath. Within a few months of taking office, Leath and McBride were communicating with each other by fax, though they used adjacent offices. After Wettlin rewrote the Rules of Order, McBride was calling for his firing also.

Reviewing the first eleven weeks of McBride's mayoral tenure, *The Sun News* editorialized on March 25, "It is simply malicious for anyone to say that the Myrtle Beach city council isn't working together. Almost every vote has been 6-1. That is a huge majority.

"The council thus seems to be working well together, except for Mayor Mark McBride, the '1' vote. Yet, he alleges fractiousness among the council. Conversely, McBride is just where he was on the last council, often alone on the minority end of majority votes."

When it came to matters of money, the council had a whole different set of issues with the mayor. Even as a city councilman, McBride
had played fast and loose with the city purse strings. Between 1994 and
1996, he ran up $2,213 in personal debt, using City Hall as a loan
office. When the city advanced him money for travel and other municipal business, he was supposed to turn in his receipts and the unused
cash. Since there was no deadline for returning the money, McBride
was clearly in no hurry. "I just didn't have the money and no one ever
asked for it," he explained to *The Sun News*. "When no one asks for it,
it is easy to let it run." Most of the debt had been run up while his
restaurant delivery business was going under and he was desperate for
cash. "That's not an excuse, that's just how it happened," he said. "I
was just struggling."

When the issue was brought to light with a *Sun News* freedom of information request, McBride quickly paid up his arrears – interest free.

Then the councilman was elected mayor and in his first four
months on the job, he maxed out his city credit card to the tune of
$3,718. About $1,500 of that was for personal expenses, including part
of a family ski trip, new clothes and a tire. Once again, McBride
pledged to pay the city back immediately – after the matter was made
public. "Next week, when I get paid, you know, I'm supposed to go in
there, and I was going to sit down and straighten it all out," he told a
Sun News reporter.

True to his word, McBride paid the credit card bill and returned
the plastic to the city, swearing off any further use of city credit or cash
advances. Nevertheless, council immediately passed an ordinance prohibiting personal use of city credit cards.

Later that year, alarmed council members started looking into the
annual mayor-and-council operating budget. The budget for fiscal
1998 had been busted by more than $17,000. Council attention
homed in on several items. It seems McBride was receiving two unpub-
licized and unauthorized monthly allowances, totaling $971.

"This is the taxpayers' money. . . ." said an incensed Chuck
Martino. "It smells of a slush fund. I think it's unethical and I think it's
not prudent management practices."

The city also provided the mayor with a cell phone. In five months in office, McBride ran up more than $700 in cell phone charges. By comparison, former Mayor Bob Grissom's cell phone bill had been about $300 for his last six months in office.

Rachel Broadhurst was beside herself. "I think it's ludicrous. I run four companies and my cell phone bill is about twenty-seven dollars a month. Who the hell do you talk to that long?"

Council responded by taking away McBride's $971 monthly allowances and curtailing his cell phone use.

It wasn't just the city's money that McBride was careless with. In August 1998, a former friend filed suit against the mayor, alleging McBride had failed to repay a personal loan. Timothy Cooper said McBride had not made a single payment to Cooper, who had loaned him $20,065 to settle business debts. According to the suit, Cooper said McBride called him "in a panic" in August 1995, begging for money to save his business, MSM Food Service, Inc., doing business as Mark's Delivery.

Cooper said McBride first agreed to write a promissory note and make payments on the loan, but after Mark's Delivery went out of business, McBride and his wife declined to sign a note on the loan. "The defendant intentionally made a misrepresentation to the plaintiff . . . ," according to the suit. The suit also stated that McBride told Cooper his political career would be ruined if he did not pay his creditors.

McBride told *The Sun News* that he had been making $500 monthly payments on the loan and was keeping faith with Cooper. Cooper disagreed. "I understand Mark McBride has a public image to uphold, but unfortunately the facts tend to discredit his statements."

McBride responded, "I am continually saddened by my friend's inability to accept the settlement upon which we agreed."

In January 1999, the matter was put to rest when Cooper accepted McBride's promissory note for $20,065 due, with payment to begin in two years. "Obviously, the final outcome has proved the validity of the debt," Cooper said.

So went Mark McBride's first year in office. As 1999 rolled around, council members looked for a way to lower the temperature, to bring council, mayor and staff together. What they settled on was a planning retreat, to be held March 2-3. Part of the retreat would be a workshop, led by professional "leadership-building" facilitator Carl Neu Jr. of Lakewood, Colorado.

"I have some serious apprehensions about this council," Neu told *The Sun News*. "There are some indications that relationships are headed toward a pathological level."

The cycle of anger, frustration and revenge was a threat not just to the council, Neu said, but also to the whole city. "If relationships continue to get bad, then the community suffers. The community becomes the walking wounded and the venom will contaminate community politics."

One got the impression that the mayor was not enthusiastic about Neu's workshop. Not only did he fail to complete his pre-workshop questionnaire, but he also showed up for only a half-day of the two-day exercise. That half-day proved very telling. Part of the exercise called for role-playing and this was the scenario: a plane crashes in the Sonora Desert. A team led by City Attorney Joe Wettlin, with council members Judy Rodman, Wayne Gray, Crain Woods and Wilson Cain, survived the "crash." Their survival strategy was simple: remain at the crash site and wait for help.

Another team, led by Mayor McBride and made up of council members Rachel Broadhurst and Chuck Martino along with City Manager Tom Leath and Assistant City Manger Allan Blum, did not fare so well. "I'm walking," McBride announced, striking out across the imaginary desert. The others followed, agreeing to send out a two-person party to look for help. But within forty minutes, the group went from strong individual opinions to rushed group decisions – and then "died" in the desert.

Reviewing the debacle, Neu said, "If you had a good team . . . the team will be brighter and smarter than its most brilliant member. You had nice, hardworking members who killed each other."

Three weeks later, Neu's bill came in at City Hall. It included his professional fee ($3,500) and expenses ($933) and the survival game ($715). The mayor sent a fax across the wall to the city manager, saying he was "concerned" about the cost of the retreat and implying that Leath had been less than honest about the $6,000-plus price. Leath answered with his own memo – "There is no reason to be concerned" – and told *The Sun News* the price was "average," considering Neu's national reputation as a facilitator. "I was pleased with the overall product," he said. McBride did not return calls from reporters.

Despite a shaky first year in office, McBride's supporters remained steadfast. Karon Mitchell probably spoke for most of them when she told me, "[McBride] says it like he sees it. Sometimes he stirs it too much. Sometimes he needs to say it just once and shut up. . . He's a good man. He's moral. He has convictions. He's a Christian. He's not politically correct all the time and that's what gets him in trouble."

At Home in Myrtle Beach

In 1995, a bad career move landed me in Rock Hill, South Carolina, a small city trapped in the fifties, its greatest assets being a little state-supported liberal arts college and close proximity to Charlotte, North Carolina. I was tired of Rock Hill, where a couple of friends had recently lectured me on the perils of dating women half my age and where even the local Wiccan coven felt more like a Baptist women's club when you got to know them. I was tired of freelancing, tired of staff writing, tired of dealing with arrogant, boneheaded editors.

To answer the mounting evidence that I wasn't as young as I used to be, I went out and bought a red Miata. Local police started pulling me over and giving me the third degree. Rock Hill wasn't ready for a red convertible. My sister took one look at it and said, "My god! You've gone middle-age crazy!"

It was definitely time for a change.

I spent the first three months of 1999 driving back and forth between Rock Hill and Myrtle Beach, where I conducted interviews and delved through the vertical files at Chapin Memorial Library. I knew I couldn't write a book about Myrtle Beach from Rock Hill, but this was more than a professional decision. As a child wishes every day could be Christmas, so I had wished – while vacationing there with my family in the 1950s – that I could one day live in Myrtle Beach. Some dreams die hard.

On the last day of March, I packed up my computer and file cabinets, pots and pans, bed and books in a rental truck and drove across the Intracoastal Waterway, past the Burroughs & Chapin tract where workers were clearing land for a new Home Depot and Wal-Mart SuperCenter, past another B&C tract where the Seaboard Business Park was under construction. It was a Wednesday and traffic was backed up on U.S. 501. Making my way to 19th Avenue North under lowering, gray skies, I parked in the lot behind my little apartment. As I freed my car from the tow-behind dolly, I looked up. Seagulls were calling and circling overhead.

It had taken nearly fifty years, but I was at home in Myrtle Beach.

My new apartment stood on the second dune line, half a block from U.S. 17, two blocks from the surf and ten blocks from the Pavilion. From the narrow catwalk in front of my door, I could peer between the horizontal floors of the adjacent parking garage and the vertical beachfront hotel towers and spy a little rectangle of the eastern horizon, with the deep gray Atlantic rolling beneath. In surrounding yards stood ancient pines and cedars, twisted by the Atlantic wind into haunting grotesques. Most of the buildings on my block were aging apartments and bungalows, inhabited by a seedy and colorful cast of cooks, waitresses, bartenders, beachcombers and other roustabouts, who pretty much kept to themselves. Like most of Myrtle Beach, the street was perpetually littered with beer cans, soda bottles, fast food wrappers.

At the northeast corner of U.S. 17 and 19th Avenue North, Xanadu was one of the rowdiest dance clubs in town. In the coming months, I would see hundreds of young drunks lurch and fall out of the club and wobble down the street in front of my apartment, singing, screaming, cursing, smashing beer bottles. Sometimes they would stage a mass urination in the hedges around my building, while their girlfriends waited patiently in the street. I laughed as they sagged against cars and trucks and chucked up their Calabash seafood dinners in the moonlight. In the spring and summer, hardly a weekend passed without a fight outside the club. Sometimes the police responded; more often, not. On the northwest corner was Yesterday's, a sports bar and former country music theater, which now filled the house with an occasional bill of prizefights. Not as raucous as Xanadu, Yesterday's nevertheless saw its share of blue lights in the spring and summer of '99.

At the southeast corner of the intersection was a Krispy Kreme doughnut shop. In my new home I was never safe from the aroma of hot, glazed doughnuts, fresh from the grease, permeating every corner of the neighborhood. But – with a few exceptions – my character proved equal to the test. A Shoney's restaurant occupied the fourth corner of this crowded, frenetic intersection, offering no peril or temptation.

In the early hours of April 1, two men left Xanadu and were walking across the parking lot of Studebaker's when they were accosted and stabbed by a third. The injuries were not serious, but the incident set the tone for the rest of the season on the block. In mid-May, a woman was murdered at the Outrigger Motel, four blocks from my apartment. It was the first of three murders that would occur over the next couple of years in hotels a few hundred yards from my front door. Within days of my arrival, I knew I was living in a combat zone. I was awakened in the night and startled in the day by screeching tires and crashing steel on U.S. 17, by the wail of sirens around my apartment.

Myrtle Beach city council met every second Tuesday, at 7:00 p.m., in municipal court chambers at the Law Enforcement Center on Oak Street. As a new resident, I thought it my responsibility to keep any eye on this fractious body. I attended my first meeting on April 13, taking my place in a deeply cushioned theater-style chair, along with dozens of others, amid the soft lighting and mellow acoustics.

Before me on the dais was the large, paneled, semicircular desk, with Mayor McBride seated in the center, flanked by the six council members – all elected at-large – the city clerk, city manager and city attorney. The most respected and talented member of council was Rachel Broadhurst, 57, owner of Century 21 Broadhurst Realty. She disliked McBride and was widely considered to have the best chance to knock him out in the next mayoral election. There was also Wayne Gray, 31, from one of the oldest families in the county, owner of a chain of local restaurants. Gray graduated Presbyterian College on a basketball scholarship and, in 1983 and 1984, quarterbacked the Myrtle Beach High School Seahawks to state football championships. The trophy case in the lobby of the Pepper Geddings Municipal Recreation Center held a large framed photo, showing a quarterback facing the opposing line, fiercely calling signals behind his center. His face was barely visible, but it was 17-year-old Wayne Gray. Trim and handsome with dark, wavy hair, Gray could have been Mark McBride's brother. In fact, they have been called bookends. But looks were all they had in common. They disliked each other intensely and Gray was said to be hungry for McBride's job.

The other council members included insurance man Chuck Martino, former educator and former director of the Grand Strand Senior Center Judy Rodman, pharmacist Wilson Cain and retired educator Crain Woods. Woods was the sole African American on council. Cain liked to play the dumb good old boy, but he was shrewd and had built a reputation as the man to see for constituent service. He held the longest tenure on council, at sixteen years. Woods and Cain seemed to be engaged in some long-standing competition to see who could wear the blazer with the most outrageous pastels and plaids to council meetings.

Promptly at 7, the mayor called the meeting to order. The Reverend Gardner Altman came forward to deliver the invocation. Praying briefly but passionately, he closed with "in Jesus' name, Amen." Then all stood as Chuck Martino led the Pledge of Allegiance to the Flag.

The first order of business was to authorize City Manager Tom Leath to execute the final memorandum of understanding and to negotiate a contract to build a Convention Center hotel. The city's financial consultant came forward to review one more time the complex public/private financing package behind the project. Councilman Gray made the motion to authorize a memorandum of understanding with the contractor. Councilman Martino seconded. After years of planning and debate, it had come down to this. With a four-star hotel attached to the Myrtle Beach Convention Center, Myrtle Beach hoped to move into the big league of convention and conference cities. But then it was the mayor's turn to speak.

McBride had fought against the Convention Center hotel for years and he took this opportunity to stick it to the project one more time. Stepping down from the dais, he used an overhead projector to show and tell his numbers. He criticized the city's financial exposure in the deal, suggesting one of the investors in the project might not be legitimate because he was headquartered in the Cayman Islands. He impugned the integrity of the city's consultant. "This [deal] is absolutely, positively the wrong way to do it," the Mayor entreated. " . . . It's time to get out of this deal." He was articulate; he was passionate – and he didn't have a clue what was going on.

When he finished, Broadhurst, Martino and Gray tore into him, demonstrating his ignorance of the law and the financing behind the hotel. McBride was forced to apologize to the consultant but stubbornly held his ground on other points. After more than an hour the issue came to a vote. McBride was joined by Woods and Cain but lost, 4 to 3. Immediately, citizens in the gallery demanded to know why public input was not allowed before the debate. McBride apologized again, saying it was his oversight. The city attorney suggested suspending the rules to hear public input. McBride called for a vote, rules were suspended and the public spoke for thirty minutes.

So went my first experience with Myrtle Beach democracy.

Hog Heaven on the Strand

May is "bike month" in Myrtle Beach. First the Harley-Davidson Rally, then the Atlantic Beach Memorial Day Bike Festival descend upon the Grand Strand like a conquering army. The fact is widely known in the Carolinas and anyone who does not appreciate the sound of two-cycle engines is advised to stay away. That long-anticipated vacation to the Grand Strand can be traumatic for those not familiar with local tradition.

In 1940, the Carolina Harley-Davidson Dealers Association invited their customers for a weekend at the beach. They've been returning ever since. Over the years the annual rally swelled, reaching at least 50,000 by 1998. The Harley reputation for lawlessness had grown with the event. Along with regular complaints about the noise of thousands of V-twin engines, there were fights, shootings, drunkenness, drugs and many, many arrests. In 1983, a group of Hell's Angels planned a showdown with the rival Pagans biker gang on U.S. 501; they were deterred only by a troop of armed law enforcement officers. Two Pagans were shot in a barroom brawl in 1990 and three blocks of Ocean Boulevard were closed to put down fighting in 1994.

City officials had considered getting tough on the event, when the Harley-Davidson Dealers Association took charge by organizing the rally, creating a task force to plan activities and spreading the event out to venues around the city. More police officers and better communications with bikers helped tame the celebration. Gang colors were banned in many bars and clubs.

To cope with the Harley-Davidson and Memorial Day bike rallies, Grand Strand municipalities banded together in 1994 to form the Bike Week Task Force. They met regularly to share information and study similar events in other cities. One outgrowth of the task force was the Friendship Team, a group of citizen volunteers who walked the streets in bright yellow T-shirts during biker events, handing out information brochures, taking questions and complaints. The Bike Week Task Force had worked well, especially in taming the Harley-Davidson event.

"The weekend sort of each year has become calmer," City Manager Tom Leath told *The Sun News*. "Now Harley has sort of mellowed into an uneventful weekend." But as "uneventful" as it was, Myrtle Beach recorded 831 arrests and violations in 1998 and North Myrtle Beach recorded 135.

As 60,000 Harley-Davidsons bore down on the Grand Strand for the 1999 revel, it occurred to me that I had never been near a motorcycle rally; I had never even been on a motorcycle. The closest I had come to motorcycles was the iconographic films, *The Wild One* and *Easy Rider*, and Robert Persig's novel, *Zen and the Art of Motorcycle Maintenance*. They are to bike culture what John Wayne movies are to American history.

Different bikes attract different followings, of course, and the Harley-Davidson crowd is the roughest, toughest, meanest, baddest of them all. At least that's the image they cultivate with their black leather jackets and boots, their tattoos and chains – and I, for one, was not about to challenge them for the title. But based on what I had read and what I observed on the roads and in the bars where I traveled, most Harley riders were outcasts and losers, alienated and angry.

If this stereotype seems harsh, the vanguard of bikers who hit town on Saturday, May 8, did nothing to dispel it. It didn't matter that the 60th Annual Harley-Davidson Rally would not start until Wednesday. These people wanted to party *now!* Parking lots filled up with glistening chrome Hogs and shattered beer bottles, while the streets filled up with black leather, graybeards and potbellies. The Harley-Davidson image does not strike the terror it once did, but the keepers of the flame still take themselves pretty seriously.

The Boulevard was lined with lawn chairs as the camp followers of these weekend road warriors watched the parade of chrome and leather go by. From hotel balconies and the beds of pickup trucks the spectators recorded it on camcorders. Women passengers on the big roaring Hogs carried their own camcorders to document the spectators in their lawn chairs and pickup trucks. The beachwear and T-shirt shops offered a breathtaking array of tacky biker T-shirts, the most popular bearing the message: "If You Can Read This, The Bitch Fell Off." Anything with a

Confederate flag painted, printed or stitched on it brought a premium.

Through the weekend the crowds and the noise built. Tens of thousands of Harley riders filled the hotels along the Boulevard and U.S. 17. From Pawleys Island in the south to Brunswick County, North Carolina, they cruised up and down U.S. 17 and the 17 Bypass, by ones and twos and forties and fifties. They focused on a prearranged "loop" from the Myrtle Beach Convention Center on 21st Avenue North to the U.S. 17 Bypass, south to Murrells Inlet and back up U.S. 17 to 21st Avenue. At both ends of the route, and several places in between, were trade shows and swap-and-shop markets for Harley paraphernalia. But this was all a pretext. The real reason 120,000 mostly middle-aged people came to town that week was to ride and drink and party. And they would not be denied. They filled the streets with the roar of their straight-pipe exhausts and megaphone extensions. There was no place in the city, no moment in the day or night when one could escape the noise. By the second night, I knew I was in for something unique in my experience: nine days of uninterrupted pandemonium, without silence or privacy of thought or a good night's sleep. Nine days of unmuffled internal combustion, coming from all directions at all times. Nine days of V-twin engines, straight-pipes and 6,500 rpm bursts.

Motorcycles are, by their nature, an antisocial technology, disrupting everything around them with their ear-splitting noise. It is not surprising that they attract an antisocial element and encourage antisocial behavior. Simply to switch on a Harley and throttle up is to violate the noise ordinance of every county and municipality in the United States, including Horry and Myrtle Beach. For most of the nine days the Harleys were in town, the decibel level at key intersections and vendor areas hovered between 90 and 110; keeping in mind that 110 is the level of a disco club and 120 is the threshold of human pain. Law enforcement officers did what they could, but noise enforcement was not on their agenda.

Myrtle Beach police were regarded as some of the toughest anywhere, and bikers got no special treatment. At Daytona Beach, Atlanta and Sturgis, South Dakota – three towns that draw huge rallies of bikers and black students – arrest rates were about half a percent of all visitors. In Myrtle Beach, the rate was one percent. And Myrtle Beach assessed heavier fines than other cities. But Myrtle Beach was also a symbol of personal freedom and the annual Harley-Davidson rally was a celebration of lawlessness. In that spirit, local police agencies tended to treat bike rallies like hurricanes – as natural phenomena, beyond human control. They advised citizens how to prepare and protect themselves, including shutting schools early and staying off the roads. But, ultimately, bikers in such numbers were a force unto themselves. They transformed the environment around them. The rest of us had no choice but to adapt or leave.

One reason Myrtle Beach was so popular for bike rallies was that South Carolina was one of twenty-nine states that did not require bikers over the age of twenty-one to wear helmets. It also led the nation in biker deaths, double the national average. About 11:30 p.m., Sunday, May 9, James Fox and wife Amanda, both 36, both of Myrtle Beach, were rear-ended by a southbound Pontiac on Kings Highway. Neither was wearing a helmet. Both were rushed to the Medical University of South Carolina in Charleston, where James Fox died the next night. He became the first fatality of the 1999 Harley-Davidson Rally.

Whether bikers are an economic boon or the spawn of Satan depends to a large degree on what kind of business you're in. Harley riders essentially do five things in Myrtle Beach: eat, sleep, drink, ride their bikes and go to strip clubs. If you're in one of those businesses, you can make a lot of money. Local bars such as Studebaker's, the Beach House Restaurant, the Dog House and the Parrot Bar & Grill drew such throngs they hired their own security forces. On the other hand, bikers do not play miniature golf or ride merry-go-rounds. If you're in the family amusement business – as Burroughs & Chapin is – biker week is a disaster. "The bikers come here with very specific ideas of what they want to do," a B&C spokesman said, "and for the most part, we don't fit the bill."

It's not just that bikers don't like miniature golf; they keep away those who do. It's a phenomenon called "segmented tourism"; it's bad for the industry and bad for Myrtle Beach, City Manager Tom Leath told *The Sun News*. "Normally we attract a pretty good cross section of people, from golfers to shoppers to beachcombers. But when you start having lots of big events geared toward specific groups, be they bikers or gay pride activists, it alienates another part of the population and certain businesses will suffer," Leath said. "People either feel left out because they are not bikers, or they just don't want to mess with it. Either way, more and more people are choosing to avoid the area during biker events."

Of course, the real losers are the folks from Peoria and Steubenville and Terre Haute who pull up the MBA Chamber of Commerce Web page and decide Myrtle Beach is the perfect place to spend their vacations. The experience embitters an untold number of them every year. Some vent with angry letters to the editor or to City Hall; most just leave with a solemn vow never to return.

Harley week roared on. Several bikers spent much of Tuesday night racing around in the concrete parking garage adjacent to my apartment building, revving their engines; the noise reverberated off the concrete walls and rattled the windows in my building. They left for a while, then came back just before dawn.

On Wednesday, bikers cruised up and down the Boulevard through the afternoon and into the night. As the sun set, the motel verandahs filled with spectators; lawn chairs lined up three and four deep in the parking lots. Bikers and their mamas packed the front porch of the Beach House Restaurant. Thousands of beer cans littered the adjacent alley and parking lot. Despite the lusty tone of the revelry, I could not escape the sense that something here was very wrong. It's one thing to drive hundreds of miles to Myrtle Beach and cruise Ocean Boulevard when you are twenty years old. But if you're still doing it when you're fifty, it's time to think seriously about getting a life. And if you're fifty years old and you have nothing better to do than sit in a lawn chair and videotape other aging hell raisers cruising the Boulevard, well, it might be too late to get a life.

That night sleep was impossible, so I lay in bed and read till dawn as Harleys howled and growled on Kings Highway. I don't know if bikers read newspapers or books or anything else. Reading, for me, is an act of reaching out, trying to come to terms with other views and realities. It seems to me the biker's life is just the opposite — a shutting out of any sensation that does not exalt the rider as the center of the universe. They surround themselves with a cocoon of noise that insulates them while it demands the attention of all around them. At traffic lights they sit revving their engines, drowning out the sound of other bikers' machines.

Thursday evening I was sipping wine with friends on a verandah two blocks west of U.S. 17; the noise was so intense we had to adjourn the soiree inside. There one of our company — a vacationing pediatric nurse — suggested that bikers were engaged in some great infantile fantasy. They reminded her, she said, of a hospital nursery: when one infant wails, the others start to cry, not out of pain or hunger, but out of a need to drown out the others and preserve their insular, self-centered universe. I took some consolation in this image of the hairy, tattooed biker as overgrown brat. Sometimes the difference between rugged individualism and infantile self-absorption is in the eye if the beholder.

In other ways bikers display a sort of childlike innocence. They seem to have few sensibilities – aesthetic, auditory or otherwise – and are shocked and perplexed to learn that others do. This leads them into frequent conflict with neighbors, communities and law enforcement over a host of dress, behavior and lifestyle issues. When they get their knuckles cracked, they turn to their first and last and only defense – personal freedom. Freedom is their highest principle and it is hard to argue against.

In a boardwalk bar Friday afternoon, I spent a couple of hours drinking beer and talking with David, a Harley rider and sheetmetal worker from Norfolk. He was forty-two years old, but his leathery face and graying beard added ten years to his appearance. He worked fifty to sixty hours a week to support three children and two ex-wives and he salted away what little he could for this one week each year. He had missed only one Myrtle Beach Harley-Davidson Rally since he was nineteen.

There was nothing about David that I found remarkable. He had the requisite tattoos, a broken incisor and a blue kerchief over his head. Furthermore, he was a bigot and missed no opportunity to tell me how blacks and Hispanics were ruining the country and ruining his life. He hated two of his three children and both of his ex-wives, including Janet, who was hammering him for more child support. It was only when I asked him the inevitable question – Why do you ride? – that this angry, simple-minded yeoman became a poet: "When I'm on the road, on the open road and the wind is blowing on my face and my eyes are watering and there ain't nothing but straight road ahead of me, then I'm like Superman. I'm like God. I'm immortal." My heart soared; I almost imagined myself on a big chrome Hog, cruising the highways with David and his friends. Then he added, "You know, it's almost like that bitch Janet ain't even on the planet." The reverie shattered like plate glass.

In Nora Ephron's novel *Heartburn*, her main character describes her faithless husband who "could make love to a venetian blind." I suspect most bikers could make love to an exhaust manifold. It is obvious many have transcended such worldly considerations as personal appearance – their own or anyone else's – which gives them the great advantage of being able to couple with any member of the opposite sex, anywhere, under any circumstances. Of course, there were plenty of police on hand to make sure nothing like that happened on the streets of Myrtle Beach, but it has happened before and one could not escape the suspicion that, if the gendarmes turned their backs for just a moment, it would happen again.

On Bourbon Street during Mardi Gras, men stand below hotel verandahs and shout to the women above, "Show your tits! Show your tits!" Harley men, being sensitive and poetic types, held up signs to women on passing bikes: "Free Them Puppies." When a Harley maiden found enough admirers lining the roads and there were no cops in sight, she would rear back in her "bitch seat," yank her T-shirt up to her chin and bask in the cheers and applause. Later that night she might dance topless on a pool table or ride the mechanical bull without benefit of support in one of the local roadhouses.

Several bars, including the Dog House on U.S. 17 and the Beach House on the Boulevard, built their reputations as "biker bars," drawing large crowds of the tattoo-and-leather set. But these joints were kickstand kindergarten compared to the one, the only, the most audacious, outrageous biker bar of them all – Suck Bang Blow.

A visiting law enforcement officer told me the closest comparison he could make to Suck Bang Blow would be the red light district of Hamburg. Even as I calculated which circle of Hell comprised the red light district of Hamburg, the officer amended his verdict: "On second thought," he said, "it's probably beyond the red light district of Hamburg." Wherever it stood on the Hamburg Scale, I wanted to see for myself.

Operating out of a wooden store front in Murrells Inlet, Suck Bang Blow was open only one week out of the year, when owner Jimmy Motley knew it would find its most appreciative fans. Here the waitresses not only showed it all; they allowed the customers to handle the merchandise. But the thing that really set Suck Bang Blow apart from those wimpy biker bars was the "burnout pit." A biker would bring his machine into the little club and set the front wheel against the bar. Then he would hit the accelerator and do a "burn" on the concrete floor, running his engine up to 100 miles per hour or more. "This is the only bar on the East Coast you can drive your bike through at eighty miles per hour or do a burnout," Motley told me proudly. The wall behind the burnout pit was splattered with rubber from hundreds of burns. Engines occasionally blew up; pistons flew; tires disintegrated. Bartenders wore gas masks to protect themselves from exhaust fumes and the acrid smoke of burning rubber. Patrons sat outside, drinking and socializing, coming into the club only long enough to watch the next burn. They stumbled back outside, wheezing, gasping and rubbing their eyes. The bike would exit through a back door of the bar and another enter through the front to take the Suck Bang Blow challenge. It takes a special kind of love to treat your Harley this way.

While bikers rumbled through the city in the early hours of Friday morning, nineteen-year-old Sandy Sue Strause, of Reading, Pennsylvania, became a statistic. Strause was riding north on Kings Highway with her father when their bike rear-ended a Chevy Blazer. She died at Grand Strand Regional Medical Center at 2:42 a.m., May 14. Her father remained in critical condition.

At 5:30 Friday afternoon, a thundershower swept through the city, drenching everything, clearing the streets of bikers. For forty-five minutes silence reigned; I could not hear motorcycles for the first time in days. Then the skies cleared, the Hogs came out and the city reverberated through the night, the next day and the next night.

The party ended on Sunday, May 16, as 60,000 bikers and their 60,000 attendants and groupies headed for the city limits. The official count was two bikers dead, dozens hospitalized from numerous accidents and two non-biker locals killed in separate wrecks. But the whole thing came off with little violence or carnage, city officials said. Myrtle Beach police reported 215 misdemeanor arrests, 16 felony arrests, 53 traffic arrests and 197 tickets written.

By early Sunday afternoon, the number of bikes on the street was dropping by the hour. About 3:00 p.m., I took a stroll down to the beach for the first time in a couple of weeks. There I discovered that, with the surf and wind roaring in my ears and the wall of high-rise hotels standing between the Boulevard and me, I was completely safe from the sound of motorcycles. I walked north, picking up shells and fossils for my growing collection. It was 6:15 when I left the beach and walked back up to the Boulevard. The motorcycles were gone. The city was silent. Harley week was over.

A kind of trembling exhaustion fell over the town. People seemed giddy and dazed by the quiet, the kind of relief I suspect people feel when they come up from their cellars after an air raid. For the first time in a week I could hear pedestrians laughing and talking on the Boulevard. A number of Boulevard shops closed early that night. I turned in by 10:30 and slept eleven hours.

But this had been merely the warm-up act. The Atlantic Beach Memorial Day Bike Festival was only days away.

Thunder in the Streets

Since its modest beginnings in 1980, the Atlantic Beach Memorial Day Bike Festival had become a huge headache for the Strand. Unlike the Harley rally, the Memorial Day Bike Festival resisted all efforts to organize it, to structure it, to provide alternative activities to get people off the streets and roads. In a celebrated fiasco in 1998, a concert and other events flopped when a promoter absconded with the funds.

I heard endless stories of public lewdness, drunkenness, urination and defecation. The festival made streets and roads impassable for days. Many restaurants closed for the weekend, claiming the young blacks were too obnoxious and too hostile to be served. They were also cheap customers and lousy tippers, as numerous bartenders and waitresses told me. Memorial Day had once been the biggest weekend of the year for the Grand Strand. Now it was a total loss for many businesses.

But along with the righteous anger came a lot of small-town Southern prejudice. Myrtle Beach has never done anything to welcome blacks and has done quite a lot to threaten and discourage them. Recent demagoguery – with talk of using police dogs and the National Guard – was just the latest example. In February, the Council of Myrtle Beach Organizations (COMBO) had fueled public fears and the rhetoric of Mark McBride when it called for using the National Guard to control Memorial Day bikers. A political action arm of the hotel, golf and other tourist-related industries, COMBO had never sought National Guard assistance against Harley riders, spring breakers or other disruptive groups.

I had witnessed this mentality for years. Living in three Southern college towns has taught me that the difference between a keg party and a civil disturbance is often a question of "Who's your daddy?" I have seen white fraternity boys riot in the streets, vandalize property and shut down much of a city for hours while the town fathers shook their heads and clucked. If the rioters had been black or held a political agenda, authorities would have declared a state of emergency.

For centuries the driving force of Southern politics and culture has been white fear of black people. Events of the last half-century have hardly diminished that fear. For many whites the fear takes two distinct scenarios – finding themselves outnumbered by black people and finding themselves confronted by black sexuality. The Atlantic Beach Memorial Day Bike Festival promised plenty of both. With an estimated 100,000 African Americans heading for the Grand Strand, blacks would be the majority on this little strip of beach for four days. And they would bring with them an aesthetic which many whites found incomprehensible, even terrifying.

In Myrtle Beach, white promiscuity is more commercialized and confined to strip clubs and massage parlors. In black pop culture, sex is out in the open and in your face, as the rhythms and lyrics of hip-hop and rap music clearly show. Black sexuality is intense and unambiguous. It drives Southern Baptists and retired Yankees crazy! Something about vast reaches of black skin, exposed and pulsing to the music, something about the spring heat and the humid air heaving with the sound of hip-hop through the steamy days and nights – I fear it was too much for some frail psyches. Several women told me, in near hysteria, of public sex acts they claim to have witnessed during past Memorial Day Bike Festivals. I wouldn't have guessed these wives and maidens even knew the words to describe such acts, but they depicted them quite vividly.

Tension was palpable along the Strand as the Memorial Day event approached. In bars and restaurants, rumors ran dark and ugly. I heard that there was a gang of black bikers mobilizing in (take your pick) Mississippi, Florida or Atlanta to make war on whites in Myrtle Beach. The list of businesses that intended to shut down – including much of Restaurant Row – grew longer by the day. Another rumor claimed there was a Web page calling for the destruction of any business that closed for the bike festival. No one knew the Web page address or had actually seen it, but that didn't stop the rumor. The only Web page related to the event that I knew anything about was www.blackbikeweek.net which called for having a good time and keeping on good behavior: "Fellas, this year, when you go to Black Bike Week, please DO NOT disrespect the ladies and please DO NOT disrespect anyone else. Over the past couple of years . . . similar black events have been getting bad publicity because of a few knuckleheads who cannot control themselves. Let's not add any more fuel to the media fire. We don't want our beach trips canceled. . . . For the few of you who plan on acting like fools this year, please think twice. Don't spoil it for everyone."

In his climb from first-term councilman to mayor, Mark McBride had not hesitated to play the race card. An easy target for his populist wrath was the Atlantic Beach Memorial Day Bike Festival. With its rowdy and lewd behavior, the festival was McBride's *bete noir*, inspiring his most vicious and virulent demagoguery. In 1997, Councilman McBride called for a referendum to ban the event from Myrtle Beach. *The Sun News* editorially denounced McBride's "demagogic showboating" and "political malarkey."

"Mark is just looking to get his name in the paper," another critic told *The Sun News*. "I don't think he's quite mature yet. Mark McBride has said a lot of things lately that are getting a lot of people mad. I think it will catch up with him in November." In November, Councilman McBride was elected mayor and he hadn't forgotten where his bread was buttered.

In 1998, Mayor McBride continued to beat the drum, calling for more law enforcement to deal with that spring's Atlantic Beach Memorial Day Bike Festival. In February 1999, he called for using special units of the National Guard to police the city during the bike rally but was rebuffed by Governor Hodges and repudiated by council colleagues. The issue was thought to be dead, but at a city council workshop on April 22, McBride stunned his colleagues by announcing that he would send a letter to the governor, seeking National Guard assistance. "Police Chief [Warren] Gall admitted that we've thrown our hands up to the motorcyclists," McBride said. "The law enforcement of the City of Myrtle Beach has said, 'We can't control those people.'" McBride's request confused the Governor's Office and drew the scorn of city council.

"I'm concerned that bringing in the Guard may place our city in harm's way," Councilwoman Rachel Broadhurst said. "With this decision, all of a sudden we're discriminating. All of a sudden we're racists. We could cause a riot with this. We could cause people to be killed."

Chief Gall responded that his department – along with some 300 police officers on loan from other agencies – would be sufficient to handle the situation. "I feel comfortable given the numbers of officers confirmed and promised, that we'll be able to field a good force out there with high visibility," he said. The chief flatly denied McBride's claim that his police were not up to the task. "I would never say anything that would undermine the confidence I have in my officers at the police department," he told *The Sun News*.

Nevertheless, McBride sent his letter to the governor requesting National Guard support for the Memorial Day Bike Festival. Again he was rejected, but he continued to raise racial tensions, this time in his weekly column in the *Myrtle Beach Herald*. Days before the event he wrote, "Memorial Day Weekend is now upon us and the City of Myrtle Beach now enters what is perhaps our most stressful moment in the year. The time for debate has passed and it is now time to do our best to protect and preserve our City with the support we have and to stand behind our Police Department and the other outside agencies that have come here to help us."

Later in the week, McBride called for the city hiring more police officers, even if it meant sacrificing a tax cut in the pending budget. He was rebuked by Rachel Broadhurst and outvoted 5-1.

As Zero Hour approached, state and local law enforcement officers were on their way to the Strand from jurisdictions all across South Carolina. Myrtle Beach police officers underwent sensitivity training and twenty observers from the U.S. Justice Department's Community Relations Division were also on hand. Police and city planners went through their final drills, getting everybody in place, contacting the Friendship Team volunteers, explaining to the public that northbound Ocean Boulevard would be closed to all but emergency vehicles.

Atlantic Beach Police Lieutenant Phil Andryshak said his department had gone through final countdown. "We're ready. So far, we've got everything in order," he said.

Atlantic Beach business owners spruced up their hotels and restaurants in anticipation of their biggest payday of the year. "On Memorial Day Weekend, if you don't get your money, you won't get it," Jacqui Gore told *The Sun News* as she cleaned up her bar. Along the Boulevard and U.S. 17, beachwear shops displayed their Black Bike Week wares. Confederate Flag T-shirts and mementos were put in storage.

Wednesday, May 26: A xenophobic town was about to meet its Annual Worst Nightmare, as the first wave of black bikers entered the city gates. By mid-afternoon, the streets were buzzing. By 9:00 p.m., traffic had congealed on U.S. 17 and throughout the city. In response to gridlock, schools along the Strand announced early closings Friday. More than 100,000 people were expected in town, according to police estimates. About a quarter of them would be on bikes; the rest would be riding four wheels. The Atlantic Beach bikers rode Japanese machines – Suzukis, Hondas and Kawasakis – "rice burners," as wags derisively called them. Unlike the dragon's roar of the mighty Harley, Japanese bikes gave the high-pitched whine of a chain saw. But they were just as hard to sleep through at 5:00 in the morning.

Through Thursday, traffic built on the streets and backed up for miles on U.S. 501. Residents began changing their schedules, their itineraries, their lives to deal with the gridlock. Television and radio stations covered the traffic crisis as they would a natural disaster, with helicopters flying overhead and periodic updates and advisories. That night I spent several hours down on the Boulevard. With the northbound side of the Boulevard closed to all but emergency traffic, the southbound lanes and the west sidewalk became a circus, a *carnivale* of flesh and music, booze and hormones. Thousands pushed and shoved their way up and down the west sidewalk to commune with the cruisers in the two southbound lanes. And commune they did. The sport of the day was "showing," and there was a lot more than "puppies" to be seen here.

"Hey, baby, show me sumpin!" the guys called to women in the passing cars. The women squealed and cursed and giggled. And they showed. When one of them threw a car door open, the men charged in, armed with camcorders and disposable cameras, to see and record. On the sidewalk the women paraded in the skimpiest of fishnets and G-strings. "Hey, baby, show me sumpin!" and the girls obliged, posing for all comers, in all positions, humping, bumping and grinding against cars, walls, lampposts and anyone who was willing. And the weekend papparazzi were there to record it.

Amid the frenzy of flashing skin and flashing bulbs was the ceaseless thump of rap music from every car, every verandah, with its violent lyrics and rhythms. . . . *I said, ain't it fun, it's just a gun . . . pull de trigger, nigger, don't be scared . . . uh-huh . . . uh-huh . . . I said, pull de trigger now . . . uh-huh . . . de bitch is dead, is what I said . . . de bitch is dead . . . uh-huh . . . uh-huh . . . kill de muthafucka, fucka. . . kill de muthafucka, fucka . . . kill de muthafucka . . . muthafucka . . . muthafucka . . . muthafucka . . . you can suck my dick . . . uh-huh . . . uh-huh . . . I said, suck my dick . . . uh-huh . . . uh-huh . . . put a bullet in his head . . . uh-huh . . . uh-huh . . . don't look now, the nigger's dead . . . uh-huh . . .*

uh-huh . . . *uh-huh* . . . *uh-huh.* It was definitely going to be a long weekend. . . . *Uh-huh* . . . *uh-huh.*

Things got off to a roaring start on Friday when Trooper Gilmore Owens of the S.C. Highway Patrol set out in pursuit of Marvin S. Summerville of St. Albans, New York, both men on motorcycles. Trooper Edward Walker joined the pursuit in his patrol car. Somehow Trooper Owens rear-ended Trooper Walker, was thrown from his bike onto the back of the patrol car, then landed on the pavement. Other officers joined the pursuit up U.S. 17. Summerville, on his 1996 Kawasaki KSL dirt bike, led them to the Dunes Golf Course, where he managed to drive his bike into the lake on the first hole. Summerville was taken into custody; Owens was treated and released at Grand Strand Regional Medical Center. Both bikes were totaled. *Muthafucka!*

That night I was back on the Boulevard, observing riders play a game called "bouncing." Unlike Harleys, Japanese bikes are built with the seat curved up on the back. A woman riding behind the driver must lean forward to put her arms around her man's waist, thrusting her butt up in a provocative manner. Men on the street liked what they saw and showed their appreciation: "Hey, baby, show me sumpin!" The girls didn't need much encouragement, leaning forward to wag their butts for the admiring crowd. But that wasn't enough. Drivers would race their engines while holding the brake, causing their bikes to shimmy from end to end. Their women's upturned butts would bounce like jelly, as men closed in with their cameras.

I saw one young girl – very pretty and not a day over seventeen – on the back of her boyfriend's bike. She was a natural draw for the men on the street, who hooted and called to her. She seemed flattered and embarrassed by the attention; she alternately smiled and hid her face against her boyfriend's back. "Hey, baby, show me sumpin!" As the men closed in, she turned away with alarm and tried to say something to her boyfriend; he locked the brake, hit the gas and her butt bounced wildly on the vibrating machine. The guys converged around her, hooting and howling, bending down to inspect and video-tape her barely clad buttocks bouncing against the leather. As the bike pulled away, one of the men smacked her on the butt with his open hand. A look of shock and pain crossed her face. I think there were tears in her eyes. She leaned forward to speak to her boyfriend, who just raced his engine and laughed. *Muthafucka!*

The black Ford 4x4 Off-Road F-250 pickup with mud tires, high-rise shocks and tinted windows probably drew little attention as it cruised the Boulevard during those tense nights. Mayor Mark

McBride was at the wheel, communicating with police and later mak-ing inflammatory reports to the media on what he observed. Others would say later he was more instigator than observer, especially when he reported that there had been rapes and sexual assaults throughout the bike rally. He repeated the charge of rapes at the next city council meeting, despite the fact that the police knew nothing about them. In a later interview with me, he said that a woman from the local Rape Crisis Center called to report a surge of rapes during the event; he would not give me the name of his source. When I asked the executive director of the Rape Crisis Center if she knew about an epidemic of sexual assaults during either of the biker events, her answer was guarded and vague: "The more people there are in town, the more of all crime there will be, including sexual assault. . . . We could be cut-ting our own political throats if we started talking about any particular kind of crime when any particular group is in town."

The mayor also told me he had knowledge of a gang rape on the steps of the First Baptist Church. Again, he could provide no names or sources for these stories. As some of his critics pointed out, rape is a legal term and is established in a court of law, not in the media or a city council meeting.

From the slight rise at 16th Avenue North, I looked south at the pulsing river of humanity that filled the west sidewalk, spilling out in the street and surging around the double line of southbound cars and bikes, with red taillights receding into the distance. Police cars cruised up and down the emergency lane. Lines of foot patrol officers moved along the line of cars, urging drivers to keep moving, urging pedestri-ans to stay on the sidewalks. It was all futile. *Muthafucka . . . muthafucka . . . muthafucka . . . muthafucka . . . uh-huh . . . uh-huh . . . muthafucka.*

At Can-Am Gifts, manager Rich Russell put in a stock of dispos-able cameras and sold them by the hundreds for ten dollars a pop. "All they do is take pictures of girls' butts," Russell told *The Sun News.* "That's why they buy all these cameras." Among the mountains of litter heaped on the Boulevard was the packaging from thousands of disposable cameras and thousands of rolls of videotape. Each night city crews picked up more garbage than they had during the entire week of the Harley-Davidson Rally, a city spokesman said.

At two o'clock Saturday morning, the police closed off the Boulevard and told the cruisers to go to their hotel rooms. The cruis-ers went out to U.S. 17 to bide their time while the trucks and crews cleared away tons of litter. Then the cruisers were back, in violation of the 2:00 a.m-to-6:00 a.m. no-cruising ordinance. The cops tried to

warn them off the Boulevard, but it was a waste of breath. . . .
Muthafucka . . . muthafucka . . . uh-huh . . . muthafucka.

I walked and watched on the Boulevard until 5:00 a.m., went back
to my apartment, then drove up to Atlantic Beach. At 6:15, I was sitting in bumper-to-bumper traffic, creeping through North Myrtle
Beach, the morning air vibrating with the sound of Japanese engines
and rap music. . . . *Muthafucka.* The roadsides were an endless landscape of garbage. Weary vendors slouched in their stalls, where they
had spent the night selling T-shirts, cassette tapes and sausage dogs. In
a garbage-filled service station parking lot, eight young men danced to
rap music pouring from the stereo of an open convertible. *Muthafucka
. . . muthafucka . . . uh-huh . . . uh-huh.*

At that little spot of earth called Atlantic Beach I turned onto 30th
Avenue South. All of the east-west streets of the tiny town were lined
with vendors and covered with garbage. The air was rich with frying
bacon, sausage and fish. Music thumped from the dilapidated bars
and restaurants of the dilapidated little town. I walked the streets for
more than an hour, talking to visitors and locals, then ate a hearty
breakfast of grits and eggs and fried fish from a Styrofoam box and felt
no guilt about dropping the box in the ankle-deep pile of garbage
around my feet. At 8:30 I headed back home to get some shuteye. It
took fifty minutes to drive ten miles to my apartment.

While I slept through the afternoon, things spiraled downward
along the Grand Strand. Describing that Saturday afternoon's traffic
in the next day's *Sun News*, reporter Clay Barbour wrote: "It was
entirely possible to walk on the hoods of cars from the northern tip of
Myrtle Beach to Atlantic Beach without once touching the ground. In
fact, walking may have been faster than driving. . . . My average speed
during the journey: a hair over 4 mph."

Traffic was at a standstill and backed up for miles on U.S. 501. At
6:00 p.m., police began forcing 501 traffic to go either south or north
on U.S. 17 Bypass. Northbound bypass traffic was prevented from
entering 501 toward the beach. Traffic was reduced to a crawl at the
bypass and S.C. 707 intersection. There were multiple accidents on
U.S. 17.

As the sun set, things got nasty. Shots were fired on the Boulevard,
on U.S. 17 near my apartment and in North Myrtle Beach. A man was
hit in the leg by a Boulevard bullet. There was an assault at the Bon
Villa, alleged rapes and assaults in North Myrtle Beach. From my
vantage on the Boulevard that night, I saw and heard none of this.
What I did see was a crowd on the verge of becoming a mob, the clos-

est I'd ever come to ground zero in a riot. At The Towers and The Islander, two low-rise motels on the 1800 and 1900 blocks of North Ocean Boulevard, hundreds of young people jammed onto the verandahs, drinking and shouting to the throng below. Something about the juxtaposition of the crowd in the cars, the crowd on the sidewalk, the crowd on the balconies above them . . . the chemistry suddenly turned volatile. The police moved in and cut off traffic from those blocks, routing it out to U.S. 17, where it encountered the stand-still wall of traffic there. But the action effectively cut off the oxygen from the smoldering spots around the motels. "If there's nothing to stare at, they move on," one officer told me. And so they did. The crowd around the motels began to break up; a potential riot was defused, but not before beer bottles and other objects were thrown from the balconies. One officer was hit in the face. *Muthafucka.*

Along Ocean Boulevard gray paddy wagons picked up handcuffed prisoners where they were arrested. Most of the charges were alcohol related — disorderly conduct, DUI, underage drinking, open containers, public intoxication. The accused were hauled downtown to the Law Enforcement Center, where they were unloaded in a covered bay behind the red brick building, run through the booking process and each allowed a phone call. Friends, families and bail-bondsmen gathered around the jail. Throughout the weekend they milled about, smoking, drinking, eating, waiting. By Monday morning, the lawn and parking lot looked like a garbage dump.

And so it went, through four tense nights and five days. The Chamber of Commerce would later say 450,000 people came to the Grand Strand over Memorial Day Weekend. The figure was controversial, but no one doubted there were far more than the 100,000 that had been predicted. It took days to clean up the garbage that lined the streets and highways. Myrtle Beach police reported 2,631 calls for service, from Thursday through Monday. There were only 700 arrests, down from 984 the previous year. The number of felony arrests was up from twenty to twenty-five. The city collected $172,866 in fines from Friday through Sunday.

North Myrtle Beach Public Safety Department recorded 755 arrests, a 56 percent increase over 1998. North Myrtle Beach police also reported being fired on, but no arrest was made. In another incident, a driver was charged with assault and battery with intent to kill after he drove through a checkpoint, hitting an officer with his pickup truck.

Authorities agreed 1999 was the smoothest the event had gone in years. The Myrtle Beach Human Rights Commission commended the improvements but said much work was still needed. Commissioners cited open containers of alcohol on public sidewalks, large amounts of trash and inappropriate attire on the streets.

"It went as well as could be expected," Myrtle Beach public information officer Mark Kruea told *The Sun News*. "Traffic was bad, there's no question about it. Trash was bad, there's no question about it. There was a fair amount of skin showing and there were some acts that easily crossed the boundaries of good taste."

There were no deaths directly attributed to the event, as there had been with the Harley-Davidson rally. On the other hand, nerves were more frayed, tempers more tested, sensibilities more shocked than during Harley week. Yet, for all the bad behavior, the Memorial Day Bike Festival did not represent a serious threat to civil order, as Mark McBride had claimed. But it was bad enough.

The Sun News printed the inevitable letters of outrage. A typical one said, "Considering Myrtle Beach looked like a giant garbage truck blew up all over it, I don't see how anyone could see how Memorial Day weekend went well. . . . We saw guys running down the middle of U.S. 17. . . with beer, girls performing sex acts right out in public, and we were told to get off the road because we were white! . . . Hopefully next year somebody will listen to Mayor Mark McBride."

Five days of racial taunts and curses, five days of pounding rhythms and violent, vulgar lyrics had taken a toll on the city. Before it was over, my own good will was severely tried. I had a camera and some cash stolen from my car and met a hail of obscene, racist invective from punks on the Boulevard. The Atlantic Beach Memorial Day Bike Festival lasted five days – half as long as the Harley Davidson Rally – but it felt like five months. It felt like a siege. It felt like a war. And it didn't end any too soon.

The next day – June 1 – was the first day of hurricane season.

Golf: The Game
That Built Myrtle Beach

You know you are in a different world when grocery stores, drug stores and liquor stores sell golf balls; when rental cars have stickers on the windows reminding passengers to remove their golf cleats; when auto dealerships install putting greens for customers to work on their game while mechanics work on their cars; when the local newspaper reports and discusses greens fees as if they were utility rates or property taxes; when the Yellow Pages offer eight pages of golf courses, golf supplies, golf instruction, golf course consultants and contractors; when one of the largest retailers in the region is Martin's Golf & Tennis Superstore, with 85,000 square feet of clothes and clubs, bags and balls.

The year 1999 saw nearly a dozen new courses open on the Grand Strand and as many others announced, including four new courses at Barefoot Resort and Golf Club, an $812 million development across the Intracoastal Waterway from North Myrtle Beach. To design the courses, the Barefoot Resort developers signed up four of the biggest names in the game: Pete Dye, Tom Fazio, Greg Norman and Davis Love III.

The golf industry is ruthlessly competitive in South Carolina, but the game has been very good to the state. In October 1998, the Department of Parks, Recreation and Tourism released a study showing that golf generated $1.2 billion on the Palmetto State's 355 courses in 1997; $577 million were spent in Horry and Georgetown counties. Golf created 10,922 jobs along the Grand Strand, paying an average of $17,379. The average golfer shot seven rounds during his Grand Strand visit, with an average of 46,716 rounds shot on each Grand Strand golf course, twenty-three percent above the statewide average. And sixty-four percent of Grand Strand golfers were from out of state, according to the PRT study, a fact not lost on anyone who has stood in baggage claims at Myrtle Beach International Airport and watched the golf bags glide down the conveyor.

It takes 10,000 additional golfers to support each new course on the Grand Strand. The competition for golfers is intense, not just on the Strand, but nationwide. According to the *Wall Street Journal*, the number of golfers in the U.S. has been stagnant at about twenty-six million since 1988; 509 new or expanded courses opened in 1999, bringing the national total to 16,747. "The supply is growing faster than the demand and we need to do something to bring more golfers," Ashby Ward told *The Sun News*.

Or, as one wag told me: "The problem is simple: too much pasture, not enough cows. The cost of grazing is going down."

Or maybe not. It is probably no coincidence that golf courses and doctors spend so much time together. Both are almost impossible to find in poor rural areas or inner cities. Rather, they tend to congregate around affluent suburbs and resorts. Both consider it beneath their dignity to price competitively. When the excess of golf courses or doctors threatens the survival of some individuals, they often respond by *raising* their fees to maintain profits with diminishing market share.

The new Tournament Players Club, a daily fee course, opened on February 1, charging $95 per round in green fees and golf cart rental. In the peak spring and fall seasons, a round at TPC could cost $150. Retirees and locals who moved here for the golf have complained for years. "Why don't our golf courses have more reasonable rates for our locals, especially our local seniors?" wrote a Murrells Inlet man in a typical letter to *The Sun News*. "Most of our seniors are on fixed incomes." The opening of TPC caused *The Sun News* to take a long look at the impact of upscale golf on this working class resort. It was all part of long-range marketing, according to Micky McCammish, executive director of Myrtle Beach Golf Holiday, a local marketing group.

"For years Myrtle Beach has been on the lower end," McCammish said. "As we have more courses, we've got to grow the market, so we've got to go to the higher end market."

In a *USA Today* feature on Myrtle Beach golf, a Burroughs & Chapin spokesman was more blunt: "We're trying to lose that beer-drinking golfer image."

Perhaps the Golf Capital of the World needed a bit of a makeover. For all its hype and braggadocio, Myrtle Beach in 1998 could not claim a single course ranked nationally in *Golf Digest's* Top 100. However, there were four Top 100 courses south of Charleston, around the upscale resorts of Hilton Head and Kiawah Island. This was a class distinction that rankled local sensibilities and may explain why the south coast – and not the Grand Strand – hosts some of the most prestigious tournaments on the PGA Tour, while the best Myrtle Beach has been able to draw is the Ingersoll Rand Senior Tour Championship and the LPGA Championship.

Golf came to Myrtle Beach early. When the Woodside brothers built their Ocean Forest Hotel in the 1920s, golf was part of their plan for a grand East Coast resort. The hotel is long gone, but its Pine Lakes Golf Course remains. At the intersection of Kings Highway and Woodside Avenue, the massive sculpted wooden sign announces, "The Granddaddy – Pine Lakes International Country Club."

The Grand Stand's second course was at Dunes Golf & Beach Club, created in 1948 by local patricians – including the principals of the Chapin Company – as a sanctuary from the town's tourist and blue-collar culture. Built on the shore north of Myrtle Beach, it was designed by Robert Trent Jones, creator of Augusta National and other great courses around the world. The notorious thirteenth hole – dubbed "Waterloo" by those it has defeated – is considered one of the most challenging anywhere. The Dunes was immediately celebrated in *The New Yorker* and *National Geographic*, which called it one of the three best seaside golf courses in the United States.

The first pro to serve at the Dunes Club was Jimmy D'Angelo, the son of an Italian immigrant laborer. D'Angelo was a scrawny, dark-eyed nine-year-old when he started working as a caddy at the Huntington Country Club, outside his native Philadelphia. By the time he was twenty-one, he was the club pro at Huntington and the youngest professional golfer in the country. When he was thirty-eight, he came to the Dunes and spent the next half-century promoting Myrtle Beach golf.

In April 1954, D'Angelo invited about a dozen golf writers to stop by Myrtle Beach for a Robert Trent Jones testimonial dinner on their way to the Masters in Augusta. The scribes were wined and dined and spent the week on the links. They returned home to write glowing reports of Myrtle Beach golf in their major Northern newspapers. Such publicity could not have been bought at any price, and it continues to this day. The Golf Writers of America Annual Tournament is a Myrtle Beach tradition.

D'Angelo's last years were a succession of accolades. "Everything Myrtle Beach has become owes a little something to Jimmy," said Dunes Club golf director Cliff Mann. "He brought the golf writers to Myrtle Beach and they brought the world," said Mickey McCammish. In 1977, Mayor Bob Hirsch officially recognized D'Angelo as "Mr. Golf."

The next great boon for golf came in 1967. A group of hotel and golf course owners pooled their resources to create Myrtle Beach Golf Holiday, a consortium to promote Grand Strand golf worldwide. It advertises in *USA Today*, *The Wall Street Journal*, on ESPN and the Golf Channel and creates "packages" of accommodations and courses.

Golf is such a huge industry along the Grand Strand that it has its own training school. Coastal Carolina University in Conway offers degrees in golf management, one of only nine such programs in the country. The highly selective four-year program covers everything from marketing and administration to food and beverage and turf management, and includes two years of paid internship at local courses under Class A professionals. To enter the program, a student must have an eight or less handicap and pass the PGA's Playing Ability Test before the third year. A graduate can expect to start out earning in the low to mid-twenties.

Only the Atlantic Ocean itself has had a greater impact than golf on the culture and the landscape of the Grand Strand. But the flood of golfers and golf courses has had two unexpected consequences. The first is environmental degradation. Golf is attracted to coastal lowlands, not just for their natural beauty, but for the challenge of playing – and building golf courses – through the maze of land and water. The appeal is only enhanced by images like the one that ran on sports pages nationwide in 1996. It showed divots flying as Lee Trevino swung through on the thirteenth hole at the Dunes Club in the Senior Tour Championship. Beyond Trevino, an enormous alligator lolled in the November sun and beyond the gator, ducks glided placidly on the water hazard.

It used to be claimed that golf – like other sports and entertainment – is a clean industry. No smokestacks. No discharge pipes. No toxic byproducts. On a small scale, the claim is probably true. But Myrtle Beach is golf on an enormous scale. The emerald-green perfection golfers demand can actually be a wasteland. Not only is a fairway an ecological monoculture, but hundreds of tons of fertilizers and pesticides are dumped on the area's 100-plus golf courses each year, to be washed into the tidal creeks and marshes and ultimately into the ocean.

Some courses are making efforts to use environmentally friendly design and turf management techniques. Newer courses are designed with berms to hold chemical-laden runoff, but the long-term effect of so many golf courses packed so densely together will be years in the telling.

The second impact of golf has been cultural degradation – though it's difficult to say whether golf has degraded Myrtle Beach more than Myrtle Beach has degraded golf. As one local patrician told me, golf used to be a gentleman's game, one of the things that allowed rich people to get together. Today, he lamented, it's Everyman's game. "Now mill workers play golf out of pretension. They shoot in the 90s and 100s. They don't care. . . . Myrtle Beach has really brought golf down. There's a raw side to [golf] and Myrtle Beach really brings it out."

A glimpse of that "raw side" can be seen in the 1961 *Saturday Evening Post* illustration of the Dunes Club lounge. Norman Rockwell, the *Post's* legendary cover artist, would have found warmth and universality in the image of middle-aged men sitting around, waiting out a thunderstorm. Artist Ben Prins brought a queasy, unsavory realism to this party of aging stags. This is no place for women, for blacks or Jews, for lovers of Yeats or Chateau Neuf-du-Pape. Take these slouching, guffawing, cigarette-smoking duffers out of their posh surroundings and their silly golf duds and they might be a bunch of deadbeats spending the afternoon in the parking lot behind a liquor store.

The vast majority of golfers who come to the Grand Strand are male and most of those males come in the company of other males, released however briefly from the bonds of hearth and home, career and community. They get in two – sometimes three – rounds while the sun shines. And when night falls, they hit the town.

What the Pavilion Amusement Park is to ten-year-olds, Myrtle Beach night life is to these weekend bachelors. For women in the service industry, golfers are an occupational hazard, albeit an extremely lucrative one. Any woman waiting tables or tending bar for more than a few months can tell tales of being groped, propositioned or otherwise insulted by roving golfers. For other tourists, golfers are simply a hazard and a nuisance. When a pack of them descend on a restaurant – drunk, loud, obscene – unattached women instinctively herd together like sheep before wolves, or pay their checks and leave.

Like a force of nature waiting to be harnessed, this unbridled flood of testosterone drew entrepreneurs, builders and dreamers. The first strip club on the Strand was Thee DollHouse, which opened on the family-oriented Restaurant Row section of U.S. 17 in 1988. By the spring of 1992, at least a half-dozen clubs were applying for business licenses. They sported such names as Pink Pony, Nuttin' Butt Horseplay, Fantails, Derriere's, Bottoms Up and Dangerous Curves.

What people call them is generally a reflection of one's attitude toward them. Some dismiss them as strip clubs. Others describe them as gentlemen's clubs, topless clubs, exotic dance clubs or titty bars. The clubs are regularly in the news over issues of litigation or lewdness. When police occasionally arrest strippers for prostitution, club owners are always shocked – s*hocked!* – to learn that sex is being exchanged for money on their premises.

Along with these clubs came other amusements for lonely guys. Oriental massage parlors flourished. With pictures of fetching young Asian women, their daily ads in the sports section of *The Sun News* promised "Oriental Staff," body shampoo, jacuzzi and other amenities until 3:00 a.m. And there were the "lingerie modeling" shops. For as much as a hundred dollars an hour, a sensitive fellow could not only shop for something special for the little woman back home, but could have it modeled for him in a private room. He could even bring his buddies along to help him make a selection. And there were adult video and novelty shops, such as Priscilla's, Cupid's Arrow and X-Citement Video with shelves of oils, lubricants, and sexual appliances, plus books, magazines, and videos for every taste and predilection.

There was nothing subtle about the market for all this temptation and titillation. The marquee above Miss Kitty's Saloon and Show Bar was very explicit:

WELCOME GOLFERS

GIRLS   BOOZE   GAMES

Ads for Palm Tree Spa invited readers to "Relax & Relieve Tension After Golf." King's Spa said, "Golfers Bring Tee for 10% Off." The Masters Gentlemen's Club not only had a room called the Hole in One Club, but actually offered a practice driving range out back. One local golf club sponsored an annual event called the Baby Masters. Dancers and waitresses from local clubs were invited to "caddy" for a select and high-paying coterie of duffers. How much clothing came off and how lovingly the drivers were handled depended on how well the caddies were tipped in the course of this boozy, day-long event.

Locals weren't blind to what was going on. The issue wasn't just the presence of dance clubs and sex shops, it was their location: three clubs and two shops just beyond the city limits on U.S. 501. Billboards with provocative ads for these clubs cropped up around the Grand Strand, extending ninety miles west on major approaches to the city. Clubs aired radio promotions comparing their dancers to the "dogs" in other clubs.

There were predictable efforts to control the flesh parlors. A city ordinance restricted all clubs to the warehouse district around the Seaboard rail line, between 10th Avenue North and U.S. 501. A 1998 county ordinance required that clubs be 2,000 feet from residential areas, churches and schools, that dancers not come within six feet of customers, that all tips be placed in a common jar. Dancers could not show buttocks or pubic region and had to wear pasties. The ordinance started a wave of litigation with no end in sight.

By 1999, the tandem of golfers and strippers was an economic fact of life. Without strippers there would be far fewer golfers and without golfers there would be hundreds of millions fewer dollars in the Grand Strand economy. Horry County residents seemed reconciled to this reality, if not happy with it. Citizens marched and prayed. They wrote letters to the editor and to their council members. Liz Gilland won a seat on county council in 1996, campaigning to clean up the county. "It's an obvious problem," Gilland said. "It's not unusual for one of the biggest golfing capitals in the world to have an inordinate amount of sexually oriented business."

Amen, brother. The Baptists may have built this town, but golf was playing through.

Sacred Sand

In the beginning . . . was the beach. Tempting. Sensuous. Shimmering. Stretching nearly 100 miles from Winyah Bay to Cape Fear, the beach was the genesis of all that followed. At low tide, eighty yards of glistening sand lies between surf and dunes. It was here that Franklin Burroughs stood, bold and bearded, like a prophet of old, and proclaimed, "Some day this whole strand will be a resort." Like Moses, he never entered the Promised Land, but he opened the way for millions to follow. Today, they preen and frolic, splash and cavort on this sacred sand. We can only guess what that puritanical nineteenth century patriarch would have thought of their behavior and their attire in 1999. Perhaps he would commiserate with Doug Wendel about the dreadful behavior on Ocean Boulevard. They would shake their heads gravely and recall how things used to be, how their balmy Eden was corrupted by easy sex and dirty T-shirts, how once you let the genie out of the bottle . . .

Curiously, in a city without history or monuments, the beach – in its most primitive, unlettered way – provides both. The black stone shards scattered along the sand are proof of life dating back millions of years – fossilized shells and shell casts, sand dollars and sharks' teeth. Even more interesting are the bits of large vertebrate bone and teeth. The remains of ancient fish, alligators, turtles, mammoths and mastodons, giant sloths, camels, bears, and beavers regularly come to light on Horry County beaches. Some of these fossils are as young as 10,000 years; others date back more than 100 million. The most recent beach renourishment deposited quantities of fossil material on the shore and drew fossil hunters from miles around.

Beach renourishment. That's what politicians and developers call the massive facelifts they periodically perform on Mother Nature. What they do not understand is that beaches are living geological formations, produced by the dynamic meeting of land and water. It is their nature to change, to expand and shrink, to drift north and south at the whim of the restless sea. Today, human intrusion into the natural life cycle of the beach is the primary cause of beach erosion. Nowhere is this more evident than New Jersey, where decades of building seawalls to protect beachfront property destroyed the beaches and seriously damaged the state's beach tourism. South Carolina may yet be spared the tragedy of New Jersey. The 1988 Beachfront Management Act banned new seawalls, though the law is under constant challenge by developers and property owners.

Still, the state's multibillion-dollar coastal tourism industry demands permanent beaches. This is achieved by pumping huge quantities of sand from the ocean bottom onto the shore – the process called renourishment. Like mowing a lawn, it is a repetitive, unending chore – and vastly more expensive. Hundreds of millions of federal, state and local dollars have been spent renourishing South Carolina's beaches in recent years. In 1996 and 1997, the Great Lakes Dredge & Dock Co. pumped six million cubic yards of sand onto Grand Strand beaches, at a cost of $54 million. A previous renourishment project took place in 1987. Plans call for $165 million worth of new sand for the Grand Strand in the next five decades, plus millions more on the state's other beaches.

There are problems with renourishment, both environmental and economic. Critics say developers use it as an excuse to loosen beachfront building restrictions. Following the recent renourishment project in North Myrtle Beach, the Office of Ocean and Coastal Resource Management moved the oceanfront setback line 100 feet seaward to accommodate new development. The ruling directly contravened the Beachfront Management Act.

"The idea that you make a beach safer for new development is so short-sighted," said coastal geologist Orrin Pilkey of Duke University.

Pilkey was a legend and a lightning rod in the battle between environmentalists and developers. Bearded and barrel-chested, Pilkey looked – and sometimes sounded – like an angry prophet in his own right, as he denounced the greed and arrogance that are destroying the South Atlantic coast. In 1992, he told a reporter, "Real sacrifices will have to be made. Some real important people – and I mean *real* important people, with some real political connections – will have to watch their homes fall into the ocean if the state is to protect its coast for the long term."

Developers are the enemy of both the environment and democracy, Pilkey told me in an interview in his office at Duke. When a weekly newspaper in Edisto Beach, South Carolina, published Pilkey's criticism of local beach development, realtors gathered up newspaper racks around the town and deposited them in front of the paper's office. Pilkey so outraged the town council of Folly Beach, South Carolina, that it passed a resolution calling his views "insulting, uninformed and radical both in content and intent." In another case, a historical road marker on the Outer Banks – a marker commemorating a great hurricane of the 1840s that devastated the islands – mysteriously disappeared. No other markers in the area were disturbed.

The prophet remained angry and unreconciled. South Carolina "is shooting itself in the foot," he admonished. "The citizens are being shafted for the sake of the fat cats. I guess that's the oldest story in the world. They had a Coastal Council of some substance. The Coastal Council has been destroyed and now, in come the tigers. The tigers are right there, helped along by our consulting geologists and engineering companies. . . . I feel sorry for the consultants. They don't have much choice but to find the truth towards their clients' needs or they want be hired again. But somebody needs to tell these guys the truth. . . .

"I understand the agony of loosing a house, but I have almost zero sympathy with beachfront property owners. . . . I really have a strong distaste for the beachfront mentality. They're destroying our beach. They're taking huge amounts of money and they are very costly people for our society. Beach nourishment would not have to be done if it was not for the beachfront property owners," Pilkey said.

More beach madness comes in the form of National Flood Insurance. Congress established the insurance program in 1968, with the idea of reducing the need for federal disaster relief. By establishing strict new construction codes, communities would be eligible for federally subsidized insurance. Prior to 1968, insurance for beachfront property was extravagantly expensive – if it could be bought at all. Banks would not loan money to build or buy structures that could not be insured. These factors conspired to make beachfront development modest and sparse.

With National Flood Insurance, mortgage bankers jumped in to finance billions of dollars of development. Walls of high-rise hotels and condominiums rose along the Southeastern and Gulf coasts. The insurance program actually paid its own way for the first two decades, but with Hurricane Hugo in 1989 and Hurricane Andrew in 1992, it went into the red. The program continues to draw on the federal treasury for a bailout when there is serious river or coastal flooding. Federally insured structures that are lost or damaged due to storm or erosion are rebuilt at taxpayer expense – often to be lost and rebuilt again. A 1998 study by the National Wildlife Federation ranked North Myrtle Beach among the top 60 towns in the country for repeat losses from storms and high seas. Attempts by Congress to amend the flood insurance program have been stymied by real estate interests and politically well-connected beachfront property owners. This program of welfare for the wealthy allowed the average beachfront property owner in 1999 to pay a little over $300 a year for flood insurance. In her book, *Against the Tide: The Battle for America's Beaches*, Cornelia Dean described "the central, glaring flaw in the insurance program: it is betting the federal treasury against a sure thing: coastal flooding."

Fueled by cheap insurance and a roaring high-tech economy, more billions of dollars in new development sprang up on America's shorelines in the 1990s. As a generation of baby boomers prepared to retire, many of them looked south, dreaming of palm trees and cabanas. In 1999, more than 80 million people lived within fifty miles of the United States' coasts. The federal government estimated that by the year 2010, more than fifty percent of the nation's population will inhabit that narrow, volatile zone. By some estimates, South Carolina's coastal population will add 450,000 by 2010. And nature is striking back. Due to the greenhouse effect and melting of the polar ice caps, sea levels are rising about a foot a century. As the Earth's atmosphere heats up, scientists predict there will be more frequent and more violent storms in the years ahead.

As a kid coming to Myrtle Beach for a week each summer in the 1950s, I found one of the most alluring spots on the beach to be the outflow from the stormwater pipes. With an ocean in front of me and miles of sand on either side, it was the trickle of water from a pipe near the Ocean Forest Hotel that captured my imagination. I recruited my brother and other prepubescent engineers from the beach and our apartment house and we dammed that trickle of water, built islands in the little pond and levies around it.

With the frail wisdom of children we hauled and pulled the sand against the rising tide, knowing that we would be overcome, that ultimately the ocean was mightier than all of us together. But that was part of the game, watching the tide overwhelm our best efforts. Each day the beach would be an empty stage on which we could again act out our engineering fantasies.

The outflow pipes were still there, still a magnet for children more than forty years later. On a trip to the Grand Strand shortly after taking office as governor, Jim Hodges remarked to a local apparatchik that his sons – both under the age of 10 – enjoyed playing in the beach pools in front of the outflow pipes. The difference was that now those pipes drained hundreds of acres of parking lots and thousands of acres of golf courses that were not there when I was a child.

In 1999, Grand Strand municipalities were still wrestling with the pipes, which jut out on their beautiful beach like metal studs from the face of a Boulevard teenager. They were still wrestling with the fact that the area had grown too fast, without proper planning or engineering, and now there was simply no place to put the water from a heavy rain except through this worn-out, inadequate drainage system and onto the beach. They were still wrestling with the fact that the water that collects in pools around the outflow sites can be a health hazard to the one group most likely to play in them – children.

The month of April closed with an Atlantic storm that brought five days of gusting winds and nearly uninterrupted rain. The beaches were empty and local bars and clubhouses filled with drunk, pissed-off golfers who couldn't get out to the links. That would have been plenty to give Ashby Ward a headache, but more trouble was coming down the pipe – literally. The five days of rain flushed bacteria, oils, heavy metals and other toxins from the landscape onto the beaches. The State Department of Health and Environmental Control posted its first swimming advisory of the season, warning of high bacteria levels on the beaches of Horry and Georgetown counties. The advisory was lifted after twenty-four hours, but the damage was done.

Two weeks after the advisory and 240 miles away, the *Greenville News* published an editorial drawing attention to the city's stormwater problems and swimming advisories. Headlined "Bacteria Will Hurt Tourism," the editorial had several factual errors, saying there were 300 stormwater pipes dumping onto the beaches, when the number was actually about 180; and saying that septic tanks and city sewage was being dumped along with stormwater. But one fact they did nail squarely: "Uncontrolled growth and poor land use planning pushed development far past the capacity of the infrastructure. Growth has increased stormwater runoff and destroyed wetlands and soil that naturally filter bacteria. . . . Developers must be required to install larger stormwater retention ponds to treat the water before it reaches the ocean."

It would take Ashby Ward & Co. *six weeks* to respond to the piece, but when he did, he took no prisoners. The editorial was "atrocious," he told *The Sun News*. "If these out-of-town papers would run this thing accurately, then it would be OK. What you end up with is an article about sewers instead of storm drains and people don't know the difference. . . . We actually have less stormwater going into the ocean now than we did 15 years ago."

Dirty Dancing by the Sea

If, as some have suggested, South Carolina is the worst-governed state in the nation, at least its leaders know how to have a good time. In 1984, the General Assembly acted boldly, without fear or favor, to make the shag South Carolina's official State Dance.

Myrtle Beach's growing international influence has caused some consternation as to the exact meaning of the word shag, and why people have contests and clubs to demonstrate their shagging prowess. To the uninitiated – and especially to the British – it is important to explain that the shag is a dance of local origin, which is performed while vertical and fully clothed.

Lynn Northrup, of North Myrtle Beach, had been shagging for years and considered it as natural as logging onto her eBay account, where she conducted hundreds of trades under the name "Shagger." Then one day she had a message from eBay: if she did not terminate her sign-on, they would terminate her account. Officials at eBay acknowledged that the S-word meant different things to different people but told Northrup, "We would not be making this request if we had not been receiving complaints."

"I'm going to fight this to the hilt," Northrup told *The Sun News.* "It's regional discrimination. Shagging is the dance of South Carolina. I don't mean anything sexual by it."

Within a week, the bluenoses at eBay backed down and apologized. "I'm happy," Shagger said. "It was something I was going to fight for and I won."

Serious scholars have seriously studied this indigenous eight-step shuffle. S.C. Educational Television has made a documentary on it. All theories link the origin of the shag to black dance clubs and music. Called by some "the lazy man's jitterbug," the shag was said to have come out of the black clubs of Columbia in the 1930s. Some trace it to Atlantic Beach, where vacationing blacks from

Harlem brought the lindy hop. Others claim it developed from a slow grind dance called the "dirty shag," performed in the 1950s on the Hill. In the days of segregation, adventurous whites would cross the color line to clubs on the Hill, in Atlantic Beach and other black neighborhoods. There they heard rhythms and saw steps unlike anything at the high school hop. They "cleaned up" some of the dance floor moves, then added some of their own steps, such as the sugarfoot and flybacks. When they were finished, a legend was born. But where did it begin? When did it happen? As with other great moments in history, many claim to have been there. They can't all be telling the truth.

Whatever its origin, the shag is today firmly attached in fact and folklore to the Grand Strand and to the "Carolina beach music" of such legendary performers as The Tams, The Platters, Billy Stewart and Willie Tee. For aging baby boomers and beyond, it is linked by memory and imagination to a simple, idyllic Southern way of life, to endless summers and beachfront dance floors, with Wurlitzer jukeboxes full of dime-a-play 45s. It was a world of bobby socks and beehive hair-dos. "I can see everyone standing around in Gant shirts, madras shirts, khaki pants and shorts, alligator belts and Bass Weejuns," one old-timer told *The Sun News*. All of this was captured in a big-budget, if little remembered, 1989 film, *Shag*.

Therein lies the irony and the tragedy of the shag. To have come out of such colorful and multicultural surroundings, it is today the exclusive province of white middle class Southerners. It represents the lifestyle of those who – for reasons of chronology or circumstance – were not touched by the music and politics of the sixties. Today, thousands of people belong to some 100 shag clubs stretching from Virginia to Mississippi. They meet regularly to polish their steps, shuffling to the old beach tunes and – more recently – to rhythm and blues. They network through newsletters, Web sites and a magazine. Twice a year, thousands of graying shaggers return to the Ocean Drive section of North Myrtle Beach for their Spring Safari and Fall Migration. There they spend evenings reliving their youth and showing their style on the polished dance floors at Ducks, O.D. Pavilion, the Pirate's Cove and Fat Harold's Beach Club.

Fat Harold's is a shagger's shrine, its walls hung with hundreds of documents, memorabilia and pictures, pictures, pictures of great DJs, great dancers and great moments in the history of the shag. Main Street of Ocean Drive is inlaid with marble stars recognizing some of the famous names of shag, including former S.C. House

Representative John "Bubber" Snow, whose statesmanship trans-formed this modest jig into the State Dance of South Carolina.

On March 13, I was at Studebaker's, the cavernous dance club on U.S. 17 and site of the 16th Annual National Shag Dance Championship. Hundreds of affluent, casually-dressed white folks thronged around the elevated dance floor, sipping beer and cocktails, renewing acquaintances. Newt Gingrich would have been right at home here, sitting up front in his Polo shirt, his elbows on a table, a glass of white zinfandel before him on a little cocktail napkin.

The average age of the crowd was on the high side of forty and many were on the high side of sixty. But there was a large contingent of young people – both spectators and contestants – who had taken up the dance and will carry on the tradition. There was even a junior division of competition for these novitiates.

Local realtor and famed shagger Barry Thigpen was master of ceremonies, explaining the rules and categories of competition. As with the Academy Awards, it seems there was a prize for just about every contestant. If you didn't win one, you clearly weren't trying. And, like the Academy Awards, the whole thing went on *much* too long. I left after nearly four hours, with the judges still handing out awards and citations.

In his bill naming shag the State Dance, Bubber Snow wrote, ". . . all South Carolinians are proud that the shag, one of the great devel-opments of terpsichorean culture, is native to this state."

On second thought, perhaps this scandalously named little shuffle is actually South Carolina's greatest contribution to civilization.

Down on the Boulevard

In the 1950s and early 1960s, my family loaded up the Ford station wagon each summer and headed off to Myrtle Beach for a week's vacation. Descending from the Piedmont to the coastal plain, we entered tobacco country. I was fascinated by the tobacco barns, where the golden leaf was hung each fall and dried over wood fires in preparation for market. The tall, narrow buildings stood like watchtowers on the broad, plain, as exotic to my young mind as the pyramids of Egypt. The wooden tobacco barns have long given way to metal, gas-fired ovens for drying tobacco, but many of them still stand across the countryside, relics of another age, slowly rotting to the ground.

The Holliday family of Galivants Ferry brought tobacco to Horry County in the 1890s. Auction markets appeared in Conway, Loris and Aynor, as the new cash crop transformed the local economy. It is still the largest crop in the county. Burroughs & Chapin Co. did not sell its tobacco allotments until the early 1990s, to concentrate on coastal development. The Hollidays are still in Galivants Ferry, the largest tobacco-growing family in the nation, according to the late John Monroe Holliday. And despite growing hostility toward their crop, the Holliday empire appears quite secure.

Cigarette smoking – along with violence, poverty and illiteracy – remains an endemic part of the South Carolina culture and nowhere is it more endemic than Myrtle Beach. Never had I seen more smokers. In bars and cars, in supermarkets and hotel elevators, people could not put down their smokes. Cigarette butts flipped right and left from cars and SUVs lined up at stoplights. They collected like snowdrifts against curbs and medians. A local joke held that Detroit would soon introduce a special edition SUV called the Grand Strand. It would get ten miles to the gallon, feature speakers that rattle windows three blocks away and have no turn signals or ashtrays.

Smoking prevention programs were virtually unheard of in Horry

County, which in 1998 had the second highest rate in the state for pregnant women who smoked. The number of pregnant smokers was due to the area's low wage scale and lack of awareness, according to Baron Holmes of the S.C. Kids Count advocacy program. "Smoking rates tend to be higher among blue-collar or working class people," Holmes said. "You have to ask what kinds of messages are being communicated in your communities about smoking and pregnancy."

I asked Shelley, one of my favorite bartenders and a smoker herself, why there were so many smokers in Myrtle Beach. Did the town attract smokers, I wondered, or did it create them? A sweet/tough girl of 23, Shelley followed her mother through a lifetime of bad marriages and relationships before landing in Myrtle Beach with a deadbeat man of her own. She was quick to grasp my question: the antisocial impulses that lead people to smoke also lead them to Myrtle Beach, she said, in somewhat less technical words. A month after this triumph of social research, Shelley announced she was pregnant.

Tobacco has been the state's largest cash crop throughout most of the twentieth century and public opinion here has been schizophrenic in dealing with it. On the one hand, ever more public places – including the State House in Columbia – have become smoke-free zones. On the other, at seven cents a pack, South Carolina had the fourth lowest excise tax on cigarettes in the nation. Of the $165 million the state received from the nationwide tobacco settlement in 1998, the Democratic-controlled Senate budgeted $3.5 million for youth antismoking programs; the Republican-controlled House budgeted nothing. The $74 million a year the tobacco industry spent on advertising here dwarfed any feeble public effort to educate smokers.

The federal Youth Access to Tobacco Law was so widely ignored in South Carolina that in 1999 the state almost lost a federal block grant for alcohol and drug abuse services. A statewide study that included twenty-five Grand Strand volunteers showed that youths, ages twelve to seventeen, were successful in fifty-seven percent of their attempts to purchase cigarettes in convenience stores, drug stores, grocery stores and restaurants. The result of these formal and informal policies toward tobacco was inevitable: twenty-five percent of the state's minors smoked in 1991; by 1999 the number had risen to thirty-six percent.

Nowhere was smoking more epidemic than on the Boulevard, where young women pushed baby strollers with one hand as they lifted cigarettes with the other; where fifteen-year-old girls licked ice cream cones from their right hands and puffed cigarettes from their left; where bands of dirty, foul-mouthed, buck-toothed teens roamed in their Winston Cup T-shirts and Marlboro Country caps; where Joe Camel, surrounded by his cool dromedary pals, gazed out from a front window display in the Castaways and other Boulevard convenience stores. Ocean Boulevard is the tobacco industry's dream.

Such behavior was not surprising along a strip of asphalt that has been a symbol of youthful defiance for generations. "The kids have seen smoking as a form of rebellion against adults," said an epidemiologist with the American Cancer Society. "What they need to see is that not smoking is a form of not being manipulated by the tobacco companies."

Smoking was one way these "Boulevard Rats," as they called themselves, won acceptance to this special club. They came to the Boulevard as refugees from broken and abusive homes, many driven out by the men their mothers chose to live with. For many the Boulevard was the closest thing to family they had known in years. If smoking was the price they paid for belonging, it seemed small enough to a seventeen-year-old.

It took weeks to win the trust of these alienated kids and get them to talk to me. Once they started, some of them couldn't stop.

Jason, 20, and Jade, 16, were both victims of violent stepfathers. They found each other on the Boulevard and lived together at the Castaways Motel. A former body piercer, Jason ran deliveries for a local sandwich shop and did day labor at the unemployment center. Jade was studying to get her GED after being kicked out of school for fighting. She hoped to become an emergency medical technician. "I want to do something in medicine so I can help people," she told me.   Jade's short life had been filled with violence and death. She went through a litany of boyfriends, relatives and others who had died of natural and unnatural causes before their time. Her brother had recently been jailed for assault and battery with intent to kill. The fellow he beat up had since died in a Charleston hospital and now her brother's charges were about to be upgraded to murder. I watched almost voyeuristically as the young couple sat together, touching, talking, sharing a cigarette with a precocious, happy intimacy. For the first time in their young lives they had found someone they could be secure with.

Burnt was twenty years old, from North Carolina, with a pierced left eyebrow and tongue. He wore his wavy blond hair in a "bowl" cut and rolled his steel tongue stud around in his mouth as we talked. Homeless for four years, Burnt dropped out of school and hit the road when he was sixteen because his father wouldn't let him play with his band. In Myrtle Beach he slept on any bed or sofa where he could crash for a night, on the beach, on rooftops and in Chapin Park. He worked making and selling hemp jewelry for an Isreali merchant in a Boulevard kiosk and was quite talented. For a kid who had seen some of the worst of the world, he had high spirits and a wry sense of humor.

Heather, 18, was from northern Virginia, petite, cute, with freckles and a pixie haircut. She wore a spiked leather collar when I talked to her, a chain hanging from her wallet in the hip pocket of her baggy jeans and small plastic butterfly clips – blue, pink and yellow – in her hair. With silver bracelets on both wrists and rings on most of her fingers, she was a walking advertisement for the little jewelry kiosk where she worked for six dollars an hour, plus five percent commission. She had recently had her tongue illegally pierced. Heather dreamed of pursuing her ballet training some day and practiced in whatever flophouse room she found herself. "Every ballerina lives on cigarettes and coffee," she told me – and she was no exception. "Wherever I can find a place to stay, I stay there. So far, I am doing all right. There's not a night I haven't had a place to stay." It was tension with her mother, not her stepfather, that had led Heather to move out of the family house three months earlier. She had called her mother recently and they had a long talk. Her mother begged her to keep in touch. Heather didn't have the heart to tell her that she was homeless. "I'm very close with my Mom," she said, her eyes misting up.

Jessie's mother didn't know where she was and probably didn't care. A seventeen-year-old from east Tennessee, Jessie had endured her stepfather's violence and sexual taunting for years until, at the end of the school year, she had joined a girlfriend on a lark and the two of them had hitchhiked to Myrtle Beach. The girlfriend had since taken up with a boy and Jessie hadn't seen her in days. Now she was lonely, broke, unemployed and sleeping in Chapin Park, at a local shelter or anywhere she could find. Tall and slender, with large eyes and short hair dyed metallic red, she wore a black Marilyn Manson T-shirt, several sizes too large, with rings in her ears and eyebrows and one in her tongue. She was thinking about going home, she said. "At least I could play my CDs at home." Then she stopped and said, "But my momma would kill me. Oh god, she'd kill me for sure." She shook her head and grinned sadly. "You don't know how crazy my momma is."

Not all the Boulevard Rats were runaways. Stacey and Brandee had just graduated from high school in Rock Hill. Stacey's mother drove them down to Myrtle Beach and deposited them on the Boulevard for a summer's adventure. They were sharing a $300-a-week hotel room and had found jobs together at Goodfella's Pizza on the Boulevard, working for five dollars an hour, plus tips. They were pretty, bright and spirited, Brandee with her pierced tongue and the slight lisp it gave her, Stacey with her body glitter.

Stacey wanted to be a fashion designer and showed me some of her sketches. Brandee said, "I honestly, *honestly* don't know what I want to do with the rest of my life." I told her she had plenty of time to think about it. Within a few weeks, the girls had gotten enough of Myrtle Beach. "It's exciting to play and vacation here, but this is *hard work!*" Brandee told me. "There's more bullshit in Myrtle Beach in a day than there is in Rock Hill in a week. I could be in Rock Hill with my people and not have to put up with all this bullshit and hassle."

When the girls weren't slinging pizza, they would dance together in the open door of the restaurant, raise their arms over their heads, let out loud, hormonal screams and shake it till it rattled for anyone who wanted to watch. Guys lined up at the bar, ordering pizza and beer, hoping to get lucky. I doubt that any of them scored, but Stacey and Brandee left their mark on the Boulevard that summer.

Runaway children came to Myrtle Beach from hundreds of miles away, with their frantic parents often close behind. In the summer of 1999, posters appeared periodically on Boulevard windows and lampposts, with the face, name and other data on missing teens. I saw a middle-aged man in front of the Pavilion, handing out fliers to all who passed, asking if anyone had seen his daughter. Some parents sent private investigators to Myrtle Beach, looking for a lead on their children.

Runaways are a problem to many beach towns, according to Margaret Frierson, director of the South Carolina office of the National Center for Missing and Exploited Children. Teens are drawn by the mild climate, the sense of excitement, the desire to find lost and lonely kindred souls. They blend in with the flood of other youth in the area and usually are not found unless they want to be. When a runaway is identified, a family court judge can issue an order for police to pick up the underage teen and hold him or her until the family makes arrangements to take custody. For kids who are ready to go home and turn themselves in to police, Greyhound Bus Lines will provide a ticket, through an agreement with the National Center for Missing and Exploited Children.

Not all Boulevard runaways were children. Eddie Wilkins was managing a convenience store in Yadkinville, North Carolina, in 1989. "Murphy's Law was kicking my butt," Wilkins told me. One day the cash register broke down, then he had to deal with a rude customer. "For five cents I'd quit this damn job and move to Myrtle Beach," he told his clerk. The guy reached in his pocket, took a nickel and flipped it to Eddie. "That was it!" he said. He walked out and headed east.

When I met him in 1999, Wilkins was forty-eight years old, a security guard at the Golden Villa Motel, two blocks north of the Pavilion. Bearded and rotund, missing his upper front teeth, Wilkins stood in front of the Golden Villa each night, watching the parade go by, always in his blue security uniform, a .45 automatic Llama IXD pistol on his hip, a flag and eagle on his cap, with the slogan, "Right to Bear Arms." Eddie Wilkins had found his place in the world. "I always wanted to live in Myrtle Beach," he said. "It's peace of mind I never had. This is the place I belong."

For Zeus, Myrtle Beach was an accident. A guitarist with a touring rock band, he was stranded here when the group's van broke down in 1992. The rest of the band had long since moved on, but seven years later, Zeus was still in town, playing gigs at local clubs, working at New York Pizza during the summer, working as a roofer in the winter. "The town has been good to me," the bearded, upbeat musician said. "There's always a gig in Myrtle Beach. There's always something to get you by."

David worked at Goodfella's Pizza when I met him, tossing and saucing dough, spreading the cheese and toppings. He was meticulous and artful — when he was sober, which wasn't often enough. In his late thirties, his once-handsome, intelligent face was ravaged by drugs and alcohol. His hands shook when he lit a cigarette. Once incarcerated at Riker's Island Jail in New York City, he had since spent time in the Myrtle Beach jail. David's wife had run off with another man to Myrtle Beach a couple of years before and brought their two young sons with her. David followed her to be near his boys. He was living from flophouse to flophouse, doing a little carpentry on the side, sustaining himself on pizza, and mooching money off everyone he could. "Hey, Will, lemme have five bucks," he would say almost every time I saw him. "I'll pay you back next week. I promise." I helped him out when I could, but he was far beyond my small powers of redemption.

EyE painted temporary tattoos in front of a Boulevard head shop. Her boyfriend, Mike, worked in another nearby head shop. She wrote her name with the first E reversed, making it a visual as well as an alphabetical palindrome. And that was perhaps the least strange thing about her. After talking to her on several occasions, I gave her my card. She vanished from the Boulevard soon after; then I got a call from her a few weeks later. She was crying, incoherent, almost hysterical as she told me how she had been ripped off for $1,000 by the store where she had worked and Mike had been beaten up and hospitalized by the same people as a warning to her to stay away. Now they were being evicted from their $250-a-week flophouse room.

In a rambling, sobbing discourse, she told me that she had "found God." I asked her if she was on drugs and she said no. "When you're on the Boulevard, it's almost like you don't have a choice [about drugs], but I don't do drugs anymore. I'm twenty-three now. I'm growing up and I'm not into the Goth no more. You can't get nowhere dressed like that, so I dress normal now and I just want to get a job so me and Mike can get a clean start and have a roof over our head. Thank God for Mike. I couldn't have gone through all this without Mike. He keeps me alive. God gave him to me to keep me alive." She told me she could not go home to Upstate South Carolina, because of "family problems," and she could not go back to the Boulevard, "Because it will kill you! The Boulevard will *kill* you!" I asked her if there was anything I could do to help. She said she would get back to me in a day or two. I never heard from her again.

Rich Rugg and Mark Paskuly were refugees from Buffalo, New York, from busted marriages and failed dreams. At Mark's suggestion, they walked away from the winter wasteland and urban decay of Buffalo and opened a sandwich shop in April 1999 in the sun-drenched land of hope called Myrtle Beach. They had two years' restaurant experience and no working capital between them when they moved into the former site of the Candy Castle, a Boulevard legend. They didn't even bother to remove the old taffy machine and glass display cabinets from the shop. They just set up some rusted lawn chairs and tables and started serving sub sandwiches and tacos. And that became the name of their shop: Subs & Tacos – no sign, no logo.

Rich, 31, had already suffered a heart attack and seen his life unravel along with his marriage. He told me about sitting on the bathroom floor in his house in Buffalo, with no electricity, with the gas about to be cut off, broke and desperate to be with his children. Living alone, behind in his child support payments, he was ready to try anything when Mark approached him in January about coming to Myrtle Beach.

"It was a way to get out," Rich said. "I'd run out of answers and run out of options. This was the last chance. This was jumping off the cliff and grabbing the rope hanging out in front of me. If I missed that rope, it was basically over."

Now he had a new life, working fourteen hours a days, seven days a week at Subs & Tacos, sleeping in the shop at night and dreaming of having his children with him. Myrtle Beach "gave me a reason to get up in the morning," he said. "It gave me a reason to push for some form of legacy for my children."

Mark's story was just as sad: forty-four years old, twenty years in the hardware business, a divorced father of four. Along the way he had met Marilyn, who was married, with three children of her own. Mark and Marilyn had a baby. Mark led me through a narrative of several years and hundreds of miles, from Buffalo, to Asheville and Winston-Salem, North Carolina, to Myrtle Beach, involving wiretaps, private detectives, guns, threats, arrests and corrupt judges, the upshot of which was that the now four-year-old son of Mark and Marilyn had been given to Marilyn's husband for custody.

To be closer to Marilyn in Winston-Salem, Mark moved to Myrtle Beach, where he had family connections. He and Marilyn had already spent $13,000 fighting for custody of their child and were trying to put together money to fight on. "I came to Myrtle Beach and opened a restaurant so I could be close to her," Mark said. "We like the beach; we like coming here; the sun is shining; the water is beautiful; the people are happy; they're on vacation; it's a nice place to be."

For untold millions, the Boulevard was indeed a nice place to be. But for many – including Doug Wendel and Mark McBride – it was not just a moral abomination, but a threat to their personal ambitions and way of life. It was their mission to clean it up and they came a step closer on April 17. That was the day the last federal court injunction ran out and Myrtle Beach's ordinance against body piercing officially took effect.

"Fuck 'em!" said David Kupstas, a piercer at one of the Pit Bull Piercing shops. "They put us out of Daytona. Now they're putting us out of Myrtle Beach! Fuck 'em! We'll go to Panama City. We'll go somewhere!"

At another Pit Bull station, Nate Fogel was packing up his needles, rings and studs from a display case. "I'm getting out of this dump," he told me.

Which dump? I asked. The store or Myrtle Beach.

"Both!" he laughed. He might pursue piercing at another time or place, he said, or he might get back into building log cabins. There was a large job in Canada where he could find work.

A sign at the Dr. Pierce venue read: "Temporarily Closed Till Further Notice – Tommy, Dr. Pierce."

At Kugi's, Josh Woolbright was philosophical. "I'm still in business – not in piercing, but in retail," he said. "I didn't want to be in piercing all my life. I wanted to get into retail. Piercing gave me a chance to save up enough money to do this." He gestured around his tiny shop full of sunglasses, jewelry, T-shirts and candles.

The next day city code enforcers were on the Boulevard, ordering the removal of all signs and promotions related to body piercing. Some piercers told me they were going to sell do-it-yourself piercing kits. Others said they would go underground and keep sticking needles in people. There was no doubt an illegal industry was about to be born. Within days police detectives were prowling the Boulevard and setting up stings. One of the first to get busted was none other than Josh Woolbright – and it wasn't sleuthing that got him in trouble. It seems Josh pierced two eighteen-year-old New York girls' noses – and the rings fell out. The indignant customers filed a complaint with police and young Josh's life suddenly became very complicated. The last time I talked to him, he had just paid a $1,200 bond to get out of jail and was not at all philosophical. Now he just wanted to sell out and leave town. "As soon as I can get my money, I'm outta here!" he said.

Score one for Wendel and McBride.

There were other crusaders on the Boulevard in 1999. Preachers, prophets and proselytes come each summer from around the Carolinas, believing this to be the most wicked place in all Creation, and to their bewildered, small-town eyes, it surely is. They bring their Bibles, their tracts and their uncompromising faith to this evil avenue. Some come in church buses, forming teams of two or three to fan out along the Boulevard, challenging the heathen, reading Scripture, beseeching sinners to repent by the light of the Freaky Tiki Club and Michael's Bar & Grill. Others come as lone prophets, entering the wilderness to meet the devil in his den. One made several appearances in the summer of '99, wrapped in a sheet, wearing a crown of thorns, dragging a cross of two-by-fours over his shoulder, facilitated by a little wheel at the bottom.

I saw another young man that summer, who appeared only once, stalking frantically up and down in front of the Pavilion Arcade, confronting people, seizing them by the shoulders, imploring, "Look at us! Look at what we've become! America must repent! America must get down on her knees!"

The dean of the Boulevard evangelists was David Hallman, 52, bearded, rough-hewn, intense and sincere. He had a street ministry in Columbia, but came to Myrtle Beach on summer weekends to "proclaim." He told me that in 1983 he found "Yahweh," his constant reference to the Old Testament Hebrew God. He left his job with a major regional dairy company and went to work as an odd-job repairman, freeing himself from the "bondage" of work-a-day corporate life. In a rambling, nonstop banter he talked about Yahweh and salvation and how he worked with his hands on his own schedule, free from the rules and schedules of mortal men. He had no need of money or man's law: "I'm free from all that."

Standing in front of Ripley's Believe It or Not! Museum each Friday and Saturday night in the summer of 1999, Hallman was joined by evangelists Lance Barr and Bill Smith, who carried a small wooden cross with "Jesus Saves" written on each beam. Occasionally they would capture a lost soul amidst the hip-hop music and parade of skin. They would take him to his knees in tearful prayer as throngs pushed by on the filthy sidewalks. Each weekend Hallman, Barr and Smith handed out hundreds of tracts depicting a bloody Crucifixion, the bliss of Heaven and the torments of Hell. At the end of the night the sidewalks around the 9th Avenue intersection were littered with their papers, but God's men were not discouraged. They returned the next weekend and the next and the next. There were so many souls to be saved and the summer was so short.

For all its transience, the Boulevard had its institutions and traditions. The greatest, of course, was the eleven-acre Pavilion Amusement Park. In recent years Burroughs & Chapin had added a number of fast, exciting new rides, but none would ever replace the Hershell-Spillman Carousel with its twenty-seven hand-carved wooden animals and two chariots. Built in the early twentieth century, it was brought to the Pavilion in 1950 and still carried hundreds of children a day. The Pavilion's other treasure was the band organ, built in Waldkirsch, Germany, by A. Ruth & Sohn, in 1900. The two-ton organ was driven by compressed air, as hand-punched cardboard scrolls were fed through the player mechanism. It had 400 pipes and eighteen life-like figures, twelve of which moved. After half a century, the music of the band organ still filled Boulevard nights with magic and memories.

For those who liked more tangible pleasures, there was Peach's

Corner, at 9th Avenue North, open since 1937, selling foot-long hot dogs and draft beer. Two doors behind Peach's was the Bowery, an old-fashioned honky-tonk that opened its doors in 1944. Before they became Grammy Award-winning superstars of country music, Alabama was the house band at the Bowery, playing for tips in the early 1980s. Out of that gig they spun this little ditty, called "Dancin', Shaggin' on the Boulevard":

> Well, the Magic Attic's where the music rolls
> And the Army-Navy's got ole Jackie Soul
> Down at Peach's Corner there are good ole boys
> And at Mother Fletcher's making lots of noise.
> These people shaggin' on the Boulevard.
> Well, the Tams are playin' at Port-O-Call
> And the Drifters underneath the boardwalk.
> At the Spanish Galleon and ole Fat Jack's
> Juke box playin' and the place is packed.
> You bet they're dancin', shaggin' on the Boulevard.

There was not much left of the old Boulevard culture that Alabama lionized. The sound of hip-hop had driven out almost all remnants of traditional beach music. An exception was the Pavilion bandstand, where well-scrubbed white folks performed harmless covers of "Carolina Girl" and "Love Potion No. 9" on Friday and Saturday evenings in the summer. In another sign of the times, the Magic Attic club at the Pavilion had been converted to an alcohol-free teen club in Burroughs & Chapin's unending effort to clean up the Boulevard and its own tawdry past. There was nothing here to remind vacationers of the 1950s and 1960s, when the company brought wrestling matches and carny shows to the Pavilion.

An Ocean Boulevard cultural highlight was the Myrtle Beach National Wax Museum, offering its bizarre blend of history, fantasy and religion. Where else could you find three-dimensional representations of Adam and Eve in the Garden of Eden, Washington at Valley Forge, Jesus at the Last Supper (á la Leonardo DaVinci), Columbus, Leif Ericson, Blackbeard the Pirate, Francis Marion, sundry Confederate generals, American presidents, astronauts, Elvis, John Wayne and Charlie Chaplin, with the Ghastly Dungeon and the Haunted Graveyard, all under one roof?

Haunted houses were a Boulevard staple in 1999. There were three of them around the Pavilion, and remnants of another that had recently closed. In another intellectual triumph, Nightmare Haunted House played a constant loop of Bach's Toccata and Fugue in D Minor from loudspeakers over the sidewalk.

More frightening than vampires or grave robbers were the arsenals on display in many Boulevard shop windows. These were collections of exotic blades for slashing, stabbing and throwing, as well as brass knucks and ninja-chucks. In their crusade to save the Boulevard, the preachers, politicians and social engineers never mentioned these implements of mayhem. The gaudiest arsenal was at the Red Hot Shoppe, where four-foot ceremonial swords lined the walls and street-front windows displayed smaller, personal weapons. On a muggy June night, two young punks stood at one of these displays, scrawny, burr-headed creatures with baggy clothes, tattoos, metal loops sticking out of their ears and faces. They fantasized out loud as they window-shopped the savage steel.

"Yeah, man, you could really split somebody's head open with that," said one as he clinched a baby pacifier in the side of his jaw.

"Yeah, look at that one! I'd like to cut somebody with that one."

"Yeah, that's neat! That's neat!"

A few weeks later, the Red Hot Shoppe and Boulevard Beachwear pleaded guilty in federal court to selling drug paraphernalia. The companies faced fines up to $500,000 for each offense of selling bongs and water pipes.

Boulevard Beachwear was operated by Jacob Garon, who apparently considered paying fines and lawyers' fees to be part of the cost of doing business. Garon was the poster child for what some called the "Israeli Mafia," a group of rogue Israeli merchants who dominated the beachwear and T-shirt stores along the Grand Strand. He had been arrested several times over the years, including the 1988 sweep that hauled in twenty-eight Israeli T-shirt vendors for peddling material the city deemed obscene. That action sparked a cry of anti-Semitism from the Israeli community and a challenge by the American Civil Liberties Union. " . . . the arrests of only Israelis on pornography charges is too coincidental to be dismissed lightly," said Steve Bates, head of the state ACLU.

Rabbi Rubin Kesner of Temple Emanu-el defended the city against the anti-Semitism charge, saying it was "merely a nasty ploy by this group that has been challenged with illegality in their business." He said he had never had an anti-Semitic experience in his twenty-four years in Myrtle Beach.

Nevertheless, in such a conservative community, it was not surprising that the Israelis would come under public scrutiny. A frequently voiced suspicion – even found on the editorial page of *The Sun News* – was that legitimate commerce could not support the huge numbers of beachwear stores on the Grand Strand; *ergo*, they must be fronting some kind of illicit business. "How is it possible for the proliferation of beachwear stores to stay in business?" asked *The Sun News* in 1988. "We do not believe in guilt by association, but the sheer numbers of beachwear stores argue for a thorough investigation."

And investigation there was. Called Beachpro – for beachwear proliferation – the task force was launched in 1986 and involved eight local, state and federal agencies, including the FBI and the IRS. Busting dirty T-shirt dealers was the easy part of the Beachpro mission. Before the investigation was over, several Israeli merchants were charged with financial shenanigans, including tax evasion, mail and wire fraud. Some were accused of wiring money out of the country illegally to avoid paying creditors. One Israeli and his lawyer were charged with submitting false documents to bring another Israeli to work in the country. In another case, the City of Myrtle Beach used health codes to close down the "Zoo," four apartments packed with illegal Israeli immigrants brought in to work the beachwear shops. A number of Israelis were deported.

The beachwear merchants were an embarrassment to Myrtle Beach's buttoned-down Jewish community. Jewish leaders deplored the term "Israeli Mafia," but Rabbi Kesner spoke for many when he said, "I and all the good Jewish people of this community hang our heads in shame for the acts of a few. The investigation of the alleged illegal activities casts a cloud among our entire Jewish community – the guilty and the non-guilty."

My own experience with the Israelis on the Boulevard was almost comical. The word circulated through the beachwear shops that I was hanging around, asking questions. Soon Israelis were crossing the street to avoid meeting me on the sidewalk or disappearing into their offices when I walked into their stores. Jerusalem Restaurant, on Withers Drive, was their favorite gathering place. The first couple of times I walked in for lunch, the joint fell silent – until they figured out I don't speak a word of Hebrew.

Since the 1950s, business and political leaders of Myrtle Beach had been aware of a potential threat. "We had a lot of visitors come down here from New Jersey, New York, those places," a lifelong resident told me. "Some of them had a tough reputation and a tough way of doing business and all their names ended with vowels, if you know who I mean. We didn't want to give them any reason to stick around."

The specter of organized crime drove city fathers to keep gambling and prostitution off the streets and out of sight. It marked the beginning of Myrtle Beach's neurotic obsession with its "family" image. Ironic that the closest thing to organized crime Myrtle Beach has seen came, not from the cannoli-and-pasta mob, but from the kosher crowd.

Suffer the Little Children

On January 20, 1999, Gene Chapman and his wife Jennifer Curtis were outside their 2nd Avenue North home, playing football with some local children, when they were approached by two rough-looking men and a woman. They told Chapman and Curtis they had arrived in Myrtle Beach from Oregon a few weeks earlier "to start a new life," but things had not gone well. They had no jobs. They were living off canned beans from the welcome center and sleeping in their 1983 Datsun with a puppy . . . and the woman's nine-year-old son. The boy was asleep in the car.

The twenty-eight-year-old mother and her twenty-six-year-old boyfriend told Chapman and Curtis that they were leaving the child with them and would pick him up the next day. The boyfriend awakened the boy and ordered him to pick up a stick by the roadside. "Get yourself your punishment stick," he ordered, and proceeded to beat the child. According to later police reports, the boyfriend said it would be best for the child to stay with Chapman and Curtis, or he "would kill him and bury him three feet underground." The three drove away, abandoning the boy, leaving without so much as a goodbye or an "I love you," Chapman told *The Sun News.*

The couple took the terrified child inside, bathed him, washed his clothes, gave him the first good meal he had eaten in days. In the process, they discovered he was covered with bruises, scratches and cigarette burns. They called the police, who located a foster placement for the boy. By the time the police came to take the child, he had bonded with Chapman, Curtis and their two small children. "He started balling up in the corner. He didn't want to go," Chapman said. "I couldn't even sleep, worrying about that kid."

"I cried," Curtis said. "I'd take him right now. . . . I'm not rich but I'd give him food and a place to live and I ain't going to beat him." The boy's mother and her two male friends were arrested the next day in an Ocean Boulevard flophouse.

In a somewhat similar incident a week later, Myrtle Beach police arrested three men and two women at the Holiday Towers, on a variety of drug charges, and took into custody a twelve-year-old boy who was staying with them. Among those arrested was a common-law couple, charged with unlawful conduct toward a child.

Another makeshift family arrived in Myrtle Beach from Missouri in March 1999. Melanie Frizzell was 21; her boyfriend, Matthew Allen Clark, was 17. There was also Frizzell's four-year-old son, seven-month-old baby and three-year-old daughter Courtney. According to *The Sun News*, they stayed first in a tent, then in a small camper on Lot 3009 at Lakewood Campground. The yard around their little camper was cluttered with lawn chairs, garbage bags, toys, an inflatable child's pool and other urban detritus. Frizzell and Clark argued frequently, according to campground neighbors.

About 1:30 on the morning of July 18, Frizzell and Clark each dialed 911. They told EMTs that Courtney had fallen out of bed and hit her head. The child was taken to the Medical University of South Carolina in Charleston, where she died on July 22. Police investigators soon had a different explanation for Courtney's death. Clark, they said, had thrown the child into the shower stall repeatedly and shaken her when she refused to take a cold shower. He then put the unconscious girl to bed and left her until she began to convulse several hours later. Investigators found "a pattern of systematic abuse" in the home: "This child had literally no portion of her body where there was not a bruise or contusion." Her brother had "bruises literally from the top of his head to the tip of his toes."

Authorities charged Clark with homicide by child abuse; Frizzell was charged with unlawful neglect of a child.

Sometimes children are an unwanted burden in the lives of irresponsible adults. Sometimes they are pawns in their parents' pathological games. In November 1998, Michael Passaro parked his Chevy Astro in front of his estranged wife's apartment in Surfside Beach. In the back was his two-year-old daughter, Maggie. Passaro doused the vehicle with gasoline and set it afire, murdering his child to spite his wife.

For all the public talk of family values, South Carolina is horribly unforgiving to its vulnerable families. In 2000, the state ranked second in the nation for the percentage of separated couples. In 1999, it ranked forty-third in overall well-being of its children, according to a survey by the Annie E. Casey Foundation. In Myrtle Beach, unstable families, a minimum-wage culture, an environment of transience, violence and lawlessness all conspire to make victims of the most vulnerable.

At 10:00 on a July night, I dropped into Subs & Tacos to have their famous tuna salad sandwich and catch up on news from the Boulevard Rats who gathered there. That night there was a young kid in the place I had not seen before. His name was Kevin. He was twelve years old, bright, articulate, with short brown hair, blue eyes and a ring in his left ear. Kevin was a natural raconteur and that night he was entertaining everyone in the place with the chameleon he kept on a string as it climbed over his head and shoulders. He lived with his mother in a room in the flophouse above Subs & Tacos. The place was a notorious drug haven, called Roach Hotel by its seedy residents. It was the latest in a series of dumps Kevin and his mother had lived in. Yet he was cheerful and outgoing – apparently untouched by the squalor around him.

How had he come to Myrtle Beach? I asked.

He and his mother were living in Wisconsin the previous summer, Kevin said. She was parking cars for a traveling carnival when she met a man who worked on the midway. The three of them loaded into her 1985 Subaru with one of the gears stripped and they headed to Myrtle Beach. "She met this guy and it was so fast and – BANG! – three days later we were gone!" he told me. His mother had married her new boyfriend on the road to Myrtle Beach. The three of them had shared a room until his new stepfather moved out a few months later.

Over the next weeks I saw Kevin on the Boulevard and in local bars at all hours of the day and night. At Marvin's boardwalk bar, he was regarded as a junior pool shark. He often had his lizard on his arm and some wisecrack about the local cops or merchants who had hassled him that day. And he always tried to panhandle me to buy something to eat. Rather than give him the money, I would take him to a Boulevard restaurant for a sandwich or pizza. The only thing he loved more than pizza was video games and he hit me up for a few quarters to play whenever we were together.

I wanted to learn more about Kevin's life and made arrangements to interview his mother, Margaret. We met one evening at the bar in Marvin's. Margaret drank Budweisers from the can and smoked Dorals, one after another. I could barely see to take notes or hear above the jukebox as she talked. Behind us, Kevin played on a Sega NASCAR simulator, interrupting us repeatedly for more quarters.

Margaret was forty-four, with plain features, thick glasses and long, straight, shapeless hair. She was a clerk in a Boulevard souvenir shop, working for $6. 75 an hour, a job she started two days after she and Kevin and her third husband arrived in town in July 1998. Besides Kevin, Margaret had two grown daughters and an eight-year-old granddaughter she had not seen in five years. Kevin had never met his father. He was conceived in a brief encounter with a man who wanted nothing to do with him. "He wants to meet his daddy and it's only natural," she said. "He takes his meanness out on me 'cause he can't see him."

In Wisconsin, Margaret had been bored with small town life, tired of the bitter winters. She met the man who became her new husband on a Sunday. They departed on Wednesday and were married on Thursday. Kevin was against the marriage, and for good reason. Margaret's third husband, like her second, abused the boy. He bought a wooden paddle from Woolworth's, she said, and used it on him frequently. Though they were still married, Margaret said she had not seen her husband since he moved out of their room in December. "If he wants to be that way, I can be that way, too." She had since taken up with another man, who shared their room and the $125-a-week rent.

Kevin had been arrested twice by Myrtle Beach police, once for carrying an illegal knife, another time for having a corncob pipe with marijuana residue. Margaret grounded him for a month for the knife arrest, but that meant that she was grounded also, to stay at home and watch him. "He likes it when I'm grounded because he knows where I am." She needed to be watched, she admitted, because she wandered the Boulevard too often, drinking late into the night. It was Kevin's job to find her and bring her home. "I wind up back at my place, passed out," she said, shaking her head.

"I know it's hard on Kevin. I wanted him to see what this side of life is like, and I want to protect him from it," she said. "I can teach him and show him and I can learn while he learns, but there's got to be more to life than that humdrum place I was in. I had to get out and find something better and I have to protect Kevin."

Margaret was staring away in silence and sipping her fourth beer when I left her at the bar. I said goodnight to Kevin and handed him some quarters. It was a good evening for a long walk on the beach.

Horry County –
Where the Frontier Lives

Perhaps the most defining characteristic of the American experience has been the frontier. For most of their history, Americans have looked west to new horizons and new beginnings. The romance of the frontier is in our blood – the freedom to build empires, the individualism to stand apart from the human herd.

On the frontier, a man was free to scorn convention, to spit in the eye of polite society. Because there was always a new horizon and a new tomorrow, a man might have little regard for what he did in this moment or this place. Not only could he leave his failures and humiliations behind, he could leave the land – as despoiled and depleted as his own name. This was the dark side to the great American romance. The frontier, wrote historian Richard A. Bartlett, "demonstrably fostered violence, lawbreaking, discrimination against minorities, anti-intellectualism, and individualism so fierce that it worked against the common good."

Unlike most of the country, Southerners have retained a largely frontier worldview. Even as our world has become increasingly urban and interconnected, Southerners have maintained a notorious aversion to government authority and regulation. The frontier is alive and well in Dixie, as reflected in the nation's dirtiest environment, highest rates of homicide and traffic fatalities and lowest standards of health, education and law enforcement.

On a bright, cold March morning, I drove north, up Kings Highway, toward Little River, past miles of mind-boggling architectural and commercial clutter. Comedy Cabana, Dynamite Fireworks, the Original Benjamin's Calabash Seafood, Carolina Calabash

Seafood, Steere's Calabash Seafood, McDonald's, Galleria Shopping Center, Players Sporting Lounge, Burger King, Wings Beachwear, Ultrazone Ultimate Lazer Adventure. Near this place – the intersection of Lake Arrowhead Road – President George Washington passed an uncomfortable night in the modest abode of Jeremiah Vereen, in 1791. There is no sign or marker to announce "Washington Slept Here" – only acres of asphalt, topped by glass and neon and billboards and streaming, honking traffic. The nation was young, the land wild and unspoiled when Washington passed this way. It was a new republic, dedicated to freedom and individualism, commerce and the pursuit of happiness. U.S. 17 is the apotheosis of these virtues.

I continued north, past Willard's Fireworks, Bargain Beachwear, Plantation Pancake House, Thoroughbred's Blue Ribbon Dining, Hardee's, Eagle's Beachwear, Fish Co. Calabash Seafood, Magnolia Plaza, the Afterdeck Club, Thee DollHouse Gentlemen's Club, Myabi Japanese Steak House, Waterway Hills Golf Club, Panama Jack's Club, Dynamite Fireworks, the Dog House, Lone Star Steak House, Rainbow Falls Miniature Golf, Mr. Fireworks, Domino's Pizza, Gullyfield Restaurant, Chesapeake House Restaurant, Chestnut Hill Restaurant, the Farmer's Daughter Restaurant, Red Lobster Restaurant.

High on anybody's list of most appalling local phenomena were the warehouse-sized beachwear stores. Scores of them lined the Strand, the most prolific being Wings, followed by Eagles, Pacific, Bargain and others. After Hurricane Hugo, the beachwear industry rebuilt in profuse and flamboyant gaucherie. Most beachwear stores along U.S. 17 had 20-foot-high glass fronts packed with bikinied mannequins, towels and T-shirts, posters and boogie boards, Hawaiian print shirts and shorts. Inside were more T-shirts, sweatshirts, caps, hats, bikinis and swimming trunks, rows of shot glasses, coffee mugs, beer mugs, beer bongs, ashtrays, sunglasses, shell sculptures, bins of cigarette lighters, key chains, candles, gold chains and earrings, conch shells, dried starfish, sand dollars, alligator heads and feet, beach balls and disposable cameras. The stores' exteriors were painted in pastels of blue and yellow, green and orange, with matching neon piping. Huge roadside marquees promised live hermit crabs with a $10 purchase and proclaimed the mantra, the slogan, the watchword of Myrtle Beach commerce and culture: "Buy 1, Get 1 Free!"

Northward I pressed, into the vast junkscape. U.S 17 through North Myrtle Beach is perhaps the most visually abusive stretch of road in America. The tone was set at the city limit, where a sign proudly proclaimed, "Home of Vanna White." The roadside was an alphabet jungle, an all-out assault of undifferentiated shapes and colors, lights and gadgets, all designed to steal your glance for just one moment from all the other shapes and colors, lights and gadgets vying for your attention and your dollars: Barefoot Campground, Alabama Theater, House of Blues, Rosa Linda's Café, Grill House, Kelly's Restaurant & Bar, Alligator Adventure ("Explore 15 Acres Live Reptile Zoo"), Q-Zar Laser Games, Preston's Seafood, Logan's Road House, Golf Ball Outlet, Bargain Beachwear, Myrtle Beach Christian Retreat, Sutter's Mill Miniature Golf, Myrtle Beach Grand Prix, Jersey Mike's Sandwiches, Grand Games & Café, Perk & Deli, Pacific Beachwear, Factory Outlet, Rockefeller's Raw Bar, Tropical Furniture, King's Famous Pizza, Golf Supplies, White Point Seafood Café, Hawaiian Rumble Miniature Golf, LJ's Lingerie, Excitement Video, Crazy Horse Gentleman's Club, 4:20 Shop, Sam Snead's Grille, Willard's Fireworks, Chance's Games, Wings Beachwear, across the highway from Eagles Beachwear, adjacent to Pacific Beachwear, Martin's Golf & Tennis Super Store, across the highway from Golf Dimensions Warehouse.

And there was more . . . House of Pancakes, Bert's Surf Shop, Plantation Pancake House, Jackaroo Australian Steak House, Crawdaddy's Oyster Bar & Grill, Bargain Beachwear, Lost Treasure Miniature Golf, Bargain Beachwear, Pro-Fit Golf, Beach & Golf Vacations, Brick Oven Pizza & Pasta, Golf Shoe Centers of America, Possum Trot Golf Course, Benny Rappa's Trattoria, Mulligan's, Over-Time Sports Bar, Outrigger's Seafoood, Krispy-Kreme Donuts, Pavilion Discount Beverage, Mexico Lindo, North Myrtle Beach Bowling Center, Don's Pancake House, Budget Golf, Waves Beachwear, Dick's Pawn Shop, Mr. Cashier, Fun World Miniature Golf, Waffle House, Wings Beachwear, across the street from another Wings Beachwear, Gator Hole Golf Course, Mayday Miniature Golf. And on and on it went.

In North Myrtle Beach, billboards towered above the ground-level blight like an urban forest canopy, pushing up to the edge of the road, adding a new dimension − physically and aesthetically − to the visual chaos. Unlike its namesake, North Myrtle Beach had made no serious effort to control its eruption of billboards. Now they blossomed like algae plumes in a water hazard. I could remember when U.S. 17 was an open, picturesque coastal highway.

At the intersection of Kings Highway and Mineola Avenue, two filling stations, a Coastal Federal Bank branch, a video casino and the

Little River United Methodist Church stood where James Cochran provided lunch for President Washington on that day in 1791. Again, there was nothing to memorialize this small moment in presidential culinary history.

Like Kings Highway, U.S. 501 was a forest of billboards greeting visitors at the front door of Myrtle Beach. Along one short stretch of 501, a landowner not only erected a string of enormous signs but also cut down acres of forest to give them maximum visibility. Years later, the angry black stumps still thrust out of the marshy ground.

The City of Myrtle Beach made a serious effort at controlling billboards, barring any further billboard construction in the city. The problem with sign control was the same problem with other development controls: the city had tougher regulations than the county, where erecting billboards was regarded as a sacred right of property owners. Billboard companies – including Burroughs & Chapin – were among the most generous campaign contributors to Horry County Council members.

Tourists, of course, were unaware of such local vagaries. They didn't understand that most of the clutter on U.S. 501 lay outside the city. They only knew they could not drive to the beach without having their senses assaulted. To them Myrtle Beach was not a corporate municipality. It was a place in the imagination; it was a memory; it was a yearning. And too often it was sullied before the visitor even crossed the city limit.

On the frontier, the physical environment was a resource to be used and discarded. That's how early Southerners treated their fields and forests. The modern Southerner still does it every time he exercises his God-given right to throw his beer can in your front yard. It's a way of life so deeply ingrained that even Myrtle Beach police officers threw cigarette butts and drink cups out of their cruisers. As for enforcing litter laws, several officers told me they don't bother.

The same was true on the beach, that spiritual and nominal source of all that is Myrtle Beach and the Grand Strand. Signs warned that littering was punishable by a $219 fine, but an officer with the Beach Patrol admitted only two or three people a year were cited. Yet tons of garbage were deposited each day by those who came to pay homage to sand and sea. They left their tribute in the form of beer cans, soda bottles, Styrofoam cups, hamburger wrappers, French fry cartons, chicken and pizza boxes, disposable diapers, plastic shopping bags, newspapers, magazines, towels, T-shirts, bed sheets and cigarette butts by the tens of thousands. South Carolina's beaches − like its roads − were the filthiest in the nation. Myrtle Beach − to say nothing of Horry County and other municipalities − spent more than $120,000 a year cleaning its beaches with giant mechanical sweepers that roamed up and down each night, collecting the garbage, making the strand pristine for the next day's communion.

Outsiders fail to appreciate the Southerner's rugged individualism and contempt for government tyranny. Hence many Northerners are shocked at the amount of garbage on our streets and roads.

On moving to South Carolina in January 1999 to take command of the hapless University of South Carolina Gamecock football program, Coach Lou Holtz made an off-hand remark to a reporter: "This is the best place in the world to live year-round, but I don't see as much pride in this state as I thought I would. . . . I say that because of when I was driving up I-26 and seeing all the trash and paper on the side of the road. You don't do that in a state where you've got a lot of pride in where you live and what you do."

It took a football coach to do it, but suddenly South Carolina's eyes were open to the shameful truth. Politicians, editorial writers, industry and tourism recruiters were all talking about litter. *The Sun News* editorialized on litterbugs: "There is a streak of carelessness, if not downright arrogance, in letting trash fly off their pickup trucks or in hefting an empty beer bottle onto the roadside. Flipping cigarettes out the window is commonplace. . . ." With millions of carefree, anything-goes visitors each year, Horry County had perhaps the trashiest roads in the state. The county's environmental services department picked up a million pounds of roadside litter a year.

Seizing the moment, Governor Jim Hodges named a litter czar and created a litter task force, replete with Web site and slogan. Hodges declared September to be Palmetto Pride Month "for the purpose of requesting the active participation of and involvement of every citizen of South Carolina to do everything they can to eliminate litter." Holtz and the USC football team made public service videos. The state started using video cameras and unmarked vehicles − pickup trucks, actually − to snare litterbugs. Fines were raised from $200 to $1,000.

Did the governor's task force and the coach's preaching make any difference? Certainly not in Horry County, where roadside garbage only increased and law enforcement only looked the other way. "We've got enough to worry about without worrying about littering," a Myrtle Beach officer told me. "I mean, people come here to have a good time, right? I'd feel like an asshole if I pulled somebody for tossing a piece of paper out their window."

Closely related to the litter problem was the question of recycling. Both the concept and the practice were fairly new to Myrtle Beach in 1999. The city provided blue recycling bags at all fire stations for those who wished to pick them up and use them, but few did. I was the only resident on my street who made the effort. James Ewing, director of public works, estimated only half a percent of household waste was recycled in Myrtle Beach – and no commercial waste, except cardboard. Recycling simply was not compatible with lifestyles and attitudes on the Grand Strand.

One of the most contentious public issues in 1999 was the placement of a new solid waste landfill. No one wanted it in his or her backyard. Tempers flared and demonstrators marched down to county council meetings to carry signs and vent their anger. Everyone had a better idea for where to dump the county's garbage. The one thing I heard no one in the public forum mention was that a tough recycling program would go a long way toward solving the landfill problem. Frontiersmen don't recycle.

A sacred tenet of Southern culture is that a person's land rights are inviolate. In a notorious incident from the early 1970s, landowners in Pickens County showed up at the courthouse with shotguns to protest proposed zoning. As a result, there was still no county zoning in Pickens in 1999.

The defenders of "property rights" in South Carolina today are not farmers with shotguns, but realtors and developers. And their weapons of choice are money, lawyers and lobbyists. One of the first pieces of business Republicans took up at the beginning of the legislative session in January 1999 was the Private Property Rights Protection Act. First passed in 1997 by the Republican-controlled House, the act would require state and local governments to pay property owners for any "loss" incurred as a result of a new law, ordinance or regulation which "inordinately burdened" a use or planned use of their land. The law was designed to block all new zoning, environmental or architectural regulations in the state and to prevent the enforcement of existing laws and regulations. The bill had died in the Democratic Senate the two previous years, but here it was,

February 1999, and the Republicans were doing their damnedest to push it through again.

In the little world of Horry County, realtors and developers were the 800-pound gorilla on all important issues, pouring a flood of cash into local political campaigns. Republican politicos came from across the state to the Coastal Carolinas Association of Realtors' Annual Legislative Pig Pickin', where they were feted and lobbied with the twin mantras of "property rights" and "local control." Association president Tom Maeser laid out his views in a statement to fellow realtors in the Sunday real estate magazine, Real Estate Plus. After denouncing a "Smart Growth" initiative from the Governor's Office, Maeser declared:

> We local boards and Associations are going to have to step up our monitoring and lobbying efforts to make sure these changes are positive and protect our private property rights. Now is the time to begin exploring ways and means to increase our political activism on the local level. . . . regulation can result in a decrease in property values due to restrictions on use or to increased housing costs due to burdensome controls and delays in the development process.

Realtors – and their developer allies – were "monitoring and lobbying" with phenomenal success. At the behest of their benefactors, the Horry County legislative delegation decreed that the state Heritage Trust Program could not buy any more land within the county to preserve from development. Realtors and developers thwarted efforts to control clear-cutting of forests and to establish stronger stormwater controls, with the effect that flooding in urban areas was a regular feature of Grand Strand life. They blocked impact fees on new development, with the result that infrastructure and services were hopelessly inadequate. (Statewide and in Horry County, studies showed that existing tax rates would not support infrastructure for future development. On February 20, 1999, the State Budget and Control Board reported that the cost of development in South Carolina would be $57 billion above existing tax projections over the next twenty years.)

When barbecue dinners and campaign contributions weren't enough, developers had other means to work their will. County building inspectors have been induced to look the other way while contractors built without permits and violated building codes – though none has ever been prosecuted.

In 1999, homeowners across the county were in litigation with more than a dozen companies that built their houses and condominiums. Complaints involved leaking roofs, windows and doors; rotting exterior walls, eaves, stairs and rails. In one case, a child's foot went through a floor. Some condo owners lost their property because they could not maintain the enormous repair costs imposed by their homeowners associations. Until recently, Horry County building codes did not require exterior wood to be weather treated.

The case of Barbara Abrams was typical. Three months after she moved into her new Kingston Ridge home, she found leaks in several places. The developer of Kingston Ridge was one Rick Greene, a member of the county planning commission, who was subsequently caught building on his personal property without a proper permit.

Grand Strand residents felt powerless in the face of development and corruption, but they weren't blind to it. In 1997, *The Sun News* conducted a survey of attitudes on the relationship between local government and developers and reported some stinging opinions. "It seems like local governments sold out to developers," said a retired educator in North Myrtle Beach. "And they build and build and build and there's no infrastructure to support it."

Said a retiree in Surfside Beach: "I don't think the planning commissioners are doing a good job. They let the developers do what they want. . . . It's a lot of special-interest, self-serving politicians. The real estate lobby is a lot bigger than the people here."

The "real estate lobby" included much of the Horry County courthouse crowd. In a rational world, the relationship between the real estate lobby and the county Republican Party would be a criminal conspiracy. In Horry County it was simply business as usual – blatant, unabashed, matter-of-fact. This was not to say that Democrats were more virtuous than Republicans, but Republicans held power and many thought the only reason to seek office in Horry County was self-enrichment. In a frontier world of transients and fortune-seekers, public trust was just another resource to be bought and sold, mined and plundered.

The depth of some county council members' cynicism was breathtaking. Councilman Terry Chambers nominated to the zoning board of adjustments and appeals one Al Bragg, a bail bondsman and former business partner, who was arrested with the councilman on forgery charges in 1993. The Bragg nomination was defeated after Bragg's background became known. In January 1998 – while he was under investigation for alleged vote buying – Chambers missed three consecutive council meetings. It was soon learned that the councilman had moved to the Cayman Islands, where he was selling timeshares. He had somehow neglected to inform his constituents and council colleagues of his change of address. The matter was resolved when Chambers faxed a brief, crudely scrawled note from the Caymans: "I Terry Chambers do hereby resign in my position as county council member representing district six of Horry county, effective this 28th day of February, 1998." End of missive. End of term.

In 1996, county GOP chairman Blaine Liljenquist explained how local politics work when he announced creation of the Business Round Table. Businessmen would pay $1,200 for the privilege of meeting monthly with the county's top Republican officials over heavy hors d'oeuvres and an open bar to discuss their problems and concerns. The money would go to the county Republican Party to finance future campaigns. "The business owners who join would certainly have better access to the politicians," Liljenquist said matter-of-factly. "They can sit down and talk to them on a one-on-one basis."

Six months later, Chairman Liljenquist gave a practical demonstration in how influence works in Horry County. As a condominium developer, he came under scrutiny for his building and sales practices. The county building code required that each bedroom in new residences have at least one window. Liljenquist was selling condos as two-bedroom units, though they had only one bedroom, under county building code, according to *The Sun News*. The county fire marshal ordered him to install sprinklers in the substandard condos, but Liljenquist ignored the order for two years. Three of Liljenquist's GOP friends on county council – including Chairman Joey McNutt and statesman Terry Chambers – moved quietly behind the scenes to retroactively amend the building code, exempting Liljenquist from installing sprinklers. Chambers even nominated Liljenquist to chair the building inspection board of adjustments and appeals, a position that would have allowed Liljenquist to exempt himself. The scheme came unraveled when *The Sun News* brought it to light. Lois Eargle, the county auditor and chairman of the county Christian Coalition, defended Liljenquist. "What I don't understand is why people are so concerned about this and people will allow abortions to be done and kill babies," she said. Local authorities investigated the Liljenquist affair, but no sanctions or discipline were meted out.

In 1997, after *The Sun News*, ran a series of stories on the cozy relationships between politicians and the interests they are supposed to regulate, Chairman McNutt had a word of caution for his colleagues and members of county boards and commissions: "People have the impression county council bows down to developers. . . . We need to be real careful that everything is proper."

It seems McNutt was not one to take his own advice. In 1994, the county was involved in dubious negotiations with businessman Ken Pippin, who wanted to buy the county railroad. It took *The Sun News* to report that Pippin was a close personal friend of Terry Chambers and was the landlord to McNutt's real estate appraisal business. But it was taxes, not conflict of interest, which marked the undoing of Joey McNutt. The rising young GOP star failed to file his state income taxes for three consecutive years, sparking an investigation by the State Law Enforcement Division (SLED) and the FBI. Under indictment for tax evasion, McNutt was suspended from office in September 1997. After denying guilt for more than a year, he took a plea to three counts of failing to file state income tax returns in December 1998. He paid fines and court costs and walked away. "For all intents and purposes, public service is out of my life right now," he told a *Sun News* reporter.

The planning commission was perhaps the most powerful and conflicted body in Horry County. Appointed by the county council, the all-white, nine-member planning commission was heavily stacked with real estate and building interests, including Chairman Don Helms, who owned a real estate company, and Vice Chairman Tony Cox, who was a builder. Two other members of the commission, which included eight men and one woman, were also in real estate.

In 1998, Cox and his business partner, County Councilman Ray Skidmore, found themselves embroiled in a controversy over the development of a proposed mobile home park. Cox recused himself from deliberations only after opponents of the project turned out to demand that he step away from the deal. *The Sun News*' scrutiny of local politicians and regulators seemed to have a cleansing effect on the commission's behavior. Members with conflicts of interest recused themselves from discussion or voting only five times in 1995; by 1998, the number was up to twenty-nine. Chairman Helms recused himself twenty-six times over a fifty-two-month period. That was thirty-six percent of the cases that came before the commission in which he had a real or potential conflict of interest.

Don Helms raised wheeling and dealing to a whole new order of magnitude in Horry County. As a real estate agent and chairman of the planning commission, he displayed a special talent for not allowing one role to interfere with the other. Though he had brokered land for International Paper Company, he declined to recuse himself from discussion in the county's negotiations with IP over the Carolina Forest development. He was questioned by the county council and chided by the State Ethics Commission in that matter, but no action was taken.

In another affair involving International Paper, Helms was accused of using his authority as head of the planning commission to threaten two businessmen who beat him out of a commission on an IP land deal. According to affidavits taken by county attorneys, Helms told a real estate broker and a member of the Horry County Solid Waste Authority they could expect trouble getting future plans approved by his commission. *The Sun News* reported that Helms became upset when the authority used broker Keith Hinson, rather than Helms, to handle the purchase of 1,100 acres of land. Hinson negotiated the sale at a lower price than Helms was willing to take. Hinson later agreed to split the reduced sales commission with the piqued chairman; Helms is said to have pocketed a cool million dollars on a sale he didn't make. But apparently that was not enough. *The Sun News* said the chairman was still angry over the $2.75 million commission he had hoped to make on the deal.

Again, no action was taken by the State Ethics Commission or any other agency.

In an unrelated Helms matter, in 1997 Burroughs & Chapin negotiated the purchase of 900 acres west of the Intracoastal Waterway, destined to become part of the Grande Dunes development. B&C employs dozens of real estate agents who could have handled the sale in-house. But the company chose to go outside, paying planning commission chairman Don Helms $300,000 to broker the deal. A year later Helms voted to support B&C on a critical zoning change for the tract he had brokered. The State Ethics Commission reviewed the matter and judged there was no conflict of interest.

Paving Paradise

South Carolina is consistently among the deadliest states in the nation to drive, ranking above only Mississippi at the bottom of national highway safety standings in 1999. Among the state's forty-six counties, Horry ranked among the two or three deadliest for drivers. The final count in 1998 was forty-six dead. By February 1999, Horry was well on its way to a new record of sixty-five traffic fatalities.

While the nationwide trend in recent years has been toward fewer traffic fatalities, traffic deaths in South Carolina were on the rise, with a rate sixty percent above the national average. There were 1,064 traffic deaths in 1999, or twenty-seven per 100,000 people. One out of every fourteen South Carolinians was involved in some kind of road crash in 1999. There are many reasons for this highway slaughter, but most of them are rooted in this state's long tradition of lawlessness. The Surface Transportation Policy Project ranked South Carolina's drivers as the most aggressive in the nation.

"I think attitude has a lot to do with it," Ree Mallison, director of S.C. Safe Kids Coalition, told the Associated Press. "We think that we don't have to buckle up because it's our God-given right not to buckle up."

"We're paying a high price so that people can exercise their individual freedom," said Harry Pastides, dean of the University of South Carolina School of Public Health.

"I've never seen any real serious effort aimed at a concerted drive to improve highway safety," said Rick Todd, president of the S.C. Trucking Association. "There's a lack of political will which goes back to the culture of this state. There's a laissez-faire, leave-me-alone-and-don't-tell-me-what-to-do attitude." Our state legislators, always eager to fulfill the wishes of their constituents, are only too happy to comply. The Insurance Institute named South Carolina among the three worst states for highway safety laws in 1999; the state spends less per mile to build and maintain its roads than any other.

South Carolina's go-to-hell attitude is amplified in Horry County, where reality is optional and many residents and visitors come to escape life's rules and responsibilities. On U.S. 17 and U.S. 501, souped-up pickup trucks and SUVs on giant mud tires race and roar, dodging in and out of traffic with impunity. Not surprisingly, Horry County has perhaps the highest rate of arrests for driving under the influence – about 1,500 cases a year in a county with a population of some 190,000. "We've always got a high number of DUI cases in this circuit," local prosecutor Greg Hembree said. "People will come here and do things they'd never do at home."

In a letter to the editor of *The Sun News*, a Myrtle Beach man wrote, "Living in NASCAR country, a majority of motorists think they are NASCAR drivers. They go fast (at least 10 mph to 15 mph over the speed limit). They draft (tailgate), then change lanes quickly – without using turn signals."

Another writer contributed: "I've driven in many states and cities, but I've never seen anything like this anywhere else. It's nearly always South Carolina drivers – probably because other states wouldn't let it become a habit as it seems to be here."

Part of the problem is the infrastructure itself. "I love the winters in Myrtle Beach. However, it has the worst traffic control system of any city I visit," wrote a woman from West Virginia. ". . . you are playing Russian roulette with your life when trying to make a left turn from U.S. 17. . . ."

Wrote another: "I have driven the freeways of California, the streets of downtown Los Angeles and from the East Coast to the West Coast, and I have never driven on a more congested, confused stretch of highway than U.S. 17. . . . No wonder I have heard the sirens from the rescue squad every day."

And there was this epistle of anger and sorrow: "I visited the Myrtle Beach area for the first time last month. I attended the memorial service for my dad, who was killed in an automobile accident . . . at the intersection of U.S. 17 and Inlet Square Boulevard. . . . You have thousands of tourists each year navigating streets unfamiliar, including a 60 mph business crowded highway. Vital street markers are lost in an incessant barrage of advertising and competing eyesores. Drivers run vegetation obscured stop signs among parking lots, access roads, and main arteries that are so randomly intermeshed that 'right of way' means 'guess and go.'"

Indeed, developers often had more control than engineers and planners over how and where roads were built in Horry County.

The fruits of South Carolina's tradition of rugged individualism could be seen in the tacky roadside memorials on U.S. 501. Crosses of wood and Styrofoam, embellished with photographs, personal mementos and plastic flowers, provided visitors a jarring welcome. Five or six people died on U.S 501 each year between Conway and the Pavilion. It was almost impossible to drive the twenty-eight-mile round trip without encountering at least one accident. On summer weekends, traffic sometimes backed up twenty miles.

A researcher at the University of North Carolina-Greensboro told *The Sun News* in 1997, "During peak tourist season, traffic and crowds practically force locals to stay in their homes. . . . .Myrtle Beach is a traffic nightmare. They have not done much about their roads in 20 years." Actually, it took more than twenty years for things to get this bad, but in a town with little public will or leadership, there was no one to offer an alternative vision.

Myrtle Beach came of age with the automobile, having no thought to public transit. In 1999, ninety-seven percent of the thirteen million people who came here arrived by personal automobiles and used them throughout their visit. The problem was compounded by the fact that U.S. 501 was the entree for seventy-five percent of those visitors and U.S. 17 was the artery that connected the whole Strand, from end to end. A 1994 computer analysis showed that U.S. 501 could comfortably handle 24,000 vehicles a day; but in 1993 the average was 49,900, with the number rising sharply during tourist season – and Broadway at the Beach and a whole generation of new attractions were being announced almost weekly. But widening old roads would not be enough. Widening roads to solve traffic congestion is like loosening your belt to solve a weight problem. New roads were needed to disperse the traffic flow around the Grand Strand.

"If we don't get some new roads built, we're going to choke on our own success," Ashby Ward warned, with no trace of irony.

In the early 1980s, Ward and other business leaders began collecting money and hiring lawyers, transportation consultants and lobbyists. To divert traffic from U.S. 501, they proposed a sixty-nine-mile connector between I-95 and Myrtle Beach. "This is probably the most studied road ever built in South Carolina," Ward told *The Sun News*.

But the I-95 connector was a disaster from the outset. According to an analysis by *The State* newspaper in Columbia, the highly paid consultants used bogus data to have the east end of the connector moved north from Myrtle Beach to Briarcliffe Acres, the most congested stretch of U.S. 17. Subsequent computer models showed the connector would dump 91,400 vehicles a day onto U.S. 17 by the year 2030. On the west end of the connector, environmentalists organized to stop the road from crossing miles of swamp and wetland forests on the Pee Dee and the Little Pee Dee rivers. Rather than face a long and expensive battle, local authorities moved the west end of the connector from I-95 to U.S. 501, west of Conway. Thus the I-95 connector became the Conway Bypass. As *The State* reported, "It started in the wrong place. And it ended in the wrong place."

"It's a nightmare," is how one county legislator described the road in a public hearing. Tempers flared between citizens and highway planners. At a county council meeting in November 1989, residents packed the chamber, throwing books and calling one another liars. The two Department of Transportation officials most responsible for pushing the Conway Bypass were later fired in connection with other misconduct. But before he was sacked for malfeasance, DOT chief Joe Rideoutte told a hearing, "I don't think the project can be stopped."

Other heads would roll at DOT before this boondoggle was played out. In 1997, the Charleston *Post & Courier* reported that the Burroughs & Chapin Co. had received what appeared to be excessive payment for seventy-eight acres in the path of the Conway Bypass. The land in question was the site of the Conway Bypass-U.S. 17 interchange – some of the most valuable real estate in Horry County. The S.C. Department of Transportation and the Federal Highway Administration originally offered B&C $15.3 million for the tract, based on the highest federally approved appraisal. B&C countered by hiring its own firm, which turned in an appraisal of $36 million.

As condemnation proceedings moved forward against the property, state and company officials reached an agreement that would give B&C $25.7 million for the land, through cash and tax credits. The deal was cut by state transportation director B.K. Jones and DOT chief attorney Victor Evans. The DOT board never voted on it and was not aware of the deal until reporters started asking questions a year later. When the story broke, the board forced Jones and Evans to take early retirement. Federal highway officials refused to reimburse any part of the overpayment, leaving state and county tax-payers to pick up the tab. DOT Commissioner H.B. "Buck" Limehouse called on the state attorney general to investigate the sale. "It doesn't pass the smell test," Limehouse said. "I've never seen this much maneuvering on something."

But the whole flap died quickly and quietly. No charges were filed.

On the foggy morning of February 6, 1994, Senator Ernest "Fritz" Hollings and some 300 dignitaries gathered on the banks of the Intracoastal Waterway near Briarcliffe Acres to thrust spades into the ground and pose for the media. The event marked the beginning of construction on the six-lane Conway Bypass bridge across the Waterway. It was a dazzling moment – and it was pure theater. For, in fact, there was no money to build the Conway Bypass. Consultants, lawyers and lobbyists had already cost some $20 million. There was just enough money left in the pot to make a gesture, and local highway commissioner Billy Alford decided that gesture would be the Intracoastal Waterway bridge. The span was duly built, but there was no road leading to either end of it. For three years the "Bridge to Nowhere" arched gawkily across the water. If it were ever to be part of a superhighway, somebody would have to come up with $465 million. Neither state nor federal government was willing to pay the tab and local officials were mad as hell.

"I don't think the state realizes that ten percent of its entire budget comes from Horry County tourism," complained Ashby Ward. "Out of forty-six counties, this one county provides ten percent of the entire state budget. We get very little in return."

If Horry County were to have its misbegotten Conway Bypass – plus a proposed north-south Carolina Bays Parkway – it would have to pay for them itself. To buy the asphalt, business and political leaders mobilized to pass a one-cent sales tax increase. The penny-tax campaign opened old animosities of class, geography and profession. "We don't need this road," Conway resident Jimmy Hammond told *The State*. "It's only going to benefit the people who own the big hotels at the beach. . . . If Myrtle Beach needs the Conway Bypass, then let the people who are going to use it pay for it. . . instead of some family that has to buy groceries and shoes for their kids."

Out of these resentments arose a grassroots protest called Of the People. Led by state Representative Harold Worley, the group printed bumper stickers calling the Conway Bypass "Dumb" and the sales tax "Dumber," playing on the title of a popular movie. Angry letters poured into *The Sun News*. Worley called for a federal investigation, saying the pro-tax coalition was using highway funds to campaign for the tax increase.

Business leaders didn't need to use public money; they had plenty of their own. They organized the Road Works Reform Committee, raised

$270,000 and hired a high-powered Columbia public relations firm to sell the new tax. They sent out mailers to every registered voter in the county, organized workshops to explain the plan to retirees and filled radio and television airways with folksy ads. Tax opponents waged a $20,000 campaign based on door-to-door contact. They claimed there was a secret "Plan B": if Horry County rejected the penny-tax increase, the state would be forced to step in and pay for Horry's roads. Tax supporters insisted there was no Plan B. Governor David Beasley came to Conway to reiterate that he would not allow an increase in gasoline tax to pay for roads.

The Sun News strongly endorsed the penny tax; publisher Michael Pate sat on the Area Council on Transportation, which had first proposed it. Another important supporter was Doug Wendel of Burroughs & Chapin. As the penny-tax referendum approached, the following memo went out from the executive offices at Founders Centre:

> TO: All Burroughs & Chapin Employees
> FROM: Douglas P. Wendel
> President and CEO
> DATE: January 24, 1996
> RE: Your Vote to Improve Horry County Roads
>
> As most of you know, Horry County is in desperate need of new and improved roads and there is no state or federal funding available to fix the problem. . . . We have a unique opportunity to fix our traffic problems and ensure economic growth in Horry County for ourselves and our families by voting "yes" on the March 5 Referendum. Burroughs & Chapin Company supports this referendum 100% because we know how important good roads are to the future of our community.
>
> As I told you in our Employee Meetings, if the road referendum passes and if you have voted in the election, I will go before the Burroughs & Chapin Board of Directors and ask for a special reward for the employees who registered and took the time to vote in this critical election. Your supervisors will arrange your morning or afternoon schedule on Tuesday, March 5 to allow you time to vote and you will be paid for that time. . .

On referendum day, 32,752 people went to the polls in Horry County – an astounding 46.5 percent of registered voters, in a county that usually draws less than twenty percent in local elections. That evening at Wild Wing Plantation Country Club, Ashby Ward and the powers that be sipped cocktails, grazed the hors d'oeuvres and awaited the outcome. They gagged when the numbers came in.

After two years of planning and a quarter-million dollars worth of propaganda, the penny-tax went down to defeat by a two-to-one margin.

Half-joking and completely bitter, an unidentified tax supporter told *The Sun News*, "I really think we need a movement to secede from the State of South Carolina and find a way to be annexed into North Carolina. They know how to build roads. They have better schools, better everything. They would love to have our tourism dollars."

An unidentified local CEO (who sounded a lot like Doug Wendel) said, "The sun will come up tomorrow and I'll go to work and we'll keep building. I'll let the other side figure out how to handle the people who are coming here."

"People thought it was their chance to say no to City Hall," anti-tax organizer Marion Foxworth said after the votes were counted. "It was their chance to say no to county council and to big business."

And so died the penny tax. That summer millions of cars descended on the Grand Strand. Traffic came to a crawl on all highways and sat glistening in the sun like a great metallic serpent wrapped around Horry County. Horns honked and tempers rose, along with the body count. Six people died on U.S. 501 alone. And the Bridge to Nowhere stood empty and silent against the blue summer sky, a monument to the county's failed leadership.

Then something remarkable happened. On June 28, 1997, Governor Beasley came to Myrtle Beach – amid great fanfare and ceremony – to sign a bill creating the state infrastructure bank, a special fund to finance bonds for a select group of highway projects. Under the plan, the Conway Bypass and Carolina Bays Parkway received top priority. The project was scaled back by several hundred million dollars, but soon the bulldozers and asphalt trucks were ready to roll. This was the elusive Plan B which penny-tax opponents had predicted.

On January 19, 1998, Beasley was the speaker for the second Conway Bypass groundbreaking – four years after the first. Standing at the Bridge to Nowhere, the Governor said, "This is a historic day. . . . This is the beginning of the future."

After nearly two decades of talking, fighting and self-mortification, Myrtle Beach would get her Conway Bypass and Carolina Bays Parkway. There were compromises and trade-offs. Looking to trim the cost of the bypass, local officials and engineers made two important modifications. First, they reduced the number of lanes from four to two on some stretches of the bypass and, second, they reduced the number of bridges across wetlands. To appease environmentalists, the S.C. DOT had originally promised to bridge ten miles of federally protected wetlands along the twenty-eight-mile highway. But politicians and accountants determined the cost was too high. By filling 182 acres of federally protected wetlands instead of bridging them, they could reduce construction costs from an average $25 million to $10 million a mile. In exchange for the filling, DOT would agree to buy and protect wetlands elsewhere. Environmentalists and the U.S. Army Corps of Engineers signed off on this "mitigation" plan. In the face of such an economic imperative, it wasn't a bad deal.

The Carolina Bays Parkway was another matter altogether. Politicians, developers and public money always make a toxic stew. In Horry County, the kitchen was full of familiar faces stirring the pot.

The Carolina Bays Parkway Task Force Executive Committee – the group responsible for laying out the path of the parkway and spending $750 million in highway funds – was an all-white, all-male panel of leading businessmen, several with real estate and development interests that could be influenced by the path of the parkway. The project director was Dr. Peter Barr of Coastal Carolina University, a paid consultant to Burroughs & Chapin. B&C president Doug Wendel was another member. His company had just signed a contract to buy 900 acres in the path of the parkway. There was also realtor and county planning commission chairman Don Helms, who was handling large land transactions along the middle portion of the parkway route, and Sidney Futch, a vice president of Canal Industries, the company that owned much of the land in the northern path of the parkway. The chairman of the task force executive committee was one Sidney Thompson – and that's where the problems began. In 1997, part of the Carolina Bays Parkway project called for a five-mile connector between the planned parkway and U.S. 701, south of Conway. The connector would go right past Thompson's ninety-six- acre farm. Opening up that part of the county with a major road might greatly enhance the value of Thompson's property – and it would certainly threaten miles of pristine Waccamaw River lowland forest.

Thompson protested there was nothing improper in his role on the committee. "The idea of a 701 connection was already part of the Carolina Bays Parkway concept when I became chairman," he told *The Sun News*. "It would have been a distortion of the process had I attempted to divert the project for any personal reason."

In fact, *The Sun News* reviewed old parkway documents and found there had been a road proposed for the area, but it didn't reach Thompson's farm. Furthermore, the executive committee met in a secret session, in violation of state law, when it voted, in December 1996, to jump-start the dormant connector project.

Public scrutiny and fierce environmental lobbying carried the day. The state DOT and the parkway executive committee dropped the 701 connector in the final version of the parkway plan. But when environmentalists tried to confine the parkway to the east side of the Intracoastal Waterway – where the heaviest development was already in place – they were stopped cold. The route would have crossed vast Burroughs & Chapin holdings, which were already being carved up for the billion-dollar Grande Dunes development and the 1.3 million square-foot Mall of South Carolina. As a member of the executive committee, Doug Wendel knew how to protect his own. So the parkway swung far west of the Waterway, exposing huge tracts of Horry County to new development.

Who was responsible for calling this bunch of good old boys to account for their improprieties, real or imaged? No one, according to *The Sun News*. Through no formal process, the executive committee appointed its own members and reviewed its own actions, *The Sun News* reported. It answered to no one but itself and on several occasions conducted business in secret meetings.

After *The Sun News* started asking questions about these conflicts, Chairman Thompson took a long moment at an executive committee meeting to caution members: "As we move along in some decisions that are going to concern the location of the parkway, I want you to be real careful that you don't create a conflict of interest. So I would like you to be a little more cautious."

On February 24, 1999, the state Department of Transportation came through with $95 million to restore two lanes to the Conway Bypass that had been budgeted out in 1997. "This is a great day. It's a great day for Horry County and for South Carolina," state Senator Luke Rankin exulted. A few days later, the legislature passed a bill formally naming the "Bridge to Nowhere" after Billy Alford, the highway commissioner who had the faith to build it and wait for the road to come to it.

Horry County's $1.1 billion road-building project was finally funded and under way. But what had the county bought? According to a 1993 transportation analysis by *The State* Newspaper, even with the completion of the Conway Bypass and the Carolina Bays Parkway, things would only continue to deteriorate along the Grand Strand. The average traffic speed will decline from 24.7 miles per hour in 1991, to 10.8 miles per hour by the year 2030.

The Carolina Bays Parkway − which opened in 2002 − was especially suspect. Florida's experience provides all the warning any tourist town should need. That state was opened to the automobile by U.S. 1, which ran along the eastern shore. When it became overdeveloped, the Dixie Highway was built to the west, to relieve traffic on U.S. 1. Then came I-95 to relieve traffic on the Dixie Highway and the Florida Turnpike to relieve I-95. Yet with all these roads, the average traffic speed in the Metro Miami area was down to nine miles per hour in 1993. Those with long enough memories can recall that the U.S. 17 Bypass was supposed to be the solution to all the Grand Strand's traffic problems when it was opened in the late 1970s. Instead, it became the launch pad to the next wave of development, including Broadway at the Beach, NASCAR SpeedPark, Plantation Pointe subdivision and the rest.

Einstein observed that, while human beings are able to pass along and compound our technology from generation to generation, the acquired wisdom of a lifetime dies with each individual. It is sad enough that homo sapiens cannot transmit wisdom from generation to generation; now it seems we cannot even transmit it across state lines.

Environment:
The Cost of Doing Business

Historically, South Carolina's environmental stewardship has been abysmal. In 1670, the first ship of Europeans to make their home in Charleston harbor brought with them African slaves to start cutting the forests. Later ships brought exotic crops – rice, indigo and cotton – which transformed the land and defined the culture for generations to come. Within months of their landing, the Europeans were at war with the indigenous Americans and within a century had driven them from the coastal plain. They heedlessly cleared the land and depleted the soil with one-crop agriculture. In three centuries, they exterminated many species, including, most poignantly, the Carolina parakeet. The only parrot native to the United States, the large green bird moved in great flocks between Pennsylvania and Florida. Farmers destroyed the birds' forest habitat with agriculture, then killed them by the thousands to protect their crops. The last small flock of the doomed creatures was seen in 1936, on the banks of the Santee River, fifty miles southwest of Horry County. Six years later, the site was flooded by the giant Santee Cooper hydroelectric impoundment. The Carolina parakeet is a ghost that haunts the conscience of environmentalists; but to most Carolinians, it is simply the cost of doing business.

Horry County is home – at least for part of each year – to fourteen federally endangered animal species and several plant species. It is also home to a skyrocketing human population, which increased 36.5 percent in the 1990s, with even greater rates in other coastal regions. A half-million new residents were expected to settle on the South Carolina coast over the next twenty years. State and local governments have been intellectually and philosophically unprepared for the great rush to the sea, which began in the 1970s. To the small extent that they have tried to regulate growth, they have been blocked, sabotaged and undermined by developers. In a state that has been singled out by the Sierra Club as among the worst in the nation for encouraging urban sprawl – 48th in protecting open spaces and 45th in transportation planning – Horry County has been singled out as the worst in South Carolina by the state chapter of Sierra Club.

"The more economic development we get, the more everybody seems to want to maximize the return on every piece of ground," said Jimmy Chandler, an environmental lawyer who worked out of Georgetown. "We're losing the tracts of land – the forests and the wildlife habitat and the natural areas that gave the land its character as people rush toward turning all the land into dollar returns. I don't really see much end to that. It's part of our whole economic system."

There is abundant irony in the flood of Yankees and their money into one of the most depressed regions of the rural South. Perhaps the ultimate irony is the water itself. It is water, after all, which attracts development. Yet it is this same water which limits it, as builders feverishly squeeze one more condo, one more convenience store onto any available land.

Saltwater marshes are called the womb of the ocean, providing shelter for many species to spawn and grow before going to sea. Yet thousands of acres of these vital waters have been filled to build marinas, houses and roads. Much of the Cherry Grove section of North Myrtle Beach was built on former salt marsh that was bulkheaded and back-filled from the 1950s to the 1980s.

Inland are freshwater wetlands, along the creeks and rivers of the coastal plain. They not only provide habitat for many species but also filter pollutants from water and provide a buffer against flooding – and they represent about forty percent of the land available for development in Horry County.

Wetlands are being ditched, drained and filled by developers and farmers in a cat-and-mouse game with beleaguered regulators, who have few resources and less authority to stop the destruction. In Brunswick County, North Carolina, just across the state line, developers rushed to ditch and drain as many acres of wetlands as they could before stricter state regulations kicked in on March 1, 1999. Some developers didn't stop at the deadline. An estimated 7,500 acres of North Carolina wetlands were lost between June 1998 and March 1999, most of it in three coastal counties.

"It goes to show what happens when you are not watching," a North Carolina environmental control official said. "There's basically a rush to develop."

An Environmental Protection Agency official told *The Sun News*, "It's different in South Carolina, because [developers] can do anything they want." That happens because South Carolina has no regulations against draining wetlands. Its feeble enforcement agency, the Office of Ocean and Coastal Resource Management (OCRM), had only four enforcement agents for the entire coast in 1999.

Wetlands protection is left to the U.S. Army Corps of Engineers, whose regulatory authority is constantly being challenged in federal courts. Thousands of acres of wetlands have been lost in the state over the past decade because of shoddy testing and enforcement by the corps. Environmentalists have charged that the corps is lax to the point of criminal culpability in its enforcement of federal wetlands regulations. Corps officials "have gone out of their way to allow more unpermitted filling and draining of wetlands in South Carolina than the corps has elsewhere," an attorney with the Southeastern Environmental Law Center in Chapel Hill, North Carolina, told *The State* newspaper. "It's a very difficult thing to get a hold of, but we think it's a big problem."

The preservation of a wetland, of course, depends on defining a wetland and that is a cabalistic art comprehended "only by God and the Corps of Engineers," a long-time observer told me. Sometimes land that is wet for long periods of the year is not a wetland. A case in point was the tract at the intersection of U.S. 501 and Seaboard Street. The land was owned by Burroughs & Chapin and was the site of the new Wal-Mart SuperCenter, Home Depot and the proposed Mall of South Carolina. Massive drainage ditches were cut across the property, but no regulatory officials seemed concerned and B&C officials refused to discuss when or how the ditches got there.

In 1996, the corps tested the 128-acre mall property and found only 2.6 acres of wetlands. "That's bullshit!" said a biologist familiar with the site. "Common sense will tell you it just doesn't happen in the Lowcountry." B&C was allowed to pay $75,000 into the wetlands mitigation bank to preserve wetlands elsewhere. They were then permitted to destroy the 2.6 acres of wetlands on their mall site. Since 1996, criticism by environmentalists has forced the Corps of Engineers to abandon the testing procedures by which they permitted development on the B&C mall tract. (Like the mall site, B&C's Broadway at the Beach tract was ditched and drained years before development plans were announced.)

There are other federal wetlands regulations with loopholes big enough to drive a bulldozer through. Timber growers are allowed to ditch wetlands on tree farms, ostensibly to facilitate the harvesting of timber. When the wetlands have drained and become "highlands," the trees are cut and the land is available for development. This is a common practice along the Southeastern coast, said an environmental engineer who did not wish to be identified. "There's a direct line from sylvaculture to ditching to development. You see it everywhere," he said. Burroughs & Chapin dug drainage canals on 200 acres of prime real estate along U.S. 17 Bypass, resulting in the loss of ninety acres of wetlands in the mid-1990s. An EPA investigation revealed that no laws had been violated.

Carolina bays are isolated wetlands, unconnected by surface water to any larger body of water. Thousands of these strange, elliptical depressions stretch along the coastal plain from Maryland to northern Florida. Horry County contains scores of bays, which provide habitat to numerous rare and endangered species. As late as the 1970s, the U.S. Department of Agriculture encouraged the draining and cultivation of Carolina bays. That policy was abandoned long ago, but today the bays face the threat of uncontrolled urban growth. With the coast nearly built out, developers are turning their bulldozers toward the deep forests beyond the Waterway.

Trees absorb large amounts of rainwater, help to recharge the region's subterranean water table, provide habitat for many species and cool the air in the torrid Carolina summers. And they are being wiped out. On a clear day, one can see columns of smoke rising from various points around the county, as trees are burned to make way for new houses and golf courses. Smoke blows across highways, closing them to traffic. Residents complain that burning poison ivy and poison oak puts toxins in the air, causing them to break out in an itchy rash. On any given day, hundreds of acres of forest are being destroyed in Horry County.

Over the years, developers have resisted any attempt by Horry County Council to adopt a tree protection ordinance. *The Sun News* editorialized: "Every effort in Horry County to restrict the cutting of trees instead of encouraging clear-cutting for no good reason other than ease of development, has failed. This 'Independent Republic of Horry' has been claimed by landowners who want what they want, when they want it, and by developers who would do what they want, when they want to do it. Nevermind [sic] the public that suffers from indiscriminate cutting of trees. . . . This county, with all its wonderful foliage, should protect its residents from unbridled tree hacking."

In 1998, Myrtle Beach passed a tree protection ordinance that might as well have been written by the developers. While it does identify protected species and sizes of trees, it has loopholes that make most trees vulnerable to any cagey builder. Among the qualifications for removing a tree is to find it "hazardous or in decline." In other words, any tree that has been twisted or broken by coastal winds – no matter how many years before – is probably not protected by the ordinance. And to certify that a tree is, indeed, "in decline" requires the word of a registered forester or certified arborist. Since the city has no such person on staff, it is up to the landowner or developer to hire his own specialist to make a finding and report it to the board of zoning appeals.

This is what Burroughs & Chapin did with twenty-three acres of densely wooded land at 82nd Avenue North and Ocean Boulevard. The tract lay at the heart of the company's luxurious Grande Dunes development, but 1,885 protected trees stood in its way. So B&C hired an arborist, filled out the paperwork and headed down to City Hall to plead its case before the board of zoning appeals. The bulldozers were rolling within months.

"Greed has taken over," a Little River resident told *The Sun News*. "Everywhere you turn, you see more trees down. It's not only affecting the scenery, but it's affecting the environment."

Clearing of trees, destruction of wetlands and covering the land with impervious surfaces – buildings and asphalt – have produced an inevitable result: urban flooding. County zoning requires new development to have stormwater ditches and retention ponds to handle a ten-year flood; city zoning requires stormwater preparation for a twenty-five-year flood. Of course, water has no regard for city limits or local ordinances; it respects only the law of gravity.

A good summer thunderstorm could put streets and whole neighborhoods under water. Areas that never flooded before the mid-1990s flooded regularly by 1999. Myrtle Beach alone was looking at millions of dollars in engineering to alleviate flooding, but the question remained: where do you put the excess water on this flat, sandy island?

"I think the biggest risk we face right now is maintaining water quality," Jimmy Chandler said. ". . . More development leads to more stormwater runoff, which puts more pressure on those wetlands in terms of being able to filter those pollutants. I'm worried about water quality and the long-term impact that's going to have just on the food chain."

After a heavy rain, stormwater becomes a toxic cocktail of pesticides, oil, gasoline, heavy metals and fecal coliform bacteria as it runs off parking lots, lawns and golf courses. For decades, Grand Strand cities have discharged stormwater through some 180 pipes onto their beaches. These pipes were unsightly and a potential public relations disaster: high levels of bacteria in the water regularly forced health authorities to post swimming advisories and close shellfish beds. Since 1972, test data found pollution in the surf, drainage pipes and tidal creeks. The U.S. Geological Survey and other agencies repeated those findings almost annually since 1991.

Some have proposed discharging stormwater into the Intracoastal Waterway, but that body already violates state and federal clean water standards, as do the Waccamaw and the Little Pee Dee rivers. Four municipal sewage plants discharge into the Waccamaw, which discharge into the Waterway, which provide Myrtle Beach with its drinking water. In 1999, mercury levels in the Waccamaw made fish inedible and E. coli bacteria counts were higher than the EPA recommends for swimming.

"We've got a stormwater law that's been in effect for ten years now," Chandler said, "but it's under-funded and it's under-staffed. . . . Horry County's probably the worst right now. The number of stormwater permit applications that comes in is so overwhelming that staff at [Office of Ocean and Coastal Resource Management] barely have time to just go down the checklist to see if all the right pieces of paper are in the application. And they spend zero time checking to see whether there are any lies contained in those documents – or just honest mistakes."

The long-term effects of polluting Horry County's water and soil will be years in making themselves known. But one effect may already be terrifyingly clear. In October 1998, the Centers for Disease Control and Prevention granted the state's Central Cancer Registry $20,500 to study the high number of pediatric leukemia cases along the Grand Strand. The state identified twenty-eight cases since 1985, with seven in 1997 alone. The grant would allow the Cancer Registry to examine environmental factors such as stormwater runoff, drinking water and location of golf courses in relation to residential patterns and incidence of cancer.

In its frantic effort to build its roads up to current needs, Horry

County set out to lay more than a billion dollars worth of asphalt through some of the most fragile swamps, wetlands and forest in the Southeastern United States, home to bears, bobcats, alligators and other endangered plant and animal species. Together, the Conway Bypass and the Carolina Bays Parkway represented an environmental nightmare. The combined sixty miles of superhighway would be not just lacerations across the landscape, but the leading edge of future development. Where the asphalt was laid today, the condos, strip malls and Burger Kings would come tomorrow.

To their eternal credit, environmentalists have fought a rearguard action for a decade, knowing they cannot stop the course of events but hoping to shape them in some small ways. And they have had their successes. They blocked a connector between the parkway and U.S. 701 that would have opened large tracts of undisturbed Waccamaw River forest and lowland to development. They saved Sandy Island in Georgetown County, and other Waccamaw River tracts. But the road-building process – driven by tourist dollars and local outrage at inadequate roads – is a force that will not be denied. The 28.5-mile Conway Bypass alone required the moving of eight million cubic yards of earth. Built by the Fluor Daniel Company, the bypass contained numerous underpasses to allow wildlife to migrate through the region without crossing the highway. This is particularly critical for black bears, several of which are killed on Horry roads each year.

Such victories were rare. The Grande Dunes development provides another example of environmental regulators who seemed more in sympathy with developers than with the environment. Grande Dunes was on Burroughs & Chapin's drawing board since the late 1980s, with the name Bear Branch Resort. Bear Branch got shelved, at least in part because the tall pines around 82nd Avenue North were home to several red-cockaded woodpeckers. Known as the "spotted owl of the Southeast," the red-cockaded woodpecker is on the federal endangered species list. Federal law protects the bird's habitat, an inconvenience that slowed or stopped several local developments.

Doug Wendel would never let a few birds stand in his way. One of the first things he did on coming to B&C, in 1993, was dust off the old Bear Branch plans, give the project a pretentious new name and start dealing with those pesky woodpeckers. B&C entered into a plan with the state Department of Natural Resources, allowing the company to relocate the birds from its Grande Dunes property to other sites. "We're looking for a means to transport them safely to another location where they will be comfortable," a B&C spokeswoman said in 1997.

Others were not so sanguine. "It's going to take a long time to find out whether, if you move these birds, they will stay," a local Sierra Club officer told *The Sun News*. "The damage will have been done when we see how well it did work or did not work."

In recent years, South Carolina has made some good-faith efforts to amend its ways. In 1976, South Carolina became the first state to adopt a program of buying environmentally sensitive tracts of land to hold in the public domain in perpetuity. The Heritage Trust Program has preserved unique and irreplaceable habitats throughout the state. In Horry and Georgetown counties, Heritage Trust bought Sandy Island in the Waccamaw River and several thousand acres along the river between Conway and the North Carolina border. One goal of the program was to create a safe corridor for black bears to move along the river in their ceaseless quest for food and mates. The most celebrated Heritage Trust acquisition was Lewis Ocean Bay Heritage Preserve, purchased from International Paper in 1989. The 9,343-acre site provides protection for twenty Carolina bays and sustains habitat for Venus flytraps, pitcher plants, native orchids, black bears, red-cockaded woodpeckers and bald eagles. Without Heritage Trust, the tract surely would have been destroyed. By 1999, it was surrounded by three giant developments – Carolina Forest, Barefoot Resort and Grande Dunes – as well as at least ten golf courses, a proposed landfill and four major highways, including the Carolina Bays Parkway.

Unfortunately, the Heritage Trust Program became a victim of its own success. In 1998, the Horry County legislative delegation, under pressure from builders and realtors, voted to allow no further Heritage Trust purchases in the county. The decision was made without public debate or notice. Heritage Trust is effectively dead in Horry County.

In 1988, the General Assembly passed the Beachfront Management Act, one of the most progressive coastal management laws in the nation. It stopped the building of walls and revetments on the beach and established a setback line to limit new construction on the dunes. The law was compromised almost immediately by a property owner who successfully took the state to the U.S. Supreme Court, claiming he had to be compensated for land in front of the setback line.

In 1992, the South Carolina Coastal Council was named the top coastal management agency in the nation by the National Oceanic and Atmospheric Administration. Two years later it was killed when

Governor Carroll Campbell folded the independent agency into the Department of Health and Environmental Control (DHEC) and renamed it the Office of Ocean and Coastal and Resource Management. During the David Beasley administration, OCRM became a toothless tiger under the thumb of the highly political DHEC board. *The Sun News* editorialized: "OCRM was treated like a red-haired stepchild, shoved down the ladder several notches. DHEC denied the intention, but that was the effect of what the powers that be in DHEC – and perhaps elsewhere in state government during the Beasley Administration – intended. They and some if not all, developers wanted coastal regulators muzzled. . . . DHEC has seemed to mistreat coastal management at the behest of developers."

In March 1999, a state Senate subcommittee reviewed a bill that would resurrect the old Coastal Council, with all its former powers. "It's a nationally accepted fact that the coast is a special place requiring management and protection under a higher standard than that appropriate for other areas," said a member of the former Coastal Council, who favored bringing back the agency.

Will the Coastal Council ever be reconstituted? "I doubt it very seriously," said Jimmy Chandler, "unless there's some political revolution in the state of South Carolina."

Republicans Ascending

In the predawn morning of April 27, 1791, President George Washington departed Wilmington, North Carolina, on the next leg of his nation-building tour of Southern states. He traveled in a white coach with brass handles and moldings and gilded paintings of the Four Seasons by Cypriani. With a small entourage, he journeyed down the Kings Highway and crossed the state line into South Carolina about midday. In Little River he stopped for lunch at the home of James Cochran, then proceeded south to spend the night at the home of Jeremiah Vereen. The next day, Washington wrote in his journal, "Mr. Vereen piloted us across the Swash . . . on the long Beach of the Ocean; and it being at a proper time of the tide we passed along it with ease and celerity to the place of quitting it, which is estimated 16 miles." It was at the present site of the Dunes Golf & Beach Club that George Washington first got some Myrtle Beach sand in his shoes.

Traveling through this god-forsaken corner of the world along this unnamed strand, he passed the place where the Ocean Forest Hotel would one day rise and fall; the future sites of the Pavilion Amusement Park, Michael's Bar & Grill, Can-Am Gifts, Ripley's Believe It or Not! Museum and many other establishments, past and present, grand and seedy. Apparently, the President did not think much of Horry County, describing the cabins and hovels he encountered as "small and badly provided, either for man or horse." By the end of his second day in South Carolina, he had cleared Horry and arrived among the wealthy rice planters of Georgetown County, where he was welcomed and feted sumptuously. "The manner of the people, as far as my observation, . . .were orderly and civil and they appeared to be happy," Washington wrote of Georgetown County. The plantation of Colonel William Alston "looked like a fairy land."

Little authentic history has been made in Horry County since that day. For all the millions of vacationers, spring breakers, golfers and other refugees from reality who came here, there was little to attract presidents or other important people with important things on their minds. That began to change in 1980, when the Republican Party scheduled the first Southern presidential primary of the quadrennial marathon in South Carolina. Since then, this humble state had become the doorway to the South for GOP presidential hopefuls. On April 15, 1999, former Vice President Dan Quayle walked through it.

Only the day before, Quayle had been in his hometown of Bloomington, Indiana, where he declared himself a candidate for the office once held by George Washington, Thomas Jefferson, Abraham Lincoln and Franklin Roosevelt. The next day he was in Myrtle Beach, polishing his image.

In the four years he stood a heartbeat from the presidency, Quayle made himself an easy target for pundits and late night comics, with his brash fraternity-boy manner, his inability to spell "potato," his criticism of the television character Murphy Brown for having a baby out of wedlock.

I caught up with Quayle in front of Planet Hollywood, where seventy-odd well-dressed, well-tanned white people, along with a troop of Boy Scouts, came to meet their champion. Standing on a riser in front of the surreal hamburger fantasy land, J. Danforth Quayle was still trim and youthful at fifty-two.

Quayle wasted no time going straight for the red meat, tearing into Bill Clinton, Al Gore and the Democratic Party. "They have trashed the White House and it's not their White House to trash," he said. "It's *our* White House and we're taking it back." He called for a thirty percent across-the-board tax cut and an end to "death taxes." "The reason you're exhausted and stressed is you're paying too many taxes." Quayle spoke for six minutes, scolding Clinton and Gore. He was still boyishly handsome and facile and empty as a gourd.

The next day he was in New Hampshire, host of the first presidential primary, still ten months away.

As silly as it all was, the Dan Quayle Show was a precursor of the long, silly year to come. In April 1999, most Americans – indeed, most Republican presidential candidates – had never heard of Horry County. But that would soon change. In the next eleven months, John McCain would come here *six times*. Elizabeth Dole, Alan Keyes, Steve Forbes and George W. Bush all would bring their campaigns to the land of beaches and golf courses.

Many in South Carolina believed that Destiny had chosen them to play a pivotal role in the nomination of Republican presidential candi-

dates. Alas, things are never that simple. In truth, it took the machinations of a native son and latter-day Machiavelli, Lee Atwater, to cast the
national spotlight on this backwater state in a way it had not been
focused since some local boys pulled the lanyards on Fort Sumter in
1861.

Atwater was a son of suburban Columbia and a graduate of
Newberry College, a tiny Lutheran school fifty miles from his parents'
front door. At Newberry in the early 1970s, he became fascinated with
politics. Those who knew him at the time say it might as easily have been
Democratic politics as Republican, but the Republican Party was on the
rise in South Carolina in the 1970s and it was the Republicans who got
to him first, who brought him into their fold, who gave him a home. In
return, Lee Atwater gave the GOP more than a decade of stunning victories and gave the American people a bad taste for the politics of attack
and innuendo.

Starting with political races around Columbia and South Carolina,
Atwater earned his stripes and a reputation as a shrewd and tireless campaign manager. It was Atwater who prevailed in having the state GOP
shift its presidential primary from Super Tuesday – with most of the
other Southern states – to the Saturday before the regional primary. In
so doing, he established South Carolina as the "Gateway to Dixie." The
move accelerated Republican gains in South Carolina by assuring
national media attention every four years to an otherwise politically
insignificant state with a historic inferiority complex.

In the two decades since South Carolina Republicans began holding their presidential primary on Saturday, the Palmetto State estab-
lished a remarkable record: no Republican had won his party's presiden-
tial nomination without first winning in South Carolina. In 1980, Ronald
Reagan's landslide victory in the South Carolina primary propelled him
past George Bush and John Connally and on his way to the White
House. Atwater was largely responsible for that victory. Eight years later,
Bush was back in South Carolina in his second quest for the White
House, in a bitter race with Senator Bob Dole and religious broadcaster
Pat Robertson. But this time, Atwater was working for him. Bush carried
South Carolina and swept the South three days later. Four years later
South Carolina provided the surge Bush needed to overcome a strong
challenge from conservative columnist Pat Buchanan. However, it didn't
have the magic to reelect him in November. In 1996, the wheels seemed
to be coming off Bob Dole's presidential campaign. He had lost two
early contests to Buchanan, but South Carolina gave him a solid victory
and sent him on his way to a fruitless GOP nomination.

So, in 1999, as Republican hopefuls queued up to make the South Carolina tour, demographics dictated that the Grand Strand would be a major stop. Horry was the fastest growing county in the state and the sixth most populous. More important, though, of those six counties, Horry had the second highest percent white population, at 81.4 percent. In Horry County there were more white people per acre than almost any place in this pivotal state and modern Southern politics were dominated by one very simple equation: White = Republican.

The transition of South Carolina and Horry County from Democratic to Republican mirrors the trend across the region. In his 1969 study, *The Emerging Republican Majority*, Kevin Phillips identified the subregion of the South he called the Black Belt: South Carolina, Georgia, Alabama, Mississippi and Louisiana. These were five states with the highest percentage African American population (by 1960 census figures); South Carolina possessed a thirty-nine percent black population (down to thirty-one percent by 1997) and was second only to Mississippi, with its forty-five percent black population. "From the early Nineteenth Century, slavery and later white supremacy have been the principal concerns of Black Belt politics," Phillips wrote. "In 1860 and 1861, the Dixie Black Belts sparked the cry for secession from the Union in order to protect the institution of slavery. . . .

"White political Negrophobia in the post-bellum South was premised on fear of Negro voting power, particularly in those Black Belt counties where illiterate Negro ex-slaves outnumbered their former masters by ratios of six- and eight-to-one. On a statewide basis, Negroes constituted a majority of the post-Civil War populations of Mississippi, Louisiana and South Carolina and more than 40 percent of the populations of Alabama and Georgia."

With the end of Reconstruction, the white populations in the Southern states violently seized control from blacks and Republicans who had been running state governments. Then began the process of disenfranchising black voters and removing them from all public offices and positions of authority, then segregating all schools and public facilities. To maintain political power, whites used the Democratic Party, with its "white primary." The Republican Party – the party of Lincoln, Emancipation and Reconstruction – was intolerable to Southern whites. The National Democratic Party took little interest in the way Southern Democrats managed their affairs.

So it went for decades, until Franklin Roosevelt's New Deal began to alarm Southern whites with its sweeping social programs. Most Southern voters remained loyal Democrats, though, until 1948, when the National Democratic Convention passed a landmark civil rights plank. "The two principal Negrophobe states – Mississippi and South Carolina – spearheaded a movement to form a third party," Phillips wrote. Dozens of Southern delegates stormed out of the Philadelphia convention and gathered at Birmingham, Alabama. There they nominated Governor Strom Thurmond of South Carolina and Governor Fielding Wright of Mississippi to head a third party ticket, hoping to throw the presidential election into the House of Representatives and control enough electoral votes to hold the balance of power. The Dixicrats, as they called themselves, carried only four Black Belt states and failed to stop Harry Truman and the Democrats from winning in 1948. But they cracked the Solid South and Southern politics would never be the same.

With passage of the Civil Rights Act of 1964 by a Democratic-controlled Congress, at the bidding of Democratic President Lyndon Johnson, Southern whites revolted against the party that had been their shield and bulwark for nearly a century. The Republican Party that year nominated Barry Goldwater for President, and as Phillips wrote, "his platform – quite conservative to begin with – was quickly propagandized as barely disguised racism in the Deep South vein. This image gained so much credence that Goldwater swung the Deep South into the Republican column but sacrificed the rest of the nation. . . . In essence, Goldwater won where Thurmond had won in 1948, largely for the same reasons. Like Thurmond, Goldwater captured Mississippi, South Carolina, Alabama and Louisiana, and added Georgia – the next-best Dixiecrat state – to the list." With the exception of 1976, when Georgia Governor Jimmy Carter headed the Democratic ticket, South Carolina has gone Republican in every presidential election since 1964.

Within a year of the Democratic landslide of 1964, Congress passed the Voting Rights Act, which abolished poll taxes, literacy tests and other traditional barriers to black voter participation in the South; it also gave the Justice Department sweeping powers to come into Southern counties and register black voters. African Americans began voting in unprecedented numbers. Most of them naturally identified with the Democratic Party, joined the party and became candidates for office. In response, whites fled the Democratic Party for the GOP; white elected officials – led by South Carolina Senator Strom Thurmond – switched party affiliation, a trend that would continue for the next thirty years. A white Southern lament I have heard throughout the South for decades is, "I didn't leave the Democratic Party – the Democratic Party left me."

By 1968, the nation was in turmoil over the Vietnam War and wrenching cultural change. There was racial violence in the urban centers and racial polarization throughout the South. The time was ripe for the jackal and George Wallace smelled carrion. The Alabama governor was first elected in 1962 as a defiant segregationist. He spent the next six years establishing himself as the voice of racial and class resentments, stirring fears of Federal authority and cultural change. He took his campaign nationwide in 1968 with a third party presidential bid, revealing the true depth of rage among Americans. He received fourteen percent of the nationwide popular vote, most of it from the Black Belt South. The result of that election was a pattern that looked much like the Dixiecrat insurgency of 1948 and the Goldwater debacle of 1964. Wallace carried Georgia, Alabama, Mississippi, Louisiana and Arkansas. South Carolina barely went for Republican Richard Nixon, thanks primarily to the influence of Senator Thurmond. Democrat Hubert Humphrey received only twenty-five percent of the total vote from the Black Belt states, most of it from newly enfranchised black voters. The Deep South had broken out of the Democratic orbit and become a two-party region. And the two parties were almost as segregated as the rest of life in the South.

With his election in 1968, President Nixon both courted and rewarded Southern whites with his "Southern Strategy," an informal policy of federal foot-dragging on desegregation. The result was that Nixon swept the South from end to end in 1972.

Despite the seismic shift in South Carolina politics, until the 1980s many whites still voted Democratic in local elections; Democrats retained control of the General Assembly, most state executive and county offices. That changed after the election of Carroll Campbell as governor in 1986, an election engineered by Lee Atwater. A brilliant party builder, "Campbell made being Republican respectable in South Carolina," according to political scientist Jack Riley of Coastal Carolina University. With the help of Atwater, Campbell brought Presidents Reagan and Bush to the Palmetto State for frequent visits and the presidents brought with them the national spotlight. White South Carolinians responded by giving their vote to the GOP in more and more local races and by changing party affiliation. The trickle of Democratic office holders switching parties reached a torrent, culminating in 1990 with the defection of state Agriculture Commissioner Les Tindal, the biggest fish the state GOP had landed since Strom Thurmond. Following the 1994 elections, the Republicans took over the House of Representatives, thanks to further desertions. They took the Senate with another key party switch after the 2000 elections.

The first party defection in Horry County came in 1984, when state Representative Lois Eargle made the switch. First elected as a Democrat in 1976 – "It was the only way you could win" – she could see which way the wind was blowing. "Today, if you want to run countywide and be elected, you've got to be a Republican," she told me.

In the 1960s and 1970s, the handful of Republicans in Horry County were largely transplants from the North. Known Republicans were pointed out and whispered about on the street. According to Eargle, a powerful state senator used to send county police to conduct surveillance at suspected Horry Republican meetings. If a county employee's car was found there, the employee would be fired. "You didn't let people know you were a Republican in this county in 1976," she said.

The father of the modern Horry County Republican Party was Al Tirrell. A child of Maine and California, Tirrell was active in GOP affairs in high school and community college. He had not lost his taste for politics when he was stationed at Myrtle Beach Air Force Base in the early 1960s, but as a member of the Armed Forces, he was barred from partisan politics. He retired from the Air Force in the early 1970s, settled in Myrtle Beach with his wife Wilma, and developed a miniature golf course on U.S. 17. And he came out as a Republican.

"The Republican Party seems very interested, and always has, in family values and high moral integrity," Tirrell told me. "The Republicans I have known and worked with always want to see everybody get ahead and have a good life." The Republicans support "patriotism and a capitalistic way of life."

The year 1979 found Tirrell serving as chairman of the county GOP and putting out the local party newsletter. Heading into the 1980 election, inflation and interest rates were sky high and President Jimmy Carter's approval rating in South Carolina was at rock bottom. Playing on Carter's unpopularity, Tirrell & Co. put up yard signs around the county, with the message: "Don't Blame Us! We Voted Republican!" It was a bold party-building measure that marked the emergence of the local GOP as a contender against the Democratic establishment.

Tirrell conducted a poll in the county newsletter in December 1979 that showed Ronald Reagan leading John Connally going into the critical state GOP primary. A few weeks later, he officially presented the results of the poll to Reagan when the candidate arrived at the Florence airport on a campaign swing. Tirrell has a framed photo-

graph of that moment in his den, along with dozens of citations, letters, newspaper clippings, campaign buttons and convention ribbons,
autographed photos of Republican presidents, governors, senators
and congressmen.

In the state GOP primary on March 8, 1980, Reagan defeated
Connally in Horry County, 1,664 votes to 1,520; George Bush got
789. Statewide, Reagan took fifty-four percent and swept through the
South three days later. Tirrell was a Reagan delegate to the GOP
convention that summer and the Republican Party became a major
force in state politics.

By 1999 the GOP had supplanted the Democrats in an essentially
one-party political system. In Horry County – as in the state of South
Carolina – many offices were filled in the Republican primary; there
were simply no Democratic challengers. Sad to say, the GOP had
become the party of white supremacy in South Carolina. The two
major parties were similar on most important issues except one – and
that one issue was race. The Democratic Party embraced civil rights
and were embraced by African Americans. Whites fled to the GOP.
Republican leaders piously denied that racism was the glue that held
their party together, but their protests sounded coy at best, menda-
cious at worst.

As far back as the mid-1970s, Lee Atwater accused white
Democratic candidates in South Carolina of belonging to the National
Association for the Advancement of Colored People. In 1988 came
the infamous Willie Horton ad. As chairman of George Bush's presidential campaign, Atwater was able to hold Bush's opponent,
Massachusetts Governor Michael Dukakis, responsible for the parole
of the infamous black rapist. There was nothing subtle about Atwater's
tactics. He understood the great divide in American politics and he
knew how to scare the hell out of white people. He played the race
card without qualm or scruple and built the modern Republican Party
in the South. In 1994 the state Republican Party put a referendum
question on the primary ballot, asking if the Confederate flag should
be kept flying above the state House. The measure was designed as
much to build the GOP as to preserve the flag, but it accomplished
both spectacularly. White South Carolinians voted in the Republican
primary in record numbers, supporting the Confederate Flag, by a
three-to-one margin. Of the 273,583 ballots cast in the GOP presidential primary in 1996, African Americans cast one percent.

You rarely heard Republicans using overtly racist language. Their
speech was "reconstructed" and distilled to the code words of race:

crime, school vouchers, freedom of choice, "welfare queens," states' rights. "Republicans constantly talk about states' rights and being opposed to federal interference," said Clemson University political science professor Bruce Ransom. "A lot of blacks simply have a visceral reaction to that. States' rights to many blacks raises the question of whether blacks are going to be treated fairly."

In the Old South, every town had a café or general store where local Democrats gathered to hatch their schemes and divvy up the spoils of monopoly politics. When Republicans gathered in Myrtle Beach to scheme and divvy, it was usually at Shamrock's, the U.S. 17 sports bar owned by state representative Mark Kelly. If the big gray Lincoln with the "Legislature 48" license plate was parked out front, it was a safe bet the District 107 representative was holding court in the northwest corner of the dining room, seated at the large round table, facing the door, surrounded by his knights and jesters. It was to this table that the sleazy parade of Republican politicos and wannabes, developers, speculators and fortune seekers came to announce themselves, to present their plans, to court favor. It was to this table that the Myrtle Beach City Council – minus Mayor Mark McBride – adjourned at the end of its Tuesday night meetings. And it was in this club that the Horry County Republican Party set up headquarters on primary nights to watch the vote counts come in on the eleven televisions.

Gruff, rumpled and bearded, Mark Kelly was a transplant from Buffalo, New York; 45 years old; first elected to the House in 1992; snugly in the pocket of developers. But he did know how to run a pub. All the beer was draft and the chicken wings were the best in town. The place was a shrine to the glory of Ireland and to American sports. The walls of the three rooms of Shamrock's were lined with framed photographs of great moments and great stars, with jerseys, hockey sticks, baseball gloves and other memorabilia – and with a full contingent of video poker machines.

In many ways, the Palmetto State has been transformed by migration, by civil rights, by a flood of new industry and commerce. That transformation was reflected in the shift of the white population from the Democratic to the Republican Party. Yet, whether Democratic or Republican, South Carolina remained what it had been for generations – one of the most corrupt and backward states in the nation. Never was the adage more true: The more things change, the more they remain the same.

Who Owns This Town Anyway?

This is how *Sun News* columnist Bob Bestler described the chief executive of the Burroughs & Chapin Co.: "Seriously now, is there anyone in the Myrtle Beach area who does not know who the Big Cheese among us really is?. . . the hands-down, no-holds barred, we-are-not worthy Big Cheese in this neck of the woods is . . . a fellow by the name of Doug Wendel."

Elsewere, Bestler wrote this of Wendel: "His company owns much of the land upon which the Grand Strand rests and not much is done on that land without the Burroughs & Chapin imprint. And it is no exaggeration to say that as B&C goes, so goes Myrtle Beach."

True enough. In the six years since taking the helm at B&C, Wendel transformed the company and the company transformed Myrtle Beach. The once-passive corporate landlord was a major shaper of public policy, not to mention the earth, forests and waters of Horry County.

Who was this unelected Big Cheese, so intent on building the Grand Strand in his own image?

Born in 1943, a native of St. Louis, Missouri, Douglas P. Wendel attended the University of Maryland on a track scholarship. There he received his bachelor's and master's degrees, though it is not clear in what fields. In a major profile in *The Sun News* he told a reporter his degrees were in political science. His official resume on file with B&C said his degrees were in public and business administration.

In 1974, the town of North Myrtle Beach advertised for its first town manager. Young Wendel was working in the budget office of Anne Arundel County, Maryland, where a former colleague remembered, "He certainly has a knack for numbers." Wendel was one of about fifty applicants for the job and was called for an interview, Rayford Vereen remembered. Vereen was mayor pro tem when Mayor Bryan Floyd asked him to come down to City Hall and talk to a hot young prospect for the manager's job. After thirty minutes with Wendel, Vereen came out and told Floyd, "Hire him!"

"He was very good on budgeting and that was critical to us at the time," Vereen recalled.

Wendel was not at North Myrtle Beach long. In 1977, Horry seated its first county council and that council hired Wendel to become the county's first administrator. A year later he went to Washington, D.C., to become chief-of-staff to Sixth District Congressman John Jenrette, of North Myrtle Beach.

Jenrette still admired the way Wendel took control and whipped his staff of twenty into shape. "It was an abrupt change when Doug came in, because he was well organized and he was a memo person. . ." Jenrette said. Wendel established a clear chain of command in the office and started demanding accountability and written results. "So he came in with that professional mentality. It upset a lot of members of the staff, because they had to produce on paper, not just mind thoughts. It upset 'em and some of my time was taken trying to settle feathers, but he did a really good job." The new regime "actually freed me up a lot to do some things that I was able to do," Jenrette said.

While in Jenrette's office, Wendel organized the powerful Congressional Travel and Tourism Caucus. When Jenrette lost his bid for reelection in 1980, Wendel took over as executive director of the Travel and Tourism Caucus. From there he went on to a post as vice president of the American Bus Association.

In 1983, Grand Strand Water & Sewer Authority, a semi-public utility serving the unincorporated regions of Horry County, was looking for an executive director. As chairman of the GSW&SA board, Rayford Vereen interviewed a procession of applicants without success. One night, standing in the parking lot after another frustrating meeting without a director, Vereen said to his colleagues, "You guys know who we should be talking to?"

"You think he's available?" one of them asked. Nobody mentioned a name, but Vereen went home and looked up a phone number. The next day he called Wendel in Washington and invited him down to Horry County "for some good old seafood and a round of golf" – and to talk about a job. Wendel met with the GSW&SA board and a deal was struck. "It was a no-brainer," Vereen said.

After a stellar decade of stellar growth at Grand Strand Water & Sewer, Wendel was tapped by B&C chairman Egerton Burroughs, in 1993, to head the huge development company.

It is said that a company reflects the values and personality of its chief executive. This would seem true in the case of the Burroughs & Chapin Co. and Doug Wendel. Both were paragons of middle class rectitude and upward mobility; both were aggressive, unsentimental overachievers. Despite their preachments and posturing, neither seemed committed to any principle that would interfere with its respective success. Though Wendel and B&C intruded constantly in government affairs, the company and its executive demanded autonomy to do business without government interference. Of the thirty-three members of Coastal Partners, a powerful developers' lobby, only four – including Wendel – voted in January 1999 to support the Private Property Rights Act, prohibiting any government control over development.

Obsession with public image was a corporate hallmark at B&C. The company had a penchant for extravagant – even pretentious – names for its properties: Founders Centre, Corporate Centre, Grande Dunes, Piper's Pointe. B&C informed local media that it wished to be referred to as "the Burroughs & Chapin Co." or "Burroughs & Chapin." No initials, please – though the company did use its initials on its own corporate logo.

Most amusing was B&C's dumping of its corporate slogan. Until the spring of 1998 the company described itself as "Boldly Shaping the Future With Pride." That season B&C became embroiled in an ugly battle to keep a gay pride rally off its Broadway at the Beach property. Suddenly the word "pride" took on a whole new meaning, which threatened B&C's buttoned-down image. The slogan was jettisoned in favor of something that reflected new cultural and marketing trends: "Family Values Since 1895." It also reflected the personal values and lifestyle of the chief executive.

To his credit, Wendel lived the values he professed. By all accounts he was an observant Catholic, devoted to his grown son and daughter and wife Paula. Taking Paula out to dinner and an evening's entertainment on Friday was a ritual respected by his associates and all who knew him. With dark, thinning hair and craggy features, Wendel was still trim and fit in his mid-50s, unimposing except for his expensive suits and ties and stylish, wire-rimmed glasses. He could be seen tooling around town with his wife in their beige Ford Windstar.

He played golf and deep sea fished with Rayford Vereen and other lesser cheeses in the Horry County business community.

Most corporate CEOs are driven and compulsive; Doug Wendel was no exception. His tight, controlled public manner barely concealed the fires inside him. Those who knew him said he was "a true Southern gentleman," "brilliant," "doesn't suffer fools gladly," and "is always the hardest worker and the last to leave the office." Others used words like "huge ego," "on a power trip," "a task master," "he wants everything done his way and done right now" – traits not uncommon among corporate superstars. Some remembered Wendel's presiding over the 1993 Horry County United Way Campaign. "He was like Hitler," one woman recalled. "I wonder if he knew we were volunteers," said another. But the 1993 campaign set fundraising records.

Doug Wendel didn't mind what people said about him. He seemed energized by conflict. "A lot of people don't like controversy, don't like waves," he told *The Sun News*. "If you're going to achieve anything that is significant, you are going to encounter problems."

Company towns once lay at the heart of Southern culture. There were textile towns, tobacco towns, lumber towns and furniture towns. Myrtle Beach was still a company town in 1999, and Burroughs & Chapin was The Company. In traditional company towns, the company sought to manage the economy, the politics, even the morality and culture of its people. In Myrtle Beach, B&C worked to control not just the future of its town but even its history. Company literature emphasized its role in founding and directing the town. To make this point, the company built the Founders Centre, in 1989, and located its corporate offices there. B&C history was told in photographs and documents on display in the first-floor foyer.

In the early 1990s, a local historian and civic leader was preparing to publish a history of Myrtle Beach, based on years of interviews and research. Unfortunately, his version of events did not jibe with the "official" history. According to the historian (who asked not to be identified) the forgotten heroes of Myrtle Beach development were the Woodside brothers, who built the fabled Ocean Forest Hotel and Pine Lakes Golf Club in the 1920s. It was the Woodsides who put Myrtle Beach on the map, who brought electricity, water and sewer service to the town, who got U.S. 17 paved and the bridge built across the Waccamaw River at Georgetown. And when the Woodsides fell behind in their taxes during the Great Depression, it was the Burroughs brothers and Simeon Chapin who paid off a $260,000 tax lien and reclaimed the Woodsides' 62,000 acres. Of course, there was nothing illegal in what Chapin and the Burroughs boys did, but it was not the image of a benevolent and pioneering spirit the company liked to project.

When company officials learned of the work in progress, they contracted local writer Rodney Gragg, who produced – for a reputed $50,000 – a friendlier version of events. The *Illustrated History of Horry County* was a glossy, easy-to-read, copiously illustrated, 104-page coffee-table volume, published by the Burroughs & Chapin Co. in 1994. Most importantly, it limited mention of the troublesome name Woodside to two references and told the history of the Burroughs & Chapin Co. from the birth of Franklin G. Burroughs in 1834. Gragg and company officials declined to be interviewed about the book. (In 2003, the alternative history remained unpublished.)

B&C's manipulations of Horry County and Myrtle Beach affairs threatened the very sovereignty of those public entities. In 1993, *The Sun News* reported that the company avoided paying more than $170,000 in property taxes on eighty-eight acres of oceanfront land it was developing in the Grande Dunes tract. With its undeveloped oceanfront property zoned "agricultural," B&C paid $1.60 an acre on land that was appraised at $160,000 an acre. It was all perfectly legal under the state's agriculture tax law. Farmers like Burroughs & Chapin had many friends in Columbia.

Reflecting its agricultural past, South Carolina has perhaps the most archaic municipality laws in the nation. For a piece of property to be annexed, a municipality must first have the consent of the property owner. This law represented a gun pointed at the head of the City of Myrtle Beach, because B&C (and Myrtle Beach Farms Co. before it) owned thousands of acres surrounding the northern and western city limits. Simply put, the City of Myrtle Beach could expand only by the terms of the Burroughs family and their stockholders. The company held all the cards and played them shrewdly.

Typical was the deal the company finagled from the city on water and sewer service. Myrtle Beach provided these services at premium prices to property owners outside their corporate limits. The city reduced utility rates as an incentive for property owners to allow annexation.

Myrtle Beach Farms agreed, in 1983, to lease to the city a 110-acre tract on the Intracoastal Waterway to build its water and sewer treatment plants. Under the lease agreement, Myrtle Beach Farms, with all its businesses and entities lying outside the city limits, would be served by the city's water and sewer system at "in-city" rates. In signing the lease agreement with Myrtle Beach Farms, the City of Myrtle Beach gave away the carrot and the stick for future negotiations on annexation. But there were no options. The city had to build its water and sewer plants *some*where and Myrtle Beach Farms owned all the available land along the Waterway.

As Mayor Bob Grissom later said, "We are at their mercy."

The company was never bashful about using its influence. To expand the Pavilion Amusement Park in 1992, it cajoled city council into closing a block of Chester Street, over the protests of local merchants and residents. When B&C built its NASCAR SpeedPark on U.S. 17 Bypass, it overrode protests from local residents and won an exemption to the county noise ordinance for its unmuffled go-carts to run near residential neighborhoods. As homes and whole neighborhoods were being threatened by road-building projects, the City of Myrtle Beach agreed to reroute two existing roads to make way for B&C's planned Mall of South Carolina. And in January 1999, while clearing land for its Seaboard Office Park, the company closed a state road for hours with no authorization.

In traditional company towns, part of the role of company managers was to monitor and control the behavior of residents. The old Myrtle Beach Farms Co. took its patriarchal role seriously, donating land to build churches and the municipal jail in the early years of the town. In more recent decades, the world has become infinitely more complex and so have the company's efforts to control the life and culture of its subjects. Nowhere was this more evident than on Ocean Boulevard, home of the Pavilion Amusement Park. To the chagrin of municipal leaders and B&C officials, Ocean Boulevard was the gathering place for the refuse of America's failed families, failed schools and churches, failed substance abuse programs and social welfare agencies. It was an unsanitized slice of American reality, as rough and raunchy as the T-shirts worn by so many of its denizens.

"That area [of Ocean Boulevard] is the heart of Myrtle Beach," said Egerton Burroughs, board chairman of Burrroughs & Chapin. "That's where it all started. But that area has a lot of problems, and families are fleeing the downtown." City Manager Tom Leath was more blunt: "There's an element that just sort of pushes the envelope. . . . If you walk down the main four blocks of the Boulevard, it's sad. We look like some block right off a military base."

A downtown redevelopment effort failed to get off the ground in the 1970s. In the early 1990s, municipal and business leaders united in a new effort to revitalize the decaying district and to clean up the Boulevard. The redevelopment group hired a designer to draw up a bold plan for a downtown shopping, dining and entertainment complex. The chairman of the redevelopment commission was B&C vice president Bill Pritchard. His presence aroused suspicions among merchants, who feared their properties were about to become fodder for Burroughs & Chapin bulldozers. There were also questions about how the grand design would be financed, along with a lack of support within the community at large. The redevelopment plan probably would have died a natural death, but on November 28, 1993, B&C officials formally unveiled plans for their giant new tourist Elysium on the bypass. With up to twenty theaters, four hotels and scores of shops, restaurants and clubs, Broadway at the Beach was the *coup de grace* to downtown redevelopment. It was a stroke of social engineering, conducted in a boardroom, with no community input. Developers and real estate speculators have been killing America's inner cities for half a century, but the fact that B&C had a hand in the downtown redevelopment effort, while simultaneously plotting the demise of the downtown district, left a bad taste in many mouths. As Bob Bestler wrote, Burroughs & Chapin had altered Myrtle Beach with the stroke of a pen more quickly and profoundly than any civilian government ever could have.

The lesson for all to learn was that corporate power works. While community leaders squabbled and dithered for fifteen years over redevelopment, B&C moved quickly and decisively, taking its bold quarter-billion-dollar development from drawing board to grand opening in less than two years. The corporate juggernaut had blitzed City Hall, had humiliated the public redevelopment effort and had shamed the democratic process.

Burroughs & Chapin would heap one further indignity on the

public before Broadway at the Beach formally opened for business. In 1994 the company announced it would seek tax increment financing to pay for the infrastructure around its Broadway at the Beach complex and its adjacent Seaboard Commons "big box" store development.

Tax increment financing (TIF) allowed a city to sell bonds based on the expected property tax base of future development, and was specifically drafted by the General Assembly to help cities redevelop blighted urban areas. The 510 acres of open countryside B&C wanted to develop along U.S. 17 Bypass hardly fit that definition. The tract was not even in the city limits. But B&C held the trump card: in exchange for the special TIF arrangement, the company would allow the city to annex Broadway at the Beach and Seaboard Commons.

The TIF deal sparked a revolt. State Representative Harold Worley brought suit on behalf of taxpayers and Horry County School District over lost tax revenues. After some bitter head-knocking, the city agreed to pay Horry County and the school district for revenues lost in the TIF deal and the company pledged a $3 million parcel of land to the school district to build an elementary school. So B&C got its special tax district with infrastructure at taxpayer expense and Myrtle Beach got to annex the giant development.

On September 1, 1995, Broadway at the Beach was officially dedicated "To the Families of the World," as a bronze plaque at the entrance proclaims. (The grand family-values venture got off to a rocky start that day. Senator Strom Thurmond was on hand, along with Grace McGowan, director of the S.C. Department of Parks, Recreation and Tourism. The ninety-three-year-old senator, recently separated from his wife, assessed McGowan for the press and dignitaries: "Not only is she good and capable, but she's good-looking, too. You know how I like good-looking women." Everyone laughed politely.)

Drawing more than ten million visitors a year, Broadway at the Beach was corporate fun, relentlessly bland and upbeat, with uniformed security guards and service personnel to oversee every detail and keep everyone in line. A speaker system broadcast a continuous stream of light pop music throughout the vast complex, along with announcements and promotions for other B&C entertainment venues. On summer nights there were fireworks shows and patriotic music, featuring Lee Greenwood's signature song, "Proud to Be An American." Under B&C's rosy rubric, even the Victoria's Secret lingerie shop and the Smith & Wesson gun shop seemed as wholesome as apple pie.

For Doug Wendel – social engineer and family values crusader – Broadway at the Beach was just the first step in cleaning up Myrtle Beach. Ocean Boulevard remained the ultimate challenge and he held the ultimate weapon. On July 3, 1996, Wendel announced that 1998 would be the Pavilion Amusement Park's last year on Ocean Boulevard. Burroughs & Chapin would open a new 100-acre gated theme park on the Disney model in 1999 at a site near Broadway at the Beach.

For generations of Southerners the news was stunning. "It seems like all my childhood memories took place there," Sal Bennes told the *Charlotte Observer*. "It's very sad."

A spokesman for B&C had a bloodless explanation for the corporate stratagem: "We don't want to lose sight of the market that has made Myrtle Beach what it is today. But this is an upscaling." Few people grasped the implications of that remark in 1996, but they would hear a lot more about "upscaling" in the years to come.

Some observers suspected from the outset that the Pavilion gambit was a bluff on the part of Wendel and the company board. Whatever Wendel's intentions, Mayor Bob Grissom and city council took him seriously. Grissom went to work, meeting quietly with Wendel, lining up help from local politicians and Governor David Beasley, writing letters of intent. On January 30, 1997, Grissom, Wendel and Egerton Burroughs held a news conference at the Pavilion to announce the amusement park would stay on the Boulevard – if the city would commit to a five-year program of downtown redevelopment. "There has to be a total environmental change in land use, new ideas for security, lighting, safety and transportation," Wendel told *The Sun News*. That sweeping agenda included cleaning up Ocean Boulevard.

Politicians worked overtime. City council, local ministers and community leaders traveled to Columbia, where they lobbied for criminal penalties to put teeth in their local laws. City council passed ordinances against the sale of drug paraphernalia and limiting the hours of cruising on the Boulevard. Over the warnings of the American Civil Liberties Union, Representative Mark Kelly introduced a bill that would make it a crime to sell, display or distribute "indecent" material to minors. "People are trying to hide behind the First Amendment to make money selling what I would consider smut," groused the Myrtle Beach tavern owner. "I don't think this is where our forefathers wanted the First Amendment to go." In October 1998, city council capped its long agenda of Boulevard regulations with a ban on body piercing. The linch-pin to the Pavilion rescue plan was downtown redevelopment. The Pavilion Area Task Force was created with a twenty-five-year mandate to remake 300 acres of the downtown and beachfront. A New York consulting firm was paid $182,000 to draft a master plan for the $55 million project.

The executive summary read in part:

> The City of Myrtle Beach and local property owners [Read: Burroughs & Chapin] are concerned about the decline in the number of families visiting downtown. Families are being replaced by a younger crowd and the retail and entertainment development is responding to this market. A general decline in the types and the sameness of merchandise being offered, a lack of variety in eating establishments, growing numbers of body piercing shops, low quality motel accommodations and gener-ally poor building maintenance all add to the perception that the area is changing for the worse. The goal is to attract more families to downtown, give them more things to do and more appropriate merchandise on which to spend their money. . . .

Consider for a moment what might happen if these same criteria were applied to another popular activity − say, golf. It was hardly a family activity and had led to a culture of strip clubs and massage parlors. City and corporate leaders did not seem concerned that 100-plus golf courses and dozens of golf supply and service stores were monotonous, repetitive and one-dimensional. To the contrary, they pointed with pride to industry predictions that there would be 200 golf courses in the area by the year 2010. When the golf and sex industries responded to market demand, the system was working and all was right with the world.

It didn't take an MBA to figure out what was going on here. A great deal of bad behavior could be tolerated if the offender was packing a platinum card on a Fortune 500 corporate account and spending $600 a day on food, lodging and entertainment. But the kid who paid $18 to get a stainless steel stud through his tongue and $16 more for a T-shirt that read "Beer − It's Not Just for Breakfast Anymore!" was a social problem that had to be engineered out of town.

Nevertheless, a corporation was created to execute this master plan. It consisted of eleven city officials and business leaders – all male, all white – including Doug Wendel and B&C consultant Dr. Peter Barr.

The New York Times, Los Angeles Times and *Wall Street Journal* dispatched scribes to report on Myrtle Beach's *Kulturkampf*. "If we were not the magnanimous, loving, caring company we are, we would abandon [the Pavilion]," Wendel told *The New York Times*.

In October 1997, Myrtle Beach got a deeper look into B&C's world of social engineering when *The Sun News* published the story of the "tourist loop," a sweeping plan to segment local tourism into three economic categories and create transportation, housing and entertainment for each. The loop called for a network of hotels, restaurants and attractions allowing tourists to spend their entire vacation on B&C-owned properties. It would be supported by a national advertising campaign and toll-free telephone number.

Lakeshore Village, a cluster of hotels around Broadway at the Beach, would house the low-end tourist segment and offer shuttle service to the beach, two miles away. For the mid-range tourist, B&C would offer South Beach Resort, on the south end of the Boulevard. At the high end of the loop would be Grande Dunes, with its four-star hotels, marinas on the Intracoastal Waterway, golf courses and other amenities. All three segments would have shuttle connections to Broadway at the Beach, for shopping and entertainment. "I'm looking for every component of our society that wishes to go on vacation and are looking for a quality experience," Wendel told *The Sun News*. ". . . I would hope the loop would continue to get broader and broader and wider and wider."

Grande Dunes had been on B&C's drawing board for nearly a decade and it had become a passion for Doug Wendel. What people needed, he reasoned, was an escape from the tackiness and mediocrity of Myrtle Beach. What he gave them was "The Atlantic Coast's Premier Destination Address."

On February 18, 1999, B&C officials presented to the Myrtle Beach Community Appearance Board (CAB) the artist's rendering of its Grande Dunes clubhouse. Designed for exclusive use of Grande Dunes residents, the 40,000-square-foot building would have a "South

Florida look," replete with stepped waterfalls along the approach drive, indoor and outdoor pools, hot tubs, a ballroom and patios for entertaining, and a panoramic ocean view. "I imagine this design will set the tone for the whole project," CAB chairman Larry Bragg announced. "I am very, very pleased with this."

"That's really what they were after – amazement, excitement and the feeling that there's a theme behind it, a level of clientele we are aiming for," B&C spokesman Pat Dowling told *The Sun News*.

"We were looking for something higher-end than we have in the Grand Strand," architect Tom Pegram said. Higher-end, indeed. The 2,200-acre development would offer six residential areas, with homesites starting in the "upper $200s" in Bal Harbor and moving to the "$700s" in Oceanside.

Grande Dunes *was* grand. From the clubhouse at 82nd Avenue North, it sprawled west, across U.S. 17 and U.S. 17 Bypass and – on a 400-foot, $5-million, Mediterranean-style bridge – across the Waterway. "It's not only a bridge, but one of the hallmarks of the development," Dowling gushed. "It is an important piece. It is an amenity that has to be first-class." On the east, Grande Dunes would occupy the one of the last major undeveloped stretches of beach on the Strand. Grande Dunes' 11,000 residents wouldn't have to worry about undesirable elements encroaching on their western flank. The development bordered a state wildlife preserve, a point brought out in its marketing material.

Over a century B&C had built this crazy place called Myrtle Beach, this Redneck Riviera, this flashing, glittering, honking wonder that drew 13 million people a year. Now the company would create the ultimate resort – a place for people to come to Myrtle Beach and never have to *see* Myrtle Beach.

B&C Plays Hardball

The *Saturday Evening Post* illustration of the Dunes Club lounge is more than just a picture of good old boys playing hooky from their wives and kids. The back-slapping, ball-scratching camaraderie is a portrait of the tribal rituals of Myrtle Beach, the informal way commerce and politics have always been conducted. While blacks and women did hold several elective offices in Horry County, no blacks and very few women had been admitted to the inner sanctum of power by 1999. Public council chambers were for show; the real power brokers met over putting greens and cocktails – or in the fourth-floor offices of the Founders Centre.

Linda Angus was thirty-six years old when she was hired, in 1996, to be Horry County's sixth administrator. She was a professional, with a degree in public administration from Marshall University; a West Virginia native, not privy to the ways and wiles of Horry County. She was not used to the courthouse culture, to the casual and unaccountable manner in which business had always been done there. Bob Bestler described the situation this way: "She is younger and brighter than most of the old boys – and girls – who are used to running Horry County; their resentment comes through frequently."

Linda Angus ran headlong into this tradition of cozy, informal business-as-usual, tangling with powerful interests inside and outside the county courthouse. When she tried to standardize county personnel policy, she made a blood enemy of Auditor Lois Eargle, who sought to maintain policy-making power within her department. She made an enemy of Treasurer Johnny Allen when she denied him a pay raise and audited his and Eargle's departments to account for $7 million in unpaid property taxes.

Angus beefed up the county's one-person planning staff, increasing it to eight. With their new muscle, planning staff did more thorough research and made more detailed recommendations to the planning commission. Soon the planning commission, composed of realtors and developers, was regularly overruling the planning staff's zoning recommendations. In one shabby affair, International Paper Co. (IP) prevailed in its effort to pack nearly seven times more apartments than zoning allowed into an eighty-acre tract in its giant Carolina Forest development. According to *The Sun News*, the planning commission granted this dispensation without requiring IP to sign a critical development agreement with the county. County council signed off on the zoning change. By the time Angus and the planning staff learned what had happened, the deed was done and the county had no legal recourse.

No explanation was ever given to the press or the public for the unilateral benefaction to IP, but some facts are known. Planning commission chairman Don Helms was a land broker for IP and *someone* from the commission tried to get the planning staff to drop the condition linking the zoning change to the development agreement. When Angus learned that a commission member – she would not divulge who – had approached staffers about changing their recommendation, she issued a directive that staff members not speak individually with any one commission member. That created more enemies for the administrator. Helms subsequently changed planning commission policy, denying the press or public the right to see staff recommendations before they went to commission members.

It was inevitable that Linda Angus would knock heads with Burroughs & Chapin. One incident with the state Coordinating Council shows how B&C played ball when it wanted something bad enough. The Coordinating Council awarded public money to private companies for infrastructure construction. County governments served as conduits for disbursement of Coordinating Council money and $4 million had been earmarked for B&C's Grande Dunes development. But procurement procedures were not followed, according to the county attorney, and B&C's money was withheld until everything was in order. The county attorney said he informed B&C officers of the problem, but company officials denied they were ever so informed. In time, the Coordinating Council and county officials were satisfied that all was in order with B&C's procurement application. The money was released to the developer, but feelings were already hardening.

Councilwoman Liz Gilland defended Angus in the matter: "There were concerns that she was going by the letter of the law, and B&C didn't want to do that. She was getting in the way of how Burroughs & Chapin does things."

But council Chairman Chad Prosser told *The Sun News*, "I have been told by the Governor's Office that we are not getting another penny from the Coordinating Council as long as that woman is there [as Administrator]."

The Governor's Office staunchly denied Prosser's claim. "There is no truth to that statement," a spokeswoman told *The Sun News*.

The attack on Angus marked a stunning change of course for the new county council chairman. Pampered and self-absorbed, thirty-year-old Chandler "Chad" Prosser was a product of private schools and Johns Hopkins University. After graduation in 1990, he took a job in the first Bush Administration. That job ended after the 1992 election and he came home to Horry County, where "his family had to find a place to put him," a former family employee said. There was plenty of room for young Prosser. His father developed and owned Wachesaw East, one of the most prestigious golf clubs on the Strand. He also owned apartments, condos and rental storage units and brokered real estate. Though Chad Prosser had no real estate experience – and according to one source, "he hated real estate" – he was put in charge of Prosser Real Estate Co.

The thing Chad Prosser really loved was politics. In 1994, he was elected to county council, where he distinguished himself. Bob Bestler credited him with "a sensibility and sophistication beyond his years." In 1998, he ran for county council chairman, receiving the support of *The Sun News* and other progressive elements, in no small part because of his support of Linda Angus. "Prosser's support of Angus . . . has been steadfast," Bestler wrote approvingly.

Prosser won the Republican nomination – tantamount to election – and was sworn in on January 3. And things began to change.

In a subsequent interview, Angus said this to Bob Bestler: "I had always been friends with Chad, but in January I noticed a change in our relationship. I was very naïve. I'm not a very good politician and it took a long time before I really understood what happened."

What happened was this: Burroughs & Chapin had commissioned a survey to learn what Horry County voters thought of various public figures – the kind of survey Dr. Peter Barr helped B&C conduct periodically as a company consultant. Among those named in the survey were the five Republican candidates for county council chairman, Linda Angus, Doug Wendel, Mayor Mark McBride and County Councilwoman Liz Gilland, a sharp critic of B&C. What the survey found was that Angus was the most popular public figure in the county, with Prosser well down the list, especially among women voters.

To manage his campaign, Prosser hired the same public relations firm that had conducted the B&C survey and – not surprisingly – Prosser also learned of the popularity of Linda Angus. With this information in hand, Prosser brought on Kathi Patrick to co-chair his campaign. Patrick was a realtor, a friend of Angus and activist on women's issues. It was her job to soften Prosser's image and make him more appealing to women voters. A critical part in that makeover was to elevate Linda Angus as a campaign issue and emphasize Prosser's "steadfast" support of her.

The ploy worked. With the election behind him, Chairman Prosser joined in the full-court press to fire Linda Angus. At the January 19 council meeting, Prosser diverged sharply and publicly from the administrator, with whom he had enjoyed a close working relationship, over the county's billion-dollar road-building plan. In another very public disagreement, Angus refused to overrule the county zoning administrator for not allowing a landfill on property that was not zoned for a landfill. "Why have zoning laws if you are not going to enforce them?" she later asked.

In this age of giant media acquisitions, a minor media acquisition raised some eyebrows in Horry County. On January 19, 1999, *The Sun News* reported that Deborah Boggs Johnson, founder and publisher of the weekly *Myrtle Beach Herald*, was bringing on partners. The company's stock would be divided into ten equal shares; nine would be sold to local investors; Johnson would retain the tenth.

What bothered some people was that one of those ten investors was none other than B&C. It wasn't clear what a development company with a $1.5 billion project in Myrtle Beach and a $1 billion project in Columbia, plus malls and amusement parks would want with ten percent of a five-year-old weekly newspaper that wasn't even registered with the *Gale Directory of Publications and Broadcast Media*. But B&C spokesman Pat Dowling was quick to explain: "Our interest is purely a business interest," he said. "We think that for the ticket of admission, it's a very good investment in a weekly that's very well done. People like it. Getting in on the ground floor we think is a very good move for us."

Dowling and Johnson went to great trouble to assure that the new partner would not influence editorial content. "We don't get to sit down and look at [Johnson's] next issue and see if we like it," Dowling said. "The news is the news and it will go on like that."

There was irony that surpasses all understanding in having a PR man explain that his development company was getting into the news-paper business purely as an investment. Whatever his pledge of edito-rial independence, within weeks Dowling was attempting to use the *Herald* to smear Linda Angus.

In May, *The Sun News* reported that Dowling recently had received from an anonymous source a package of information detailing "the sins of Linda Angus." He faxed the documents to the *Herald*, including B&C's telephone number, but with no editorial direction, he said. From there the surreptitious papers "found their way into the general public," *The Sun News* reported obliquely. In a subsequent conversa-tion, *Herald* publisher Deborah Boggs Johnson told me that a dis-gruntled former employee pirated the B&C documents out of the newspaper office and made them public.

"There is absolutely no corporate decision that has been made by the board, the president or the staff to undermine Linda Angus," Dowling told *The Sun News*, when his involvement in the matter became known.

Angus' enemies used other channels to undermine her. One of those was conservative talk radio station WRNN, which functioned as a Republican on-air chat room. Another was the Horry County Republican Party, which put out the word that Angus was emotionally and mentally unstable following the birth of her second child, in 1997. "She just went crazy," a GOP hack told me. "It must have been hor-monal or something." *The Sun News* defended Angus editorially, as did most of the letters on the editorial page. Kathi Patrick publicly denounced Prosser and apologized to friends for supporting him.

The centerpiece of the county council case against Angus was an audit of her three years as administrator. In those years, she had received good annual job evaluations by the council and her salary was raised from $80,000 to $120,000 a year. But in May 1999, the council audit cited more than thirty instances where Angus "acted or directed or approved an action" violating state law or county person-nel or procurement policies. There were also allegations that she did not return phone calls, came to meetings late and on one occasion stormed out of an informal lunch meeting with a councilman and a businessman at a local café. Many of the charges in the county council audit were listed among the "sins of Linda Angus" that Pat Dowling faxed to the *Myrtle Beach Herald*.

On May 18, Horry County Council met in a special session for the sole purpose of firing the administrator. Too late, Angus' enemies realized they could muster only five out of 11 votes. It was a humiliating setback for Chairman Prosser. A rancorous 30-minute meeting ended only when the chairman accepted a motion to delay the vote for one week.

Two days later, at upscale Myrtle Beach Martinique Resort Hotel, friends of Chad Prosser held a fundraiser to help retire his $218,000 campaign debt from the previous November. Sponsors for the "Campaign Debt Retirement Party" included none other than B&C President Doug Wendel, as well a local realtor, a highway engineering firm and a transportation consulting firm that did business with the county. B&C consultant Dr. Peter Barr gave $1,000 to Prosser before the election and $2,000 after, according to *The Sun News*. (Barr disputed this figure.) "I just think that the county is moving forward under Chad Prosser's leadership . . . and obviously that's not cheap," Barr said. Other contributors to Prosser's campaign debt relief included the Burroughs & Chapin Co., an outdoor advertiser with billboards around the county, attorneys and individuals with business before county government. Twice since Prosser's election in 1998, meetings were held in B&C's boardroom, in which those in attendance were urged to raise money to retire Prosser's campaign debt.

Explaining B&C's philosophy of campaign funding, spokesman Pat Dowling said, ". . . we focus on candidates who have talent and are committed more to the community than to their own political careers."

On May 25, county council met again and this time they were ready. This time, Marvin Heyd – the critical swing vote they thought they had in their pocket the week before – had seen the light. This time – in front of a packed chamber of angry citizens – council voted 6-5 to fire Linda Angus. Heyd maintained steadfastly that his employment as head of the residential real estate division at Burroughs & Chapin had nothing to do with his decision. Likewise, B&C maintained that it had no hand in the firing, though there is no question the company wanted Angus removed and worked to poison the public attitude toward her.

For her part, Angus brought suit against Doug Wendel, Pat Dowling, Deborah Boggs Johnson, Chad Prosser, Marvin Heyd and other council members, claiming defamation, civil conspiracy and personal damages. The suit was dismissed in state court. I investigated her claims against the defendants, finding some of them refuted by documentary evidence and the memories of others. Furthermore, in months of trying to interview her, I found her behavior quite bizarre and evasive.

Despite her faults, Linda Angus had been a fresh breeze through the musky locker room of Horry County politics. The day after her firing *The Sun News* editorialized, "This is a sorry day for Horry County government in a decade of stormy days that seemed to perpetuate themselves, one political *faux pas* after another. . . . This is a watershed day for the council, because it has not proved publicly that its decision was proper. . . . This case is not over. We fear it has only just begun. Until it reaches closure, or beyond, Horry County will be the loser."

Doug Wendel Wants A Park

For more than three centuries, South Carolina has been under the sway of a small group of wealthy and powerful white men, who controlled both the state government and the state economy. In recent decades, the old julep-sipping plutocrats have been shunted aside by a rabidly pro-development class of *nouveau riche*, *nouveau* Republicans. Like the old ruling class, their instincts are elitist and undemocratic. They work tirelessly to keep unions out and wages low. They are ideologically opposed to government regulation of any economic activity. They seek to expand the private sector to include education, law enforcement, utilities and other traditionally public areas of civic life.

The result of their influence was obvious to anyone who had spent much time in South Carolina, one of the least developed, most economically and culturally backward places in the United States. South Carolina had the lowest percentage of unionized workers in the nation. Labor and environmental laws were among the weakest anywhere. The South Carolina Chamber of Commerce shamelessly boasted of low wages and lack of regulation in recruiting industry to the state.

To the state's *parvenu* class, government was viewed as a bunch of meddling, bureaucratic ninnies. Yet there was one government role that was never questioned: industrial recruitment. South Carolina had joined other Sunbelt states in a "race to the bottom," to see who could give away the most tax breaks and other incentives to lure new industry across their borders. South Carolina had won the battle for new jobs but lost the war to improve its way of life.

In 1998, the state's largess induced 1,395 companies to locate or expand in South Carolina, according to the state Commerce Department. Since 1990, the state added 200,000 jobs, 300,000 people and 43,000 school children. Yet its roads and schools were crumbling; its teachers and law enforcement officers were among the lowest paid in the nation; its education and public health systems ranked among the worst. Its infant mortality rate was comparable to that of Third World countries. Most of the social ills that plagued South Carolina when it was knee-deep in cotton still haunted it a century later. The reason is too subtle for most people to grasp and the state's leaders were happy to keep them in the dark. The truth is that South Carolina had mortgaged its future with an array of corporate incentives, slashing taxes on movable businesses by $2.7 billion, even as its population was exploding and infrastructure was collapsing.

A little-noticed legislative study released early in 1999 showed that the state would need to spend $57 billion on roads, schools, sewers and other infrastructure by the year 2015 – even though it could not deliver adequate services in 1999 and its industrial tax base was actually shrinking. In this atmosphere, state and local governments raised taxes on real estate, retail sales, restaurant sales, vehicles, gasoline, entertainment admissions, hotel rooms and telephone service, plus utility rates and other fees. The new taxes inevitably sparked a backlash and fueled conservative resentment of all government and social services.

For those in the construction, real estate and financial service industries, the 1980s and 1990s were decades of unprecedented prosperity. Yet the state's average manufacturing wage rose only five percent from 1994 to 1998, less than the rate of inflation.

South Carolina's corporate incentives were "promiscuous," Wall Street financier Darla Moore told *The Baltimore Sun*. "South Carolina will give everything away not to lose a business to Georgia or Florida. . . . If something isn't done, they're going to be beyond the point of recovery. Nobody has put this together: What's happening with the businesses, what's happening with the schools."

BMW was the crown jewel of South Carolina's industrial recruitment – and the shining proof of its folly. When the German automotive giant opened its plant in Spartanburg County in 1994, it brought 2,500 jobs and twenty-two auxiliary companies with it. Less publicized were the giveaways: more than $150 million in tax breaks, $40 million for an airport for BMW planes, millions more for training BMW employees. Under BMW's sweetheart deal, the company paid one dollar a year to lease its $36 million piece of real estate and paid no property tax to Spartanburg County.

In 1998, BMW paid $8.1 million in state and local taxes – less than two percent of the company's worldwide taxes for the year.

In the late 1980s the General Assembly sweetened the deal for corporate gypsies, introducing two new incentive packages. One was the tax increment finance district; the other was the multicounty business park. Both were based on the principle of allowing a company to pay "fees in lieu of tax." Under "fees in lieu" agreements, counties and municipalities could authorize companies to use money they would have paid in local property taxes to build infrastructure to support their own developments. These giveaways came on top of whatever tax breaks and other concessions a company could squeeze out of state government.

"It's a feeding frenzy," said the chairman of an upstate textile company that had operated a century without such incentives. "Not only do you have the state doing incentives, but you've got localities . . . doing it. What are the infrastructure needs that are not being funded?"

In 1994, Burroughs & Chapin kicked a hornets nest of angry taxpayers when it bamboozled the City of Myrtle Beach into creating a tax increment finance (TIF) district to pay for the infrastructure in the giant Broadway at the Beach and Seaboard Commons developments. After months of public outrage and threatened litigation, B&C reached an agreement to pay off Horry County taxpayers and the school district for lost tax revenues. In a warm and fuzzy news conference at City Hall in November 1994, all parties met to announce an agreement had been reached. "We've learned our lesson well," a contrite Doug Wendel said, seeming to refer to his lack of communication with elected officials.

Five years later, some people would wonder just what lesson Wendel had taken away from that brief skirmish.

On April 28, 1999, *The Sun News* reported that Burroughs & Chapin would ask county council to create a 7,175-acre business park. It would be the largest business park in South Carolina and the first in Horry County and it would encompass the Mall of South Carolina, Grande Dunes and twenty-five other B&C projects. "This is one of the most monumental projects we've ever been involved in," Wendel exulted. And this time Wendel would be ready for his critics. His strategy was to strike fast, to overwhelm his adversaries with an avalanche of figures, projections and legalisms, then demand a quick decision on the project before the opposition could mobilize, as it had done against tax increment financing, in 1994.

In May 1999, very few people in Horry County – including city and county officials – had any idea what a multicounty business park was or how it worked. "It is something that's new, so there are a lot of issues we've got to look at," county council chairman Chad Prosser told *The Sun News*. But B&C officials had been planning for eighteen months and had all the answers.

The business park was similar to the TIF district, but unlike TIF, which captures all taxes generated within the district, the business park would leave residential property taxes untouched. But taxes from commercial, tourism and industrial development would not go into the public coffers, as other taxes do. By a jesuitic stroke of the pen, they would be converted to "fees" and divvied up in a complex formula: 49.5 percent would be split between the City of Myrtle Beach and Horry County; one percent would go to an adjacent "partner county," to be determined at a later date; and 49.5 percent would go to B&C to build roads, sewers and other infrastructure for the company projects. These expenses had traditionally been paid by developers as a cost of doing business.

The business park provided huge advantages for B&C and huge problems for almost everyone else. Connected to the business park would be a development agreement with the city and the county. The city and county councils would change zoning to meet B&C's development plans and then freeze zoning for the thirty-year life of the business park, with an option to renew the park for another thirty years. Within the 7,175-acre park, the city and the county would exempt the company from drainage, impact and other fees. In exchange, the city would be allowed to annex more than 2,500 acres of B&C property. The county would help the company float $30.5 million dollars in low-interest revenue bonds to build roads and sewers to support its 1.3 million-square-foot Mall of South Carolina. Ultimately, the business park would finance as much as $600 million in infrastructure to support B&C's projects.

The bond issue to pay for the mall infrastructure was absolutely critical, Wendel said. Without it, the company would have to pay for its own infrastructure. "If you included that in the equation, it would consume the profit," he explained with no trace of irony.

"I would like to have had that [development incentive] without having to put everything in myself," Joe Garrell, co-owner of a real estate company that competed with B&C, told *The Sun News*.

Environmentally, B&C's sweeping proposal was a disaster. In March, Myrtle Beach and Horry County had adopted comprehensive land use plans, which took tentative steps to control sprawl and create a more pedestrian-friendly environment over the next twenty years. B&C's brave new world – drawn up without input from city or county planners – called for thousands of acres of cul-de-sac suburbs and detached shopping centers. It was a blueprint for decades of further sprawl and traffic congestion.

But the greatest alarm was reserved for the plight of the schools. Under the multicounty business park law, the Horry County School District would be completely cut out of the funding equation and dependent on the city and county to give it a portion of their fees. Myrtle Beach and Horry officials were quick to assure that the schools would be properly funded, but it said more than words could ever speak that South Carolina's General Assembly would create this monstrously complex form of corporate welfare with absolutely no regard for its impact on public education.

There were other objections to the business park. Authorized by constitutional amendment in 1988, the multicounty business park was designed to help counties bring high-paying manufacturing jobs into their borders. Of course, B&C was already in Horry County and its land was quite fixed and immovable. Furthermore, the thousands of jobs B&C promised to create would not be high-paying or manufacturing. They would be retail and service jobs, averaging six dollars to eight dollars an hour. Of more than 200 business parks created since 1988, B&C's would be the first to serve the tourism industry. "Tourism is as legitimate an industry as smokestacks," Wendel told *The Sun News*. But that was beside the point. The business park law was never drafted to promote tourism and it was never meant to promote development that was clearly going to take place anyway.

There was another feature of B&C's proposed business park that seemed to stretch the intent of the law. Under the business park legislation, smaller parks were entitled to fewer benefits and, most importantly, shorter periods to have zoning frozen. The larger the park, the longer the zoning freeze, up to thirty years. To make its business park qualify for maximum benefits, B&C bundled together twenty-seven noncontiguous tracts and called them one business park. That was also a first in South Carolina and another creative abuse of the law.

But nothing demonstrated the company's shameless opportunism more than its unseemly haste. While B&C had taken a year and a half to develop its vast multicounty business park scheme, it would allow the county and the city only two months to study the plan and vote it up or down. Development agreements with both entities must be signed no later than July 1, B&C officials said; otherwise the $160 million mall would be dead. B&C's development partner would pull out, along with the anchor stores, which had committed to the project. If the business park were not approved by July 1, the county would lose thousands of jobs and millions of tax dollars. July 1 was D-Day for Horry County.

But wait a minute. Could this really be?

The Mall of South Carolina had been on the drawing board since at least 1997. A major out-of-state mall developer had signed on as a partner to build the behemoth. Anchor stores and smaller retailers were already on board. But Burroughs & Chapin had waited until the end of April 1999 – barely two months before the drop-dead date – to unveil the most critical element of the entire venture – the multicounty business park. Were B&C planners and executives really so stupid? Or did they hope to ram the business park through the city and county councils before the public could figure out what an insidious vehicle it truly was?

The Sun News never asked those questions and Burroughs & Chapin steadfastly refused to give me an interview. So the questions have never been answered. But B&C vice president Bill Prichard gave a simple explanation for his company's haste: "Because we're ready to move." In Horry County that was good enough.

As reporters, politicians and the public settled in to digest the details of the vast multicounty business park plan, other data were coming in. The Travel Industry Association of America released figures in May, projecting South Carolina would not be among the top ten states for tourism in 1999. Ashby Ward was incredulous that Washington State was listed No. 9. "Washington State is going to get more visitors than South Carolina? I don't believe it's going to work out like that. I can't believe that." Ward preferred the findings of Stan Plog Research, Inc., which showed Myrtle Beach tied with Orlando, Florida, as North America's No. 2 vacation spot. The American Automobile Association predicted Myrtle Beach would be the second most popular destination for its members in the summer of '99, behind Orlando.

A new report, out of Old Dominion University, in Virginia, confirmed Horry County's standing with one of the lowest pay scales in the nation: $20,291 per capita, against a national average of $22,331.

The last week of May was bad for children and retirees. First came the release of the 1999 Kids Count report on the condition of children in the United States. Not surprisingly, South Carolina ranked forty-seventh in the nation for children living in vulnerable and impoverished families and forty-ninth for children dying before the age of fourteen. In Horry County in 1997, 40.6 percent of births were to single mothers; 23.8 percent of children lived in single-parent families and 26.8 percent of children lived in poverty in 1995, according to the study funded by the Annie E. Casey Foundation.

"That's something that happens with younger families," the state director of Kids Count told *The Sun News*. "Families are a lot more disadvantaged when they are young."

That same week the latest edition of David Savageau's *Retirement Places Rated*, ranked Myrtle Beach No. 94 out of 187 retirement destinations in the country. The mediocre rating was based on a higher-than-average cost of living, high crime rate and high incidence of hurricanes. But more bitter than the ranking itself was the fact that Hilton Head Island came in at No. 51 and the Charleston Sea Islands were No. 2.

Among lists of best places to live, this was only the latest poor showing by Myrtle Beach, causing *Sun News* business editor David Wrenn to go into a deep meditation on what it all meant: ". . . as fast as this area's population is growing," he wrote, "so is a sense of discontent among residents who feel this area's sense of community slipping away."

Wren interviewed Duke University sociologist Linda George, who explained that the Grand Strand attracts most of its population from the two extremes – retirees who have already done their community building and now look for a quiet place to fade away; and young transients who come to the beach for the low-paying service industry jobs.

"The healthy middle is disproportionately small compared to most places in the United States," George said. Without that "healthy middle" to bind together the extremes, it's hard to plan for growth or development, because the perspectives of the two extremes are so different. "Developers probably will have an easier time doing what they want to in an environment like that," George predicted.

"People are going to feel assaulted on many fronts," she told Wrenn, "so things will slip through the cracks. If it's just one thing, like a shopping mall, people can get together on that, but there's going to be so much development and so many problems, from traffic to schools deteriorating to environmental protection, that the community will be fragmented, and that lessens the chance that any one of those issues will be handled effectively."

Myrtle Beach seemed destined to become an ever larger collection of individuals pursuing different lives in different ways, George said. "It's going to be more and more of an anything-goes kind of place."

May 25, 1999: At the meeting of Myrtle Beach City Council, Mayor Mark McBride's colleagues excoriated him for his continued obstruction of the Convention Center hotel project, which was already approved by council. McBride doggedly grilled the city's bonding attorney, questioned the integrity of contractor's representatives and the competence of City Attorney Joe Wettlin. Councilman Wayne Gray apologized to the contractor's representatives and turned to McBride. "Where have you been for the past two years?" he demanded hotly. McBride tried to gavel him down, but council voted unanimously to give Gray privilege to speak. "We've gone through this for the past two and a half years," Gray continued. "When are you going to get it?"

McBride snapped at Gray and Councilman Chuck Martino for trying to rein him in, then gaveled down Councilwoman Rachel Broadhurst for criticizing him.

Next item on the agenda: Doug Wendel, Peter Barr, Pat Dowling and other Burroughs & Chapin lieutenants came forward to formally present to council the company's plan for its multibillion-dollar, thirty-year, 7,175-acre business park.

They stood in stark contrast to the elected representatives before them. In the contentious, psychotic atmosphere of the council chamber, these men − and they were all men, white, middle-aged, impeccably corporate − were a model of discipline and cooperation. They brought their maps, charts and spread sheets. They answered questions on command. They all knew their lines. No one spoke out of turn. There was just enough grinning and hand-shaking to give the show a touch of folksiness, but no one who saw Wendel & Co. sweep into the chamber and make their presentation could doubt this was the real thing. These were the Pros from Dover. These were the can-do guys. They did not come to supplicate. They came to negotiate. They were socially and economically superior to the officials on the dais before them. They were deferred to and treated as visiting sovereigns. Rarely have I seen democracy appear so impotent or incompetent.

In Conway, at that very hour, Horry County Council was unceremoniously sacking Administrator Linda Angus on a 6-to-5 vote. It was a very good night for Burroughs & Chapin.

Larceny in the Blood

South Carolina is reputed to have the most corrupt legislature in the nation, and Operation Lost Trust provided the proof. In 1989, U.S. Justice Department agents quietly moved into Columbia, set up a false company to promote pari-mutuel betting, used a convicted lobbyist named Ron Cobb as their sting and made it known there was money available for those willing to support a pari-mutuel bill. The crudeness of the offer was exceeded only by the enthusiasm of the respondents. Lawmakers lined up at Cobb's door. When the feds closed down the operation and issued indictments in July 1990, twenty-eight legislators, lobbyists and assorted state officials had been snared.

Operation Lost Trust provided a segment for "60 Minutes" and a topic for months of speculation and debate in South Carolina. It led to sweeping reforms in state ethics rules, expansion of state grand jury powers, massive reorganization of state government – and years of trials, appeals and retrials. Eight years after the trap was sprung, former state Senator J.M. "Bud" Long was the last person awaiting justice. He had long ago been convicted of bribery. Jurors thought the videotape of the senator stuffing twenty-eight hundred-dollar bills into his pocket as he discussed the pari-mutuel bill with Cobb was thoroughly convincing.

In 1992, Long got his conviction thrown out on a technicality and a new trial was granted. After more years of maneuvering and delays, the seventy-two-year-old former prosecutor and Myrtle Beach city judge had run out of options. Standing before Federal Judge Charles Haden in Columbia, on June 30, 1999, Long pleaded guilty to the simple charge of lying to federal investigators when he denied receiving the $2,800. Because he was not under oath at the time, he had not committed perjury. Most importantly, it seems Long was able to convince federal prosecutors that the money was a personal gift from his longtime friend Ron Cobb.

Cobb certainly had reason to feel beholden to the Horry County senator. Long had introduced Cobb around the county and had been instrumental in helping him land $61,000 in local contracts. "I was impressed with his ability to get things done and with his relationship with leaders of the House. . . . " Long told *The Sun News* in August 1990. "I figured he would be less expensive than some others." Through Long's introduction, Cobb received a $15,000 contract with the Area Council on Transportation to lobby for funds to build the Conway Bypass and other roads. And Long got Cobb through the door at Grand Strand Water & Sewer Authority, where he pulled down $46,000 over four years. On his resumé to GSW&SA's then-executive director Doug Wendel, Cobb described himself in 1986 as "active professionally and socially with a majority of the members of the General Assembly, many state agencies including the Dept. of Highways and Public Transportation." The first reference on his resumé was Bud Long.

From 1986 to 1990, Cobb earned his check from GSW&SA, landing state and federal grants worth $1.4 million for the utility company. He also worked for amendments that would shield GSW&SA from a wetlands protection bill and worked on a municipal annexation bill for the company in 1987. Cobb got results, for sure. But he also got greedy and as his price went up, company directors decided they could do without his services. "We appreciated what he did for us," Wendel told *The Sun News*. "But he felt he was underpaid and the board felt he was getting expensive."

Corruption is so endemic to the business and political culture of Horry County that the public becomes inured. Because prosecutors and courts rarely have the guts to send white-collar criminals to jail, selling the public trust carries little risk and much opportunity. When everything has a price and making a dollar is the highest human endeavor, even the schools are not safe. In 1995, Horry County school board Chairman Richard Heath and school Superintendent Gary Smith were indicted on charges of bid-rigging in connection with computer purchases and accepting gratuities from IBM. Charges were dropped against Smith in return for his resignation. In dropping charges against Heath, local prosecutor Ralph Wilson cited the high cost of going to trial and the "burden upon the citizens and taxpayers."

Corruption could be as sinister as building inspectors allowing contractors to put in whole developments without county permits. Or it could be as petty as furnishing false documents that allowed friends and associates to avoid paying taxes on their automobiles. That's what Horry County Auditor Jack Gerrald pleaded guilty to in 1989. State investigators said the thirty-two-year veteran auditor cost the county $40,000 in unpaid taxes. In return, he received such gifts as a new set of tires, a dishwasher and a refrigerator. He also received a three-year sentence in state prison; his deputy auditor and a clerk got probation and a fine.

Among twenty-three people who pleaded guilty to furnishing false documents to Gerrald were developer Philip Permenter and landscaper Willie Lee Todd. Their attorney was Bud Long, who praised his clients after their May 10, 1989, court appearance: "They've spent most of their lives performing public service to the community. I'm proud, as we stand here today, to call them my friends."

Also pleading guilty that day was North Myrtle Beach developer Rayford Vereen, former North Myrtle Beach City Council member, chairman of the board of GSW&SA, friend and benefactor of Doug Wendel. Vereen was sentenced to a year's probation and ten days of community service. Community leaders rushed to excuse his "error in judgment." Among them was GSW&SA executive director Wendel: "It is with regret and sadness that we have learned of Mr. Vereen's plea to a misdemeanor," Wendel said in a prepared statement. "This is a personal matter affecting Mr. Vereen and his business and not the Grand Strand Water & Sewer Authority. . . . in all dealings with [GSW&SA] he has been a gentleman beyond reproach."

The list of characters charged with public corruption in Horry County would read like the begattings of the Old Testament – a tedious recitation of insignificant and forgotten figures. But among the host of crooked cops and clerks, mayors and magistrates, one stands above the rest like Moses on Mount Sinai. Indeed, "Young Moses" is what some of his supporters called Sixth District Congressman John Jenrette. To many of his black constituents across the rural Pee Dee wasteland, Jenrette was a new messiah. A Democratic operative told me he had been in African-American homes in the 1970s in which there were three pictures on the wall: Jesus Christ, Martin Luther King Jr. and John Jenrette.

To his colleagues in the U.S. House of Representatives, he was a rising star, destined, some said, to be Speaker. With craggy, handsome features and brown wavy hair, the populist Democrat was a passionate, instinctive politician. "No one ever worked a room like John Jenrette," one of his admirers told me.

Jenrette grew up working cotton, corn and tobacco on his family's fifty-acre farm in the interior of Horry County. A star on the Loris High School football team, he was gregarious and charming, the center of attention at shag clubs in North Myrtle Beach. He won a football scholarship to Wofford College, followed by the University of South Carolina Law School, where he was elected president of the Student Bar Association. Everything he touched turned to gold. He married, started a family and opened a law office in North Myrtle Beach. In 1964, he was elected to the state House of Representatives.

Eight years later – against all odds and the advice of friends and pundits – Jenrette challenged thirty-four-year veteran Congressman John McMillan in the Sixth District Democratic primary. He won the nomination in a runoff but was defeated in the general election by Republican Ed Young. Two years later Jenrette ran again and defeated Young. At age thirty-seven, he was on his way to Washington, where he was elected the first-ever freshman Majority Whip.

But the charmed life of John Jenrette was about to take a dark turn. His drinking came to control his behavior and judgment and his marriage broke up in 1975. A year later the *Charlotte Observer* reported that Jenrette borrowed $870,000 to develop real estate in North Myrtle Beach, using as collateral tracts of land he did not own, which were under water or were mortgaged. A federal grand jury investigated but returned no indictments. Yet he still seemed to have the golden touch in 1976, when he took as his second bride a blond bombshell from Texas named Rita Carpenter.

In January 1980, Jenrette and a business associate named John Stowe went to a townhouse in the Georgetown area of Washington, D.C. There they met a man they were told was an Arab sheik who needed a special immigration bill allowing him to stay in the United States. He was willing to pay his "friends" in Congress a lot of money to introduce and pass the legislation. The sheik offered the South Carolina congressman $100,000, with $50,000 up front. Jenrette, who was drunk at the meeting, infamously responded, "I got larceny in my blood; I'd take it in a goddamn minute."

The answer became infamous because it was taped by FBI agents in history's most famous sting investigation – ABSCAM. Seven congressmen, a United States senator and other politicos were netted and, in June 1980, Jenrette was indicted on three counts of conspiracy and bribery. Maintaining his innocence, he claimed he was a victim of his own alcoholism and an FBI vendetta. Back home in the Sixth District, his constituents seemed to buy his story. Less than two weeks after the indictment they nominated him for a fourth term in Congress. His wife Rita stood by her man, walking with him arm-in-arm to the courthouse each day of his five-week trial, winning wide notice both for her faithfulness and her beauty. On October 7, 1980, a federal jury in Washington convicted Jenrette on all counts. Still, he refused to withdraw from the congressional race and nearly defeated Republican John Napier on November 4.

Jenrette's life went into free-fall. Rita left him in February 1981 and made a memorable "statement" in a *Playboy* magazine "pictorial essay" that same month. Later that year she published her tell-all memoir, *My Capital Secrets*, then went on to a brief acting career that involved some off-Broadway and two low points in film history, *Zombie Island Massacre* and *Malibu Bikini Shop*. In July 1981, John and Rita were divorced.

For John Jenrette, the nightmare had only begun. In December 1981, he was sentenced to two years in prison and fined $20,000. For three years Jenrette and his attorneys fought for a new trial, but in April 1985 he reported to a federal prison near Atlanta, where he served fifteen months. Released on parole, he returned to Horry County to open a public relations firm and start over.

Jenrette's name still carried great cachet and he traded on it well. Even prison could not diminish the boyish charm, the populist fire, the hunger for adulation. He started working the fried chicken circuit, shaking hands, being seen with the right people. Most importantly, state and local Democrats were not afraid to be seen with him. He spoke publicly of his triumph over alcoholism and established the John Jenrette Center for the Children of Alcoholics. Few doubted he was planning a run for his old Sixth District seat in 1990. The golden boy still had the touch.

On December 7, 1988, Jenrette was in Fairfax County, Virginia, when he decided to do some shopping. That afternoon, cameras and security guards in a Tyson Corners department store caught Jenrette altering price tags on several articles of clothing and walking out of the store in a pair of shoes he had not paid for. He was arrested and, on February 24, 1989, convicted of shoplifting, fined $1,000 and ordered to serve fifteen days in the county jail. Jenrette was allowed to return to Horry County to serve his 200 hours of community service doing research in the public defender's office.

This time the golden boy did not rise from the ashes. This time the humiliation and self-destruction were complete.

In 1999, Jenrette was living with his third wife – an elementary school principal – in their comfortable oceanfront house on North Ocean Boulevard. He seemed to have no further political ambitions, though he did get around to political events and still loved to press the flesh. He supported himself as a professional deal-maker. A Democratic operative called him a "facilitator," somebody who brought people, money and ideas together for a fee.

When I went to interview Jenrette at his home, he met me at the door, wearing dark blue nylon sweats, wire-rimmed glasses and a thick gold chain around his neck. There was gray in his swept-back brown hair. He had developed a slight potbelly, but his face was still lean and tanned. What struck me was that he was subdued and resigned. The energy and charisma that once electrified audiences were gone. His moment had passed and he knew it.

He ushered me into the sun room overlooking the beach and asked me to excuse him while he completed a phone conversation in another room. I had several minutes to admire the colonnaded arbor across the front of the house, the exquisite antiques and oriental carpets, the bamboo blinds and plants, the writing desk and leather executive chair, as I gazed across the beach to the vast gray ocean and pondered the wages of sin. From a back room I could hear the former congressman talking excitedly about golf courses and contracts, photographers and satellite uplink services.

Though he served as Jenrette's chief-of-staff during the congressman's last two years in Washington, Doug Wendel was never linked to Jenrette's misconduct and downfall. Wendel found his way back to Horry County in 1983, when Rayford Vereen, as chairman of Grand Strand Water & Sewer, promoted him for the job of director.

Through the years, Vereen and Wendel had remained close friends. By contrast, Jenrette and Wendel lived only a few blocks apart in their respective oceanfront houses but saw each other only occasionally. "Doug I would consider a friend and I think he considers me a friend. We don't stay in touch a great deal. . . ," Jenrette told me. "We've had lunch, we've had dinner. He's been a guest in my home. . . . We're not buddy-buddies every day, by any means." The former golden boy grinned wanly. "He gets up too early and starts too early for me."

In 1999, Doug Wendel's star was rising like a comet across the Grand Strand and South Carolina. Along the way, two of his associates – John Jenrette and Rayford Vereen – had met public disgrace and settled into quiet obscurity. Like the sands of a beach, memories are in constant flux and flow, constantly in need of reshaping and rebuilding to better serve our needs. John Jenrette, for example, proudly remembered getting Wendel hired as city manager of North Myrtle Beach – a claim not borne out by documentation or the memories of others. To Jenrette – whose business card carried the Seal of Congress and the designation "Former Member United States Congress" – Doug Wendel was still a friend. On his official Burroughs & Chapin resume, Wendel stated only that he was administrative assistant to an unnamed Sixth District congressman.

Timing, they say, is everything. On July 1, the day after former Senator Bud Long pleaded guilty to lying to federal investigators, *The Sun News* reported the FBI was investigating the relationship of politicians and developers in Horry County. Seven people told the paper they were interviewed by federal investigators; five had turned over documents. Among the issues the FBI seemed most curious about were campaign donations by area companies and their officers to local politicians; relationships between political appointees and developers; an alleged conspiracy to get Linda Angus fired as county administrator; efforts by county council to sell the county railroad; and alleged efforts by county council chairman Chad Prosser to overrule the zoning administrator, allowing Land South Partners to get a site rezoned for a landfill.

The newspaper quoted a lot of name-calling among the usual suspects. I got a few ugly phone calls and e-mails myself. Since my arrival in Myrtle Beach in April, there had been speculation – and I had heard some of it – that I was an investigator for Burroughs & Chapin, for Linda Angus, for various politicians or other interests. Now the word was out – *I was a Fed!* Three of my sources contacted me after *The Sun News* story, demanding to know who I *really* was. I was able to mollify two of them, but the third refused to have any further contact with me.

Welcome to Never-Never Land

Under Doug Wendel's leadership, the Burroughs & Chapin Co. has made several forays beyond the parochial confines of Horry County, attempting major developments and entertainment venues in several Southeastern cities. Those projects have been stopped or stymied in almost every case. Most notable was the $1.5-billion Green Diamond development, which the company proposed for the Congaree River flood plain, outside Columbia, South Carolina. "The company's strategy in presenting its argument has really put the community off to a great extent," said Kit Smith, chairwoman of Richland County Council. "It has not served them well with that aggressive strategy." Environmentalists and community leaders joined forces to kill the project, despite two years and hundreds of thousands of dollars in corporate lobbying.

But in Horry County, B&C still had the magic touch, still had the power to wrap politicians, the media and the public around its diamond-studded pinky. There are many reasons for this. The most obvious is the public's love of bread and circuses.

For many residents, Myrtle Beach is a land of escapism, of fantasy and wish fulfillment. They come to get rich on a quick development deal; they come to have a mid-life crisis or to prolong their adolescence, some well into middle age. Whatever draws them, they are not here to become citizens, not here to vote or get involved in public policy issues. That stuff is for grownups – people like Doug Wendel. Myrtle Beach is Never-Never Land, where Peter Pan and Wendy sing and dance the night away. And if they are lucky, they never have to go home.

Over California rolls in a North Myrtle Beach sushi bar I mentioned Doug Wendel and the business park to a young lady named Traci, who could not disguise her indifference. She was a waitress who had lived in North Myrtle Beach nearly two years. As her eyes glazed over, I took the opportunity to explore her ignorance of the region.

Seems she had never heard of Myrtle Beach Mayor Mark McBride, or her own mayor in North Myrtle Beach; had never heard of Burroughs & Chapin or the multicounty business park. She had heard that some-one planned to build a giant mall somewhere in the area and that seemed to excite her. The young lady wrestling with the chopsticks across the table from me was typical of the transient, hedonistic young people of the Grand Strand. Her awareness of the world began with pop culture and ended with consumerism.

Filling the food, beverage and entertainment service jobs along the Grand Strand were thousands of such twenty-something women with names like Ashleigh and Kristi and Heather, with their liposuc-tioned thighs and silicone-implanted breasts; and thousands of twenty-something guys with names like Kevin and Jason and Sean, with their gold chains and their spiked, tipped hair. They tend bars, wait tables, manage clubs and restaurants and take their clothes off to entertain strangers. Some of them do it only for a summer or two; others for a year or two. Some get addicted to the easy money and fast life – to say nothing of the drugs and alcohol – and they stay long after they should have moved on with their lives. Like the kids on the Boulevard, they come for the thrills and the freedom. They are older, better educated, but just as lost and alienated in their own ways. Their lives appear to be one endless Michelob commercial – an homage to cheer-ful, stylish hedonism. On closer examination, one suspects there's something darker going on.

Sheila was nearly thirty when I met her, trying desperately to hold onto her youth with daily workouts, pills and every fad diet that came along. She came to North Myrtle Beach on spring break during her junior year at Appalachian State University. On a fateful, moonlit, beer-drenched evening, she fell in love with a bartender named Michael and her life was never the same. She returned to campus long enough to pack her bags and tell her sorority sisters she was going to get married and live happily ever after.

Back on the Strand, she moved in with her new beau and got a job as a hostess in a calabash seafood restaurant. When she turned twenty-one, she moved up to working as a cocktail waitress in a North Myrtle Beach club. She was making lots of money, meeting lots of new people and having the time of her young life. And she was getting tired of Michael's wandering eye and cocaine habit. They split after several of Michael's violent outbursts and she spent the next eight years in a suc-cession of service jobs and unhappy relationships. Her family tried to convince her it was time to leave the beach. They arranged a sales job for her in the Greensboro area. But "things didn't work out," she told me cryptically. Within six months, she was back in North Myrtle Beach, tending bar.

Sheila was briefly married to a restaurant manager, followed by other short-lived affairs. One of them was violent and ugly, but she didn't leave the guy until he put her in the hospital with cracked ribs and a torn rotator cuff. In the weeks she was out of work with her arm in a sling, she moved back in with her former husband. She told me it was the happiest life she could remember since childhood. But he could not control his cocaine use and she did not want to follow him down that path. By the time I knew her, she had two DUI arrests, as well as convictions for shoplifting and marijuana possession. She was living alone, dabbling in Eastern religion, trying to quit smoking, trying to make some sense of it all.

Sheila was emblematic of thousands of women on the Grand Strand. Like Sheila, most came from broken homes and makeshift families. They typically had one or two years of college and spoke vaguely of going back some day to study art or early childhood education. I never met one who displayed any interest in art or education, but these were perceived as fields that require minimum academic labor. For those who had stopped kidding themselves about college, there were careers as models and flight attendants. All they had to do, they told me, was make a few phone calls and fill out the application. Some of them had been promising to do it for years, but they were going to wait until the season was over, because right now they were making too much money and having too much fun.

There was plenty of both for a young woman who didn't mind keeping late hours and putting up with the boorish side of masculine nature. For those who did not like the late hours, there were the golf courses, where "beverage girls" cruised the links in golf carts with coolers full of beer, bottled water and sodas. On a good day, one girl told me, she could make $200 or more. "They just hand me a five dollar bill and say 'keep the change, sweetie.'" On the down side, she had to put up with almost daily propositions.

Closely related to the food and beverage servers were the "exotic entertainers." Melanie and her boyfriend Lew came to Myrtle Beach from Muncie, Indiana. They were watching the news on a cold winter night two years earlier. Outside, the world was covered with snow and ice. On the television screen was Florida, warm and sunny. They counted up their resources and knew they would not have enough to reach Florida. But there was Myrtle Beach. They loaded what they could in their car and headed south, arriving late at night on the Boulevard. The town was quiet, dark and empty. Melanie told Lew to stop in a hotel parking lot. The two of them sat in the warm car, looking out at the waves breaking on the dark beach. They were in the Promised Land.

Lew took a job behind the bar at a Myrtle Beach restaurant and Melanie went to work in one of the low-end strip clubs. No audition. No experience needed. "I never dreamed of doing anything like this," she told me in genuine surprise. "I come from such an old-fashioned sort of family. . . . People make such a big deal out of it, like it's dirty or something, but of course it's not – not unless you make it dirty. I mean, it's just *dancing*."

There were hundreds of women in the Myrtle Beach area who made their living as Melanie did – and a good living it was, for many of them. Several hundred dollars a night was not unusual. Melanie said she once had a golfer give her seven hundred-dollar bills through the course of an evening, then come back and do it again the next night.

A popular trick with some dancers was the old tuition scam. Once a girl had some poor fool eating out of her hand, she explained that she was dancing the night away to put herself through Coastal Carolina University and she needed just $300 more to make tuition. It's a line that rarely failed and some girls made tuition several times a night. Somewhat riskier were the men who tried to arrange an after-hours rendezvous. They would offer a price and suggest a time and place to meet. A savvy and cynical young lady told me she countered by demanding half the price up front. If the pigeon is drunk enough to fall for it, he found himself alone and feeling stupid at the end of the night.

Some clubs had policies against their dancers "dating" the customers. But once you've taken your clothes off and lap-danced for a guy, it almost seems a courtesy to meet him after hours to consummate the evening. Perhaps that was why so many dancers slide across the line into prostitution. That's the way Cyndee got into it. She would meet a cute guy at the club where she danced three or four nights a week; he would make an offer and she would go back to his hotel room or bring him to her apartment. It didn't take long to figure out that she could make as much money at home in a couple of hours as she could bumping and grinding in the spotlight all night. Her boyfriend, who worked in the pro shop of a golf course, put her name and phone number around to caddies and pro shops at other clubs. These customer service specialists were happy to pimp a woman to a friendly duffer, if they could expect a little extra tip at the end of the day.

As a freelance hooker, Cyndee was making between $1,000 and $3,000 a week, depending on the season, and spent her extra hours working on her tan, her hair, her nails. "I'd die if I was still doing this when I turn thirty," the 26-year-old Kentucky native told me. "I'm going to keep putting my money away and staying out of trouble and in a couple of years me and Barry are gonna move to Florida and buy a house and get married. Then I'm gonna open a hair and nail salon, which is what I came to Myrtle Beach to do anyway. . . . I always knew what I wanted and what I was willing to do to get it. I mean, I wouldn't kill nobody and I wouldn't let nobody hurt me, but this – hey, this is just natural, you know?" she laughed. "Why shouldn't I make some money off of it?"

Unlike Cyndee, most of the upscale hookers around Myrtle Beach worked for escort services, fantasy consultations, massage parlors and lingerie modeling shops. There were ten pages of listings for escort services in the local telephone yellow pages in 1999, with illustrations as explicit as GTE would dare in such household reading. The purveyors of these services knew their market well. One escort service was called the Back-9; others were Fairway Delights, Golfer's Connection, Golfer's Delight and Golfer's Choice. The Toy Box promised, "We Cater To Golfers." Caddy Shak offered "golf packages" of caddies, dancers and "companionship," plus a website (www.caddy-shak.com) and a slogan: "You Can't Bogie The 19th Hole." Dozens of these ads also mentioned that they were accepting applications. An escort service ad in the Horry Telephone Company yellow pages promised $3,000 to $6,000 a week to girls who made the grade. "All we require from you is a willingness to work for our agency and you will benefit from our marketing . . . on a national & international scale, in all major hotels and golf courses along the Grand Strand."

"I think it's horrifying," Horry County Councilwoman Liz Gilland told *The Sun News* in 1997. "I think it's a horrible reflection on our community. The yellow pages are blatant. It's right in your face. Here's prostitution if you want it."

Local police acknowledged that most of the 70-plus escort services were, in fact, fronts for prostitution. But they also said there was not a great deal of impetus to stop it. Staging a sting and catching a girl in a compromising position involved renting a hotel room, setting up audio and video recording equipment, using a number of officers over an extended period of time and filling out reams of paperwork. "It takes a lot of man-hours, money and equipment to set up a sting operation to get one person for prostitution for a $200 fine that might or might not get paid," a Myrtle Beach police captain said. And, except for Liz Gilland, no one seemed to care – not even Ashby Ward.

"If [escort services] were more widely publicized, it would probably have a negative impact on the image of our family beach," Ward told *The Sun News*. Indeed, image is everything in Myrtle Beach and call girls work behind closed doors. Streetwalkers, on the other hand, are out in the open. Local authorities have taken notice and taken action.

The largest collection of these lower class hookers work the Yaupon Drive neighborhood on the south end of Myrtle Beach, between Ocean Boulevard and U.S. 17. Yaupon Drive is not the place to find golfers and account executives. This is where out-of-town construction workers and blue-collar locals come for a quick fix. And this is where Corporal Brenda Christy of the Myrtle Beach Police Department vice squad sets her sting.

Before the bust goes down, officers sweep the area, telling the working girls to get off the street. When she has the market all to herself, Christy shows up wearing short shorts, a bathing suit top or tank top with no bra, dirty hair and no makeup. "I just want to look like I'm one of the street girls," she said. She is wired, with at least three undercover and two uniformed officers backing her up. It doesn't take long for some *schmuck* to cruise by, looking for a little fun. The standard offer is twenty dollars for oral sex, Christy said. Once the sexual act is mentioned and the money is offered, the bust goes down and the john is hauled off to jail. After an evening of listening to men proposition her, Christy said she feels "verbally violated. . . . I'm emotionally drained – and all I'm doing is talking." The police department releases the names of all johns to the media, though they are rarely published.

In the winter months prostitution increases sharply, Christy told me. Businesses close for the season or cut back their staffs. That cute "coed" who served cocktails or did lap dances in August may be taking calls for an evening's "companionship" in February. Older women, less attractive or less educated, may find themselves plying their trade on Yaupon Drive. Christy estimated the average education of a Yaupon Drive hooker is probably tenth grade; their ages range from eighteen to forty.

Another difference between Cyndee and most Grand Strand women in the "service" industry is their patterns of consumption. Cyndee was thrifty, a planner and a saver. Most young women live for the day, the hour, the moment. Money is quick and easy. That's the way they make it. That's the way they spend it. When they get off work at night, they hit bars like Gypsy's, Drifters, Macatz and Droopy's and drink till near dawn, buying each other rounds of beers and exotic shooters of mixed liquors and liqueurs, with names like Buttery Nipple, Purple Slut, Black & Blue and Pit Bull on Crack. Or they go to dance clubs, dressed to the nines. They spend their in-pocket fortunes on clothes, hair, tans and massages. And they live to shop! Fashion is their life and *Glamour* and *Cosmopolitan* are their bibles. They talk clothes and hair and men, compare notes, plan shopping trips to Charleston, Columbia, even to Atlanta. But a $200 trip to Inlet Square Mall will provide an afternoon's amusement in the middle of a boring week. "The only thing I love more than clothes is shopping for them," a former beverage girl told me with a sigh of complete satisfaction.

Though they make tens of thousands of dollars a year, many of these young women go home to a lower middle class life of trailer parks, run-down apartments and sleazy motels. They drive new SUVs and Camaros and spend hundreds of dollars a week on clothes and entertainment, but live in dormitory-like conditions, three or four in a two-bedroom apartment. One "exotic entertainer" drove thirty-five miles inland to a dumpy apartment she shared with her two teenage children. This working class lifestyle is as much a result of their upbringing, I suspect, as their spendthrift ways. Domestic comfort and privacy are alien concepts to most of them.

The guys were no smarter than the girls. They lived for cars, clothes and women. They read *Penthouse, Men's Health* and various automotive magazines. They drove SUVs, BMWs and muscle cars with thousands of dollars worth of sound systems and accessories. Like their female counterparts, they were often a year or two shy of a degree in business administration or accounting. After sex, money occupied their every waking thought. They talked about it, dreamed about it, schemed for it. They would go back to school next year, they said, or get a real estate license and make a killing in condominiums. Of course, that requires getting out of bed in the morning and having a plan – and most of them just weren't there yet. To a frightening degree, they were racist, cynical and ignorant. To the extent they had any political views, they were Republican – violently, loudly, aggressively Republican.

For many male bartenders, club managers and bouncers, drugs were as much a part of their lifestyle as their gold chains and Ford Explorers. Drugs were a status symbol and a source of income. Many male bartenders and bouncers were into body-building because they occasionally had to deal with rowdy customers and because, well, they just liked to buff up and showboat on the beach and around the club. Of course, where you find body builders, you find steroids, which flow through Grand Strand health clubs and nightclubs like bottled water. Having pumped-up, steroid-crazed bouncers might be some managers' idea of avoiding trouble; but they can also be a threat to public health and safety. Bouncers have savagely beaten some poor bastards who couldn't behave themselves. One incident at Broadway at the Beach led to a lawsuit against the city.

According to a study by the Australian Institute of Criminology, there is a correlation between excessive force exerted by bouncers and public violence. Though it was conducted on the opposite side of the world, the study spoke directly to the problem of official violence in Horry County, reporting that bouncers and doormen had been observed initiating and further encouraging fights.

"Many seem poorly trained, obsessed with their own machismo, and relate badly to groups of male strangers," the study said. "Some of them appear to regard their employment as giving them a license to assault people."

Several factors lead to the violence in bars and clubs, the study continued. These include the presence of large groups of male strangers, low comfort levels, high boredom, extreme drunkenness and aggressive, unreasonable bouncers. "In practice, many bouncers are not well managed in their work and appear to be given a job autonomy and discretion that they cannot handle well."

Drugs were epidemic in bars and clubs along the Grand Strand. Marijuana and cocaine reached the Strand from South Florida; LSD and designer drugs – Ecstasy and GBH – from the Northeast. In the summer of 1999, LSD was making a comeback in some circles, though it was said to be laced frequently with the artificial hallucinogen PCB, making it a dangerous and unpredictable trip. The hot new designer drug on the Strand was gamma-hydroxybutyrate – GBH – often used as a body-building aid, and chemically simple enough to be manufactured in a basement chemistry lab. *The Sun News* reported that GBH sent several people to Grand Strand emergency rooms each weekend. "It's very easy to get a little too much, and when mixed with alcohol, people can easily end up in a coma," an emergency room physician said. For that reason, it has been used like Rohypnol, the notorious "date rape" drug.

Ecstasy and GBH were the drugs of choice in the dance clubs and on the rave scene in the summer of '99. Raves are parties of young people engaged in high-energy dancing to high-decibel electronic music. A rave was in progress at the Hole-in-One Club, part of the

Masters Club complex on 10th Avenue North, on the Sunday morning of September 5. In the cavernous dark room some 350 people were bouncing and gyrating to the techno beat at about three o'clock, when 27-year-old Kevin J. McMichael walked in with two friends. McMichael was a body-builder and former fashion model. He worked in his family's North Myrtle Beach seafood restaurant and was training to make the U.S. Olympic bobsled team. As McMichael and his friends entered the club, he spoke briefly to a hostess. Then three other young men – all strangers to McMichael and his companions – stepped up and angrily confronted the new arrivals. One of the men, 21-year-old Charles Kevin Carraway, drew a knife and stabbed McMichael three times in the chest. He was pronounced dead two hours later at Grand Strand Regional Medical Center.

It was the most spectacular murder of the year in Myrtle Beach, just another diversion in a town that had too many distractions for its own good.

A Gentler Side of Myrtle Beach

On Saturday afternoon, July 10, Elizabeth Dole was in town, on her ill-starred quest for the GOP presidential nomination. She met her public at Broadway at the Beach, a few hundred yards from the site of Dan Quayle's forgettable appearance in April.

I took the day off from politics. The only ladies I was interested in were the ones playing China for the World Cup soccer championship. I watched the game on the television above the bar at the Tiki Hut Cafe at the 2nd Avenue Pier, along with an enthusiastic cheering section of fishermen, bait cutters, drunks and drifters, most of whom didn't know a thing about soccer and couldn't find China on a globe. But this game, we all knew, was important, though we probably couldn't have agreed why. We watched Brandi Chastain kick the winning goal and swoon to her knees on the deep, green grass, her fists clinched triumphantly, in an image destined to become an icon of feminist power. That evening, hastily scrawled signs in bars, restaurants and store windows congratulated American's women on their victory. One suspects those signs were made by Myrtle Beach women, who don't usually have much to cheer about.

South Carolina has never been kind to the fairer sex. In 1998, this state led the nation in the rate of homicides against women – more than twice the national average – and in the rate of domestic violence. Along the Grand Strand, the abuse was more exotic. Yes, women got paid well to take off their clothes and dance under strobe lights, or just to serve cocktails and hamburgers in skimpy shorts and push-up bras. When the unexpected happened, they had to go to Columbia or Charleston for an abortion; such a service was not to be found in this family-values sanctuary. Local churches erected billboards urging women who had a "problem" to pray and seek alternatives to abortion.

Myrtle Beach is a man's town. Men like to drive down Kings Highway in their muscle cars and pickup trucks, looking in the beachwear stores at the truncated female mannequins, sporting their post-age-stamp bikinis on their headless, faceless, armless torsos. They like the billboards, featuring come-hither models glancing over bare shoulders, with an invitation to one or another strip club. They probably even liked Kelly Gray's employment announcement on the business pages of *The Sun News*. A public relations firm hired Gray to write press releases and brochure copy. Apparently, she felt her copy would read better if the public knew she was a former Miss New York City. In this town, it couldn't hurt.

There have been a few women of genuine power and influence in Horry County. The most notable, of course, was county Administrator Linda Angus – and her fall was an object lesson to any women wanting to play ball with the good old boys. More than a year after her firing by county council, Angus filed a sexual harassment suit against her former employers. Among her allegations: being called a lesbian; being questioned about her ability to function competently because she had children; being told to wear more makeup, curl her hair and hire more attractive female employees; and being described as the "prettiest candidate" during a press conference to announce her hiring as county administrator in 1996. She said council members subjected her to harassment and created an abusive work environment.

Councilwoman Liz Gilland supported Angus' charges: "Everything she alleged in the lawsuit, I know it happened," she told *The Sun News*. "I didn't do anything about it because it's sort of a way of life for some folks down here. If you take issue, it gets worse or they laugh at you like you're making a big deal over nothing and it gets worse."

Bob Bestler saw it and called it in one of his columns: The boys on county council, he wrote, "have always seemed to have a serious problem treating women as equals.

"It was obvious for years during their dealings with former county Administrator Linda Angus. Invariably, certain councilmen turned especially belligerent when they spoke with Angus. I never saw them speak the same way to men.

"Since her departure . . . the nastiness has been directed at Liz Gilland."

Bestler was just warming to his subject: "Nor are the boys at Burroughs & Chapin entirely innocent when it comes to playing the gender card. Their dealings with the Horry County Board of Education have been patronizing, at best, and one reason may be that two women head the school system here – board Chairman Helen Smith and Superintendent Gerrita Postlewaite."

Women with political muscle were a relatively new phenomenon in Horry County. The first one on the scene — and still one of the leaders — was county Auditor Lois Eargle. Some of her detractors called her a political has-been, but she knew how to pull the levers to get Linda Angus dumped. Did she feel any regret, any feminist solidarity with Angus? Don't bet on it. She gasped when I asked if she considered herself a feminist. "Certainly not!" Yet, in the same breath, she complained that there is a double standard in politics, that women do not have the financial connections that men enjoy.

If that was a paradox, it is only one in a long and complex story that had no end in sight in 1999. Eargle's life story sounds like a country music song. She was a tenth-grade dropout who got married, then got her GED. In 1976 she ran as a Democrat and won a seat in the state House of Representatives. In 1984 she switched parties and was elected chairman of the Horry County GOP the next year.

I interviewed Eargle in her office at the county administrative complex in the old Burroughs School in Conway. She was a high-energy sixty-three-year-old, trim and attractive, with bouffed, tinted hair, who dropped the names Jesus and God into her conversation as if they were her personal trainers. She had earned the right: she also chaired the Horry County Christian Coalition. Her office walls were hung with awards, plaques, citations. There were photographs of Lois Eargle with Famous Republicans, including Ronald Reagan, George and Barbara Bush, former governors James B. Edwards and Carroll Campbell, senators Strom Thurmond and Phil Gramm, Vice President Dan Quayle, late knave Lee Atwater, along with other faces and moments from her career. Just below her office window, her big, gray Lincoln sat on the lawn, a "Forbes 2000" bumper sticker on the window and a vanity plate that read "Audit 1." In a quarter-century political career that included losses as well as victories, Eargle earned a reputation as a bare-knuckles campaigner who could kick, bite and claw with the best of them.

Eargle took pride in being the first woman auditor of Horry County, the first woman to run for the General Assembly and for Congress from the county. In 1999, many women held office throughout the county and they all owed a debt to Lois Eargle. "I've always felt the pressure of being first," she said. "One woman's behavior will affect the way people look at all women." And she came back to that old double standard. Former Congressman Robin Talon (whom she ran against unsuccessfully in 1984) was four times divorced, she reminded me – "and it was *never* an issue! If it had been *me* that was divorced, they would have followed me with that question everywhere I went. . . .

"I'm at the point where people respect me for my track record," she said. "And I'm also in a position where I can help people. And I have. I think I've helped many people over the years."

Indeed she has. And she'll help you, if you ask. Just don't call her a feminist.

Another well-manicured political animal was Sally Howard. A small-town North Carolina girl by birth and upbringing, Howard married when she was eighteen, started a family and got involved with local Democratic politics. She liked the company and rose to become secretary of the North Carolina Democratic Party. Governor Jim Hunt named her to head his Women's Commission, where she lobbied for legislation on a number of women's issues, including domestic violence, rape and abortion. At least one member of the North Carolina General Assembly called for abolition of the Women's Commission, accusing it of recruiting and training women to run against male legislators.

Howard's marriage ended in the mid-1980s and she moved to Horry County, where she owned real estate, had friends and loved to shag. South Carolina was a culture shock for the former First Feminist of North Carolina. When friends back home asked about women's issues in South Carolina, she replied, "Well, at least they let us vote now."

Howard soon fell into her old ways and was elected chairman of the Horry County Democratic Party. She led local Democrats to a resurgence in the late eighties and early nineties, putting out a newsletter, filling the back room at Akel's House of Pancakes with their monthly first-Monday meetings. She recruited and successfully ran Luke Rankin for state Senate and served on the steering committee of Hillary Clinton's National Women's Leadership Forum. In 1999, Sally Howard was a 50-something businesswoman and grandmother, blond, with quick, blue eyes and quick, deadly wit. She was proof that American life does offer second acts for those who pursue them. She was a charter member of the OD Shag Club and lived with Don Yonce, a fellow Democrat and an associate in her mail-order costume jewelry business. In her cluttered office/warehouse/political headquarters she had as many awards and citations as Lois Eargle, but all of her photographs featured Sally Howard smiling with Famous Democrats.

There are powers in this world that are not of this world, and women understand this better than men do. Eleanor Schiller has seen many terrible and wonderful things revealed in her lifetime. She was a child in America, safe from the madness of World War II, but as a Jew she knew the war had special meaning for her people. Later she met Hugo Schiller, who would become her husband. A European Jew, Hugo had not been so fortunate. He was rescued from a concentration camp by Allied forces, but he lost friends and relatives in the Holocaust. The anguish and survivor's guilt remained with him still.

As a social studies teacher at Chabad Academy in the late 1990s, not only was Schiller charged with teaching her fifth and sixth grade classes about the Holocaust, but she also was responsible for providing Holocaust materials and background to other Chabad teachers. Part of the problem with talking to children about the Holocaust, she told me, is magnitude. The sheer number of human beings murdered by the Nazis is overwhelming and – to a child – incomprehensible. To make it more lucid, Schiller chose to use smaller numbers – and smaller victims. Of six million Jews killed in the Holocaust, 1.2 million were children.

In January 1998, with Holocaust Remembrance Day approaching in April, Schiller was responsible for creating an observance that would be fitting and instructive. She stood before the other eight teachers of Chabad Academy, troubled by the burden of history but inspired by God and memory. "It came out of my mouth," she told me a year later. "'Suppose we could put out in the field there 1.2 million butterflies.' And everybody seemed to be nodding."

So it was spoken; so it was done. But not so easily.

In her class the next day, Schiller got a very enthusiastic response to the idea. The children drew out their crayons and pencils and started to work. They crafted stencils and started running them off on the copier, then colored them with all the imagination of childhood. But Hugo Schiller understood the truth. Enormous deeds require many hands, great will and huge passion. These children could produce no more than 2,000 butterflies a week, he said. More hands were needed. More will. More passion.

Eleanor Schiller got word to the local schools that paper butterflies were needed to remember 1.2 million forgotten children. An occupational therapist put seniors in a local retirement home to work making butterflies. *The Sun News* picked up the story and soon schools and synagogues around the country were mailing boxes of butterflies to Myrtle Beach. Operation Butterfly got a mention in *USA Today* and National Public Radio sent a reporter to Myrtle Beach to do a story. But her "big break," Schiller said, was the story in *Time for Kids*. It included butterfly patterns for teachers and the address of the school.

As April 23 approached, Schiller didn't know what to expect, but she notified the post office that Chabad might be getting more mail than usual. Then came the deluge. In the week before the deadline, the post office was delivering butterflies by the truckload from around the nation. Schiller mounted a large map on the wall and children stuck pins to identify each location that sent butterflies. They cheered when Hawaii, the last state, came in. The children organized the arrivals, recorded addresses for "thank you" notes and mounted butterflies on sticks to place in the yard. Volunteers came from around the city to offer help. But even this task was overwhelming. Hugo came forward again to suggest they mount the butterflies on cloth strips.

On Holocaust Remembrance Day – April 23, 1998 – 1.35 million paper butterflies fluttered in the Chabad Academy yard. Hundreds of friends of Chabad came out that morning to sing and hold hands and mingle their tears with the spring rain. There were prayers and words of hope from a rabbi, a Baptist minister and a Catholic priest.

"Sometimes some of the things we do are just sort of answering a call," Schiller told me. "I said, 'Okay, this is God's project. He has just let me be the implement.'"

There was a sanctuary on rural Highway 1008 in Little River. The sign out front read, "Evans Book Outlet – Church Supplies, Afrocentric Books & Robes." Inside, Charlotte Evans watched over her flock.

Evans was friend and counselor to her community, a tutor to their children, an advocate for their rights, a minister in their church and a philosopher of practical living. In 1989, she was a leader in demonstrations to have a black teacher reinstated at Conway Middle School after he was unjustly fired. The teacher, H.H. Singleton, was reinstated by court order two years later.

"Life is too precious to spend it not doing the things you love to do," she told me.

I first met Charlotte Evans as she sat at a small table in her 1,000-square-foot store, preparing her sermon for St. Elizabeth Missionary Baptist Church. As we talked, we were interrupted by phone calls and friends coming in to share a greeting, to ask for advice or support. Barely five feet tall, Evans weighed less than a hundred pounds, but her shoulders carried a heavy burden. She did it with grace and laughter and a quiet intensity.

Evans came to Horry County from her native Missouri when she married Wallace Evans, in 1969. They raised two children and had five grandchildren. Along the way, she earned a degree in psychology from Coastal Carolina University. She and her husband opened the bookstore in 1994, as much a community outreach as an enterprise. One of the things she found striking about Carolina culture was the resistance to women holding any formal authority or opinions – especially in matters of the church. She always considered herself a good and faithful wife, she said, "But the deacons would come up and quote me Scripture. They would say, 'Wives, be submissive to your husbands.'" She could laugh about it now, but the experience was painful and confusing.

Her husband left his job in the chemical industry in 1978 to enter the ministry. It was a wrenching decision, which he resisted for years, but she supported him through it all. In 1989 he became minister of St. Elizabeth Church in Aynor.

In 1997, Evans felt her own life starting to change. "As a child, I had dreams and, being a child, I didn't understand them," she said. Now she began to perceive where her dreams were taking her. She was being called to join her husband in the ministry. "I resisted it," she said. "I fought it for months." She had seen the toll that the ministry had taken on her husband. "He found it very lonely and demanding." But God kept troubling her sleep. "He would wake me every morning at the same hour to pray. It was all I could do," she said.

In October 1998, during a crisis over her daughter's health, she "gave in," she said. Guided by her dreams and prayers, she heard God's voice speak to her during the Sunday morning service at St. Elizabeth's. She told her husband the moment had come, then stood and told the congregation she had been called to preach the Gospel. She spoke of a dream she had about one of the members, who stood and acknowledged the dream was true. The Spirit ran through the congregation like fire that morning. Two members came forward and were saved, while the congregation prayed and sang and clapped in response.

When I met her, she was acting as assistant to her husband, delivering the sermon at St. Elizabeth's once a month and studying for an extension degree at local Cathedral Bible College. She was taking her new life one day at a time, still unsure of her course. "I haven't set any long range goals for myself," she said. "All things will be revealed in time."

I never met Elizabeth Chapin Patterson; she died in 1980, completing a long and remarkable life. The daughter of Simeon Brooks Chapin, she drove an ambulance Stateside in World War I and was one of the first woman insurance brokers in America. She traveled the world and one of her journeys, aboard the icebreaker Malygin, carried her within 200 miles of the North Pole. Years later she would recall that seeing that vast, silent icescape was part of her spiritual awakening.

All of her life had been a preparation for November 8, 1931, the day she journeyed to Harmon-on-the-Hudson, in New York State, and met the little man with the impish smile and the dark, shining eyes. He was born Merwan Sheriar Irani, in Poona, India, in 1894, but to his thousands of followers worldwide, he was Meher Baba – the Compassionate Father. "When I first met him, it was just as though I had always known him," Patterson said of that moment. She would be his disciple for the rest of her life.

Patterson spent seven years in India, receiving spiritual training from Baba. She drove a bus thousands of miles across that vast, impoverished country, carrying Baba and other disciples on a mission to feed the hungry, wash the lepers, build hospitals and schools. Crowds of 100,000 were said to come out to hear Baba speak and to receive his blessing.

When Patterson returned to America in the early 1940s, she was on a mission of her own. Baba had charged her with finding a site in the United States to become a spiritual retreat for his followers, a place of good climate, abundant water, and fertile soil. And he told her, it had to be given from the heart for the support of his spiritual work. She found the perfect location: 495 acres of her father's pristine pine forest between U.S. 17 and the beach. She persuaded her father to give her the tract, along with the two fresh water lakes, the mile of beachfront and the peace, beauty and tranquillity of the forest. There she established the Meher Spiritual Center and there it is today, an unspoiled oasis in the heart of the neon ghetto, between Myrtle Beach and North Myrtle Beach.

Most residents of the Grand Strand had never heard of the center and had no idea what lay hidden on the undeveloped tract of pines on U.S 17. There was no sign marking the entrance to the retreat; the pilgrim had to look for the little dirt road across the highway from Hooter's Restaurant. But thousands from around the world found it each year. Most came for day visits; others stayed in one of the small residential cottages, spending their time in the well-stocked library, in meditation and prayer, in discussion with other Baba followers. There is inspiration in the magnificent woods, where deer abound and alligators slip silently through the clear, glassy lakes. On my first visit there, I saw an enormous snapping turtle crossing the sandy road in front of our car. There was not a scrap of litter – not a cigarette butt, not a gum wrapper – on any the miles of paths I walked that day. Staff and visitors greeted and spoke to one another in quiet tones. Some had met Baba and they exchanged stories and sayings of their master. Photos and paintings of Baba, along with his words, were framed on the walls of every residence and conference building in the center.

The Meher Spiritual Center has survived savage hurricanes and an attempt by the county tax office to revoke its tax-exempt status. In 1999 its greatest threat was development. The Conway Bypass, scheduled to open in 2000, would dump thousands more cars a day onto U.S. 17, a quarter-mile from the center. A Wal-Mart SuperCenter abutted the south edge of the property along the highway. Condo towers rose along its southern beach perimeter. The center shares a north border with Briarcliffe Acres, a quiet, upscale neighbor that appreciates its values and stewardship.

Baba visited his center in 1952, 1956 and 1958. He was sometimes accompanied by his brother, whose Indian accent rendered the name of the area in the ironic pun, "Mortal Beach." Baba was a Persian and a Zoroastrian by birth, but his philosophy drew from Buddhism and abnegation of self. "Selfishness in thought, emotion and action must be completely driven out so that there may be an unretarded release of unimpeachable Divine Love," Baba wrote. "Not by seeking individual happiness or safety, but by again and again offering one's life in the service of others is it possible to rise to the unsurpassed completeness of realized Truth. God is not to be sought by running away from life, but by establishing unity in the One with the many. . . . The false separative ego has to be annihilated and the individual soul has to realize consciously its original and inviolable unity with the God or the Oversoul."

On July 10, 1925, Baba told his followers, "I shan't be speaking today," and indeed, he never spoke again for the last forty-four years of his life. He communicated with an alphabet board and later, with gestures, through an interpreter. The day is observed each year at the Meher Spiritual Center as Silence Day. Followers gather for a day of silence and meditation. So there was no cheering at the Meher Center that day when Brandi Chastain kicked the game-winning goal against the Chinese soccer team. The disciples of Baba were celebrating a greater triumph.

Faith of Their Fathers

On January 1, 1741, evangelist George Whitefield was traveling south on the Kings Highway when he came to a tavern near Little River. There he found the locals celebrating the New Year with dancing, fiddling and demon rum. He admonished the miscreants to cease their wanton ways, then preached a mighty sermon as they laid down their fiddles and lent their ears. He even baptized one of their children that day. Later, after Whitefield had retired for the night, the merrymakers took up their fiddles and flagons and resumed their celebration.

Whitefield's sojourn along the Carolina coast was portentous, for he brought new and dangerous ideas about the nature of Man and his relationship to God. A stern Calvinist and associate of John and Charles Wesley, Whitefield challenged Anglican orthodoxy and the hierarchies of British society. In the eyes of God all were equal, he proclaimed. What mattered in a person's life was his relationship to God, based on a religious conversion, or "new birth." These seeds of individualism and equality found fertile soil in the American wilderness. Due in part to Whitefield's passionate sermons, a fever of religious revival called the Great Awakening swept through the seaboard colonies, foreshadowing greater movements soon to come. In his journey down the Kings Highway that New Year's Day, Whitefield hastened the day when George Washington would travel this same road as the president of a new republic.

Whitefield's theology had other implications. From the earliest years of Carolina, travelers had described the licentious, hedonistic ways of these Southern colonials. George Whitefield offered to these sinners the stern salvation of an angry God and it became the bedrock of Southern Protestantism. For more than two centuries Southerners have tortured their souls in a divine schizophrenia, walking the thin line between worldly pleasure and Calvinist damnation, weighing the balance between Saturday night and Sunday morning. In the process they made Myrtle Beach an inevitable oasis of indulgence in the vast desert of Calvinist repression.

Next to the ideology of race, nothing has so shaped the mind and the culture of the South as religion. "The South is by a long way the most simply and sincerely religious country I was ever in," a British traveler wrote at the beginning of the twentieth century. "In other countries men are apt to make a private matter of their religion. . . ; but the Southerner wears it upon his sleeve."

In Myrtle Beach, religion was not just the relationship between God and mortal; it was a public statement, a proclamation made by private and public figures at every available opportunity. It was the prayer that opened every city council meeting and closed with the words, "In Jesus' name we pray, Amen." It was the National Day of Prayer rally in front of City Hall – attended by the mayor, of course. It was the little "Jesus fish" on the tailgates of mighty SUVs that plied the Grand Strand highways. It was the hand-painted wooden sign nailed high on a utility pole on the U.S. 17 Bypass that read simply "Jesus or Hell." It was the steeples of the First Baptist, First Presbyterian and First United Methodist churches that dominated the downtown skyline. The downtown churches represented a sort of "state religion" of Myrtle Beach, a collective "high church," where many political and business leaders gathered on Sundays with very mixed motives.

While Myrtle Beach religion was quite public, its moral censure was directed at the most private behavior. For most white residents of Horry County, the range of human wickedness started and ended with sex. Some might include drugs or alcohol. Crime and violence were considered public policy issues, not spiritual failings. As for greed, pride, covetousness, environmental degradation and sleazy business practices, these were matters beyond the purview of Southern Protestant ethics and no Horry County minister would address them without risking his career.

Yet there were signs of a more humble, "hands on" Christianity in some of the lowlier quarters of Myrtle Beach. They included Street Reach Mission, Myrtle Beach Haven and the Promise [sic] Land, three Christian-based ministries helping Myrtle Beach's homeless and indigent. In a rooftop bungalow on Ocean Boulevard was a branch of Teen Challenge, a ministry founded by famed evangelist David Wilkerson. Teen Challenge was a Christian-based "boot camp" to get young men off the streets and off alcohol and drugs. Slacker 77 looked like any other rowdy teen club: concert posters on the walls, shaggy-haired young people, pierced and tattooed, moshing madly to a band that was incomprehensible to my middle-aged ears. But this club was not as it first appeard. No drugs or alcohol were sold or used at Slacker 77, club owner Jeff Weathers told me. Smoking was allowed outside only. The incomprehensible songs were Christian in theme and the club was a local manifestation of a burgeoning "Christian underground" music culture.

Beyond Christianity, Baha'is were active on the Grand Strand, with groups meeting in Conway and Myrtle Beach. There was a small Islamic mosque in Conway and a thriving, if fractious, Jewish community, with Conservative and Orthodox synagogues and Chabad Lubavitch Jewish Center. Falling in the cracks between Christianity and Judaism was a small contingent of Messianic Jews.

Millennialism is deeply rooted in the Southern psyche and the shadow of George Whitefield stretches long across Horry County. When the manager of the Horry County Solid Waste Authority told *The Sun News*, "Trash disposal hasn't changed much in 2,000 years," I was tempted to ask, "How did they handle it before Year 1?" Of course, the garbage guru was implying that history began 2,000 years ago and for many in Horry County there was a rising fear that it would end in the year 2,000.

In front of some fundamentalist and Pentecostal churches signs appeared early in 1999, counting down the days until December 31. On September 1, *The Sun News* ran a quarter-page ad with the headline:

8 Compelling Reasons Why:
Christ Is Coming Very Soon!
How To Be Prepared For History's Greatest Event

Those reasons included the usual proof of the "end times": the rebirth of Israel, decreasing morality and increasing famines, wars and earthquakes. The "New World Order" was said to foreshadow the coming of the antichrist as the incarnation of Satan. "Beware the mark of the beast," the ad warned, and beseeched the reader to accept Jesus before it was too late: "God's judgment is, indeed, coming on the world in rebellion. He cannot deny His nature. His attributes of perfect holiness and justice demand judgment for sin, of which we are all guilty."

Letters to the editor of *The Sun News* reflected an angry God looking down over Horry County. Correspondents denounced the Supreme Court, the satanic power of Harry Potter and the "intrusion of satanic influence via the TV media." A typical letter from Conway said: ". . . I would like to point out that this country is, in fact, a Christian nation. . . . Anyone who thinks this is so wrong should take a look at what has happened since we took prayer out of the classroom. The Constitution is . . . a guideline for a workable republic, a republic that was strong until the current crop of liberals began their efforts to tear it down. . . . We have to return to the strong Christian faith that has guided us for more than 200 years. . . . "

Another letter read: "Followers of atheistic, evolutionary humanism and Supreme Court traitors would do well to stop carping about Christian prayer in public school and read the Mayflower Compact."

Some letters revealed the racist side of Christian conservatism. When the painting of a dark-skinned Jesus was featured in a story about a local artist, a writer fumed: "You have got to be kidding me! If this does not make the people of this country take notice, I fear all is lost. It is things like this that foment racism. . . . It is time for the moral conservatives to take back the country. This is a Christian country, founded on Christian beliefs and codes. Those who do not care for that fact I would encourage to secure a one-way ticket to a socialist country of their choice."

The village atheists of the Grand Strand were Samuel Daniels and Gordon Dew Sr., who regularly wrote letters to the editor – as much to goad fundamentalists, I suspect, as to elucidate any theological issues. And they never failed to get a response.

In a typical letter, Daniels wrote: "The miracles that Jesus performed never happened. They are fairy tales, like much of the Bible.

"I would assume that Gordon Dew writes his letters attacking religion, for the same reasons I do. I'm tired of Biblical fairy tales being promoted as facts. These fairy tales cause hate, persecution, violence and start wars."

Dew's and Daniels' letters drew predictable fusillades from angry believers: " . . . as Christians already know, Satan is real and that he makes converts wherever he can. It's a bit unsettling, however, to realize that he has made such an avidly overt convert of someone so close at hand."

Another writer declared: "Ever since Charles Darwin presented his theory of evolution people have compassed heaven and earth trying to find the missing link. They never have found it and they never will. . . . I can imagine Daniels standing before almighty God and telling him it is all a fairy tale.

"No, evolution is the fairy tale."

And so it went, week after week, month after month, on the pages of *The Sun News*. It's probably safe to assume that anyone so obsessed with the impending end of the world was not terribly concerned with what was happening in county council chambers or the inner sanctum of the Founders Centre.

I wanted to discover some of the less mainstream Christian observances along the Grand Strand and perhaps none was less mainstream than J.P. "Beaver" Greenway's shag-and-prayer service in North Myrtle Beach. On Sunday morning, July 18, I found the Reverend Greenway with his flock of about sixty middle-aged, well-tanned, dissipated shaggers and beachcombers on the beachfront portico of OD Pavilion. They wore T-shirts, bathing suits and flip-flops. The reverend was in khaki pants and loafers with no socks. The cocktail tables and chairs were arranged around an electronic keyboard and small pulpit where the potbellied sixty-two-year-old evangelist and fire alarm salesman delivered his laid-back homily on the need for salvation. "You need to bow your head and say, 'Lord Jesus, I'm a sinner. I need to be saved. I need a savior.' " Behind him in the pavilion, boys played video games and shot pool. A disk clattered on an air hockey table. In front of him the beach thronged with well-oiled sun worshippers. A hundred yards to the north stood the Ocean Drive Beach & Golf Resort, where opponents of the multicounty business park had gathered three days earlier for a huge pep rally.

Greenway came by his talents naturally. His father was the noted radio evangelist W. Norman Greenway, who introduced a strain of evangelism called pre-millennialism to the South in the 1940s. Coming of age in South Carolina in the 1950s, Beaver Greenway spent summers on the Strand, wrestling with his soul and shagging with his friends. "We learned early that the better you danced, the prettier the girls you got," he told me with a raucous chuckle. He still shagged and enjoyed the company of shaggers, he confessed to me. But Jesus would not have shagged. "Some forms of dancing are wrong and vulgar. Shagging would not be his lifestyle." Greenway did it, he insisted, just to keep in shape.

The reverend passed an offering plate, led his flock in one more hymn and closed the service at 11:00 sharp. The jukebox came on. The bar opened for business and the congregation hit the dance floor.

It's a shame Greenway and his congregation did not offer a prayer for the environment. Even as they sang their hosannas, a clogged sewer line at Ocean Drive Resort was dumping raw sewage into the hotel's indoor pool, laundry room and ground floor toilets. It went into a storm drain and down to the surf. Health officials closed the beach to swimmers for 500 feet north and south of the drain. Lifeguards posted the area and kept swimmers out.

For many Christians, no place is more dangerous for their children than the public schools. Not only has God been barred at the door, they say, but all the secular and Satanic influences from which they seek to protect their children are allowed to enter, spawn and hybridize in the hothouse of young minds.

To make their schools safer and holier places for their children, a group of Horry County Christians organized Save Our Schools. Coleman Turner, a member of S.O.S., heard on a Christian radio station about a Jericho March in the Midwest, patterned on the Old Testament story of the Children of Israel, who marched seven days around the walls of Jericho, praying and singing. If Christians could not pray inside their schools, Turner reasoned, they would pray outside and, through the power of their faith, they would keep Satan at bay.

Turner contacted James Hewitt, who had led a recent March for Jesus in Loris. With others they organized the S.O.S. Jericho March, having the ambitious goal of leading Christians to march around each of the forty-three public schools plus the administrative offices of the Horry County School District over a period of about five months.

The Jericho March required participants to meet at assigned schools on Saturday mornings. I met a biracial group of about thirty-five in the parking lot of Whittemore Park Middle School in Conway, at 9:00 a.m. on October 23. The group was largely middle-aged people, probably grandparents of children in the public schools. They included Turner and Hewitt; Frankie Jordan, with her fourteen-month-old granddaughter on her arm; and Brian Tompkins, a county employee and resident of Myrtle Beach.

Few people from Myrtle Beach participated in the Jericho March, "because they do not appreciate the things our forefathers gave us," Tompkins told me. "It's time to lift up the valley and exalt the Lord. . . . If good does not wake people up, evil will take over."

The leaders of the group distributed song sheets in the parking lot and led the group in singing "Stand Up, Stand Up for Jesus" and "God Bless America." Coleman Turner led a prayer: "Lord, we're serving notice on Satan. He's got no choice but to leave this school. . . . Lord, place a band of angels around this school to keep Satan out."

Then we marched from the parking lot, around the modern brick school building, around the sprawling grassy grounds, around the band room and back out to the parking lot on U.S. 378. A few walked and sang with their arms around one another. A young mother carried a tattered Bible in her right hand and led her small blond daughter with the left. The child reached down, picked a dandelion from the ragged lawn and lifted it up to her mother. A man in a Braves sports jacket mumbled an incantation as he passed each door of each building. Frankie Jordan, with granddaughter Stephanie Edge on her right arm, muttered something as she made a small violent swish of her left hand at each door. She told me later that she was putting Satan on notice, "declaring to Satan that he is losing these grounds and we are taking them back for Jesus Christ." As a child, she never left home without a family prayer, she said. "We clothed ourselves in prayer. People don't understand how important it is when God said to clothe ourselves in the power of prayer."

Back in the parking lot, the Jericho Marchers loaded into pickup trucks and SUVs, drove to Pee Dee Elementary School, five miles away, and marched again around the walls to tell Satan he was not welcome in Horry County schools.

All the accoutrements of Southern Protestantism were instantly recognizable at St. Elizabeth Missionary Baptist Church of Aynor, if on a smaller scale than I was accustomed to seeing: the choir loft, the tinted windows, the cross, pulpit and altar, the eight pews on each side of the aisle. The congregation of about sixty reflected the demographic reality of the African American community. Women outnumbered men three to one. The seven-member choir, including the two pianists, was all women. Women led the opening of the service from the floor with the reading of Scripture and leading of hymns, "Leaning on the Everlasting Love" and "This Little Light of Mine." The piano came in spontaneously, as the congregation clapped and rocked and sang the familiar words: "This little light of mine, I'm gonna let it shine."

In his lavender vestments, the Reverend Wallace Evans sat to one side of the pulpit, his wife Charlotte at the other. The singing, clapping and responsive prayers continued for the first hour of the service. The date was October 31 and I had come to hear the Reverend Charlotte Evans deliver the sermon, as she did the last Sunday of each month. At the appointed moment, she rose from the large chair and anchored her tiny frame behind the imposing altar. Her Scripture reading came from Peter II: "For so an entrance shall be ministered unto you abundantly into the everlasting kingdom of our Lord and Savior Jesus Christ. Wherefore I will not be negligent to put you always in remembrance of these things, though ye know them, and be established in their present truth."

Setting her Bible aside, she began her sermon in steady, even cadences, recalling the promises God has made to Man and kept and the promises Man has made to God and broken. Suddenly the spirit came over her as her voice rose and tumbled in the ancient cadences of the black clergy: "Didn't the Lord *promise* Moses a land of milk and honey? . . . Didn't he *promise* Joshua a great victory? . . . Didn't he *promise* David a great kingdom?" After each question the congregation responded with claps, shouts. "Didn't the Lord *promise* us a Savior? *Yes*, he did! He promised us *Jesus Christ*. He promised us his *own son* to be our Savior." With each cadence her voice became more urgent, more strained; the responses from the congregation more passionate.

It was fascinating to behold this small, soft-spoken woman swept up and carrying her congregation along with her for nearly an hour. Her face glistened with perspiration and her presence electrified the room as she called and the congregation responded. She dabbed her lips with a small white handkerchief, stomped her foot on the floor and gave a shriek of ecstasy. Her head rolled back with each cadence: " I will *stand* on the promise of the Lord. . . . *You* can stand here with me. . . . *Stand* here with me now . . . . There's room for *every* sinner, there's room to stand up and *repent*. . . . There's *room* here, brothers and sisters, 'cause the Lord's promises are *big* and his promises are *everlasting*. . . . "

The congregation surged in response to each cadence: "That's right, sister! . . . That's right! . . . Amen." The Spirit ran through the crowd like fire.

"No wonder the old song says, 'I'm *standing* on the promise of God.' . . .That's a promise you can stand on *forever*. . . . *Stand* here with me, brothers and sisters. . . . Come up here and *stand* with me. . . . *Stand* with me." She gave a little shriek and turned to look back at the choir. The piano came up softly in the frenzy of chant and response. Evans collapsed backward into the chair behind her. The choir came in with "Standing on the Promises of God," as the congregation rocked and swayed and I swayed with them.

Weeping, tears streaming down his broad face, Wallace Evans came down from the dais and walked up the aisle, his great arms outstretched. "Don't let it pass, brothers and sisters," he implored. "Don't let it pass. It's here right now. Don't you feel it? Don't you feel it now? Reach out and take it. Don't let it pass."

On the evening of July 29, I drove north in bumper-to-bumper traffic to the Meher Baba Spritual Center. In a small, unair-conditioned conference building deep in the woods, I joined a crowd of about ninety other seekers who had come to hear Bhau Kalchuri. The seventy-three-year-old disciple had served Baba as personal secretary and attendant and had written a twenty-one-volume biography of the "Perfect Master." A small, plump, swarthy man with a fringe of silver hair around his bald pate, Kalchuri moved around the room, exchanging embraces and greetings with all who approached him. Two followers stepped forward to read poems they had written to Baba. A teen named Patrick sang a song he had written called "Baba Who?" The crowd came in on the "Baba Who" chorus and suddenly the place reminded me of church camp and singing rounds of "Kum Ba Ya."

Sitting in a chair on the stage before us, Kalchuri spoke in his gentle, Indian accent of Baba's meeting with Gandhi, of his teachings and sayings. We must surrender reason, he said, for reason is only manipulated to serve our ends. The mind is all illusory. It makes us ask why, when "why" is a meaningless word. "I am not against material progress," Kalchuri said, "but we have no time for anything else. . . . We meditate on paying our bills." We must seek a simple life, free from thoughts and desires and wishes. A simple life requires meditation and discipline. It is the opposite of the complicated life of desire and materialism. "That is very simple," he said.

Kalchuri read a passage from Baba, which reminded me of Jesus, telling his followers to speak his name in their final breath, that they may come to him in the next life. It is our purpose to wait for his call, to keep him in our heart, Kalchuri said. "Before you go to sleep at night, just remember him and say his name."

When the meeting ended, I drove through the dark woods out to U.S. 17, where the headlights and taillights were lined up as far as I could see in the drizzling rain. The traffic light changed and I crossed the highway to the Hooter's Restaurant, directly across from the front gate of the Baba Center. Inside, I was greeted by the pounding rock of a jukebox and customers leering at waitresses in hot-hot short-shorts and tank tops. At the bar I ordered iced tea and a fish sandwich.

Since moving to Myrtle Beach, I had conducted a little survey, asking dozens of bartenders, waitresses, cashiers and clerks if they could direct me to the Meher Spiritual Center. Not one had ever heard of it or had a clue where it was!

When the bartender – her name was Lissi – brought my tea, it was her turn. "Excuse me," I said. "Could you tell me where the Meher Spiritual Center is?" She seemed intelligent enough, but drew a complete blank – "The *what*?"

I repeated.

"What's *that*?"

"It's a spiritual and meditation retreat," I said. "People come there from all over the world. I'm sure it's around here somewhere."

Her face fell momentarily slack, then sprang back to its perky, pretty self. "Oh," was all she said, withdrawing into the safety of her very complicated life.

A Long, Hot Summer on the Strand

Law enforcement and other agencies prepared for a wild Fourth of July weekend. "All available troopers will be on the road through the seventy-eight-hour holiday period," a spokesman for the state Department of Public Safety said. "Unmarked Camaros and saturation patrols will be used in those areas where DUI and other violations have been known to cause accidents."

Emergency medical personnel were braced. "We anticipate possible delays due to traffic volumes, but we've kind of become accustomed to dealing with those and doing the best we can," Horry County EMS director Randy Webster told *The Sun News*.

After the bikers and the high school seniors, the Independence Day crowd would be a welcome change. "We're into the family season," Myrtle Beach city spokesman Mark Kruea said. "The mix will be a little bit different from those in May and June."

The National Weather Service called for a beautiful weekend. Innkeepers expected ninety-five percent occupancy. "It goes without saying that this is traditionally the biggest weekend of the year and it will be again this year," Ashby Ward said.

I didn't need to see for myself. I was headed out of town on the evening of Friday, July 2, for a little R&R when I nearly became I holiday statistic. Two cars were drag racing on Kings Highway when one ran the red light at the 16th Avenue North intersection and slammed into a minivan, knocking it into another minivan. Three people were hospitalized. The driver of the car that ran the light was arrested. I heard the impact and saw the aftermath as I approached the intersection on 16th Avenue. Not everyone on the Strand was so lucky. Four people died in a wreck on U.S. 501 the next night. Beach-bound traffic was backed up for miles as authorities cleared the road. A twenty-nine-year-old woman died in a three-car wreck on U.S. 17 Bypass three days later. July was a deadly month for man and beast.

A 175-pound black bear was killed on U.S. 501 in front of Myrtle Beach Factory Stores on July 17. A sixty-nine-year-old man died in a single car wreck on the former Myrtle Beach Air Force Base the next day.

July was also a horny month and it kept police busy. Horry County authorities arrested a woman for prostitution at Tokyo Spa, a massage parlor; another was arrested at Europhique, a lingerie modeling shop, half a block from my apartment. A few weeks later, undercover cops arrested thirteen men and women on prostitution charges in the seedy Yaupon Drive area. Three lifeguards, ages seventeen to twenty, were arrested for having sex with three underage girls. *The Sun News* reported several incidents of men exposing themselves.

On several occasions I saw police pursue fleet-footed suspects through parking garages and hedges, around buildings and dumpsters near my apartment. They converged in cruisers, on bicycles and street carts, shouting and chattering over their radios. Most incidents did not make the paper.

The Sun News did report the July 6 arrest of seven gang members – four men and three women – for possession and trafficking in a multitude of drugs in local strip clubs and dance clubs. Police said the four males were members of the Lost Boys, an outfit affiliated with the Pagan motorcycle gang. Two of the suspects lived in an apartment at 407 21st Avenue North, two blocks from my front door. Two days after the Lost Boys went to jail, Myrtle Beach Police collaborated with the FBI to apprehend three Charlotte residents in connection with a bank robbery and trafficking in cocaine. One was arrested at the Florentine Motel; two others at the Blue Bay Motel. These were Boulevard flophouses a few blocks from my apartment.

In September, someone in the apartments across the street from me discharged a burst of automatic weapon fire into the air. The police SWAT team swarmed through the neighborhood, surrounded the building and arrested the disturber of the peace without incident. There were no injuries.

More than an inch of rain fell on the city in a July 6 thunderstorm with predictable results: streets flooded, traffic snarled and polluted stormwater poured onto the beaches. The next day city staff met for two hours in a closed-door session with state Department of Health and Environmental Control officials to discuss how best to alert the public of high bacteria levels in the surf. "I know we're headed in the right direction and I think we're moving fairly rapidly toward concrete proposals toward stormwater runoff," city spokesman Mark Kruea said.

The new system got an early test on July 14. Following another rain, bacteria levels around the mouth of Withers Swash tested high. Orange and black signs went up near the swash with this message: "A swimming advisory has been issued by the city of Myrtle Beach for this section of beach. High bacteriological levels have been detected in this section of beach and swimming is not advised until these levels return to normal."

"It's rain water hitting parking lots, roads and lawns and running out through the creek into the ocean," Kruea explained. The swimming advisory was lifted after twenty-four hours.

Chamber of Commerce chief Ashby Ward said there had been no fallout from the latest swimming advisory. A notice was even posted on the chamber's Web site, Ward said. "There's no doubt in anybody's mind that the public needs to be advised."

On August 9 a sewage spill closed 1,000 feet of strand in North Myrtle Beach. Three days later, *The Sun News* sounded off with a bold editorial: "Job One for the Grand Strand is to rid the beaches of storm-water runoff drains. . . . After all, it has been 20 years since Myrtle Beach was put on notice to direct stormwater runoff – and its resulting bacteria and pollution – away from the public beach."

The Grand Strand's reputation was catching up with it and a public relations bombshell went off on July 25. In the first of a seven-part series on coastal development in North Carolina, the Raleigh *News & Observer* cited Myrtle Beach as the inevitable result of too much development and too little regulation:

> Myrtle Beach, S.C., a vacation behemoth that brings in $5 billion annually, offers everything a tourist could desire: 2,000 restaurants and entertainment ranging from ostrich races and jousting knights to the obligatory wet T-shirt contests. And if the beaches aren't closed from sewage spills or dirty parking lot run-off, people can even swim. . . .
>
> Condominiums 19 stories tall cast shadows on the beach all the way to the surf. The only birds flying were pigeons. The concussion from car stereos shook the concrete-block motel rooms.
>
> Pools of green water stood on the beach, fed by drainage pipes from streets and parking lots.

North Carolinians "don't want to see Grand Strand-style growth carving up their own coast," reporter James Eli Shiffer wrote. "The prospect of growth *à la* Myrtle Beach terrifies homeowners and dune-hugging environmentalists. . . ."

"It is just wall-to-wall buildings, concrete and asphalt and a gazillion cars," is how one North Carolina developer described Myrtle Beach in the story. Some feared that North Carolina's old coastal preservation law "can't counter forces that favor fairways, condos and highways over dunes, marshes and beaches." The state would need new regulations if it were to save its fragile coast from being "Myrtled."

The story quoted Duke University geologist Orrin Pilkey: "If we're going to save our beaches for future generations, we're going to have to think the unthinkable. We're going to have to really move back. That means a lot of buildings that have to be demolished."

Or what? asked Shiffer.

"As soon as the big money is here, it will be like Myrtle Beach," Pilkey answered.

The front page story was dominated by a huge crab's-eye-view photograph of a crumpled Budweiser can lying on the beach in the foreground; in mid-ground, a little girl played in the sand with a high-rise hotel towering behind her. The photo caption described the child playing on "the littered coastline of Myrtle Beach."

Ashby Ward wasted no time in stoning the messenger. The MBA Chamber of Commerce would consider dropping all advertising with the *News & Observer*, he announced. As for the beer can photo, it was "ridiculous," because local beaches were cleaned daily. Ward was right, of course, but they were also trashed daily.

Then *Sun News* columnist Bob Bestler jumped in. At his best, Bestler was the eyes, ears and heart of Myrtle Beach. At his worst, he was Ashby Ward's stooge. Referring to Shiffer's story on July 30, Bestler sneered: "The horror, the horror."

"Now I hate to sound like some kind of parochial hometown Babbitt," wrote Bestler, describing himself perfectly, "but most of what this guy wrote was so ignorant it hardly deserves a response." Bestler proceeded to demonstrate his own ignorance by challenging whether there were, in fact, pigeons on the beach. Then he came to the infamous Budweiser can: "Now, I'm not going to say you can't find a beer can on a Grand Strand Beach . . . but I can say I have been walking the beach for 11 years and the only litter I have seen are the broken sea shells washed in from the ocean. Beer cans? For me, the next one will be the first one."

I nearly had an aneurysm as I read Bestler's whopper. Grabbing my trusty camera, I rushed down to the beach and, in less than an hour, shot a roll of film documenting not just pigeons, but piles of beer cans, beer bottles and other debris, as well as green pools of standing water around drainpipes. I had the film developed and mailed the photos off to my erstwhile hero. Not only did he fail to acknowledge my "gift," he wrote a follow-up column a week later, questioning Shiffer's accuracy and fairness.

Shame on you, Bob.

In mid-July a murderous heat wave settled over most of the eastern United States, killing more than 200 people, including about a dozen in South Carolina. Local hospitals treated scores for heat-related illness. Utility companies generated record levels of power almost daily to keep air conditioners humming. Temperatures between 100 and 105 degrees were recorded throughout the state. "I can't take another minute of this," a tourist told *The Sun News*. "I feel like I'm going to melt." She was not alone.

At Barefoot Landing some shops closed for several days when the air conditioning went out; others kept right on working through the heat. On July 21, I turned on my air conditioner for the first time. The feeble unit was powerless to cool my sweltering apartment but it drove my power bill from $50 a month to $220. Day after day, the unrelenting sun glinted off miles of black asphalt, crawling traffic and the white sand parking lot in front of my apartment. The sky seemed to burn, straining my eyes and numbing my brain. The days of heat were surreal, like a fever dream or a sleep-walking nightmare. I canceled appointments to stay out of the heat and joined thousands of others who sought the cool air of malls, theaters and Boulevard arcades. So I happened to be in Myrtle Square Mall on July 31. A typical cavern of commerce, the mall was packed with refugees from the heat − aimless teenagers, screaming infants, bored tourists. A Halloween shop was already open for business. In the check-out line at Eckerd's Drugs was a bucket of golf balls with the iconic Christian fish and the inscription, "I once was lost but now am found."

Owned and operated by Burroughs & Chapin, Myrtle Square Mall was built in 1974, the first mall on the Strand. And it would be the first to be demolished after B&C opened its enormous Mall of

South Carolina. Because this was a B&C mall, it housed a B&C employment office, so I dropped in to pick up a job application. Who knows? Maybe Doug Wendel needed a chauffeur. The list of available jobs ranged from staff assistant in a real estate sales office, paying $10.31 an hour, to a variety of food service and amusement park jobs in the $6.00- to $7.50-an-hour range. On second thought, Wendel could drive himself.

The hot, deadly summer wore on. Debra Boyd of Conway was killed in a two-car wreck on U.S. 501, the first of three Horry County traffic fatalities in August. A shark bit a 10-year old boy in the surf two blocks south of the Pavilion. It took 200 stitches to close the wounds on his back and head. In other misadventures, sixteen riders got stuck in the air for an hour when a ride at North Myrtle Beach Grand Prix broke down. Three people were injured when a go-cart went out of control at Myrtle Beach Grand Prix South. At the Pavilion Amusement Park, a three-year-old girl was injured when her leg was caught under the moving platform of the historic carousel.

Undercover officers arrested a twenty-two-year-old man for illegal body piercing at the Dead Head Shop on Ocean Boulevard. A tourist was robbed at gunpoint on Withers Drive, a few blocks from my apartment. A thirty-seven-year-old man, arrested by Myrtle Beach police for drinking in public, was found dead in the city jail. Down at Goodfella's Pizza, David said he knew the guy. They had shared some time in jail and local shelters.

In a story destined to become a "Movie of the Week," the FBI arrested the three Bellamy brothers, from Little River, in connection with a string of nine bank robberies from Calabash, North Carolina, to Myrtle Beach. Larry, Claude and Alvin Bellamy made off with some $700,000 over a period of seven years. What's more, Larry Bellamy was a former lieutenant with the Myrtle Beach Police Department; Claude was a former patrolman with the Horry County Police Department. An early tip in the case came when someone noticed on the bank surveillance tapes that one of the robbers used a police shooting stance when he held bank employees at gunpoint. Former co-workers looked at the tapes and said, "That's James Larry Bellamy."

As tropical storms whipped around in the Caribbean, temperatures scorched the air and the political rhetoric. An impending gambling referendum, the Burroughs & Chapin business park and a growing controversy over the Confederate flag dominated public debate. Down at City Hall, the issues were more personal.

On July 20, Mayor McBride missed a flight to New York with City Manager Tom Leath and other officials to review the city's bond rating. A flurry of interoffice memos ensued. Within days copies of the memos were making the rounds through fourth estate and political circles. Inevitably, they reached Bob Bestler and the pages of *The Sun News*:

> To: Tom Leath – City Manager
> From: Mayor Mark McBride
> Re: Memo 99-60 New York Bond Trip
>
> You would not believe the morning I had. It was one of the few times I actually left the house on time. Unfortunately, a mixture of no working cash machines and traffic lights kept me from making the trip.
>
> I hope the meeting went to your satisfaction, and I am looking forward to an update. In fact, I believe this update should be added to the Council workshop scheduled for Thursday so that all of Council can be informed regarding our bonding activities. . . .

> To: Tom Leath
> From: [Councilman] Wayne Gray
> Re: New York Bond Trip
>
> I was in the process of sending you a memo to request an addition to Thursday's workshop agenda regarding the trip to New York by yourself, Mike Shelton and the Mayor. I am interested in the response from the rating agencies regarding the proposed bond issuance and general perspective of the City's financial status.
>
> However, I was surprised to learn the Mayor was unable to attend due to missing the flight. I am somewhat embarrassed for the City, given the importance of such an issue, that the Mayor was scheduled to attend the various meetings with the rating agency representatives and hope his unexplained absence did not receive a negative impression.
>
> In addition, what is the cost to the City in terms of plane ticket, room reservation, etc., that was not used and is there a policy requiring reimbursement by council members when such an event occurs?

To: Councilman W. Wayne Gray
From: Mayor Mark McBride
Re: Memorandum to Tom Leath

I am in receipt of your memo to the City Manager regarding the trip to New York. I am sure that all of Council is aware of the true spirit of public service and concern that sparked this correspondence and I can assure you that I appreciate it for exactly what it is.

I am also pleased at your ability to feel embarrassed on another's behalf, and I am grateful for your honorable example.

However, as you are apparently unaware, the City Manager and I already discussed an early return in order to attend the funeral of a friend. Further, our bond rating is a direct result of the management of the city by Mr. Leath and his designated assistants.

Apparently, I have more confidence in Mr. Leath's ability to explain my absence than you, but I am sure that you and he can work that out. I am confident that he and I will be able to reach an equitable resolution regarding expenses . . . as we did when you were so intent upon joining us in Atlanta. Hopefully, this will not require an illegal session of the Council to attain closure.

To: Tom Leath – City Manager
From: Mayor Mark McBride
Re: Memo 99-65 New York Trip Response

I am in receipt of an extremely interesting memo from Councilman Gray regarding the Bond trip to New York. While I am pleased that the councilman has followed my example of memorandum correspondence, I am somewhat disappointed that he is unaware of the City Expense policies. I recall that he was at one time so concerned about them that he stopped a Council Meeting in order to rewrite the policy to his taste.

As I recall, the councilman was also rather upset about our trip to visit the Mayor of Atlanta. By the way, was the City reimbursed the $800 plane ticket when Mr. Gray found last minute schedule changes to be acceptable?

It is reassuring that Mr. Gray is eager that all policies be followed. And I am sure your answer will lack the unfortunate rancor of his request. . . .

I am gratified by Mr. Gray's ringing endorsement of my abilities and belief in the necessity of my attendance. . . .

I am looking forward to the briefing from this meeting on Thursday, and hope that all will be explained to Mr. Gray's satisfaction.

Perhaps it was the August heat, perhaps tension over an approaching storm. Whatever was happening, it brought out the worst in people. In Georgetown County, a county councilman and a local realtor had a chance meeting in a Mexican restaurant, exchanged words and were soon pummeling each other amidst the chips and salsa.

The 1999 hurricane season hit high gear on the steamy Tuesday of August 24. Attention along the Southeastern coast focused on three tropical storms. Emily and Cindy did not seem to pose any immediate threat, but Dennis was moving north along the Bahamas, taking aim on the Carolina coast. That morning *The Sun News* had a front page story introducing us to Dennis, with its forty-five mile per hour winds and its twelve mile per hour drift toward the west-northwest. "I don't understand what's happening out there, but things are popping," said Jerry Jarrell, director of the National Hurricane Center in Miami.

On August 24, an unusually surly crowd of about a hundred came out for a county council meeting in Conway to protest a proposed landfill in Red Bluff. They carried signs demanding, "No More Dumping On Us – More Roads, Less Landfills."

That same evening, Myrtle Beach City Council had its regular seven o'clock meeting at the Law Enforcement Center. It was a civil and uneventful affair, dominated by B&C-related issues, including the business park and a controversial plan to expand Myrtle Beach International Airport. By ten o'clock, the council had gone through its agenda and went into executive session to discuss a delicate personnel matter.

It seems that a couple of weeks earlier, a Myrtle Beach police officer, making late night rounds, had approached a vehicle parked in the tall pines near the intersection of U.S. 17 and 21st Avenue North. Inside the vehicle, according to the officer's official report, he found Councilman Gray and a female member of the city budget staff in a compromising position. Upon questioning by Tom Leath, both Gray (who was married) and the woman denied any misconduct. Nevertheless, McBride had the police report and felt he had the upper hand when he called the executive session to "air out" the accusation.

I had heard rumors of the police report, but it was far from my mind when I left the council chamber with other stragglers that night. We went out into the muggy, late summer night, confident the city was in good hands.

Citizens remaining in the chamber were soon startled by the muffled sounds of furniture banging around in the executive chamber. Mayor McBride ran out of the room into the council chamber, calling for police. The other council members emerged and dispersed quickly into the night, without comment or explanation. I was already on my second beer down at Shamrock's when Councilwoman Rachel Broadhurst charged into the darkened bar, looked around anxiously, then sat down with some other politicos, ordered a drink and went into deep consultation.

It was two days later before *The Sun News* reported that McBride and Wayne Gray had come to blows in the executive session. The police report of the melee cited Gray as the "subject" and McBride as the victim, saying the mayor had red marks on his face and scratches on his hands. Subsequent accounts suggested that while assistant city attorney Jamie Crolan locked his arms around Gray to restrain him, McBride took bare-knuckled jabs, bloodying Gray's mouth and bruising his face.

McBride expressed no regrets, except to say, "It was a bad day for the city. But I will not stop doing what I believe is in the best interest of the city." He said he was the victim of repeated verbal attacks by council members.

Councilman Chuck Marino dismissed McBride acidly. "We have a rogue individual who is hell bent on destroying the city and the city council. . . . He seems incapable of understanding the difference between opposing his stand on an issue and opposing him personally."

Councilwoman Judy Rodman said, "I was scared. It was startling, ugly and mean." If McBride and Gray couldn't behave themselves, she said, she would resign. "This is no way for a group of adults to act."

Rachel Broadhurst concurred. "I'm really disappointed. These are grown men we're talking about. Men in their thirties, not children. You'd think they'd be able to behave."

The Sun News also concurred. " . . . Before Monday's city council meeting, Gray and McBride should beg the community's forgiveness and apologize to their council peers. They should do so in front of cameras and tape recorders. For a town's credibility as it faces a potential hurricane, anything less would be abysmal."

Gray heard the call to contrition. On the morning of September 2, following a special meeting of city council, he stepped before the cameras in front of City Hall. His wife and parents stood behind him. His voice trembled and his eyes teared as he said, "I am extremely embarrassed. I want to sincerely apologize to the city's employees, to my colleagues on council and to the citizens of Myrtle Beach." (*The Sun News* also revealed that Gray had been arrested in June for simple assault and battery in an altercation with a tow truck operator; the charges were later dropped by the operator.)

The mayor steadfastly insisted he had nothing to apologize for, but Councilman Martino thought otherwise. "There is no way the mayor can consider himself a victim," Martino said. "He cold-cocked Gray repeatedly while Gray was being held back. That's not defending yourself. The only victim in this thing was the city, which deserves an apology from its mayor."

One person who couldn't resist getting in a few licks of his own was local NAACP chief H.H. Singleton, who called on McBride and Gray to resign immediately and for Myrtle Beach police to arrest them for disturbing the peace. "Had this violent and atrocious confrontation occurred between two nongovernmental citizens, they would have already been arrested," Singleton told *The Sun News*. "There should and must not be a double standard."

Gray did not respond to Singleton's dig, but McBride rose to the bait: "I can appreciate Reverend Singleton's concern of a Myrtle Beach matter, living in Conway. But I will not apologize and I will not resign from doing my job."

A correspondent to *The Sun News* captured the irony – or hypocrisy – of the situation, suggesting that the solution to brawling city officials was "to request the National Guard appear at Myrtle Beach City Council meetings in the future."

Stuck In Minimum-wage Hell

At three o'clock in the afternoon, 365 days a year, black women lined up along Ocean Boulevard, tired, disheveled, carrying their shabby possessions in plastic grocery bags, wearing the dirty smocks from the hotels where they had just spent the day changing beds, washing linens, cleaning bathrooms. They stood on the sidewalks, sat on retaining walls and sometimes on curbs as they waited for the procession of buses to take them home. The fact that there were no bus shelters or benches on Ocean Boulevard – or anywhere else in Myrtle Beach – was a perfect measure of the city's attitude toward public transportation and toward the subsistence-wage employees who kept this town running.

Resort towns everywhere are faced with a similar problem: the cyclic nature of the work, coupled with low wages and compounded by high real estate prices, make it difficult to find workers living nearby to staff the service industry. In Jackson Hole, Wyoming, and Aspen, Colorado, workers have been known to sleep in the woods and walk miles to work for the honor of serving Barbra Streisand a cappuccino. This blue-collar town rarely offers its service workers the benefits of celebrity hobnobbing. While it does provide a decent living to the kids who tend bars and wait tables, for thousands of others – mostly black – there are only $6.25-an-hour jobs in restaurant kitchens, amusement parks and hotel laundry rooms, exacerbated by mind-numbing commutes from homes up to seventy miles inland, on dilapidated labor buses, some with no air conditioning.

In 1998, Horry County's average annual wage was $18,551, according to the U.S. Bureau of Labor Statistics, while the average wage nationwide was $31,908. In personal income Horry ranked 311 out of 313 metropolitan statistical areas. Manufacturing accounted for six percent of jobs in the Myrtle Beach area, with that percentage dropping.

"You have a situation where a few people in Myrtle Beach are making a lot of money, but most of the people aren't making very much at all," economist William Fruth told *The Sun News* in 1997. "While the area is creating jobs, the quality of those jobs is suspect."

Working two or three jobs for fifty to seventy hours a week was a way of life for thousands of local service and retail employees. For the rest of us, bad service and slow checkouts were a way of life. Everybody in the service industry seemed resigned to this eternal verity. Service and retail workers tried to hurry, to apologize, to explain. They were generally polite and philosophical – and you would be, too, if you lived on the Grand Strand long enough. Myrtle Beach, said a bartender friend, was the perfect blend of Las Vegas charm and Southern efficiency.

"Your Achilles heel is finding, training and keeping employees," tourism consultant Al Nucifora told the Myrtle Beach Area Chamber of Commerce at its 1999 banquet. Overworked, underemployed personnel are not happy and unhappy employees make unhappy customers. To meet the rising wave of tourism, "you will need to train continuously and pay more," Nucifora told the Grand Strand's economic leaders. He might as well have been talking to the ocean.

With the unemployment rate at 2.6 percent, "Help Wanted" signs started appearing along U.S. 17 in the spring of 1999. "I think some of the businesses aren't going to be able to hire as many employees as they'd like," said Ashby Ward, demonstrating his grasp of the situation. Cashiers stuffed flyers into shopping bags, offering jobs to their customers. Businesses gave bonuses to employees who brought in a new hire. Others offered golf rounds and even vacations to Disney World to selected employees. They did everything but raise the pay scale; that they couldn't do without wrecking the economic structure of the Grand Strand.

As the area boomed through the 1990s, the one thing that did not keep pace was the service industry wage. "The labor market is strange. You have a shortage, but you won't raise the wages. That never makes sense," said Frank Hefner, a College of Charleston economist.

It's no mystery why Grand Strand wages were so low. Business leaders long ago started importing labor for the tourist season. One of the first sources was the Caribbean, where a consortium of beachfront hotels found a steady supply of black labor to do their housework. Others looked inland, to the "Black Belt" counties of the Pee Dee and the Santee, where some of the poorest people in the United States lived. Hotel owners organized transportation companies, assembled

fleets of old buses and sent them deep into cotton and tobacco country, where the unemployment rate was typically above ten percent.

On a steamy July morning, I caught a Pee Dee Regional
Transportation Authority bus in Marion, a town forty-five miles from
the Grand Strand and as remote in culture and spirit as the cornfields
of Kansas. We departed Marion at 6:30, drove to Mullins to pick up
workers, turned around, came back to Marion, stopping periodically
for more riders. The fare was three dollars each way, for employees
who made approximately $6.25 an hour and could work only six or
seven hours a day. Most businesses were careful to keep their employees' hours below forty per week, avoiding overtime pay, insurance
and other benefits.

The bus filled up with African Americans, young and old, mostly
women, several wearing the smocks and aprons from their jobs. I sat
next to Henry Thompson, a middle-aged dishwasher at one of the
large pancake houses on U.S. 17. He was a native of the Pee Dee, the
son of a sharecropper, he told me. Thompson spent most of his adult
life in Rochester, New York, where he made good money as a shipping
clerk. Like many expatriate South Carolinians, he dreamed of returning home, but when he got back to Marion County, the only work he
could find was washing dishes in Myrtle Beach. So he rode the bus for
ninety minutes each morning to get in five hours of work. If the bus
got stuck in traffic and Thompson missed his 8:30 starting time, that
was just lost pay. He got off at 1:30 and killed the next hours in the
library or Myrtle Square Mall, until his bus headed back at 4:00 p.m.

Riding toward the coast that morning, the passengers slept or
talked softly in the widening dawn. As we approached Myrtle Beach
on U.S. 501, the bus stopped at fast food restaurants and at Legends
Country Club to let passengers off. Traffic congealed, coming to a
bumper-to-bumper crawl before we crossed the Waterway. We inched
into Myrtle Beach, stopping periodically to discharge passengers by
ones and two. Finally, on Ocean Boulevard, the last dozen got off and
headed to their hotels.

Between 3:00 and 4:00 that afternoon, buses moved up and down
the Boulevard picking up their riders. I got on at 10th Avenue North,
joining the weary, sweaty workers, subdued in the mid-afternoon heat.
The bus' air conditioner strained fitfully against the ninety-degree-
plus temperature. The driver told me the bus had to go fifty-five miles
per hour for the AC to work efficiently, something it was rarely able
to do. Some of the women opened windows to get fresh air. We
stopped along U.S. 501 to pick up workers at their restaurants and the

country club. As we hit the open road west of Conway, the air conditioner kicked in. The bus began to cool down; the passengers came to life with talk and laughter.

It was nearly 5:00 p.m. as we approached Marion, dropping off workers in front of grimy little roadside stores, shanty houses and sprawling tobacco fields. At 5:30, the last riders debarked, ending their day eleven hours after they started and about thirty-five dollars richer — before taxes.

In the early 1990s, Grand Strand businesses discovered another huge — and infinitely more appealing — source of labor. For thousands of foreign students, a summer in America was a dream come true — even if it meant working for less than $7.00 an hour and living in barrack-like conditions. And for employers, there was an additional benefit: the students were *white!* Well-scrubbed, young and happy, they were vastly more presentable than the weary, stoic workers hauled in daily from the agricultural wastelands of Marion and Williamsburg counties. This meant they could work in restaurant dining rooms; they could be hired for retail and other "front" jobs. By 1999, more than 700 foreign students were on the Grand Strand.

Working through the U.S. Labor Department's Alien Labor Certification Program, employers had to demonstrate that they had exhausted efforts to hire qualified American workers. They agreed to offer the prevailing wage in the area. Workers were assigned to work at a specific business and perform a specific job. The largest employer was Burroughs & Chapin, of course. The company's human resources department recruited and brought in hundreds of students each year to work at its Pavilion and other amusement parks.

The greatest number of student workers came from Russia and the former Eastern Bloc countries; Ireland and France ran a close second and third, with some fifty other countries sending their young people to run merry-go-rounds and wait tables. Each summer Myrtle Beach became a veritable United Nations of youth. Their many languages blended in the streets, bars and restaurants. Students lined up at the door an hour before Chapin Memorial Library opened each morning to reserve a computer to e-mail back home.

Companies such as B&C helped arrange student passports and travel, but it was up to students to pay their own way. They also had to pay for their housing when they arrived. Expenses were so great that many sought second and third jobs to make ends meet. Of course, one of those expenses was having fun, which is what youth of all nations come to Myrtle Beach for. Nightspots such as Neal's and the Hogan Stand catered almost exclusively to foreign students during the summer months.

Lodging was a challenge for the students and the companies that recruited them. Several older motels, such as the Rainbow Court, turned themselves into student dormitories for the summer months. B&C owned two old motels – the Kings Road Inn and the Oceanic Inn – where the company put its foreign student employees up in bunk beds, four to a room, each paying about seventy dollars a week. Not only did the company control its employees' housing, but it had the students under contract and held their visas. With this arrangement, B&C was more than ever like the old company town proprietor, controlling almost all aspects of its employees' lives.

For thousands of other seasonal employees – people like Margaret and her son Kevin, people like David, Stacey and Brandee at Goodfella's Pizza – finding a place to live was a constant challenge. Because they had no operating capital, they were stuck in flophouse rooms – with a kitchenette, if they were lucky – paying up to $300 a week rent. Under such circumstances people took on any roommates they could find and did whatever else – legal or otherwise – to make the rent on their Myrtle Beach wage. By contrast, I paid $475 a month for a 640-square-foot apartment. But that meant having a month's rent, security deposit and utility deposit, all up front. This amount was simply out of reach for most seasonal employees.

Families needed at least a $700 stake to move to Myrtle Beach, said Chuck Bachelor, director of Helping Hand, an emergency help agency that assisted hundreds of homeless and near-homeless families each year. But too many arrived with only their dreams and no knowledge of the local economy. "They come with no food, or money, no clothes, or furniture," Bachelor told *The Sun News*. "Just themselves and a car that's about out of gas." A recurring theme in the story of homelessness on the Grand Strand was automobile breakdowns. A repair of even $100 was out of reach for most seasonal workers. Without their cars – and with such poor public transportation – they could not get to work, so they wound up living on the street or in their broken-down automobiles.

"They come here thinking this is the land of milk and honey," said Capt. Michael Horton of the Salvation Army. ". . . There are no cheap hotel rates during the summer. It takes a father's full-week pay to simply pay hotel rent."

"In the summer, they can find lots of jobs, but no affordable housing," said Libby Carter, director of Street Reach Mission. "And in the winter, they can find cheap hotels but can't find as many jobs."

The shortage of affordable housing was no mystery: "You have a lot of high rollers coming in and buying expensive condos and vacation property, so the cost of property is high," economist William Fruth said. "Now where do the workers live? I'm sure you have a lot of people moving there, looking for work because they hear jobs are available. But when they get there, they find they can't afford a place to live."

Business leaders recognized that the shortage of affordable housing was one of the greatest challenges facing the Grand Strand. "That has been the roadblock to getting more people in here to work," said Ashby Ward. "There's going to have to be more affordable housing." According to a survey by the John S. and James L. Knight Foundation, sixty-two percent of local residents said that lack of affordable housing was a problem, *The Sun News* reported. That problem was compounded when builders could not find workers due to the lack of housing; the shortage of construction workers drove up the cost of building new houses, making it harder to create affordable housing. "It's a chicken-and-egg kind of thing," Ward said.

One solution to the affordable housing crisis was "manufactured housing." Horry County led South Carolina, with 26,000 mobile or manufactured housing units in 1999, and developers were scrambling to put in more developments west of the Waterway. Residents were in an uproar, in one case demonstrating in front of county council chambers to express opposition to a new mobile home park. Mobile homes, they said, depressed property values and attracted crime.

By whatever means, Myrtle Beach desperately needed affordable housing in 1999. Three shelters – Street Reach Mission, Promise Land Ranch and Myrtle Beach Haven – were full much of the year. A survey showed there were some 300 homeless people on the streets of Myrtle Beach.

To meet the housing shortage, a private consortium hoped to establish a center to help move the homeless into permanent housing. The plan called for rezoning four acres in the Futrell Park planned urban development to build the transitional housing center on 10th Avenue. At the October 12 city council meeting, council voted 6-1 to allow the zoning change. The dissenting vote belonged to Mayor Mark McBride, who said, "I believe it sends the wrong message to the homeless community across the area and the state. I don't think we should encourage homeless people to come to Myrtle Beach." At least McBride was consistent. As a councilman two years earlier, he had opposed municipal support for the Community Kitchen, a private relief organization that served meals to the poor five days a week.

Labor conditions in Myrtle Beach were hardly unique in the state which ranked dead last in the nation for the percent of its labor force who were in unions. The South Carolina Chamber of Commerce advertised the state's low union activity to recruit industry and trained new companies on how to keep unions out of their shops. The Myrtle Beach Area Chamber of Commerce had taught seminars "on how to treat employees so they would not be prone to try to organize," Ashby Ward told *The Sun News*. "I don't know if there's very much interest in unions here. There are a few unionized properties, but it has just not been a hot topic in South Carolina."

On September 7-9, the state chapter of the AFL-CIO held its annual convention in Myrtle Beach so it could protest the area's low wages and hostility toward organized labor. In this working class resort, many tourists were union workers, state AFL-CIO president Donna Dewitt said, but the political and business leaders of the city showed no respect for organized labor. "The attitude is, 'We'll take working people's money, but we have no respect for their way of life.'" Some members had not forgotten Mark McBride's words the year before, comparing organized labor to the Ku Klux Klan and skinheads.

Union members used their convention to stage a demonstration in front of City Hall, then marched across the street to the Chamber of Commerce to sing their songs and carry signs reading "S.C. Chamber promotes Third World Labor Force."

"We just observed Labor Day in South Carolina," Dewitt told *The Sun News*. "What does that mean for working families? What does that mean when you ride down past Broadway at the Beach and see beautiful buildings, and you see people working at minimum wage?"

The forty-third convention of the South Carolina AFL-CIO met in the Holiday Inn-Oceanfront, the only hotel on the Grand Strand with a unionized housekeeping staff. John Sweeny, national president of the AFL-CIO, was on hand September 9 to address the small group in the ballroom. It was a boilerplate speech, with a litany of references to corporate abuses, greedy CEOs and underpaid, overworked Americans trying to keep their families together as they held down two and three jobs.

"Income disparity and human suffering are not integral parts of a healthy economy," Sweeny said. "We absolutely must not stand for the status quo."

After the address I stepped out of the hotel into a thunderstorm that was washing over the city. For the second time in three days, millions of gallons of water poured off parking lots and roads, rooftops and construction sites, overwhelming the stormwater system, flooding streets and neighborhoods, washing out large chunks of beachfront landscaping, dumping bacteria into the surf. In front of some of the discharge pipes four-foot deep gashes were carved through the beach by the torrents of water. Ah, just another day in paradise.

A Flag of Dubious Honor

The day was April 10, 1956 – one day after the ninety-first anniversary of the Confederate surrender at Appomattox. Newspapers that morning carried stories of President Eisenhower's proposal to create a national Civil Rights Commission.

On the floor of the state Senate, John D. Long of Union County asked his all-white, all-male colleagues to hang a Confederate flag in the front of the Senate chamber. "The battle flag of the Southern Confederacy inspires our dedication to the resurrection of truth with glorious and eternal vindication," his resolution read in part.

As a member of the House of Representative in 1936, Long had placed a Confederate flag in that chamber. In neither house was there any debate on the resolution or the meaning of the flag.

Commemorating the Confederacy and defending segregation were the twin demons that animated John D. Long. Following the U.S. Supreme Court's 1954 *Brown v. Board of Education* decision, which struck down the doctrine of separate-but-equal in public education, Long introduced a resolution asking Congress to impeach the nine justices. "South Carolina has segregation in the schools and it intends to keep it," he declared in 1959. A year later, he introduced a resolution asking Congress to convene a constitutional convention for the purpose of repealing the Fourteenth Amendment, which was the basis for federal civil rights efforts.

"South Carolina's Confederate soldiers and brave Confederate women, the original Ku Klux Klan and Wade Hampton and his Red Shirts, their names and characters are as precious today as they were the day they were placed in sacrifice upon the altars of our country," Long told the Senate in a 1960 speech celebrating the centennial of secession. "We honor them and we are proud of them. We will defend them from defamation to the death."

In that same speech Long told senators to "dismiss from your consideration any little-sister sob stories about the South's brutality to the slaves and its inhuman treatment of captive and fugitive slaves."

In February 1962 the General Assembly passed a concurrent resolution to fly the Confederate flag above the State House dome as part of the Civil War centennial celebration. Alabama had raised the flag over its State House in 1961, symbolizing defiance of the federal courts. Though the concurrent resolution was passed six weeks after the first black student applied for admission to Clemson University, South Carolina lawmakers who remembered that day said they meant no hostility toward African Americans or the federal government. "We did it to celebrate, not to divide the state," said former House Speaker Rex Carter of Greenville.

Whatever the motives of the General Assembly, the Civil War centennial passed but the rebel banner never came down from the State House dome. "There was no thought, at least on my part, of it flying forever," Carter told the Assocated Press in 1999. Yet there it was – the conflicted symbol of a conflicted state – fluttering from South Carolina's most honored staff.

"The past isn't over," Faulkner wrote of the South. "It isn't even past." Never more so than in South Carolina.

July 15, 1999: The National Association for the Advancement of Colored People was meeting in New York when the South Carolina delegation brought an emergency resolution before the body, calling for an economic boycott of the state until the Confederate flag was removed from the State House dome, the Senate and House chambers. The resolution resounded through the state like the boom of cannons across Charleston harbor.

"There is no limitation as to what business and how long and how widespread the sanction will be," said the Reverend H.H. Singleton of Conway, a member of the NAACP national board. "The resolution gets the support of the national [board] in whatever the South Carolina conference decides to do in bringing down the flag."

It was a day of reckoning for the Palmetto State, as advocates on both sides recognized. Not only was the NAACP questioning a sacred symbol and a hallowed cause, but the descendants of South Carolina's slaves were dictating terms in a realm where they were still economically and politically second-class citizens. And they were doing it – not with the threat of federal intervention – but with the media and economic muscle. The NAACP overture possessed brazenness and sophistication that caught the state's white Republican establishment completely off-guard.

Glenn McConnell of Charleston, the Senate's most outspoken flag supporter and owner of a Civil War memorabilia shop, denounced the NAACP's "mean-spirited" action: "They have touted themselves as a civil rights organization and here they are carrying on a boycott. . . . They have almost reversed the tables. The oppressed are now the oppressors."

It was not immediately clear what shape the NAACP boycott would take, but there was no question that South Carolina's No. 1 industry – tourism – would take a hit. The prospect sent chills through the Grand Strand and sent Ashby Ward and other tourism promoters scrambling for their calculators. Figures on African American tourism were sketchy, though the NAACP's resolution on economic sanctions claimed sixty-eight percent of all African American family reunions were held in South Carolina. Myrtle Beach certainly got its share. Black families came to town on chartered buses and rented whole floors of Boulevard hotels during the summer months.

The state Department of Parks, Recreation and Tourism offered these statistics: There were no numbers available on black tourism on the Grand Strand, but two million black tourists came to the state in 1997 – or about seven percent of the 28.5 million total – and accounted for $280 million in direct spending. The Grand Strand saw 10.3 million U.S. visitors who spent $2.24 billion in 1997. Extrapolating from these figures, *The Sun News* reasoned that some 721,000 blacks came to the Grand Strand in 1997 and spent about $95 million.

Of course, there was more at stake than African American dollars, as Bob Bestler pointed out. When Arizona refused to recognize Martin Luther King's birthday in 1987, blacks called a boycott, costing that state some $340 million in tourism – including the 1993 Super Bowl. "That wasn't all black money," Bestler warned.

And Bestler reminded his readers of something else: "To many Americans outside South Carolina – not to mention many more who live here, black and white – the Confederate flag is a visceral symbol that represents our country's worst instincts. It's the Ku Klux Klan. It's the neo-Nazi. It is an in-your-face insult to black America."

Such well reasoned, idealistic arguments were utterly wasted on the ones who most needed to hear them. For not only was the Confederate flag a symbol of racism to most of the world, it was also a measure of the isolation, self-absorption and morbid sense of inferiority that have haunted generations of white Southerners. I had always viewed the Confederate flag with some amusement. If anything, it symbolized unreconstructed ignorance. If it made South Carolina appear backward and doltish, well, that's what we were. But it took years for me to understand the connection between the flag and racism. African Americans were never so ambivalent.

The man most responsible for making the flag an issue was Senator Kay Patterson, one of the first African Americans elected to the General Assembly in the twentieth century. Shortly after he was sworn into the House in 1975, he asked his colleagues to remove the Confederate banner from the State House dome and the two chambers. "Nothing from the other side. Silence," he said a quarter century later. "I was a lone voice crying in the wilderness."

The issue could have been quietly resolved when it briefly flared in 1987. With his political skills and telegenic, clean-cut image, Governor Carroll Campbell might have cast himself as a figure of moral authority and high principle. Like Jimmy Carter, he might have been a symbol of change and progress in Dixie. Campbell listened instead to the dark and primal voices of South Carolina, who warned that white people would turn against him if he turned against their flag. An opportunity for everyone was lost.

By the 1990s, Kay Patterson's little spark of protest finally caught flame. In 1994 the Democratic-controlled Senate passed a compromise bill that would have removed the flag from the dome, and assured that all other memorials, symbols and public names honoring the Civil War and its heroes would be preserved. With Campbell watching from the sideline, the Republican-controlled House killed the bill.

After eight years of public pieties and moral vacuity, Carroll Campbell walked away from the flag imbroglio. His hand-picked successor, David Beasley, was not so lucky. Elected in 1994, the young Christian conservative read the early notices describing him as potential vice presidential timber and took them much too seriously. Before he could be presented on the platform at a national convention, he had to address the flag issue. Beasley called for bringing it down and putting it on a monument to Confederate dead, to be erected on the State House grounds. His effort met the same fate as the 1994 compromise, but he paid dearly for it. Bumper stickers and signs appeared around the state suggesting, "Dump Beasley – Keep The Flag." They were a precursor of the rage that would make him a one-term governor.

Now, in 1999, the bitter banner was threatening to sweep up a new governor and take a bite out of the state's burgeoning tourism industry. In a state that had spent a century and a half stumbling from one disaster to the next, the Battle of the Flag represented only the latest failure of leadership.

Like the dogma of transubstantiation, Southern history remains a sacred mystery, even to those of us who have lived with it all our lives. How could a disastrous war, in defense of an unholy institution, be transformed into the shining and glorious "Lost Cause?"

Faced with the consequences of their folly, faced with the ghosts of 258,000 dead and the burden of 150,000 disabled, faced with the memory of all they had believed and loved and lost, white Southerners turned inward in the years after the Civil War. Through a self-conscious act of intellectual alchemy, they transmorgrified their loss into the Lost Cause. Southern history was not just retold but reinvented and internalized to create a whole new mythology. In the creed of the Lost Cause, the antebellum South was a bucolic paradise of dashing cavaliers, hoop-skirted maidens and their faithful, affectionate black servants. Into this Eden of magnolias and moonlight crept the serpent of Northern industrial capitalism – greedy, profane, irreverent of place or tradition, fueled by waves of Catholic and Jewish immigration. The disastrous but honorable war was fought, not to preserve slavery, but to preserve the ineffable Southern Way of Life. It was the responsibility of white Southerners to remember the sacrifices of the Confederate nation and to preserve the last vestiges of that tradition – states' rights and white supremacy. These two shabby tenets were all that remained, all that white Southerners could salvage from the bleeding and dying. The mythology of the Lost Cause became the South's secular religion, imbued with the spiritual qualities of memory, kinship and sacrifice. Generations of white Southerners have felt called to defend this religion with rope and torch.

For two generations after the Civil War, Southerners dedicated monuments and cemeteries to the memory of all they had lost. At each lugubrious ceremony they trotted out the sacred relics and shibboleths.

The Reverend Dr. John L. Girardeau of Charleston spoke on Confederate Memorial Day 1871, on occasion of the reinterment of South Carolinians killed at Gettysburg. According to historian Walter Edgar, Girardeau's address was "a detailed guidebook for the Lost Cause and a justification for the overthrow of Reconstruction."

"Let us cling to our identity as a people!" the reverend doctor intoned, and "tenaciously hold to the fragments of a noble past." He urged resistance to the Reconstruction government and told his listeners to institute "peculiar customs and organizations" to preserve the past; to set aside memorial days and create memorial associations; to collect and publish "materials of our own history"; to perpetuate memory and honor "by making our nurseries, schools and colleges channels for conveying from generation to generation our own type of thought, sentiment and opinion."

White Southerners have made a religion out of perpetuating "our own type of thought, sentiment and opinion." It has marked us as a people and set us apart from the rest of the nation and the world. For generations it was ingrained in our political rhetoric, in our public rituals, in our educational system. From the 1930s to the 1980s, South Carolinians were taught state history from the textbooks of Mary C. Simms Oliphant. Oliphant was the daughter of a Confederate Army officer and granddaughter of William Gilmore Simms, one of the antebellum South's leading writers and polemicists on slavery and secession. Oliphant's elementary and junior high school texts went through numerous editions and were the mandated texts for teaching state history in the public schools. Later editions of her books were purged of their most egregious material, but generations of young South Carolinians − black and white − were exposed to Oliphant's parochial and paternalistic views.

"Most masters treated their slaves kindly," she wrote in her 1964 edition of *The History of South Carolina*. "...the law required the master to feed his slaves, clothe them properly and care for them when they were sick." Elsewhere she wrote: "Most slaves were treated well, if only because it was to the planter's interest to have them healthy and contented." Slavery really wasn't so bad in Oliphant's South: "The Africans were used to a hot climate. They made fine workers under the Carolina sun." And besides, look at all the benefits: Slave owners "said that Africans were brought from a worse life to a better one. As slaves, they were trained in the ways of civilization. Above all, the landowners argued, the slaves were given the opportunity to become Christians in a Christian land, instead of remaining heathen in a savage country."

That there were so few slave uprisings in South Carolina "speaks well for both whites and Negroes," she explained.

Oliphant approved of violence done to abolitionists caught in South Carolina before the Civil War, including the Charleston mob that seized abolitionist literature from the post office and burned it. She devoted no less than sixteen pages to the founding of the Confederate government, the battles of the Civil War, the inevitable defeat. Yet she dared not confront the great truth behind the tragedy – that sixty percent of South Carolina's population in 1860 was black, the vast majority of it owned by white people. This demographic and economic reality dictated every important aspect of South Carolina's culture and politics, then and for generations to come. The Confederate flag controversy was only the most recent manifestation.

The Civil War – or Confederate War, as Oliphant insisted on calling it – inspired her most passionate prose. She was clearly captive to the reckless romanticism of Margaret Mitchell, as when she described the depredations of wicked Yankees: "Sherman's soldiers burned houses, ran off livestock, destroyed crops, and took everything that could be carried away. Many fine houses were destroyed by Sherman's men. Among these was Woodlands, the home of William Gilmore Simms. . . ." One family was burned to death in their home, she reported somberly.

"South Carolina suffered dreadfully at Gettysburg," she wrote. "Of the 472 men of the Fourteenth Regiment, only 82 came out alive. Of 39 men of Company K of this regiment, 34 fell at the first fire." At Fredericksburg another South Carolina hero died: "Here Colonel Maxcy Gregg charged, at the head of his men, directly into the enemy's fire, his horse rearing and pitching in terror. Gregg was mortally wounded in the fighting, but the battle ended in a great victory for the Confederates."

And this is Oliphant's paean to her hero, General Wade Hampton III: "On the State House grounds, he rides in bronze, a towering figure on his mettlesome steed, the symbol of all that is best in South Carolina and the South." Yet, in her sixteen pages of fire and fury, Oliphant could not bring herself to mention the single bloodiest battle of the Civil War on South Carolina soil – the assault on Battery Wagener by the black troops of the Massachusetts 54th.

As for the slaves during the war, "The Negroes for the most part stayed on the plantations or farms. . . . The relationship between the whites and Negroes on the plantations was at this time very friendly. Most of the slaves had proved their affection and loyalty to their masters. . . . For more than four years the women and children had remained on the land with only the Negroes to protect them."

Oliphant took a very unreconstructed view of Reconstruction. "For the following eight years South Carolina was governed largely by a ruthless band of thieves," she wrote. Reconstruction allowed Oliphant to portray blacks as passive and easily manipulated creatures. Carpetbagging Republicans "took advantage of the ignorance and lack of experience of the Negroes. . . . Those who did not vote Republican were threatened and mistreated."

She described the heroic defenders of white supremacy – the Red Shirts and, to a lesser degree, the Ku Klux Klan. Both were terrorist organizations whose violent excesses Oliphant smugly justified. "The sight of the mounted klansmen in their white robes was enough to terrorize the Negroes. When the courts did not punish Negroes who were supposed to have committed crimes, the Klan punished them." Vigilantes known as Red Shirts hijacked the election of 1876. Or as Oliphant tells it, the Reconstruction government collapsed "and South Carolina was once more in the possession of its own government." What she meant, of course, was that the forty-percent white population was in control of the government.

History is one of the most important resources of any people. Who owns that resource and how it is used is a critical determinant in who controls a society. For three centuries the history of South Carolina was owned by white people – more specifically, aristocratic white people. When African Americans were even acknowledged in official histories, they were treated as childish creatures, requiring the moral guidance and correction of their white superiors. African American history – such as it was – was little more than oral tradition, but it was a vibrant tradition and it held families and communities together for generations. And it bore witness to centuries of oppression and humiliation. It was a witness few Southern whites ever heard. When they were forced to pay it some attention – during Black History Month, for instance – they were likely to scorn. There was no black history, white folk would say. It didn't exist. Mary Simms Oliphant said so.

White history, on the other hand, is sacred and public – no matter how perverted. In Myrtle Beach, it could be seen in Confederate flag bumper stickers all along the Strand; in Confederate flag T-shirts, towels, sports caps and shot glasses in the beachwear stores. It could be seen in the Civil War Museum, a private collection of Civil War artifacts and Confederate memorabilia, warehoused with a gun shop and shooting range in a rundown building on U.S. 17 Bypass. It could be seen in the three Confederate flags that fluttered year-round in front of the Ocean West Motel, on U.S. 17, in downtown Myrtle Beach. The owner of the nineteen-unit motel was George Trakas, a pudgy, pipe-smoking little man, with a bristly mustache, in his early forties. He was a member of the Sons of Confederate Veterans (SCV) and the League of the South, and wore a Confederate flag T-shirt when I interviewed him in the tiny, cluttered office of his motel. A chihuahua ran around our feet yapping while we spoke.

Trakas was a secessionist who wanted to resurrect the Confederacy, he told me. The federal government was sending Yankees down South to intermarry with us and destroy our ethnic and cultural identity, the Greek American explained. He was contemptuous of "social engineering," "these bleeding heart liberals," and "socialists and idealists . . . who want to bring about utopia."

As the official historian of the League of the South and SCV, Trakas considered himself authoritative on matters of Southern history. Indeed, he talked for nearly an hour about Southern history and culture, about tariffs and constitutional theory, about the conflicts between England and Scotland, without mentioning the subject of African Americans until I brought it up. He seemed startled that I should speak of it.

"The war itself was not fought over slavery," he assured me. "The slave issue was meant to incite insurrection within the Confederate interior, which that never happened {sic} . . . . If the blacks really hated and despised white people, then why did they not rise up in insurrection and revolt and join the Yankee cause?. . . Yankees stirred – and Carpetbaggers stirred – hatred in the South."

With a perfectly straight face Trakas told me that 90,000 blacks served in the Confederate Army.

"During Reconstruction, when the Carpetbaggers came down here, they always set fear tactics [sic] into the blacks to use them as a way to subjugate the Southern whites," Trakas said. "And still today, they do the same thing. Just like the flag issue. The majority of blacks have no beef against the Confederate flag."

This was news to me, I said.

"The Yankee government has done everything it can to indoctrinate the South and its people through the media, through the public school system. . . . We've had about 130 years of public school indoctrination, thus we have the result we've got today. . . . The flag – taking it down – is part of that process. . . .

"The blacks had no hatred of the Southern whites before the Yankee government came down here and instilled hatred. They drove a wedge between the races in order to subjugate the Southern white people. Before that, there was no racial animosity. Everybody had their social and economic role until the Yankees caused hatred between the races. . . . "Trakas said. "Those blacks who have studied history for what it is understand that this war was not over slavery. . . . Now I know the NAACP has come down and stirred the blacks up and called the flag racism and all that kind of stuff, which we don't believe that to be the case. {sic} We believe we've got a right and a duty to preserve history, the truth in history. . . .

"The Confederate flag goes to the heart of all Southerners. . . . It reminds us that we are a conquered nation and we have in common with each other certain cultural values. . . . We fear no man. We fear Jesus Christ only. Christianity and Southern thought and ideology go hand-in-hand with each other; whereas Christianity in the North changes with the time, whatever is politically correct at the time. But Southerners' belief is strict biblical belief. If it says it in the Bible, then it's true. There's nothing to question about it. It says it, that's it, case closed. . . . There's nothing to do but do what the Bible tells you to do . . . whereas, we're gonna have a rational, intellectual debate from a Northern point of view. . . . The Bible says no homosexuals. Homosexuality is wrong. It's as simple as that. There needs to be no debate. There's not a whole lot to think about. It says it and that's it and most Southern people think that way. . . .

"The Northern people have never really took to heart history like the Southerners do," the historian continued. "The Southerners look to the past and they like things to sort of be like they used to be. They're more conservative about things, whereas the Yankees don't care a hill of beans about what happened 150 years ago. We believe our ancestors, for what they did, these things should be revered and taught to our children and to our grandchildren, so that history is not forgotten. And this treachery that has been bestowed upon the Southern people, we're not just gonna let it walk away [sic]. As proud Southerners, we're gonna let our posterity know what the truth is. . . ."

Southerners are "people who think in a conservative fashion, those who do not believe in central government and tyranny," Trakas said. "Southerners are more laid back. They have more Christianity in their lives. They are more friendly to you and less formal. . . . A Northerner sort of gives you this impression they've already seen it all, they've already done it all. They're above what you think. Somehow they know more than the good Lord does. They know what's best for you. It's an attitude. It's a look about it. It's hard for me to explain. . . .

"If you read history and you look at how things are today and if you've studied history, you can see why things are the way they are at this point in time. . . . "

The Confederate flag controversy touched something primal and angry. Nowhere was that anger more evident than in the letters to the editor of *The Sun News* – and their venom was only intensified when that paper called for furling the flag: "What has definitely happened as a result of this renewal of the Confederate battle flag disagreement is that this state has seldom seen in print as much separatist invective as has been expressed," *The Sun News* editorialized on August 11. "The very fact that the flag issue keeps arising is proof of the need to reach a compromise and get this behind us.

"We can do better than this. We must do better than this. Our livelihoods are at stake."

The Sun News published scores of letters on the flag, sometimes pages of them at a time. The great majority was in support of the flag and, taken as a whole, they provide a picture of a large portion of the white population strangling in their rage and resentments.

Erich Fromm said the first step toward genocide is for a people to cast itself as a victim in battle with an omnipotent evil. It seems time and circumstance had transformed African Americans from simple-minded puppets of Northern imperialism to a demonic force bent on destroying the Southern Way of Life. This was the world described by many of the letter writers. Their most frightening rhetorical device was to present the NAACP as a malevolent octopus, manipulating and intimidating all who stood in its way. It seemed that many of the authors were incapable of distinguishing the NAACP from Jesse Jackson, from Martin Luther King Jr. What they saw was a Cosmic Negro, whom they variously described as being in unholy alliance with the Kennedys, the Clintons, the Democrats, the American Civil Liberties Union, and the "liberal media." In a bid for the Sigmund Freud Hall of Fame, several correspondents pointed to the Miss Black America Beauty Pageant as an example of black racism, vindicating their own poisonous attitudes.

These are a few of the more toxic letters that were published in the months after the NAACP announced its boycott:

"In answer to [another correspondent's] question, 'What has brought us to this sad, sorry state?' It is the National Association for the Advancement of Colored People and its corrupt and kowtowing accomplice, the Democratic party . . ." wrote a woman from Surfside Beach. "Enter the puppet master, the NAACP, and see how people like members of the media dance."

Wrote a Conway man: "If we move the flag, they will just start whining about something else. Why work if, when you complain loud enough, there will always be a Knight Ridder paper or a liberal Democratic party to comfort you?"

From another Conway man: "I am sick and tired of hearing officials from the National Association for the Advancement of Colored People whine and make threats from one thing to another. They don't condone the Ku Klux Klan – I don't condone the NAACP."

A Myrtle Beach woman wrote, ". . . The NAACP already has the black beauty pageant, black college fund, Lou Rawls funding for colored people – and more. We have none of that. . . Leave it to the NAACP and we will have a race war started. . . ."

"The National Association for the Advancement of Colored People wants the Confederate flag down and done away with," wrote a furious woman from Surfside Beach. "It is one of the few things the white people of the South still have.

"We have no white history month, no white Miss America pageant, and no white monument to be built on the State House grounds. What right does the NAACP have to dictate anything to us?"

From a Myrtle Beach woman: "When did the National Association for the Advancement of Colored People take over control of the United States?"

And a Myrtle Beach man: "*The Sun News* should stop being an agent for the National Association for the Advancement of Colored People. . . . It seems your reporting is lopsided. *The Sun News* should try to be neutral in this affair and just report the facts."

And this from a writer in Conway: "Businesses with both black and white employees should consider adopting and publishing guidelines stating that black employees would be first to be let go and last to be rehired if financial conditions caused by the boycott warrant such actions."

The possibility that the NAACP boycott might keep some of the Memorial Day bikers away was not lost on several letter writers. One bigot wrote all the way from Melbourne, Florida, to say, "Fewer blacks coming to South Carolina will mean the standard of living for whites will greatly increase due to the fact that there will be less crime, less drugs and lower welfare costs to the productive white citizens of South Carolina. . . .

"If we're really lucky and the boycott really begins to catch on, blacks may actually begin to leave South Carolina, resulting in South Carolina being the most desirable state in the country in which to live."

Of course, there were letters opposing the flag and expressing their grief at the flood of hate mail. A woman from Calabash, North Carolina, wrote eloquently: "I do not believe I have ever read such consistently small-minded and bigoted comments in my life. . . .

"I was appalled at the hatred that was evident in some of the letters. I find it difficult to comprehend such chauvinistic remarks at the end of the 20th century."

Editorial page editor Jerry Ausband addressed the matter of some of these offensive letters in a Sunday column. Many letters he received were not printed, he said, "in part because they are so vitriolic, dripping with hate for blacks, and in part because they contain certain language that really is not suitable for letters to the editor. . . .

"It is not really possible to describe these letters in this newspaper at this time. I could say that they most often denigrate blacks with the 'n-word' and the 'f-word' and with hopes that every black will be driven to Africa by the consequences of the flag debate as it flies over the State House. . . .

"Racism – not heritage, not slavery – is at the root of this whole business. The Confederate flag is a mere symbol of the differences that divide us. . . ."

As news of the NAACP boycott spread, columnists and political cartoonists from coast to coast addressed South Carolina's flag imbroglio. Garry Trudeau devoted a week of his "Doonesbury" comic strip to the matter. Many syndicated columnists ran in *The Sun News*, including Molly Ivins, William Raspberry, Philip Terzian, Sandy Grady, Armstrong Williams and Kathleen Parker. Even conservatives like Williams and Parker said it was time to furl the Stars and Bars. Only Cal Thomas failed to make the right call, denouncing the NAACP instead.

Miami Herald columnist Leonard Pitts waxed eloquent contemplating the hoary banner on the State House dome: "Every day the sunrise finds it there, South Carolina shames itself, shames its ancestors, shames the nation, shames the very truth – and profanes the ideal of liberty and justice for all.

"Yet, there it hangs anyway, a cloth lie, flapping in the Dixie breeze.
"Look away, look away."

On August 6, *The Sun News* reported that the N.C. Academy of Trial Lawyers and the Progressive National Baptist Convention were the first groups to cancel scheduled events on the Grand Strand. Six other groups had indicated they might drop meetings or conventions in South Carolina. In the weeks and months to come, state leaders in business, labor, education and politics called for finding a compromise to remove the flag. Some cited economic reasons, others ethical. Whatever their reasons, they were denounced by an increasingly shrill coterie of flag defenders who apparently felt themselves alienated from the mainstream economy, education and politics of the state.

Within a week of the NAACP's boycott announcement, something new appeared on Ocean Boulevard. Large Confederate flags sprouted from the back of pickup trucks cruising up and down through the muggy nights. Rowdy whites would cheer from the sidewalks. In the trucks, rednecks pumped their fists and gave rebel yells. Yet, the music of the Boulevard was the cadences of hip-hop and rap. Snoop Doggy Dogg, Heavy D & the Boyz, Coolio and Getto Jam pounded from pickup trucks and cars. Was I missing something? Irony has never been fashionable here.

And what was I to make of Tasha Sanford?

Walking down the Boulevard on an August night, I passed Wild West Old Time Photos – where fantasists posed for the camera in outrageous costumes and backgrounds – when I came up short. Lounging on a chaise was a young black woman, wrapped in nothing but a Confederate flag, a Confederate cavalry hat cocked jauntily on her head, a cavalry revolver held languorously on her hip. I stopped and gawked while she primped herself into just the right pose and – FLASH! – she became a celluloid paradox. Others stood watching with me on the sidewalk. It's hard to say if they were simply admiring an attractive young woman in a revealing moment of if they, like me, were struck by the clash of pigmentation and politics.

I caught up with her after she changed into her clothes. She and her girlfriend were admiring her new picture in front of the photo booth. She told me her name, that she was on vacation from Philadelphia and she knew nothing about any Confederate flag controversy. Honest! It was just a neat flag, she said.

I had long suspected many young white people made no direct

racial connection to the flag. To some it's just a vaguely Southern symbol, like magnolias or mint juleps. To others, it is a symbol of defiance to authority, black or white, Northern or Southern. As for blacks, well, Tasha Sanford was pleased with her Myrtle Beach souvenir. I hope she still has it and it is a source of only happy memories.

Searching for Intelligent
Life in Myrtle Beach

On November 29, 1993, a group of businessmen announced the launch of Fantasy Harbour, a restaurant, shopping and entertainment complex west of the Intracoastal Waterway that would eventually be home to fourteen theaters and ten theme restaurants, drawing thousands of people a night to ice shows, country music shows, circuses and more. The developers' hopes were high, their vision clear. But somebody got the jump on them. The day before the Fantasy Harbour announcement, Burroughs & Chapin announced their own $250 million restaurant, shopping and entertainment complex on the U.S. 17 Bypass. B&C's project would have a dozen theaters – perhaps twenty – they promised. It would be such a grand aggregation of theaters that it could only be called Broadway at the Beach.

"We are on the verge of a boom the likes of which has not been seen before," Ashby Ward euphorically predicted that week

Six years later, Broadway at the Beach had opened only three theaters – an IMAX, a 16-screen multiplex and the 2,700-seat Palace Theater. The Palace was the premier entertainment venue on the Grand Strand, offering everything from the Bolshoi Ballet to the Beach Boys to *A Chorus Line*. Broadway at the Beach won the Governor's Cup as the state's top tourist attraction in 1996 and drew nearly 10 million visitors in 1999. The concept was clearly working for B&C.

Barely a mile south – across the Waterway – Fantasy Harbour was a sadly different story. Five theaters had opened in five years. Of those, three had seen the revolving door of bankruptcies, changed names and changing shows as desperate owners tried to find the right act to compete with the growing multitude of theaters and attractions. One show famously closed with the producers fleeing in the dead of night, leaving cast, crew and creditors unpaid. At various times the Fantasy Harbour theaters had served as venues for professional wrestling and taping of the QVC Shopping Network Show. The fact was that by the mid-1990s, the Grand Strand was overbuilt with theaters. Like developers who create golf courses to sell residential real estate, the developers of Fantasy Harbour and Broadway at the Beach hoped to use the stage to draw visitors to their shopping and restaurant venues. What they were not doing was responding to market demand for more theaters.

Myrtle Beach's theater boom started in 1986, when entertainer and entrepreneur Calvin Gilmore came from Nashville to open his Carolina Opry country music theater. Within a few years Gilmore had built two more country music venues on the Strand. In the sincerest form of flattery, Nashville entertainers flocked to the area over the next decade. New venues included the Alabama Theater, the Gatlin Brothers Theater, the Myrtle Beach Opry, Dixie Jubilee, Southern Country Nights, the All American Music Theater, the Ferlin Husky Theater, the Billy "Crash" Craddock Celebrity Theater, the Ronnie Milsap Theater and Bobby Helms' "Special Angel" Theater. The majority of these stages had heard the final curtain call long before 1999, their buildings recycled into restaurants, nightclubs, even a skating rink and an evangelical church.

For those who wanted a change from country, there was Legends in Concert, a theater of impersonators. Dolly Parton's Dixie Stampede Dinner Theater offered guests "a 32-horse show themed in a friendly North/South rivalry and huge musical production reminiscent of 'Gone With the Wind,'" according to its brochure, plus − my favorite part − ostrich races! Another "dinner theater" was Medieval Times Dinner and Tournament, set in an ersatz castle, with ersatz lords, ladies and battling knights who clunked dangerous-looking objects against one another's helmets.

It all sounds like good clean fun, but there was something darker in these cornpone shows than mere tackiness and sentimentality. You could get a hint of it when you entered most of these "opry-style" theaters and saw the all-white audiences and the all-white casts. Travel writer Arthur Frommer fired a warning shot in 1995, telling Myrtle Beach it was headed down the wrong road − the road to Branson, Missouri. "Myrtle Beach is on a roll," Frommer told *Sun News* business editor David Wrenn. "But you could ruin it all if you don't learn from Branson's mistakes."

The first mistake, Frommer said, was turning that little town into "an ecological disaster," with an explosion of tacky, unplanned development around Branson and its more than thirty country music theaters. But there was also the question of the culture being promoted inside those theaters. Frommer said he was offended by the religious-right politics and fist-pumping patriotism forced on patrons at most of the Branson theaters. There was also a strong whiff of racial bias in the Branson air, he said.

"What really concerns me is that I hear some of the theaters in Myrtle Beach are doing the same types of things," Frommer said. "Newt Gingrich might like vacationing in Myrtle Beach, but I wouldn't if that was the only thing available to me."

In his magazine, *Arthur Frommer's Budget Travel*, the writer was even more blunt, accusing Myrtle Beach theaters of "filling their shows with unadvertised but blatant right-wing propaganda and open religious proselytizing." He specifically mentioned Dixie Stampede. Letters he received said the dinner show "trivialized" the Civil War, asking the audience to take sides by sitting in sections marked "North" and "South." There was no mention of slavery in the three-hour production celebrating Southern culture and no African-Americans in the cast.

The majority of the shows along the Grand Strand clearly were crafted for white, working class, older audiences. A black friend said of her Carolina Opry experience, "You mean to tell me they couldn't find one single black person who could sing a song or dance a number?" A black acquaintance related the story of going to Dixie Stampede with an all-white group of female friends. At one point in the show, a friend leaned over and whispered, "Kendra, I don't want to make you nervous or anything, but you're the only black person in here."

The Gatlin Brothers Theater provided an apt portrait of theater life on the Strand. The three Gatlins — Steve, Larry and Rudy — were well-scrubbed country crooners who looked like a family of Glenn Campbells. They brought their act from Branson, Missouri, in 1994, and opened their showplace 2,000-seat theater at Fantasy Harbour, featuring country variety shows, Christmas shows, Broadway musicals and Steve's solo shows, such as "Celebrate America with Steve Gatlin and Friends." Before each Gatlin show, audiences were subjected to a video of George H.W. Bush praising the brothers' act.

When the group split up at the end of 1998, they sold the theater to a Nashville production company, headed by South Carolina native and impresario Jim Owens. His plan called for using the theater as a summer broadcasting base for "Crook & Chase," a talk show carried on The Nashville Network. "Crook & Chase" has been called the "Regis & Kathy Lee" of country entertainment and, while I had never heard of them, they were known to millions of viewers of TNN. Their arrival for a season of taping in Myrtle Beach was heralded as a major boost to the area's national profile. Jim Owens was married to Lorianne Crook, the feminine half of the chat team. She and Charlie Chase would tape their show before a live audience five mornings a week at the rechristened Crook & Chase Theater.

I decided to see what all the excitement was about and attended an August 12 taping. The lobby of the Crook & Chase Theater was a shrine to the namesake stars. In the gift shop, retirees in Bermuda shorts, T-shirts and tank tops browsed among aprons, key chains, refrigerator magnets, Christmas tree ornaments, coffee mugs, porcelain thimbles and other gewgaws featuring Lorianne and Charlie. On a display rack were autographed copies of the 202-page book, *Crook & Chase – Our Lives, the Music and the Stars*, with back-lighted color photos of the blow-dried duo on the front and back of the book jacket. The lobby was hung with large, full-color pictures of the two stars and some of their guests, many posed with the gaping, open-mouthed laugh that would get them kicked out of charm school. In a glass case, a mannequin modeled Lorianne's wedding dress. There were photos of the nuptials, the bridesmaids and the fifteen-foot wedding cake, along with small plaques explaining the historical significance of each artifact. There were also pictures of Charlie, his wife and kids, his Silver Wraith Rolls Royce, and a copy of his 1970 high school yearbook.

Visitors were encouraged to sign the enormous guest book, as had thousands before them: "Charlie, we share the same birthday, you're just five years older. Hope you liked the brownies, Lorianne. You are just great. Good luck with everything you & Jim & Charlie do. – Keith & Alice Young, Titusville, Florida."

I thought of writing my own message, but words failed me.

The sixty-minute show was a smooth blend of glitz and grits, featuring the Amazing Kreskin and country singer Connie Smith. There was a cooking segment, in which the stars joined Elvis' cousin in the kitchen to whip up Jungle Room Banana Split, the King's favorite dessert, as described in the cousin's new Elvis family cookbook. A caller from Tampa won the day's trivia contest by correctly identifying "Heartbreak Hotel" as the Elvis song written by Hoyt Axton's mother.

During commercial breaks, the stars had their faces touched up as they bantered with each other and with the audience. In a page straight out of the Johnny Carson-Ed McMahon play book, Lorianne ribbed Charlie about his drinking and Charlie did his Elvis *shtick*. The show closed with a professional Elvis impersonator – one of many local Elvises – who came out in sequined jumpsuit and sang "That's Alright Mama" with appropriate body language. We closed out with thunderous applause as the credits rolled.

To fill the huge hall in the evenings, producer Jim Owens had just the ticket. He gave the world an autobiographical musical fantasy called *Summer of '66*.

In 1966, young Owens was managing and promoting a rock band called The Villagers, booking them at the Pavilion Arcade. The skimpy plot of the musical involved the creation of the group of clean-cut young male musicians and female vocalists, how they performed together and lived together in a big house on the beach. The high-jinx of these horny, angst-ridden youngsters provided the backdrop for the real show – more than thirty vintage pop songs, such as "C.C. Rider," "Hang on Sloopy," "Leader of the Pack," "I Love Beach Music" and "Under the Boardwalk," performed live by the group. Forty-something Steve Gatlin played twenty-year-old Jim Owens.

Promotions for the show promised "an evening of entertainment the entire family will enjoy. . . . Relive Myrtle Beach's Age of Innocence through the loves and laughs of the Grand Strand's favorite teens." The show was as trifling and predictable as an episode of "Gilligan's Island," except for the bosom jokes and the fart jokes ("Who cut the cheese?" "Who smelt it dealt it!"), to which the audience roared their approval. As the band performed "Carolina Girls," audience members were invited onstage to shag with cast members. The costumes were disco and high-pop from the mid-sixties. Except for the technical effects, the whole thing might have been a high school production.

I never saw the real Villagers – never even heard of them – during their brief summer of fame. In two hours of silliness and nostalgia, this cornball operetta did get one thing right, though. These kids were a near-perfect reflection of the insular life of white, middle class Southern youth even as the nation writhed in racial unrest and the agonies of Vietnam. There was no hint of the national trauma going on around them, of the country that was being changed, of the lives that were being destroyed. I remember it vividly from the summer of 1966, yet it doesn't happen in *Summer of '66*. But what do I know about showbiz? *Summer of '66* was recognized as South Carolina's Entertainment Attraction of the Year.

Few towns the size of Myrtle Beach offer a greater convergence of people from all over the country and the world, but the atmosphere is more like a frontier mining camp than a cultural melting pot. For most residents life revolves around fast money, fast women, fast cars, abun-

dant drugs and booze and gaming the local political system. The resulting culture is depressingly cynical and lowbrow. Some love it, others
hate it, but everyone is obsessed with it.

The features that make the Grand Strand exciting to tourists –
simulation race car tracks, theme restaurants, strip clubs, beachwear
stores and dozens of miniature golf courses – look quite different to the
people who live with them 365 days a year. *The Sun News* commissioned a series of focus groups of Horry County residents in 1997 to
learn what people thought of their quality of life and culture. The
answers were not pretty. Participants variously described their county
as "tacky," "a haven for alcoholics," a "neon sandbox," and the perennial favorite – "Redneck Riviera."

"You can see three Elvises running errands on a given day," one
resident said. Another described the Barnes & Noble bookstore as the
cultural high point on the Grand Strand. Said a third, "I can't go to the
library on Sunday, but I can buy a T-shirt and play Putt-Putt."

When Horry County's small but struggling arts community does
try to do something edgy, it usually gets its knuckles cracked. The area
is blessed with no less than five theater troupes, which struggle for
funding and venues and often sanitize the scripts they produce of any
strong language or sexual references. Self-censorship is the general
rule, as explained by Diane Scroggins of the Theater of the Republic:
"We go for family values, plays that generally will not offend people.
We generally are pretty conservative."

And if she should forget that caveat, there were plenty who were
happy to remind her. Before he was removed from office for his own
crimes and misdemeanors, county council chairman Joey McNutt
declared that publicly supported arts groups should be held account-
able to the public – especially if the art does not reflect the political
climate of Horry County. "Everything is political," he told *The Sun
News*. "We have to remember what the makeup of the county is. I
would venture to say that a majority of people are by and large conservative. And I would say a lot of the fine arts aren't conservative."

The arts community got a lesson in this *realpolitik* in 1997, when
A.R. Gurney's play *Sylvia* was to be performed as part of the annual
Vivace! arts festival. The comedy is about a talking female dog named
Sylvia who comes between a middle-aged man and his wife. Played by
an actress, Sylvia is an acerbic and horny canine whose observations on
human behavior have drawn laughs around the world. Myrtle Beach
would be a tougher sell. The venue for the production was to be the
Magic Attic, a Boulevard club in the Pavilion Arcade, owned by

Burroughs & Chapin. When Doug Wendel and corporate PR officials learned of the play's subject matter, the production was moved from B&C premises to a lecture hall at Coastal Carolina University. "When we're using a sponsor's dollars, its my understanding that you have to defend them," a Vivace! official explained. "There are provocative scenes in the play, scenes that are inappropriate for children. . . . It just wasn't appropriate to be held in a venue that has family entertainment."

Another victim of this small-town mentality was artist Mike Todd. In 1982 Todd opened an exhibit of his work at the Myrtle Beach Convention Center. Three of his paintings were female nudes. Within days City Hall – landlord of the Convention Center – closed the exhibit without any legal process. The case drew national attention for its high-handedness and small-mindedness. Todd won a temporary injunction to keep his exhibit open, but the city used obstructions within the exhibit hall to effectively block the public's access to the exhibit. The publicity from the spat caused other scheduled exhibitors around the state to withdraw their invitations. Two decades later Todd felt that his career had been permanently damaged by city authorities.

The morality police busted Todd again a few years later when he mounted an exhibit of paintings in the North Myrtle Beach branch of Horry County Library. The exhibit was actually a commentary on his closed show at the Convention Center, with one of his nudes displayed with the message "Censored." Some local clergy complained, accusing Todd of practicing Satanism and occultism in his use of surrealism. The library exhibit was also closed.

In a city famous for crime, litter and traffic, the thing I found most depressing was the general intellectual climate. There were no movie theaters that showed anything the least bit exotic or "artsy." The Algonquin Coffee House opened in April 1999 – offering folk music, theater and art – but lasted less than a year. I could find no writer's group anywhere in this county of nearly 200,000. What I did find was a vast emptiness, a spiritual and intellectual vacuum that left me gasping like a fish on the bank. Most of the people I encountered did not read a newspaper and had not read a book in years. They had never heard of National Public Radio; there were people from Minnesota who could not identify Garrison Keillor. For conversation and companionship, I occasionally drove to Charleston, to Columbia, to Charlotte, anywhere I might find a few friends who had heard of Toni Morrison, Aaron Copland or H.L. Mencken's "Sahara of the Bozart."

Perhaps it's as unfair to fault Myrtle Beach for its dearth of cultural amenities as to criticize Greenwich Village for its lack of roller coasters. But lowbrow culture is the trademark of the Grand Strand and poking fun at it may be regarded as a trenchant form of affection. A Lowcountry politician cracked, "People come to Charleston for culture; they go to Myrtle Beach for T-shirts." As I walked with a visiting friend down Ocean Boulevard on an August afternoon, he came up short in front of one of the "haunted houses," where a loop of "Toccata and Fugue in D Minor" blasted onto the street. "Moredock," he said, "what do you mean there's no culture in Myrtle Beach? This town has Bach on the Boulevard!"

What Myrtle Beach lacks in culture, it compensates for in cult. Nothing except the Republican Party so unites the disparate factions of Horry County's white population as cosmetology and cosmetic surgery. Housewives and waitresses, school teachers and strippers line up to get tucked and lifted, suctioned and implanted. Young women turn themselves into cartoons of Pamela Anderson proportions in hopes of increasing their tips, their popularity, their happiness. They discuss their latest treatment or their next "fix" as casually as their mothers talked about accessorizing their wardrobes. They study the models in their fashion magazines, calculating what it would cost to get themselves completely redesigned – and what the benefits would be. In an environment where landing a photo spread in *Penthouse* or *Playboy* magazine is regarded as a long-range career goal, such reckoning is as common as it is self-deluding.

The ads in *The Sun News* fed this cult – and fed off it – with pages of advertising for "miracle" weight-loss formulas and programs, including the herbal patch, which allows the wearer to lose weight without diet or exercise. Full-page ads screamed the latest wonders: "The Amazing New 'Skinny Pill' that Empties The Fat Right Out of Your Body's Fat Cells. . . ." Or, "NOW! You Can Burn Off Body Fat Awake or Asleep, Hour by Hour, Every Day, Safely."

And how about "Apple Cider Vinegar Tablets – The Key to Weight Loss!"? There were highly dubious "before" and "after" photographs to "prove" the product really "melts away fat."

There were testimonials: "Hello, my name is Pam. There was this guy I admired at work. He never gave me a second look when I was overweight. Recently I got on the elevator with him. He asked me out, didn't even recognize me. I told him my calendar was too full to go out with him now! By the way, I've lost over 40 pounds."

Men were hardly immune to this chicanery, as attested by ads that promised "A Full Head of Hair in 30 Seconds!" and herbal "Viagra from China"

The beauty cult touches almost every aspect of Grand Strand life. In April 1999, Myrtle Beach High School freshman Sarah Belden won an award from the state Department of Health and Environmental Control for her school science project. And what was her contribution to the health and environmental quality of South Carolina? She demonstrated the effectiveness of titanium dioxide as a sun screen additive in blocking UV rays. "I'm out every day in the summer at the pool or on the beach," Belden said, "and sometimes I get so red." At the same time, Myrtle Beach High School junior Ryan Cleary won first place in the medicine and health category in the Sandhills Regional Science Fair. His discovery: too much tooth whitener could lower dental calcium levels.

Yet, when the wisecracks and cheap shots are done, it must be said that Horry County was trying to feed its brain cells. Largely invisible to tourists and transient residents, there were two choral societies, a symphony orchestra and four concert series organizations that brought nationally recognized artists to the area. The Waccamaw Arts & Crafts Guild boasted some 300 members in Horry and Georgetown counties, though the work they represented was generally conservative and tourist-oriented. Members of the WA&CG led the effort to close the controversial exhibit by Mike Todd at the Myrtle Beach Convention Center in 1982.

The Horry County Cultural Arts Council, organized in 1986, was an umbrella organization to support local arts. Funded by corporate and individual donations and local accommodations tax, HCAC was recognized in 1994 as the leading arts organization of its kind in the state. It promoted arts-in-education and, in 1996, launched Vivace!, a ten-day festival of art, music, theater and dance.

The Franklin G. Burroughs-Simeon B. Chapin Art Museum operated out of a three-story 1920s beach house that was saved from the wrecking ball and moved three miles to its present site on the south end of Ocean Boulevard. Funded by public sources, plus a grant from Burroughs & Chapin Co., the 10,000-square-foot visual arts museum stood on land donated by B&C and housed the permanent collection of the Waccamaw Arts & Crafts Guild as well as rotating exhibits.

Another impressive cultural project was the million-dollar renovation of a burned-out movie theater on Main Street in Conway, to serve as the new home of the Theater of the Republic. Established in

1969 and performing wherever it could find a venue, TOR held its inaugural production in the Conway building in November 1999.

Myrtle Beach was also home to the South Carolina Hall of Fame and the Children's Museum of South Carolina. Located in the foyer of the Myrtle Beach Convention Center, the Hall of Fame was a portrait gallery of noted South Carolinians – overwhelmingly white and male – spanning more than 200 years. The Children's Museum was organized and established in 1993 by several businesswomen who realized that South Carolina was the only state not to have such an institution. In 1999, the 7,500-square-foot museum drew some 30,000 visitors, half of them tourists. I spent two delightful hours building a circuit board with oversized electronic components and perusing the collections of fossils, shells, rocks and bones. There were terrariums and aquariums, birds' eggs from around the world, collections of leaves and insects. Interactive exhibits demonstrated gravity, magnetism, centrifugal force and electric generation and flow. Other exhibits taught astronomy, geology, meteorology, health and physiology. There were musical pipes, books and computers, maps and pictures, rooms for classes, drawing, painting and other activities. And, this being Myrtle Beach, there was even a demonstration of how the height of grass affects the roll of a golf ball.

The Children's Museum was located in a building adjacent to Myrtle Square Mall on U.S. 17 and like the mall, was owned by the Burroughs & Chapin Co., which donated the building for use by the museum. Before it was home to the Children's Museum, the building housed Mark's Delivery, a restaurant delivery service owned by MSM Food Service, Inc. and operated by Mark Struthers McBride.

Mark's Delivery went out of business in 1996, in a welter of debt and acrimony. Twenty-six thousand dollars of that debt was owed to the landlord – Burroughs & Chapin. Because it was corporate debt, McBride claimed no responsibility for it and B&C apparently did not press the young city councilman on the matter. "It was a contractual agreement of the corporation," Mayor McBride said coyly during an interview in his City Hall office. Yet, it is not clear if the books were ever closed on the debt. There is no filing on record for MSM Food Service at the Federal Bankruptcy Court for South Carolina and the company has not been dissolved.

For Burroughs & Chapin, the $26,000 debt became a write-off. Or maybe it was an investment. Whichever, it created a unique relationship between the mayor and Myrtle Beach's most powerful developer.

A Bad Season for Democracy

Myrtle Beach was created to offer a diversion from the workaday world and it has succeeded beyond all expectations. Unfortunately, it has also kept itself thoroughly diverted for much of its history. The result is that local politics are among the most corrupt anywhere, the fragile coastal environment is being ground into money, roads are impassable and the town is virtually unlivable for much of the year.

Nobody knows just when it happened, but people started waking up a few years ago and noticed that things weren't working well. This was not the town they remembered growing up in; this was not the place they had retired to. When they tried to complain, their elected leaders ignored them and Ashby Ward condescendingly explained that tourism is a blessing they should all be grateful for.

The Burroughs & Chapin Company's demand for a business park to pay for the infrastructure of its future projects was the last straw for many. It coincided with two other issues – video gambling and the Confederate flag – to make 1999 one of the most fractious years since the 1960s.

To the millions who visited Myrtle Beach that year, the town was as mindlessly engaging as ever. Carousels turned, strippers danced, golfers hacked, gamblers lost, motorcycles roared. In May an elderly woman was murdered in a motel three blocks from my apartment. Almost daily, *The Sun News* reported robberies and assaults along the Boulevard and around my neighborhood. Police sirens and the crash of vehicles on U.S. 17 awakened me and interrupted my work at all hours of night and day. Beach advisories continued to warn of high bacteria levels in the surf. Ashby Ward was beside himself when a large photograph in *The Richmond Times* showed tourists wading in a gully cut into the beach by stormwater outflow, with the caption, "Swash Awash In Germs." Republican presidential candidates came shaking hands and kissing babies.

Despite the prevalence of politicians and politics, South Carolina has a rather shaky grasp of the concept of democracy. That should not be surprising in a state which, for most of its history, defended and encouraged the institution of slavery.

The grandees of Carolina have never been eager to share power with anyone – white or black. Until 1867, the General Assembly – not the general public – elected the governor and the General Assembly was elected by white men, whose suffrage was limited by property ownership and poll taxes. Under the state constitution of 1895 – still the governing document of South Carolina – power was centered in Columbia; there were no county governments until passage of the Home Rule Act of 1976. The 1895 constitution – which was never submitted to the people for approval – disenfranchised blacks and women and barred them from jury duty. Poll taxes and other restrictions kept many whites from voting. In the presidential election of 1936, three-quarters of all voting age adults in the East, Midwest and West cast ballots; in the South it was only one in four; in South Carolina, it was fewer than one in five. During World War II, South Carolina did not give absentee ballots to its sons and daughters serving in the armed forces.

Such an environment has not instilled much appreciation of democratic principles, to say nothing of the patience, diligence and hard work critical to the democratic process. Democracy requires a sense of mutual respect among citizens, mutual ownership of the political and economic systems and mutual trust that differences will be amicably resolved. This is the antithesis of the Southern experience, in which one race, one class, one region has always dominated another – always by force or threat of force. All too often, "popular sovereignty" has been expressed in mob violence and sometimes individual violence. In broad daylight on a January afternoon in 1903, Lieutenant Governor James Tillman shot to death the unarmed editor of *The State* newspaper, N.G. Gonzales, in front of the State House, for editorials Gonzales had written about the politician. Tillman was acquitted by a jury, which deemed the killing justifiable.

There hasn't been much gunplay in South Carolina politics in the last century, but vitriol and violence are never far from the surface. It was particularly evident in the debate over the Confederate flag, as letters to the editor of *The Sun News* made clear.

From Myrtle Beach, this was typical: "I am tired of a bunch of weak-kneed, lily-livered people wanting to get rid of the Southern flag. . . .

"It's gotten so bad in this country, if the uppity troublemaking blacks want something, the government makes sure they get it. . . .

"If we are to give up our Southern heritage that we hold very dear, then the NAACP should be abolished, the black Miss America contest eliminated and everything else that is black-only."

Former Ku Klux Klan Grand Wizard David Duke cast the issue in the starkest terms when he addressed 300 flag supporters on the steps of the State House in Columbia. The non-white birth rate was higher than the white birthrate, he warned, and whites might soon become a minority (ignoring the fact that whites had been a minority in South Carolina for most of the state's history).

A poll in September showed that a plurality of South Carolinians favored removing the flag. They were joined by a growing list of public and private institutions, including the Episcopal Diocese of Upper South Carolina, several city and county councils and the boards of trustees of Clemson University, the University of South Carolina, The Citadel, and even the arch-conservative Bob Jones University, which cited the biblical admonition that one "should not give unnecessary offense."

With their angry rhetoric, the flag wavers painted themselves further into a corner, leaving no escape, no compromise. The growing number of high-profile flag opponents only demonstrated how politically and culturally isolated the Confederistas were. Like Islamic radicals on the other side of the world, they became ever more fanatical in the face of hopelessness, denouncing all things modern and rational. Anyone who failed to support them was labeled a traitor to the South and became an object of their rage.

Compromise and empathy were alien to the experience of flag supporters. Something similar was true in the ugly battle over video gambling. To gambling opponents, it was a sin and a social scourge. To supporters, it was an inalienable right of free people in a free society. There was no room for compromise, either in the General Assembly or in Horry County.

The Sun News editorialized: "The video poker industry in South Carolina has gotten too big for its britches. . . . The poker industry has gobbled too much political power and overstuffed itself with arrogance. . . . if the industry does not know how wrong it is becoming and how irritating it has already become, then it has not taken the pulse of the people."

Throughout the cranky, vitriolic legislative session that began in January, fifty different video gambling bills were introduced. There was a filibuster by angry Senate Republicans and various obstructions and skullduggery by House Democrats. The gambling lobby had already spent $387,000 by mid-April. When there was no video gambling bill at the end of the regular session, Governor Hodges called legislators back for a special session, threatening to hold them hostage until they had a bill he could sign.

On June 30 – the last day of the special session – it looked as if the solons would fail again to produce a gambling bill. "There's no leadership here," said Republican Representative John Graham Altman III.

"If there's going to be a downfall of the Republican Party, it's going to be video poker," said GOP Representative Jake Knotts.

"Screw it!" said Democratic Senator Ernie Passalaigue.

Finally, after a fourteen-hour legislative ordeal, the sausage got made. On July 2, Governor Jim Hodges was all alone as he signed their work into law. There were no trophy pens handed out that day. There were no proud legislative fathers and mothers standing behind the governor. No one wanted to be seen with this bastard bill, and for good reason.

While it set a number of new regulations on the poker industry, the bill was, in fact, all smoke and mirrors. Unable to figure out what to do with video poker, the General Assembly punted and left it to the public to settle the issue in a special November 2 referendum. If the referendum passed, the new rules and regulations would go into effect. If it failed, video gambling would become illegal after June 30, 2000. Either way, the General Assembly was off the hook.

Scholars and pundits were quick to point out that the 1895 constitution allows statewide referendums only to approve constitutional amendments, and since a video gambling referendum did not fit that definition, it was almost certainly unconstitutional. The bill was a duplicitous abdication of legislative responsibility, but why quibble? The ploy got the lawmakers out of Columbia for the July 4 holiday.

But into this specious bill Republican Representative Terry Haskins slipped a kicker: If the November 2 referendum were challenged and found to be unconstitutional, then video poker would automatically be banned, effective July 1, 2000. The Haskins clause was a brilliant parliamentary booby-trap, but got little notice in the excitement over passage of the bill. The impending referendum immediately took center stage as South Carolina braced for the most expensive and brutal democratic exercise in its history.

Meetings, meetings, meetings. The summer and fall of 1999 were a blur of meetings and rallies, as the forces of good and evil – whichever was which – mustered their troops to battle over video gambling and the Burroughs & Chapin business park. It looked like democracy, it felt like democracy; but beneath the civic tone seethed visceral anger and suspicion. All sides tended to cast their struggles in apocalyptic terms. Victory or death! It was a very Southern way of thinking, but many Northerner transplants got caught up in the passion of the day.

County council used the heat and smoke of the season to slip an old item back onto the agenda: a controversial plan to build a second runway at Myrtle Beach International Airport.

The airport issue was originally resolved in 1993. City and county councils agreed that Myrtle Beach International would remain with only one runway. At some unforeseen date, the county might buy land and build a giant regional airport deep in the interior of the county. With that settled, the city moved ahead to create the Myrtle Beach Air Force Base Redevelopment Authority, which began developing real estate around the airport. By the summer of 1999, there were already a number of small businesses, industrial sites and a housing development on the drawing board and on the ground.

How quickly things change.

County council was feeling the heat from tourism and development interests to build a second runway at Myrtle Beach International Airport. A new regional airport would be too expensive, they said, so they would have to make do with what they had.

The county wanted a new runway with a 3,000-foot separation from the old runway, allowing for simultaneous takeoffs and landings on the two runways, under federal regulations. It would also gut most of the new development on the site. The city was willing to go along with a new runway with a 1,000-foot separation, sparing the new development and allowing near-simultaneous takeoffs and landings.

An independent consultant concluded that a new runway with a 1,000-foot separation would meet the area's needs until the year 2060. Still, the county was pushing for the 3,000-foot separation.

The Sun News editorialized: "The 3,000-foot separation would destroy more than it would restore, with little or nothing resulting except a county land grab. Sound familiar?"

No, not to a town with a notoriously short attention span, a town built as a refuge from reality.

Even to experienced political observers, there was just too much going on, too many balls in the air, too many shells moving around on the table. I was bewildered by the sheer glut of local development and land use issues, while others were swept away on the passions of video poker and the Confederate flag. I suspect that's exactly how our local politicians wanted it.

The region got some drought relief from two hurricanes and random thunderstorms. Myrtle Beach received 29.25 inches of rain in September, more than five times the monthly average. Time after time, neighborhoods and houses were flooded, roads were impassable, the beach was mutilated by the stormwater discharge. I went on several walking tours of neighborhoods with angry residents and defensive city officials as they surveyed the damage. There were meetings, meetings, meetings to discuss stormwater. At one City Hall session, assistant city manager Allan Blum pointed to a wall-sized map of Myrtle Beach, delineating drainage basins, neighborhoods, roads and construction sites. Speaking slowly and carefully, he explained how development at one place can affect drainage and cause flooding miles away. Suddenly, the light bulb went on for one of the older homeowners. "So you're saying the city needs to integrate the neighborhoods in some kind of long-range, comprehensive plan," he suggested tentatively.

"That's right," Blum said, as the homeowners looked at one another and nodded in a moment of transcendent clarity. It was a victory for reason and a small triumph over the development industry, whose strategy is to dismember neighborhoods, municipalities, counties and states in the name of "local control."

Protestations to the contrary, Burroughs & Chapin's proposed multicounty business park was the ultimate dismemberment of the Grand Strand. The complexities of B&C's business park and corollary development agreements with the city and county were mind-boggling. The final draft document-which was to be the blueprint for some $5 billion dollars in development over the next thirty years – weighed in at 1,436 pages. And as Bob Bestler wrote, "The boys from Burroughs & Chapin seem to rewrite their script at every turn and it is difficult to know where they are at any particular moment."

Information – or disinformation – would be the principal tool of both sides in this war for the hearts and minds of Horry County. B&C's argument was that its business park would be so profitable for the county and the city that new tax revenues would more than offset revenues taken from Horry County Schools. To support their claims, the company brought on a team of economists to explain the numbers, led by Peter Barr. The B&C team was introduced at a news conference at the MBA Chamber of Commerce. Horry County School Board had already hired its own panel of economists, headed by Dr. Harry Miley, who had drafted the business park legislation in the late 1980s. It was Miley's contention that the General Assembly never intended the law to be used for tourist and residential development such as B&C proposed. His analysis showed that the business park would result in a $256 million deficit for Horry County Schools over the life of the project.

Both sides produced a staggering volume of numbers and documents – "wheelbarrow loads," as one school board partisan put it. *The Sun News* did a creditable job of following and explaining the business park battle over the months. Local television stations barely touched the story; it was simply too complex and there was an orgy of ambulances, police cars and hurricanes for them to chase. Time Warner Cable ran four half-hours of public service programming on the business park.

As with many modern public policy debates – national health insurance, prescription drugs, global warming – the issues are too arcane, too complex for the average citizen to grasp. This was certainly true of the flood of data coming out of the business park debate. In such disputes, the day is often carried by "public information" campaigns. And nobody outspends corporate America on public information. To assist the public's understanding, B&C launched a series of half-page ads in *The Sun News* (full-page in the *Myrtle Beach Herald*) "explaining" the benefits of the business park and "correcting" the errors of their critics. Taking the form of "Open Letters to Residents of Horry County," the ads were condescending in tone, loose with the facts and heavy-handed with the numbers. According to its third Open Letter, of June 10:

> At Burroughs & Chapin's request, Dr. Peter Barr, Dean of the Wall School of Business at Coastal Carolina University, analyzed the potential economic impact that residential projects in our proposed development agreement and multicounty business

park would have on the Horry County school system. . . . Dr. Barr's analysis shows that the property taxes generated by Burroughs & Chapin's new residential development will more than pay for that development's impact on the school system. Indeed, after that impact has been accounted for, excess property tax revenue will be available to help subsidize the school system else where in the county.

In other words, the good doctor's numbers showed that the business park would actually generate excess property tax revenue of $3,153,210!

On June 13, Bob Bestler responded to B&C's latest Open Letter, calling it a "Rube Goldberg word contraption":

The folks who run Burroughs & Chapin have more clout than Superman – more powerful than the Horry County

Council, faster than the Myrtle Beach City Council, able to leap tall mayors. . . .

Most public agencies around here don't spend a lot of time questioning Burroughs & Chapin. What's the use, they figure.

In some communities, businesses learn you can't fight City Hall. Here City Hall has learned you can't fight the fourth floor of the Founders Centre. . . .

Like a good corporate citizen, Burroughs & Chapin is doing what it can to respond [to criticism] without actually getting its hands dirty.

No, it's not having press conferences. Lord, that can get messy. . . .

Instead, Burroughs & Chapin has begun publishing, each week, a kind of royal proclamation, the same kind of decree the kings of yore used to send down to the masses. . . .

Anyway, the latest proclamation asked: "How will our proposed development agreement & multicounty business park impact Horry County's school system?"

Burroughs & Chapin didn't flinch as it answered its question. In fact, I thought it did a nice job of keeping a straight face.

B&C used its next weekly Open Letter to settle scores with Bestler, taking him to task on several points and calling him "Bob," as if he were the yardman at Founders Centre.

Despite the fortune B&C poured into its public information ads, it could not seem to buy a break. Opposition to the business park organized under the banner of We the People of Horry County, an organization composed largely of property owners and retirees who feared the business park would mean higher property taxes to fund public education. We the People sent out a flyer to every registered voter in the county that was at least as misleading as any of B&C's ads.

Angry residents filled pages of *The Sun News* with letters: "Burroughs & Chapin Co. feels it is entitled to all kinds of zoning and tax breaks. . . . such as not contributing taxes for schools, roads and utilities," wrote one. "It is confident its requests will be approved because of the number of Horry County councilmen who have incomes from developers, either directly or indirectly."

On June 6, *Sun News* business editor David Wrenn delivered a scathing column directed at "Grand Strand business leaders."

> If education really is the key to a strong economy, why are these business leaders promoting special tax districts that siphon off money for themselves while making money for new schools and better pay for teachers difficult to find. . . ?
>
> Burroughs and Chapin claims its unprecedented development can't happen unless it gets those special tax breaks.
>
> Well, maybe it shouldn't happen if those new golf courses and shopping malls are going to be built at the cost of a decent education. Corporate profit shouldn't come at the expense of new schools and better pay for teachers.
>
> With every tax break that is granted to developers, Horry County seals its fate as just another glitzy tourist attraction with little to offer permanent residents except for $7 an-hour shopping and restaurant jobs.

A series of reports in late summer made it clear what was really at stake in the business park debate, for Horry County and for the state. South Carolina's Scholastic Assessment Test scores again ranked last in the nation in 1999, with a state average of 954, more than six percent below the national average of 1,016. Horry County's average SAT score was 967.

Within weeks another report, this one from the U.S. Department of Education, placed South Carolina in the bottom five states in ranking of school children for writing skills. Another report, compiled by the Associated Press, showed that South Carolina was losing high-paying, high-tech jobs, despite huge incentives to corporate gypsies, because we did not have an educated, trainable work force ready to meet the challenges of the twenty-first century.

As its first deadline for the business park came and went, B&C was feeling the heat. The company launched a series of full-page ads in *The Sun News*. Doug Wendel threatened to withdraw his offer to allow the city to annex company property and in another, completely ludicrous gesture, he threatened not to build his prized Mall of South Carolina.

On September 30, Maryland consultant Paul Tischler addressed county council, in a packed chamber, with Wendel, Barr and Dowling sitting down front. Tischler had been hired by the council to analyze the overall impact of development on Horry County *before* B&C had proposed its massive business park and reallocation of taxes. With an overhead projector to display a stupefying array of numbers, Tischler showed that current growth projections could not pay for themselves at the current tax rate, especially with the large number of low-wage employees seeking multi-family, low-income housing. "The bottom line is that you have an untenable fiscal future here," Tischler told the crowded room. "There are very, very few communities where we work where findings are so bleak," he said, as Doug Wendel looked on grimly.

On the heels of Tischler's report, the Waccamaw Regional Planning Agency issued its report on the $169 million worth of roads B&C wanted to build with money out of the county school budget. Twenty-one of the forty-six road improvement projects the company wanted – including those serving the Mall of South Carolina and Grande Dunes Resort – were private issues and should not be included in the multicounty business park, the report said. "You look at who the road is serving," said Waccamaw Regional transportation engineer Mike Penney. "We were looking at roads that would service more than Burroughs & Chapin."

B&C demanded that Waccamaw Regional Planning Agency reevaluate its findings. Wendel summoned Penney and WRPA officials to his office at Founders Centre to discuss the issue and review "supplemental documents." On October 11, County Councilwoman Liz Gilland, the strongest B&C critic on the council, showed up for the meeting at Founders Centre and was denied admission.

"It confirmed to me how Wendel and his crew do business," she told *The Sun News*. B&C flack Pat Dowling said it was nothing personal. No elected officials were allowed in the meeting.

But Gilland said she saw County Council Chairman Chad Prosser walk out of the Founders Centre minutes before the critical meeting was set to start. Prosser told the paper he did, indeed, meet with Wendel that afternoon to discuss the business park and development agreement, but he assured the public that there was no talk of Waccamaw Regional Planning Agency and he did not attend that meeting. "I'm just doing what a chairman is supposed to do," he said, "negotiating on behalf of the council to get the best deal for the county."

At the same time Gilland was being cut out of the loop at the Founders Centre, she was being silenced in council chambers. B&C allies on council moved to limit debate to five minutes at a time on any given issue. The effort came after Gilland's council critics accused her of playing to the television when she questioned the wisdom of moving ahead on the business park. "We are in the middle of the most important deliberations on some of the most important issues," Gilland told *The Sun News*. "Isn't this an interesting time to limit debate and discussions?"

The war over B&C's business park got a story in *The Wall Street Journal* and ABC News blistered the company in a report, part of a series on the deteriorating condition of America's schools. The ABC report showed cramped portable classrooms, as reporter James Walker intoned, "In Myrtle Beach, South Carolina, schools could suffer because a large developer wants to grab scarce dollars for his own projects. Doug Wendel is using the promise of jobs to get the state to help him build condominiums, golf courses and shopping centers with money collected from property taxes." B&C flack Pat Dowling wrote a 2,200-word letter of protest to ABC News Anchor Peter Jennings. Editors at the *Myrtle Beach Herald*, the company's unofficial mouthpiece, considered Dowling's words so precious they printed every one of them – verbatim.

Despite the evidence that the business park was a bad idea, despite the fact that B&C kept changing the details of the vast document almost weekly, the business park and development agreements moved inexorably through city and county councils, receiving necessary readings and approval. *The Sun News* editorialized for caution: "It is beyond comprehension that the development permitting has gotten as far as it has without having this rewritten document. Even the Horry County Planning Commission voted earlier without knowing in detail what it was voting for." Other editorials criticized the proposed thirty-year zoning freeze and doubted that the business park would diversify the tourist economy. Doug Wendel dismissed all criticism, saying it was important that the approval process begin, even if all the details were not in place, in order to "send a signal" to the company's development partners.

The business park had a sense of the inevitable about it. Watching it move through the legislative process was like watching a train wreck in slow motion. I wanted to jump up and scream, "Wait! Can't you see what's happening?" But I admit to a morbid curiosity in watching this travesty played out in full public view, knowing that no one had the power to stop it.

Public fury over the business park tore at the fabric of Horry County society. It left its mark with angry letters to the editor. It ruined relationships on county council, where B&C supporters often ganged up on Gilland, insulting and demeaning her publicly. Their haste in pushing the business park through the approval process without proper study or analysis added to public cynicism. Both the council chairman and the chairman of the planning commission cast tie-breaking votes to hasten the approval and both had been beneficiaries of B&C business arrangements and campaign fund-raisers.

With a historic November referendum on video gambling approaching, the gambling industry was sassy and confident. It had already defeated a governor at the polls. This referendum looked like a cakewalk. Life was sweet for video gambling.

Gambling forces started buying TV ads and billboards, organizing the industry's thousands of employees. Bumper stickers appeared on vehicles, signs appeared in bars and convenience stores across the state with the simple message: "Vote Yes." Video poker ads claimed that poker taxes would eliminate the need for automobile taxes and banning it would mean economic ruin for the state. The facts supported neither of these claims, as editorialists pointed out, but that did not stop the ads.

The battle was especially intense in Horry County, which once again led the state in gross video poker receipts for the first quarter of 1999, with a staggering $88 million. At pro-gambling rallies, speakers sounded like Patrick Henry and Thomas Jefferson, demanding their God-given rights. By contrast, anti-gambling rallies looked and felt like temperance meetings from a century earlier. At one I attended in Conway, there were hymns, prayers, hallelujahs and testimonials, led by a procession of ministers, with a pledge to the American flag, a pledge to the Christian flag and a pledge to the Bible. Dozens of ministers from the area were asked to come forward and stand on the stage with the speakers. Anti-gambling literature left no doubt that this was a holy crusade: "On November 2 we have an opportunity to do something about Video Poker in South Carolina. Let the Christian Voice be heard and Vote 'NO' to the Video Poker Referendum."

As the rhetoric and the cost of the referendum soared, there came one final twist in the long, convoluted story of video poker in South Carolina. Hoping to stop the referendum, a small upstate video poker firm called Joytime Distributing and Amusement Co., filed suit, claiming the referendum was unconstitutional. Two weeks before the vote was to be held, the decision came down from the state Supreme Court: the referendum was indeed unconstitutional and would not take place. And with that decision, the Haskins clause automatically kicked in, killing video poker, as of July 1, 2000.

The $2.8 billion-dollar industry, which had taken over the state without ever being put to a vote, which had used every loophole to mock the law and thwart regulation, was now shut down without a vote, in a dazzling feat of legislative chicanery. Guile had trumped hubris, as ever it will. But I was left with a feeling that the whole exercise had been a fraud. It seemed the courts and legislators regarded the public as little more than an inconvenience and were determined to govern the state without us.

George W. Bush came to Myrtle Beach in his quest for the White House. At a GOP breakfast at the Myrtle Beach Convention Center in August, he refused to take sides on the Confederate flag, choosing instead to pontificate on Bill Clinton's personal behavior. Emcee for the event was country singer and Bush family friend Steve Gatlin. "He and his father are wonderful, wonderful people," Gatlin told an enthusiastic room full of Republicans. "We would be honored to have him as our next president."

In Conway a few days later, I took a cruise into the Waccamaw backwaters with charter Captain Dick Davis. It was a hot, clear day as Davis piloted the small open boat across the glassy black water, pointing out ospreys, egrets and other wildlife.

Along with me on the tour were five rather noisy Yankees. To me the black water bayou was a cathedral, commanding reverence and silence of all who entered. To my Northern mates it must have been an amusement park. They laughed and chattered incessantly, trying to draw me into their banter. I ignored them as best I could, watching the dark riverbanks in hope of seeing an alligator. But the Yankees were not without redemption. One of them was wearing a Banana Republic T-shirt and in a flash of inspiration I had a title for my book.

Memory and Metamorphosis

September 13 was a melancholy anniversary for Myrtle Beach. On that day in 1974 the Ocean Forest Hotel was brought down by a dynamite implosion. The blast wasn't as dramatic as Hurricane Hazel or Hurricane Hugo, but when the dust had settled, Myrtle Beach was none the better.

For nearly half a century the Ocean Forest had been the proud reminder of a fabled age. At its opening in 1930 it was one of the grandest hotels in the world, offering fresh and salt water baths in its 220 elegant guest rooms, indoor and outdoor swimming pools, high-ceilinged dining and ball rooms, chandeliers of Czechoslovak crystal, floors and columns of Italian marble. Liveried doormen, maids and waitresses polished the sterling silver doorknobs and catered to every need. Balconies and terraces draped the ten-story central tower and two five-story wings. The brick and steel structure – painted white – stood gleaming against the gray Atlantic and the vast green Horry County forest.

With the coming of the Great Depression, the Ocean Forest went into foreclosure and then to a series of owners. Even so, there were grand times in the ballroom and the Marina Patio, where Tommy Dorsey and Tex Beneke played. In the 1950s, the Ocean Forest was ranked seventh best in the nation by Actors Equity for summer stock theater. Original Broadway plays came to the hotel, with such productions as *A Streetcar Named Desire*, *Witness for the Prosecution* and *Teahouse of the August Moon*. Gloria Swanson, Veronica Lake, Shelley Winters and Arthur Treacher were among the stars who performed for Ocean Forest audiences.

In the 1960s times caught up with the aging behemoth. A jungle of new family-priced motels cut into the Ocean Forest's meager profits, offering larger rooms and – most importantly – air conditioning. The hotel went into decline as maintenance was deferred and staff cut back. Two small businessmen – Sonny Stevens and Dexter Stuckey – bought the building in 1970. They had dreams of restoring it to its former glory, but costs were prohibitive and insurers ordered them to upgrade the wiring and plumbing or close it down. In the condo boom of the 1970s, the 250-yard beachfront was worth more than the shabby old building.

Some still argue that the Ocean Forest could have been saved. Its sister hotel, the Cavalier, in Virginia Beach, still stands. But Stevens and Stuckey did not have the resources to pay the mortgage while they renovated the inoperable hotel. So the explosives were set, Stevens pressed the button and Myrtle Beach said good-bye to the only elegance it had every known.

The Ocean Forest is emblematic of what Myrtle Beach has done to all of its history. With no traditions, no architectural or aesthetic standards to guide them, developers have filled the Grand Strand with miles of glass and pastel buildings, neon and flashing lights, ugliness piled upon mediocrity, garnished with vulgarity.

The demolition left psychic wounds that have not healed. In the quarter-century since its demise the hotel came to occupy a mythic place in the collective imagination. An industry sprang up in relics and renderings. Paintings of the Ocean Forest, with gauzy skies and endless white sand stretching to the horizon, hang in fashionable homes and offices. Businesses boast windows, doors and mantelpieces salvaged from the hotel. A cluster of condos and shops in the area of the late hotel now use its name.

To fill the psychic vacuum, local businessman Bill Hussey briefly entered into negotiations, in 1978, to buy the Eiffel Tower, have it dismantled, shipped from Paris and reassembled on the Grand Strand. Others talk of building a 200-foot lighthouse, which would cast a rotating beam many miles across the sea.

A good psychiatrist would be a lot cheaper.

At City Hall a long, ugly season was far from over. Mayor Mark McBride made himself famous for coming up on the short end of 6-1 votes. He denounced his two strongest council adversaries – Rachel Broadhurst and Chuck Martino – for voting for a $500 city grant to the Boys & Girls Club while they sat on that organization's board. He called press conferences to criticize city staff and council and circulated a petition calling for a mayor-council government that would make his job full-time – and greatly increase his salary. He accused city staff of unethical conduct and called for the firing of Tom Leath. "You can't let him destroy your life," a philosophical Leath told *The Sun News*.

Council members worried publicly that city staff might get enough of the mayor's abuse and leave. Said Councilman Martino: "I can't imagine anybody putting up with an employer who belittles them publicly, demeans them in front of their peers and chastises them without any regard for the facts."

In the spring of 1999 McBride started running a weekly column in the *Myrtle Beach Herald* – paid for out of his own pocket – in which he roundly attacked city staff and council. In a typical piece, the mayor described going to the city-owned baseball park to watch the Myrtle Beach Pelicans. He ordered some boiled peanuts and soft drinks, but did not get a receipt. "In fact," he wrote, "I couldn't, because there were no receipts. . . . This is totally ridiculous. I am shocked that the city staff would have allowed for a contract that has no way to verify revenues or seek income from a project that uses the people's money. . . . I am also surprised that the council . . . would have voted for such a contract."

McBride's column was a free lunch for Bob Bestler: "Now I don't know a lot about the baseball business," *The Sun News* columnist wrote. "But I've been to many games, here and elsewhere, and I have never received a receipt from a beer vendor. Usually, by the time the beer gets to me, I'm happy if most of it is still in the cup." He quoted Pelicans general manager Steve Melliet as saying the team relies on inventory count to keep track of sales, a fact the mayor could have learned for himself, if he had picked up the phone and asked. "I guess [McBride] wants the vendors to wear little cash registers around their necks," Melliet told Bestler.

The jabs between the dueling columnists got personal. On June 9, Bestler wrote: "In most cities, mayoral messages are used to explain to residents why the city is doing the right thing. Here, the mayor's message tells why the city is doing the wrong thing – often by totally ignoring him.

"An example came right after Memorial Day weekend, when most everyone in a public position was saying things went fairly smoothly.

"Not our mayor. He used the column to renew his call for the National Guard to help keep order – an extension of his apparent modus operandi of confrontation over conciliation."

McBride fired back in his own column: "This columnist [Bestler] . . . seems to believe that the only reason a politician or elected official ever votes 'no' is for political gain. You see, in his world, there is no such thing as conviction, belief, individuality or fighting for what you believe. Only worn-out words of forgotten ideals that echo from an era of protest and liberalism that we are all trying desperately to forget."

In former Mayor Bob Grissom, Myrtle Beach had a back-slapping, joke-telling, good-will ambassador in plaid sport jacket, who would go anywhere to extol the pleasures and virtues of his town. Perhaps he lacked the dignity some would have liked in their mayor, but there was something even more disturbing about the young Christian conservative who replaced him. When he wasn't blasting City Hall or alarming the populace with his weekly columns, he was cruising the streets in his black Ford F-250 Super Duty XLT pickup, with tinted windows and giant mud tires. Shortly after he announced his desire to keep a gun in his City Hall office, the mayor addressed a convention of the National Rifle Association in North Myrtle Beach. At least one woman in attendance was alarmed at what she described as the mayor's call to arms. City council was so alarmed at his behavior that they stripped him of his power to declare emergencies and curfews.

At a council workshop – with visiting dignitaries present – McBride surprised and embarrassed council members by introducing Cameron Viebrock as his new chief of staff – an unprecedented, unsalaried position without office or job description. The mayor learned that he could tie up city staff for hours with personal "requests for information." The requests became so numerous and time-consuming that the city manager asked for relief. Council responded with a rule that any request for information requiring more than fifteen minutes of staff time be approved by full council.

In October 1999, McBride thought he had found a foolproof issue to discredit city staff and council incumbents before the November elections. He accused city council of failing to roll back the millage rate enough following a recent property reassessment. As a result, the city would illegally overtax its citizens by some $2.6 million, McBride said. He called a surprise news conference to declare that he was ready to fight City Hall on behalf of the overtaxed people of Myrtle Beach.

"I had a problem with him calling a press conference to distribute 'his' numbers and say the council didn't care about this and wouldn't work with him," Councilman Martino told a reporter. "That's an out-and-out lie."

Angered by the mayor's sneak attack and what they regarded as spurious tax figures, council hired an independent accounting firm to review their numbers. The firm pronounced the millage rate to be sound and the council took out a full-page ad in the *Myrtle Beach Herald*, defending their budget and explaining their numbers. McBride responded by threatening to file an ethics complaint against council, saying the *Herald* ad amounted to political advertising with taxpayers' money. The mayor retained an accounting firm – at $2,500 personal expense – to review the city books. He and the council then sent their respective findings off to the state Department of Revenue.

In his weekly column in the *Herald*, McBride wrote: "I have listened time and again to members of the Council try with all their hearts to avoid this issue. I have sat with them in meetings while they ask for staff to state that they are right, over and over again. But it is not about justification; it is about serving the people, which a blind reliance on staff makes almost impossible."

The 1999/2000 city budget was prepared by Budget Director Michael Shelton, widely respected in his field, a seven-time recipient of the award for excellence in financial reporting by the national Government Finance Officers Association. The University of South Carolina Institute of Public Affairs published and distributed Shelton's booklet of instructions for local finance officers around the state. Now he was being challenged over the efficacy of his budget by a man who had notably failed in several business ventures; who had been accused by a former friend of trying to cheat him on a personal loan; who had so abused his city credit card, cell phone and car allowances that they were curtailed by city council. *The Sun News* reported that the stress of McBride's constant badgering over the budget had caused Shelton to start smoking again after six years on the wagon.

At a special council meeting on December 7, a representative of the state Department of Revenue gave the city budget a clean bill of health, saying "the collection rate may have been a little high," but there was nothing illegal or improper in the budget estimates.

McBride would have none of it. "I want more realistic assumptions," he said.

Councilwoman Judy Rodman could take no more. Her face red with anger, she said to the mayor, "A budget is a budget. A budget is a budget. A budget is a guideline. This is not a cut-and-dry document and I am tired of these innuendos. You are making a mountain out of a molehill, Mark. That is what you do about everything." With that, she stood up and walked out of the meeting.

In August 2000, the final figures were in. Myrtle Beach had in fact overtaxed its property owners by $499,000 – far short of the $2.6 million the mayor had estimated. State law specifically allowed for the overpaying of property taxes, provided the city applied the surcharge against the next year's budget. Nevertheless, the City of Myrtle Beach agreed to rebate excess property taxes to residents. The first round of checks went out to 9,936 residents, at a cost to the city of $10,000. Most of the checks were for about three dollars, though many were for less than one dollar. The mayor pulled down a cool $4.97.

Throughout 1999, Mark McBride continued to brew tempests in every teapot. He had harassed Tom Leath and his staff with innuendo and accusation, and called for the National Guard to control the Memorial Day Bike Festival. He was the champion of the righteous and the angry, and never missed an opportunity to speak up for God, America and family values.

Yet, behind the mayor's constant war with city staff and council, some thought they saw a quiet pattern in his behavior. On every important issue of 1999 – and especially on the matter of the multicounty business park – McBride was solidly in Burroughs & Chapin's camp.

And then there was the issue of the proposed runway at Myrtle Beach International Airport. With the business park holding center stage since April, the runway issue had quietly simmered while business interests lobbied and lined up support for a new runway with a 3,000-foot separation from the old runway.

At the October 12 council meeting, Judy Rodman said she had never been lobbied by so many people, with such money and influence, as on the airport runway issue. Chuck Martino said the city needed to stand by its commitment to the Air Force Base Redevelopment Authority and the small businesses that had already located there. As Martino addressed the crowded council chamber, the mayor rolled his eyes, squirmed in his chair and twisted his mouth with disgust. He then presented a stack of letters and resolutions he had received from the Chamber of Commerce, golf course owners, hotel owners, trade associations, developers and others (but not B&C), all calling for the 3,000-foot separation. As he spoke, shaking the stack of letters in his hand, I marveled at how this chameleon had transformed himself. Could this actually be the young crusader who had campaigned two years earlier to take city government away from the big money interests and give it back to the people? Only his name and his perfect hair remained unchanged.

Living In Hurricane Alley

Early sailors to the New World soon discovered the Caribbean and regions north were stalked by a monster. Europeans had lived for centuries with lashing, cold North Atlantic storms, but in the tropics they met a storm of unearthly power and unimaginable devastation. Each summer, warm, moist air rises from the ocean surface, cooling in the upper atmosphere and falling back to earth. If conditions are right, great convection currents set up as air rises and falls in a towering "chimney" between sea and sky. As the currents move faster, the chimney of air starts to rotate counterclockwise, with internal wind speeds reaching well over a hundred miles per hour and a wind radius of hundreds of miles from the storm center. Once formed, such storms tend to track into higher latitudes and grow in size and strength. The Taino Indians of the Caribbean called this monster *hurakan*. We call it hurricane and it still stalks the Caribbean and southeastern regions of the United States.

In 1524, the Italian explorer Giovanni da Verrazano encountered a great storm off the Carolina coast. He marked the place where his ship took refuge by naming it the "Cape of Feare." A few miles away, in 1587, the English attempted a settlement on Roanoke Island, off the North Carolina coast. When a relief party reached the site in 1590, they found the settlers and all their homes and buildings had vanished. Some historians speculate the colony may have been lost when a storm surge swept over the island. In 1686, the fledgling settlement of Charleston was saved when a great storm struck a Spanish expedition moving up the coast from St. Augustine.

Throughout the colonial period, the Southern seaboard was sparsely populated and few hurricanes were observed or reported. When a storm did bring attention, it usually brought devastation as well. There were major storms in 1700 and 1713. On September 15, 1752, the eye of a hurricane crossed the coast at Charleston harbor on an incoming tide. The huge surge tossed all but one of the ships in the harbor onto the streets, destroyed all the wharves and many of the houses of the city. It left a forty-mile path of destruction through the countryside and a death toll of more than 100. Fifteen days later, another hurricane struck the city a glancing blow.

The nineteenth century saw more than twenty-five storms lash the South Carolina coast. In late September 1822, a hurricane made landfall between Charleston and Georgetown. Several hundred people drowned around Winyah Bay and hundreds more on North Island. A large house on North Island was swept out to sea. Horrified observers watched it drift away with its doomed occupants and lamps still burning in its windows. In August 1885, a Category 3 storm struck Charleston, damaging or destroying ninety percent of the homes and killing twenty-one. A series of eight hurricanes hit the coast between 1893 and 1911, destroying what was left of South Carolina's once-fabulous rice culture. Two of those storms struck in 1893. The June storm made landfall on Edisto Island, destroying the town of Eddingsville and killing an estimated 3,000 people between Savannah and Charleston. The second storm struck north of Georgetown in October, drowning many more.

A handful of great storms hit South Carolina in the twentieth century, including the hurricane of 1928, which killed 1,800 people in South Florida before arriving in this state. In October 1954, Hurricane Hazel became the first named storm to leave its mark on South Carolina. Most of its damage was done on the Outer Banks of North Carolina, but the Grand Strand was hit with 106-mile-per-hour winds and a seventeen-foot tidal surge. Hundreds of cottages were lost from Pawleys Island to Cherry Grove Beach. Hurricane David did $10 million damage in 1979. And in 1989, there was Hurricane Hugo, which did $6.2 billion damage and forced state leaders to finally understand they had a major urban area in hurricane alley.

Two important things have happened to change public policy toward hurricanes in South Carolina. The first was the National Flood Insurance Act of 1968, establishing federally subsidized insurance under the National Flood Insurance Program (NFIP). Homeowners who could never have bought insurance in the private sector were now protected to build their dream houses on the dunes. NFIP sparked the beach boom, which has transformed the Southeastern coast since the early 1970s. In 1992, Hurricane Andrew struck South Florida, racking up $28 billion damage, much of it covered by National Flood Insurance. The message was clear to all: As long as Uncle Sam keeps picking up the tab, people will keep building and rebuilding their houses and hotels as close to the surf as the law allows. As columnist Carl Hiaasen observed: "People's mad dash to relocate at the ocean's edge, and lawmakers' cowardly refusal to curb it, shows how quickly Andrew was forgotten."

The second policy change came in 1979, when South Carolina passed its first law requiring hurricane preparedness. An outgrowth of 1950s civil defense planning, the law was still little more than paper when Hugo struck a decade later. Hurricane Hugo forced the Federal Emergency Management Agency (FEMA) to produce the Federal Response Plan (FRP), detailing how the national government should deal with specific disasters. South Carolina took the FRP concept and developed its own emergency plan, first published in 1994. That year, the state hired its first hurricane planner, Paul Whitten. An active duty military planning and operations officer, Whitten cut his teeth working with FEMA in the aftermath of Hurricane Andrew.

Whitten helped draft the 1994 plan, which divides South Carolina's coastal counties into three "coastal conglomerates," with Georgetown and Horry counties in the northern conglomerate. The plan addresses media markets and road networks throughout the coastal counties and for 100 miles inland and creates standardized evacuation times and routes in the three conglomerates.

South Carolina is the only state in which the governor has sole authority to order mandatory hurricane evacuations. This is good for planning and coordinated response but puts enormous pressure on the governor to evacuate thousands of people. Helping the governor make the call during an emergency are public safety officials, law enforcement officers and political leaders in the threatened coastal counties. They analyze the approaching storm with a HURREVAC computer simulator program as they monitor public safety functions in their respective counties. Their information and recommendations are passed along a conference line to Columbia, where the state emergency management director analyzes and massages the flood of information − including updates from National Weather Service offices in Charleston, Columbia and Wilmington − and passes it along to the governor.

For all the progress that has been made in hurricane analysis and prediction, there is still a terrifying range of uncertainty. That is never more true than in the critical hours as a storm approaches the coast. In tracking a hurricane, planners and analysts figure there is a forecast error of 100 miles per twenty-four-hour period. With that in mind, they know it takes seventy-two hours to call up the National Guard for an evacuation. In a mandatory evacuation, it can take up to twenty-six hours to clear the coast. A voluntary evacuation can take up to twelve hours. But at the end of the day – when all personnel are in place, when all the data are collected and analyzed, when hundreds of thousands of people are sitting by their televisions and radios, waiting to hear what to do – only the governor can give the order to evacuate.

"There is a point of no return" in calling an evacuation, Whitten told me. "[The governor] doesn't want to evacuate unless it's absolutely necessary, but by the time it's absolutely necessary, it's too late. That's the governor's dilemma. . . . That's why he gets to live in the big house."

Whitten was tall, personable and energetic, thirty-eight years old, with a crown that seemed to have been swept clean of all hair by some past storm. In 1997, he came to Horry County as emergency pre-paredness director. Behind his desk was a two-and-half-inch thick loose-leaf binder of double-printed pages containing the state's emer-gency hurricane plan. It listed key roads and intersections and who would man them around the clock in an emergency, as well as shelter resources and hundreds of other details. His office was in the M.L. Brown Building in Conway, along with the Horry County Police Department and other public safety agencies. On his office wall was an autographed photo of a late-night conference in 1996, as Whitten briefed Governor David Beasley from a laptop computer on the approach of Hurricane Bertha. Arrayed behind Whitten and the gov-ernor in the picture were staff and law enforcement personnel, look-ing as alert as could be expected at 11:30 p.m.

Hurricane Bertha missed Horry County but struck the great jaw of North Carolina, which thrusts out to the east of Horry. Too bad for North Carolina. But next time Horry County might not be so lucky.

"I'm worried," state climatologist Mike Helfert told the House Agriculture and Natural Resources Committee, in Columbia, on April 13, 1999. "This thing looks like it is coming on hard, coming on fast."

"This thing" to which he obliquely referred was the hurricane season. Average temperatures were four degrees above normal, Helfert said, and Atlantic Ocean currents resembled those of the 1940s and 1950s, when many more hurricanes occurred than in the following thirty years. Furthermore, ocean temperatures in the areas where hurricanes form were significantly higher than normal, conditions that could generate more storms and earlier storms than usual.

On the South Carolina coast, the average time between hurricane hits is nine years, Helfert said, and the last severe hit was Hugo, in September 1989. For 1999 there were "more than double the chances of a hit on the mainland" of the East Coast, he said.

Helfert repeated his warning to the committee in mid-May. South Carolina was in for a hot, dry summer, he said. "And hurricane occurrence from Miami to Cape Hatteras will be up to 185 percent of normal," he said. "I won't say we are due, but statistically we should be prepared for a strike in this region."

Colorado State University meteorologist William Gray echoed Helfert's dire predictions. Fourteen Atlantic storms would form in the 1999 season, he said. Nine would become hurricanes and four would pack winds of 111 miles per hour or more.

On May 5, emergency preparedness director Whitten put county employees through a drill, simulating the aftereffects of a direct hit by a Category 3 hurricane. The *faux* hurricane, with sustained winds of 122 miles per hour, hit Garden City Beach, killing 400. The next day, Ashby Ward and state tourism officials bubbled with the good news that the summer tourist season was off to a roaring start. "We hope all the traffic on our Internet site means a lot of traffic heading toward the Grand Strand," said a spokesman for the Department of Parks, Recreation and Tourism. Ward predicted hotels would enjoy a ninety-percent occupancy rate during the season. Only one thing could spoil the party, he said–a hurricane.

The six-month hurricane season officially began on June 1. Nine days later, several hundred people turned out for the annual Public Hurricane Conference at Socastee High School. Sponsored by the Horry County Emergency Preparedness Office, the conference had a whiff of the gravedigger's grim opportunism, but Myrtle Beach had mastered the art of turning every natural resource to coin. Why should hurricanes be any different? The event looked like a county fair. Television and radio vans were in the school parking lot. In the foyer, dozens of promoters staged a "disaster bazaar," selling insurance, storm windows, propane gas, electric generators and other survival technology from their trade show booths. Along with hurricane tracking charts, key chains, refrigerator magnets and ball point pins, there were brochures, booklets and many vivid photographs depicting what can happen to *you* if you are not prepared. I moved among the charmers and hucksters, picking up my windshield decal security pass, which would allow me to return to my home after a storm. The whole Strand was broken into regions and assigned a decal color. Surfside Beach was red; Little River, green; Atlantic Beach, orange; etc. As a resident of Myrtle Beach, I received a blue decal.

In the gymnasium, residents listened to an odd mix of politicians and scientists, including Jerry Jarrell, director of the National Hurricane Center in Miami. Not only was the coastal population of South Carolina exploding, Jarrell said, but most of the new residents had no experience with hurricanes. "Emergency officials need more [warning] time because so many people live on the coast now who come from other areas," he said.

Two days after the hurricane conference, the National Hurricane Center sighted the first tropical storm of the season and named it Arlen. It was some 375 miles southeast of Bermuda, with winds of sixty miles an hour. I pinned my hurricane tracking map to my living room wall and started plotting coordinates. Arlen turned out to be a false alarm. The storm wobbled around in the Atlantic for several days and disappeared. But I was on notice and so was all of South Carolina.

Myrtle Beach Dodges a Bullet

It's hurricane season in Myrtle Beach when you walk into a sports bar and every television is tuned to the Weather Channel. And everyone is watching!

That's what I found in one of my regular Boulevard watering holes on the afternoon of Saturday, August 28. The object of all the sullen interest was a hurricane named Dennis, making its way up from the Caribbean with eighty-mile-per-hour winds. Ignoring the corny remarks about "Dennis the Menace," I settled in with my newspaper and a beer as a bartender tried to organize a pool to bet on where the storm would make landfall. A couple of unsavory regulars suggested it should strike Atlantic Beach "and wipe out that nest of niggers once and for all."

Along the Grand Strand, you would hardly guess that anything was amiss. High school football teams had played the night before. George W. Bush had just left town following a campaign appearance. Mayor Mark McBride and Councilman Wayne Gray duked it out after a city council meeting a few days earlier.

Throughout the summer, meteorologists repeated their warning of nine hurricanes, four of them major. Days earlier Hurricane Bret had made landfall at Corpus Christi, Texas, with 125 mile-per-hour winds – far enough away not to trouble our sleep, but close enough to be noticed. Now Dennis was knocking at our door and it had our undivided attention. The county opened its emergency operations center on August 27 and Governor Jim Hodges ordered 1,000 National Guardsmen to report to their armories. On the last weekend of August, the Strand was nearly deserted of tourists. *The Sun News* reported there was a run on bottled water at local supermarkets and Lowe's had sold out of electric generators. The paper ran a public service page dedicated to hurricane preparedness and State Farm Insurance bought a full-page ad offering an 800 number to assist its policy holders in making claims.

Sunday morning, August 29: I drove up to North Myrtle Beach under threatening skies to drop in on Reverend Beaver Greenway's beachfront service. Along the way, I passed merchants boarding up their storefronts on U.S. 17. Television news vans from Atlanta and Charlotte were in town, chasing the storm.

The beach was almost empty of life at 10:00 a.m. as waves pounded the sand and ran almost all the way up to the pavilion, where Greenway opened his service with scripture and prayer. He inevitably used the approaching storm as a metaphor for life's many storms, then referred to Jesus speaking to the stormy waters of Galilee, saying, "Be still."

"Jesus was centered with that storm," Greenway said, sounding more like a Buddhist monk than a shagging fundamentalist.

Greenway launched into a bathed-in-the-blood soliloquy on the sacrifice of the Lamb of God and cited Revelations to warn of "the judgment that's coming upon this earth," then denounced all the faiths and religions of the world which did not acknowledge Jesus as the Savior. I had heard enough and slipped away from the pavilion to spend the next couple of hours driving around the Strand, watching people prepare for Dennis.

By 2:00 I was on the Boulevard. There was not a tourist in sight. Wind whipped the palm trees violently and a drizzle fell across the city. On the boardwalk, sheets of plywood were going up over the windows at Marvin's, Boardwalk Bill's, the Gay Dolphin and Oceanfront Bar & Grille. Many of the precut, well-used boards were spray painted with the names of other recent storms: Fran, Bertha and Bonnie. Kyle and Karon Mitchell had boarded the office of their Sea Palms Motel. Pavilion Amusement Park employees worked like ants to cover the windows of their concession stands, ticket windows and other buildings. They had already removed the go-carts from the speedway and were securing benches and tables around the arcade. Only Michael's Bar & Grill and the beachwear shops remained open.

In my apartment, safely distant from the surf, I watched Dennis move up the coast. Near midnight I walked down the Boulevard, through the slashing wind and rain, to the boardwalk. There I encountered about a dozen other idly curious. Together we watched the waves lacerate the beach and run all the way up to the boardwalk.

That was all the drama there was. The governor issued no evacuation order. By 8:00 a.m. the next morning, the sky was clearing. By 9:00, the plywood was coming off shop windows all over town. It turned out to be a breezy, clear day, cooler than any we had seen in months. With light crowds on the Boulevard, the Pavilion remained closed for the day. By 7:00 p.m., at least one beachwear shop was sporting T-shirts that read, "I survived Hurricane Dennis – August 29, 1999."

Down at the bar, the joke was that we were all in more danger from thugs and drunk drivers than from hurricanes. After brushing the coast with its 112 mile-per-hour winds, Dennis stalled near the Outer Banks for five days before coming ashore, dumping torrential rains and sparking tornadoes in eastern North Carolina. The storm flooded roads and whole towns and destroyed scores of loggerhead turtle nests at the peak of the hatching season.

By Labor Day Weekend, the tourists were back. In the last great bacchanal of the season, thousands of young people jammed the Boulevard with cars, pickup trucks and SUVs, their stereos pounding the air. Several large Confederate flags streamed from the back of trucks. On Saturday night, I watched two Myrtle Beach foot patrol officers stop a Mustang with Tennessee tags, a spoiler on the back, and three young smart asses inside. "Turn it down!" one of the officers shouted. "We take our noise ordinance seriously here." That night, other cops conducted an undercover sting, arresting Jacob Garon and two of his employees at Boulevard Beachwear on charges of illegal piercing.

The fever, hormones and video cameras of spring were all present for one last street orgy. But there was an air of desperation and breathlessness on this weekend. It was the last chance to get laid, last chance to get rich, last chance to save a soul. The gutter around 9th Avenue North was thick with religious tracts from the regular band of apostles. The cops arrested dozens of guys that night, lining them up, handcuffed, in front of Mother Fletcher's and Ocean Beachwear. Somewhere in the night Kevin McMichael and his friends were out club-hopping around the town. In a few hours he would lie bleeding to death on the dance floor of the Masters Club, as the "hundred-day" Myrtle Beach tourist season ticked down to its final hours.

There was a strangely somber mood on the Boulevard the next week as shops began to lay off workers. Friends I had seen almost daily for months quietly vanished. The Boulevard Rats packed up and went back home – or wherever it is they go for their next season of thrills. Part of the mood may have come from the mobile replica of the

Vietnam Memorial Wall, which drew hundreds to the Myrtle Beach Convention Center. Jews quietly observed Rosh Hashannah and most of the Boulevard beachwear stores closed for the religious observance.

The days grew short and the shadows long as that melancholy that settles on me every year at this time began to creep in. The shortness and uncertainty of life is never so palpable as in the death of summer, especially in this town, which lives and dies by the seasons, as surely as any farm village. It was brought home again on September 12, when ten-year-old Marvin Washington became the Grand Strand's first ocean drowning victim of 1999. The boy and his parents had driven from Conway to Myrtle Beach State Park for an afternoon of fun that ended with the parents weeping on the beach as rescuers searched the surf for their son's body. The ocean had another fearful surprise that day when *The Sun News* introduced us to Hurricane Floyd.

Floyd was a massive storm, centered some 700 miles west-south-west of the Grand Strand, at latitude 22.7 north, longitude 64.5 west, moving west-northwest at twelve miles an hour, packing winds of 110 miles per hour. Twenty-four hours later, Floyd was approaching Category 5 status, in a league with hurricanes Hugo and Andrew, as it bore down on the central Bahamas and Florida. "It's extremely well developed and well formed," said senior meteorologist John Hope of the Weather Channel. "In fact, it's about as well formed as a hurricane ever gets."

This time there was little humor in the local taverns. Barflies clutched their drinks and followed anxiously on tavern televisions as Floyd churned its way across the Atlantic. Even hundreds of miles away, this one looked serious. People seemed to sense that Floyd was on a mission – and it just might have our number.

On Monday, September 13, more than a million people in Florida were ordered to leave their coastal homes. So began the largest evacuation in United States history as refugees took to Interstate 95 and headed north. By now Floyd was one of the largest storms ever recorded, larger even than Hurricane Andrew, which tore into South Florida in 1992, causing $25 billion damage and leaving 160,000 homeless. Forecasters said it would strike land within two days, between central Florida and South Carolina. Governor Hodges ordered 600 National Guard troops and 500 state police to the coast in the event of evacuation. Emergency shelters were opened and *The Sun News* published shelter locations and evacuation routes.

As it approached the mainland, Floyd bumped into a high-pressure front off the seaboard, which deflected it from a westerly to a more northerly course. Hundreds of thousands of nervous Floridians and Georgians jumped in their cars and joined the lemming-like rush up I-95. Yet, it was South Carolina that was suddenly in the cross hairs.

At 10:30 Tuesday morning, evacuation traffic was jammed on Ocean Boulevard and U.S. 17, inching its way out to U.S. 501. It took me a half-hour to drive the mile to City Hall, where I had an appointment with city spokesman Mark Kruea. I found Kruea and other staffers hauling boxes of files to secure locations. It looked like the last hours of the U.S. embassy in Saigon. Kruea and I rescheduled.

Governor Hodges helicoptered into Beaufort, then Charleston, inspecting storm preparations, thinking all was going well. He was clueless. Hundreds of thousands of evacuees were headed inland, only to encounter two million refugees from Georgia and Florida, who were jamming the state's roads and filling up hotels. On Interstate 26, traffic was backed up, bumper-to-bumper, from Charleston to Columbia. Cars overheated and ran out of gas. People had to relieve themselves on the side of the road. At least one elderly woman died in an ambulance during the sixteen-hour trek. Yet, incredibly, the eastbound lanes sat open and empty, as Hodges, his staff and S.C. Department of Transportation officials dithered over opening the lanes to westbound traffic.

At noon, the Governor "pulled the trigger." Flanked by the Adjutant General, the chief of the State Law Enforcement Division and the director of the Emergency Preparedness Division, he ordered the evacuation of 800,000 people from the coast. Back in my apartment, I watched on television as I did preliminary packing and microwaved a cup of instant soup. Then I made a few phone calls and sent e-mails to friends to find out where they were and let them know where I was.

A friend in North Carolina e-mailed to say that he was watching the evacuation, along with the rest of the country, "and it looks like the lunatics are running the asylum."

It was true. Not only were DOT employees charging evacuees a dollar toll to use the Hilton Head Cross Island Expressway; by early afternoon, the order to reverse traffic in eastbound I-26 was still on hold. Charleston Mayor Joe Riley, who earned his stripes ten years earlier in Hurricane Hugo, was livid. State officials were incompetent, he said. "This isn't rocket science, for crying out loud."

In Horry County, emergency preparedness director Paul Whitten urged people to get as far away from the coast a possible. "I'm talking out of South Carolina," Whitten told *The Sun News*. "People need to look at Asheville, North Carolina, or Atlanta. . . . This storm is a monster. This storm could be a killer. . . . I've been in this business for a number of years and to tell you the truth, this is the first time I'm scared."

With notebook in hand, I headed down to the crowded Boulevard, where plywood was going back up everywhere. It didn't need much cutting or fitting. This was veteran storm board. City crews were taking up curbside garbage cans and anything that could become a projectile in Floyd's 140-mile-per-hour winds. Pepsi Cola workers were collecting their vending machines from the sidewalk and loading them into a giant tractor-trailer that blocked two lanes of the Boulevard. Incredibly, several beachwear stores were open, as if nothing were going on. But there was not a customer in sight.

I walked uptown to Main Street, where every street and road approaching U.S. 501 was a stand-still parking lot of honking, fuming motorists. Some of them were tailgating from the back of their SUV's. Others pulled out lounge chairs and worked on their tans while they waited for traffic to move. At Miscue Billiards and Bar, Lillian Wiggan was open to serve soft drinks and water to motorists simmering in the late summer heat. Terry Sasser mounted plywood over the windows of his Beach Craft Upholstery & Fabrics Shop, then painted on it a bold message: "Then he arose and rebuked the winds and the sea; and there was a great calm. What manner of man is this that even the winds and the sea obey him? His name is Jesus."

I talked to a number of tourists who sat in their vehicles on Main Street, listening to their radios, incredulous that they could be trapped in downtown Myrtle Beach with an epic storm moving directly on them. After only a few hundred yards in more than four hours, Katherine Kimball, of Winston-Salem, tried to keep her sense of humor. On the back of her Explorer XLT was a hand-lettered sign: "Everyone's Annoyed − Thanks, Floyd."

Reid and Angie Peterson, of Belleville, Ohio, had their honeymoon interrupted. "We didn't know we would spend our honeymoon with Floyd," Angie laughed.

D.W. Hartman, of Danville, Virginia, said he had just arrived on Sunday, planning to stay a week. I told him to write to Ashby Ward and ask for a refund.

Teresa Koch, of Syracuse, New York, said she would get a refund from her hotel, because she had waited until the mandatory evacuation to leave. But now she was stranded. She had moved less than a mile in an hour, she told me.

I stepped into Smoothie's Billiards & Snacks, the only restaurant downtown that seemed to be open, and ordered a grilled cheese sandwich and glass of tea. The walls were covered with NASCAR pictures and memorabilia. There was a country jukebox, three pool tables and pinball machines along the wall. The five Pot-O-Gold video poker machines were all in use. Around the little horseshoe-shaped bar sat weary-looking men and women who might have been refugees from a Damon Runyon story. And all their eyes were on the big screen television, where the Weather Channel kept us apprised of Floyd's every burp and shudder. The red-orange monster was now 600 miles in diameter, moving inexorably up the coast, its "cone of probability" centered on Myrtle Beach.

I returned to Main Street to talk to more motorists, many of whom had less than kind things to say about our way of doing things in South Carolina. From their radios they knew that roads were jammed all the way down the coast. For all the years of planning and preparation that went into this moment, the state's hurricane evacuation plan was a disaster. "What kind of idiots run this state?" asked Chet Williams, of Richmond, Virginia. I didn't tell him I had been wondering the same thing for years.

Governor Hodges arrived at Myrtle Beach International Airport at 3:50 p.m. "This could be a storm unlike any other," he declared. "Unfortunately, this is a storm that has the potential to do damage to a third of the state if it continues on its course." Only then did he order the eastbound lanes of I-26 reversed. People had been sitting in a 120-mile traffic jam for eight hours.

An hour later, Hodges was back in Columbia and the first thing he demanded to know was whether the lane reversal had been completed. Not yet, he was told by DOT officials. Why not? He couldn't get a straight answer. It was going to be a long night for all of us.

Teresa Koch ran up to me on Main Street and said, "Look! Two hours and we've moved one block! There's got to be a better way." Not in South Carolina, I told her, and headed back home through the standing traffic. It was late afternoon and the Boulevard looked like a valley of plywood. Most of the evacuation traffic had cleared the area; police cars cruised up and down the Strip.

"Hey, Will!" I heard the young voice behind me. "Where you goin'?"

It was Kevin. I hadn't seen him in weeks. He had his pet chameleon on his shoulder and seemed cheerful enough, despite dirty clothes and shaggy hair. He wore his Tommy Gear sport cap backward, of course, with the bill pointing down the back of his neck. His apartment key hung from a knit chain around his neck, with "Stone Cold" stitched into it, a tribute to one of his wrestling heroes. I was delighted to see him, but afraid as always to learn too many details of his tragic young life. Where were he and his mother planning to wait out the storm? I asked. He gave a shrug. "I don't know." Where *was* his mother? He shrugged again. Did she know there was a storm coming? "Sure!" He looked at me like I was an idiot.

I had to think fast. While Margaret was totally unfit to raise a child, I had no legal standing to take Kevin with me. I might carry him to a shelter, but would his mother be able to find him there? I could take him to the police station, but he had already had several minor run-ins with the gendarmes and was scared to death of them. He would never go voluntarily. It was beginning to rain and I suddenly felt very depressed and vulnerable. I had visions of choking Margaret. Finally, I told Kevin to go home and wait for his mother and to call me in one hour to let me know his situation. We parted, both of us walking home in the rain.

I spent the next hours watching television updates and waiting for Kevin's call. It didn't come. On the tube, Dan Rather and battalions of video flunkies were in town on their hurricane chase. Outside, the rain was pouring. I disconnected my computer and set it by the front door, along with my files, selected books, a few pictures and mementos and a bag of clothes.

In Columbia, the governor met with state DOT officials at 7:00 p.m. and was told the eastbound lanes of I-26 would be reversed at 8:30. At 7:10, he held a press conference to announce the good news, but it was all for naught. The lanes were not opened until 10:00 p.m., more than six hours after his original order. In Charleston, Mayor Riley held his own press conference, pounding the podium and waving his arms in anger. "It was just . . ." he took a deep breath, "*terrible!*"

The evacuation went on through the night. Friends and family called to know when the hell I was leaving. Soon, I said – don't worry. I always sleep well when it rains; this night was no exception.

I rose a little before 10:00 on Wednesday morning, showered and shaved, then made a cup of coffee and a few last-minute phone calls, with the Weather Channel in the background. Floyd was several hundred miles out and bearing down on the Grand Strand like a freight train. I wrapped my computer, books and other valuables in towels and hauled them through the rain to my Miata. At the stroke of noon I hit the ignition and headed for U.S. 501. Myrtle Beach was deserted. The streets and roads were empty of traffic, but flooded. On my way out of town, I stopped by 10th Avenue North, at the ratty little apartment where Kevin lived with his mother and whatever man she was with this month. There was no one at home, and I wondered if I would ever see the kid again.

Even having the road to myself, it took five hours to drive the 175 miles through the blowing rain, to my parents' upstate home. From my safe vantage I continued to follow Floyd on the Weather Channel. As the evening wore on, something amazing happened. The great storm moved up the coast, following the curve of the Strand, arcing back farther and farther to the east, until it passed the North Carolina border. Against all odds and forecasts, Myrtle Beach was spared! Horry County was spared! Some trees were down. Some roofs and awnings were damaged. In North Myrtle Beach, Cherry Grove Pier had both ends swept away. Parts of Ocean Boulevard were washed out. And there was rain − torrents of rain, days of rain − as the 600-mile-wide storm crept inland, over North Carolina. Hurricane Floyd made landfall near Wilmington at 3:00 a.m., Thursday, September 16, spinning off tornadoes with its 110 mile-per-hour winds, then moved up the coast, pouring up to twenty inches of rain all the way to New England. Along much of the draught-parched Atlantic Seaboard, the rain was welcome, but eastern North Carolina was still drying out from fifteen inches of rain Hurricane Dennis had dumped ten days before. Across North Carolina's broad, flat coastal plain the flooding was biblical and it lasted for weeks. Pouring out of North Carolina, the Waccamaw River soon reached flood level.

The eastern part of that state was home to the largest cluster of industrial hog farms in the nation, with millions of hogs warehoused in giant sheds, their untreated waste held in huge open lagoons. Under thirty inches of rain from two hurricanes, the lagoons burst across the landscape and into the rivers, sending untold millions of gallons of raw sewage roiling toward Pamlico Sound, off the Carolina coast.

On Thursday, Hodges reversed the westbound lanes of I-26 without incident to begin the return of thousands of still-fuming evacuees to their homes. But the damage to Hodges' and the state's image was not so easily reversed. Tens of thousands of angry motorists blamed the governor for their day of sitting in traffic. Furious letters appeared in newspapers around the state; Internet sites sprang up, allowing people to vent their fury. The Charleston *Post and Courier* delivered a blistering editorial against "Tuesday's outrage": "The state was unconscionably inefficient in its evacuation effort. . . ." wrote the editor. "Though the traffic was bound to be bad, the state's inept strategy made it much worse than it had to be. . . . This unfortunate episode reaffirms the urgency of proper intergovernmental cooperation for safe and speedy hurricane evacuation. . . . Because the state wasn't ready to do its job, the negative legacy of Floyd now extends to the potentially tragic perception that staying at home during a hurricane beats trying to leave."

In a news conference on Friday, the governor abjectly apologized: "A message today, folks. I'm sorry. For the people who sat in the traffic on Tuesday for ten, fifteen, sometimes twenty hours, I'm sorry for the traffic jams on Interstate 26. It was simply inexcusable." Republicans seized upon the botched evacuation and promised to use it as a campaign issue. Some Charleston Republicans in the General Assembly held hearings on the evacuation.

I returned to Myrtle Beach on Friday and sat on Pier 14 the next afternoon, sipping a Budweiser beneath a brilliant, blue sky. Planes crisscrossed overhead, streaming their beach banners: "CRABBY MIKE'S 120 ITEM SEAFOOD BUFFET" and "MAMMY'S ALL YOU CAN EAT SEAFOOD BUFFET $10.99" Below me vacationers played on an almost empty beach. A few blocks to the south, dump trucks, back-hoes and tractors patched up what was left of the beach where it had been gouged out by waves and stormwater discharge. Great sections of corrugated stormwater pipe lay scattered like beached whales along the Stand.

As bad as things were in Horry County, they were horrific in North Carolina. On Monday, September 20, up to three inches of additional rain fell on the devastated region as President Clinton made an aerial inspection of the eastern part of the state with Governor Jim Hunt. "We know we have a responsibility as members of the American family to help you get back on your feet," the President said. "And we intend to do it."

Temporary shelters went up across eastern North Carolina as private and public relief started pouring in from around the country. The Federal Emergency Management Agency started writing relief checks and buying condemned homes. The Southern Baptist Convention dispatched hundreds of volunteers and tons of food and building materials. The Coors Brewing Company gave 33,000 bottles of water. Health workers sprayed for mosquitoes and gave tetanus shots, as an 18,000-square-mile cesspool of sewage, hog waste, animal carcasses, fertilizer, pesticides, gasoline and other pollutants spread out across the land. Coast Guardsmen retrieved scores of coffins that popped out of the ground in Princeville. Workers pulled furniture, carpets and interior walls from thousands of flooded homes, piling them on roadsides to be carried to landfills.

Through late September the great flood moved slowly down the Waccamaw River, toward Conway, as workers built sandbag berms to keep U.S. 501 open and save downtown commercial areas and the town's sewage plant. Residents in boats and hip boots salvaged what they could from flooded homes. On Saturday, September 18, the usually sluggish, black water river broke flood records at the town of Longs, above Conway.

The Waccamaw rose steadily, creeping onto the streets and yards of Conway, as hundreds of families fled their homes. By Friday, September 24, some 800,000 sandbags were in place along the river in Conway and Socastee. Several times I drove over to the blighted town to spend the last hour of daylight with others on the downtown bridge, looking out over the brown water. Each day it was higher, more turbid, more threatening. Residents could only pile sandbags and pray. Some of them did just that on the bridge one evening as I watched and listened. A tall woman with outstretched arms led a small group of followers as she chanted an incantation: "Lord of the river, Lord of the storm, Lord of the wind and sky, Lord, give this river peace, let this river rest, let this river run quiet and true and gentle. Let this river know your power in this universe, O Lord. Spread out your almighty hand over these waters and make them still, let them flow untroubled to the sea, O Lord."

But the river continued to rise. On September 24 the river gauge at Longs recorded forty-two million gallons of muddy, polluted, debris-choked water per day moving down the channel toward Conway. On a normal day the Waccamaw carries 515,000 gallons. On September 25 it crested at 17.5 feet at Longs and started to fall as the crest moved south toward Conway. Hydrologists predicted it would crest at more than thirteen feet on Monday, September 27, breaking the Waccamaw's historic flood record, set on September 30, 1928.

At 8:00 a.m. Monday – nearly two weeks after Floyd struck – the Waccamaw crested at 13.2 feet, just short of the 1928 record of 13.4 feet. On Wednesday, Governor Hodges was in Horry County to give a pep talk and give an example by rolling up his sleeve for a tetanus shot. That night, Hodges was back home in Columbia, but thousands in Horry County were sleeping in emergency shelters and trying to pull their lives back together. The Waccamaw River would recede over the next month, leaving a trail of filth, debris, destruction and scarred lives, some of which would never heal.

In the cosmology of the Taino Indians, *hurakan* was a capricious and jealous god who visited earth periodically to remind mortals of our insignificance. The Taino have long vanished, but *hurakan* lives on, immortal and vengeful as ever, stalking our dreams, mocking our designs, reminding us all – developers, politicians and pundits alike – that we are but grains of sand on the beach of Eternity.

Postscript to Hurricane Floyd: The day I returned to Myrtle Beach, I encountered Kevin on the Boulevard. I wanted to hug the little guy; he looked as scruffy and nonchalant as ever. He said he hadn't called me on the day of the evacuation because his apartment didn't have a telephone. He and his mother had taken a bus to an emergency shelter on the old air base. No big deal, he said. It was just a bunch of rain anyway. How 'bout some pizza?

What could I say?

Robert L. McDonald, of Pawleys Island, wrote a letter to *The Sun News*, saying that he and his friend had saved the Grand Strand from hurricanes Dennis and Floyd through their intercession with the Almighty: "The day before Hurricane Dennis arrived, God spoke to a friend of mine, a New Testament prophet, to throw a hand of salt in the ocean and command Dennis to move off land. . . . I watched, fascinated, as the day progressed to see Dennis act as if an unseen hand had unleashed a curveball."

Ashby Ward did not let the weather distract him from his mission. Within days after Floyd passed, he conducted a survey of local hotels and reported the storm had cost the Grand Strand as much as $100 million dollars in direct tourist spending. The Myrtle Beach Area Chamber of Commerce ran a quarter-page ad in *USA Today*, announcing the area was open for business. "Thanks for your Prayers," the ad proclaimed. "They worked."

Environmentally, the flooding of North and South Carolina rivers pointed up the importance of freshwater wetlands in controlling flood-waters. It's not clear if anybody outside the environmental community got the message. Scientists and engineers warned that much of the flooding was the result of rampant development and poor planning. Roads built across broad flood plains acted as berms, backing up water and contributing to the crisis. Impervious surfaces were an additional factor in urban areas. Flood maps, developed decades earlier, were use-less in predicting the direction and intensity of the flooding.

The Army Corps of Engineers reported 200,000 cubic yards of soil was washed into the Intracoastal Waterway from two giant construction sites: Burroughs & Chapin's Grande Dunes Resort and Barefoot Resort and Golf Club, in North Myrtle Beach. The sediment made the channel unnavigable, forcing the Corps to dredge and clear the Waterway. In November, the Corps issued B&C a cease-and-desist order on construction at Grande Dunes until the company could show proof that it had done everything possible to prevent further erosion. They also billed the company for its share of the cost of the dredging, according to *The Sun News*. Whether the company would pay for the dredging "is an issue that is under discussion," B&C spokesman Pat Dowling cavalierly responded.

A month after Hurricane Floyd shattered their lives, residents of the Grand Strand and eastern North Carolina opened their newspapers to discover another storm was moving up the coast. This was Hurricane Irene, much smaller the Floyd and much weaker, with 75-mile-per-hour winds. There was no mandatory evacuation this time, but many left without orders. The storm wobbled up the coast on Sunday, October 17, and skirted the Outer Banks in the early hours of Monday. And it brought with it more rain − at least six inches in Horry County and more in parts of North Carolina. The Waccamaw flood, which had been receding for weeks, immediately started to rise again. Streets flooded in Myrtle Beach; in North Carolina, residents started returning to emergency shelters. "I'm getting to the point I can't take it any more," Herbert Person, of Rocky Mount, was quoted in the Associated Press. "I've worked hard all my life and paid taxes, and now I feel like I have nothing. . . . I'm so stressed out I don't know what to do."

At least fifty-two deaths in North Carolina were attributed to the hurricane floods of 1999. More than 54,000 homes were damaged: 7,100 were destroyed; 16,674 were declared uninhabitable. In Horry County, more than 1,000 homes were damaged by water. About twenty were condemned. The estimated cost of Floyd was six billion dollars. A year after the storm, thousands were still living in temporary shelters in North Carolina.

By the end of 1999 hog farmers were rebuilding their open lagoons in North Carolina. In Horry County, houses were going up on the banks of the Waccamaw River, within sight of other houses that had "Condemned" signs on their doors. A Best Western Motel was being built at Savannah Bluff, where four feet of water had stood ten weeks before.

Used car dealer Wayne Cooper spoke for many residents as he built his new house in Savannah Bluff: "The government doesn't need to tell people what they can do with their own property. There are too many fees and restrictions and mess now."

Things were getting back to normal in Horry County.

A Miserable End to A Miserable Year

Halloween should be one of the simplest and happiest occasions of the year – an inexpensive opportunity to have some fun and be a kid again. The day before the spooky night, I bought a pumpkin and took it to a friend's apartment. While she baked lasagne, we carved a jack-o-lantern and polished off a flask of chianti. But in Myrtle Beach, as I had learned, nothing is simple. Religious leaders worried what effect the secular holiday, with its pagan origins, would have on young minds.

"We're staking a claim and making [Halloween] a night for the Lord Jesus," said Ken Rowe, youth pastor at Coastal Christian Center. "Why should it be the devil's holiday?"

The Sun News reported that several churches would sponsor alternative activities. First Baptist offered "Judgment Night," an alternative to the traditional Halloween haunted house. Jim Tippins, First Baptist's minister of music and drama, said he could remember when churches sponsored haunted houses. "But then as we went on, people's attitudes changed to where they thought that Satan and evil were getting too much coverage," Tippins said. "Fall festivals became the alternative to Halloween."

"Judgment Night" was an interactive dramatic performance with a positive message, Tippins said. This year's focus was on teen pregnancy. "This is similar to a haunted house, but this is based on reality and truth. That makes it scarier than your typical haunted house."

No sooner were the pumpkins and paraphernalia hauled to the landfill than Christmas lights began appearing around the Strand. In a town that is somewhat surreal anyway, Christmas is an invitation to go way over the top. Especially bizarre were the palm trees draped in white lights, suggesting icicles and snow. At Broadway at the Beach, Burroughs & Chapin Co. decorated the vast grounds with huge light displays, comprised of hundreds of thousands of bulbs. And there was Treasures by the Sea, Myrtle Beach's $300,000 light sculpture collection of seashells, mermaids and sea serpents. Other light sculptures included reindeer, snowmen and sleighs. As one wag put it, you would sooner find a reindeer in Myrtle Beach than three wise men and a virgin. It was an old saw, but it drew a hearty laugh and was good for a round of beers at Blues Alley.

In local bars, jukeboxes spun out a stomach churning smorgasbord of Christmas melodies – everything from Alvin and the Chipmunks' "Christmas Don't Be Late" to Perry Como's "Silent Night," to any number of versions of "Little Drummer Boy." Down at Shamrock's Sports Bar, Curtis Fredericks and other regulars passed the hat to raise money to buy toys for local children. Fredericks, with his white hair and beard, was the perennial Santa Claus for this event. Country crooner Steve Gatlin announced his annual Yuletide show, "Christmas With Steve Gatlin and Friends." Dixie Stampede and Carolina Opry planned Christmas specials and the Palace Theater trumpeted the return of the Radio City Christmas Spectacular for its annual run. First Presbyterian Church got into the act with their Montovanni Orchestra Christmas Show.

In Myrtle Beach, city council politics filled the public stage. On the at-large council, three members – Rachel Broadhurst, Wilson Cain and Crain Woods – were up for reelection. Six challengers – including Susan Grissom Means, daughter of the late Mayor Bob Grissom – were vying to replace them. Mark McBride was out to defeat Broadhurst and put his machine to work for several challengers. Broadhurst's campaign was managed by Larry Bragg; Means' campaign, by Sally Howard. Means had called Howard at 9:00 a.m. before the noon filing deadline in September and asked if she would run her campaign. Howard said, "Let's go!" Now Means' campaign signs lined the streets of Myrtle Beach and the remnants of her father's old machine quietly lined up behind her. Her run for council was widely seen as a warm-up to vindicate her father's 1997 defeat by McBride.

On Election Day – November 2 – I voted at Coastal Lane I in the county administration complex on 21st Avenue North. Crain Woods was out in the parking lot clutching hands. It was a light turnout. Polls closed at 7:00 p.m. I was already at the Law Enforcement Center with dozens of others to watch the precinct totals come in. City spokesman Mark Kruea used an overhead projector to show precincts and candidates on a large grid. It was a civic and social ritual that has been acted out in various forms in courthouses and schoolhouses, churches and taverns since the founding of the republic. There was a festive mood among candidates and supporters as the first precincts reported in. It was a welcome reprieve from the stressful, strife-filled year in city government. Councilman Wilson Cain strolled in and punched me on the shoulder jauntily. He was wearing a raspberry red blazer and an American flag tie. Though they were not up for reelection, Wayne Gray, Judy Rodman and Chuck Martino were all there, enjoying the buoyant spirits. Broadhurst and Bragg sat down front, watching the vote totals pensively, while Means mingled with her mob of jubilant supporters. Mark McBride was conspicuously absent.

As the votes came in, Kruea marked them on the transparent grid, projecting them on the screen at the front of the room. By 7:40, it was clear that Means had won a seat on council and that Crain Woods was out. Many were surprised that Broadhurst had only finished second and failed to win reelection outright. At 7:57, the mayor came in and hung around in the back of the council chamber, talking quietly with friends. He seemed pleased with the outcome. Nearby, Crain Woods held on to some dejected supporters, their arms around one another.

The last precinct did not report until 8:47 – and it didn't change anything. A total of 10,744 votes were cast that day. Means won her seat. By a complicated formula, Broadhurst, Cain and Michael Chestnut were left in a runoff for the two remaining seats.

The exercise in democracy was adjourned to Shamrock's, where Broadhurst had prematurely planned her victory party. There was no victory, but there was a hell of a party. Broadhurst made some upbeat remarks, telling her supporters not to throw their signs away. There was a round of applause and another round of drinks. From Shamrock's I moved down to Akel's House of Pancakes, where Susan Grissom Means was holding her victory party in the back room. It was a testimony to the small-town nature of Myrtle Beach and the power of personal relationships. Most of her supporters were middle-aged friends, some of whom she had known since high school. There was a framed photograph of her late father in the middle of the buffet table. "He's looking down right now from Heaven and smiling," one of her supporters said.

The runoff campaign began immediately but was overshadowed by B&C's maneuvering on the business park. After weeks of negotiations among the company, the county, the city and the school district, city and county officials agreed that Horry County Schools should receive 56.1 percent of the revenues generated by the business park – the same amount they would have received without the business park in place. School officials indicated they were satisfied with the arrangement. In making this decision, county officials cut in half the funds B&C expected to put toward its infrastructure.

On November 3, Doug Wendel struck back. He sent a letter to city council members, withdrawing the company's permission to annex most of its proposed business park. The company cut the proposed annexation from approximately 2,500 acres to 185 acres, citing the city's lack of support for the business park and the shrinking share of revenues from the park in negotiations with the county and school board. B&C's decision would block Myrtle Beach from crossing the Intracoastal Waterway and greatly reduce the amount of funds for schools and other participants in the multicounty business park.

"From Burroughs & Chapin's standpoint, the near collapse of the grand plan of providing funds for extensive infrastructure before development occurs is very disappointing," Wendel wrote.

Council members Wayne Gray and Rachel Broadhurst criticized Wendel, saying he was using the city to leverage the county and school board in negotiations. "I feel as if the city has been somewhat used to garner support," Gray said.

Mayor McBride naturally sided with the company, blaming city council for the lost annexation opportunity. "The city's negotiation stance has jeopardized the city's future," he said.

Some city officials thought they saw more sinister manipulations in the annexation dispute. Perhaps the county was using annexation as a leverage to get the city to agree to the 3,000-foot buffer for a new runway at Myrtle Beach International Airport. City officials had held fast to a 1,000-foot buffer, creating tension between the city and county councils.

County Councilwoman Liz Gilland said the county discussed a *quid pro quo* agreement, by which the county would help the city annex the full 2,500 acres, in exchange for the city dropping its opposition for the 3,000-foot runway separation. Wayne Gray denied any such agreement: "There is no quid pro quo regarding our support of a 3,000-foot separation as it relates to the annexation."

When County Council Chairman Chad Prosser was asked about a *quid pro quo*, he said, "I'm not going to answer that question."

The city council runoff campaign was uneventful. The one thing the three candidates did agree on was that they would vote against the business park as it presently stood. "I think we've been bushwacked," Wilson Cain told *The Sun News*.

Two days before the runoff, Broadhurst received a thumping endorsement from *The Sun News*: "Rachel Broadhurst . . . must be returned to a second term for her leadership abilities. And goodness knows, Myrtle Beach needs active excellent leadership. . . .

"She represents the progress that five to six members of city council have united for in the past two years, despite a disruptive atmosphere centering on the mayor, Mark McBride. . . .

"We endorse Broadhurst for her leadership, and we ask that voters choose carefully between two worthy candidates, [Wilson] Cain and [Michael] Chestnut."

Voters did not share the newspaper's enthusiasm for Rachel Broadhurst. On the night of the runoff election, the usual suspects gathered at the Law Enforcement Center. As the votes came in through the early evening, it was evident that Broadhurst was in trouble. Voters were supposed to pull the lever for two candidates, but many voted for only one. This was especially prevalent in black precincts, where "single shot" votes went to Michael Chestnut in an effort to keep at least one African American on the council. In Dunes I, for example, Chestnut got 351 votes to Cain's 69 and Broadhurst's 68. Furthermore, McBride's organization had worked overtime to get out the vote with the mission of electing Chestnut and Cain. Now Broadhurst, who had finished a strong second in a field of nine candidates two weeks before, was last in a field of three.

By 7:45, all precincts were counted except Dunes I and Myrtle Wood I. In the back of the auditorium, Chestnut's supporters chanted, "We like Mike" and cheered as the numbers came in. Sitting in the front row, looking up at the screen with Larry Bragg, a subdued Broadhurst chatted with supporters. At 8:10, a crowd of nearly 100 still murmured and milled about the auditorium, waiting for the last two precincts to report. Myrtle Wood I finally came in at 8:40 and offered Broadhurst no help.

At 9:10, Mark Kruea cleared his throat and announced in his measured bass voice that there would be no final count until Wednesday morning. It seemed one of the electronic voting machines at Dunes I had failed to print out the results, he said, and some 217 ballots appeared to be lost. But the unofficial results were clear: Chestnut had received 1,720 votes; Cain, 1,605; Broadhurst, 1,393.

Election officials brought the faulty voting machine to the Law Enforcement Center and secured it in the police department's evidence locker. "I've never seen this happen before – ever," said an eighteen-year veteran and former director of the county Voter Registration and Elections Department.

In the meantime, Chestnut's supporters headed down to Queen's Café, the legendary soul food restaurant on the Hill, where there waited a buffet, with the biggest pan of wings I have ever seen, potato salad, marinated beef tips and more. On the walls around the dance floor were African masks and art and a large picture of Martin Luther King Jr. A disc jockey stood by, with two turntables and stacks of soul and R&B records for "scratching."

At 10:10, Chestnut entered with his wife and entourage, to thunderous applause. He made a few barely audible remarks, then the DJ kicked off the music and the dance floor filled up.

Less than a mile away, at Shamrock's, the mood was much quieter. Balloons, crepe and streamers festooned the rooms, but dozens of paper party horns lay untouched by the buffet. Rachel Broadhurst, Chuck Martino, Susan Grissom Means, Jack Thompson and other politicos listened attentively as Larry Bragg explained Broadhurst's options and urged her not to concede. Broadhurst nodded glumly between sips of rosé.

The hearing into the election debacle started at the Law Enforcement Center at 11:00 Thursday morning. I didn't arrive until 12:50. Larry Bragg was outside, smoking a cigarette in the breezeway. He gave me the bad news: the voting machine at Dunes I had eaten the ballots; they could not be recovered. Inside the chamber sat Chestnut and Broadhurst with their lawyers and seconds, along with city and election officials and media reps. Cain was not present but had his representatives there. As I entered, local officials were on the phone to the state Election Commission in Columbia. The candidates and their representatives went behind closed doors with local election officials to sort out what had been learned from Columbia. When they returned, a nervous young county technician named Sammy Johnson was sworn in to explain to the best of his ability why the four-year-old voting machine had malfunctioned.

"It's just like no one ever voted on it," he said.

Next morning, the city Election Commission met at City Hall, went into an illegal executive session and certified the election, with a note that 217 votes had been lost. Broadhurt immediately filed a protest, calling for a new runoff election.

Friday, November 19, 11:00 a.m.: The city Election Commission began hearings at the Law Enforcement Center into the misbegotten runoff election. For the rest of the very long day, a procession of witnesses and technicians took the oath to tell what they knew and what they saw. Maintenance worker John Marlow told the chamber that the faulty voting machine "went into test election mode and zeroed itself out. . . . We've never seen anything like that" in ten years of working with the machines, he said. Broadhurst's attorney grilled Marlow on how the machine's fail-safe device was supposed to work, plus other legal and technical questions. Marlow was perplexed. He squirmed. He furrowed his brow and pursed his lips before the crowd of more than sixty participants and onlookers. In the back of the room Chestnut's supporters videotaped the proceedings, while cell phones beeped and buzzed all around. (One of them played "Jingle Bells.")

Linda Page Scranton, a clerk at Dunes I Precinct, described how she saw the printer tape curling out of the voting machine. She called several times for assistance from city maintenance but continued to use the machine anyway. She was upset over the foul-up, speaking of her sense of citizenship in working at the polls and protecting the democratic process. "I have seen the difference one or two votes can make," she said. "This is a lot of votes to be lost."

A number of Broadhurst's supporters who voted at Dunes I came forward to declare their outrage that their votes would not be counted.

At the end of the day, the commission voted 3-0 to reject Broadhurst's protest and certify the election. "I'm pleased that they came to that decision," Chestnut said. "The evidence did not warrant having another election."

The election commissioners may have had good reason to reject Broadhurst's protest. She would have had to win all the lost votes from the Dunes I machine in order to overtake Wilson Cain for the second council seat. But the whole thing smelled bad. Bob Bestler summed it up for a lot of people:

> By every analysis, [Broadhurst] is the victim of single-shot voting, a kind of hardball political strategy that tends to thwart the will of the electorate. . . .
>
> Her supporters cannot believe her loss. They see dirt behind every curtain because Broadhurst has been a persistent critic of a mayor who many think is not quite suited to be chief executive of this growing tourist capital.
>
> In fact, Broadhurst is being touted as the most likely candidate to run against the mayor in 2001 – if only she can get through this election. . . .
>
> The plot thickens as election workers testify that there are three fail-safes on every machine, but at Dunes I two of them failed and a third was not operational. Hmmm.

I left the Law Enforcement Center, where Broadhurst's protest was being heard. At 5:30, I was driving north on U.S. 17. It was a beautiful, warm day and the top was down on my Miata. The afternoon rush was on as I passed 19th Avenue North and noticed the GMC utility truck, with a boom on the deck, charge up on my left side, then brake suddenly behind a line of stopped traffic. It was the kind of obnoxious, aggressive driving that I observed every day in Myrtle Beach and had become inured to. As I passed on the right of the large truck, it cut into my lane and rammed my car just behind my seat. The truck driver did not see me nor feel the impact. He kept pushing his truck against the side of my car as we cruised along in heavy traffic at thirty-five miles an hour. My Miata suddenly pivoted on the right corner of his bumper, then swung around against the bumper and was pushed sideways up U.S. 17, just as the driver realized what was happening. He jammed on his brakes and we came to a stop in the middle of the road. I looked up from the white knuckles on my steering wheel and turned to my left. The massive grille of the truck was pressed against the side of my car, inches from my face.

A moment after it was over, the truck driver jumped down from his cab and was kneeling beside the passenger door of my car, saying, "Is anybody hurt? Oh, please, God, don't let anybody be hurt!" The driver was an uninsured nineteen-year-old. The plate steel bumper of his truck crushed my little car from bumper to bumper. I walked away without a scratch, but with a new appreciation of the randomness and frailty of life.

A few days later I was down on the Boulevard in the early afternoon, when I heard the familiar voice: "Hey, Will, where you goin'?" It was Kevin, of course. I asked him why he wasn't in school. He told me he was sick.

"You don't look sick," I said.

He looked at me and grinned. "Aw, you know. . . . It was one of those five-minute things."

As we approached Ripley's Pizza, he said without a glimmer of self-doubt, "It's lunch time. Why don't you buy me a slice of pizza?"

We went in and ordered two slices of pepperoni pizza apiece and giant, cineplex-size fountain sodas. While we were waiting for the pizza, he took a quarter to play one of the video games, Cosmic Kick

Boxer. The kid had obviously played it before. He went almost ten minutes on that one quarter.

As we ate our pizza, I asked him about the Band-Aid on his right ear. He told me one of his lizards had bitten him several weeks before and he tore the skin trying to pull it off. It had recently become infected, he said. Then he told me something even stranger. He said his four chameleons died a few days after the biting incident when he left their cage in the direct sunlight for a half-hour. I don't know what part of this story sounded least plausible, but I did not challenge him. Then he topped it off with one last, strange detail. He told me he had carried the bodies of his four dead lizards and placed them at the spots where he had first captured them.

Why had he done that?

"So their spirits will find them," he said simply.

We ate in silence for several minutes. I asked what subjects he was studying now that he was in seventh grade. He told me he took classes in history, science, math and language skills.

Which was his favorite?

He answered without hesitation: lunch. He said he had pizza for lunch every day. "That's definitely the best part of school."

I asked what he did for lunch when he skipped school.

"Nothing, usually," he told me. "Sometimes I eat Star Bursts." He reached into his pocket and pulled out several pieces of the candy. "Here, have one."

I declined. We finished our pizza and Kevin asked me if I wanted to shoot some pool. I didn't really, but I was interested in learning more about his life on the street. I followed him down to the boardwalk and into Marvin's, assuming I would be paying for the games, but Kevin led me straight to one of the tables near the bar. He looked around furtively, then jammed the coin intake on the table with some body English and wrist action. The balls dropped and rolled down to the pick-up slot.

"You rack 'em," he told me.

And so we played for more than an hour without paying for a game. At times I felt like I was abetting his delinquency but, in truth, he was abetting mine.

There was little joy in the season as Christmas approached. The S.C. Press Association criticized the City Election Commission for its crucial closed-door session in which it ruled against Rachel Broadhurst.

The city condemned the Bon Villa Motel, the most notorious, dilapidated and dangerous flophouse on the Boulevard. A block from my apartment, bulldozers moved in and started knocking down a wood frame structure, one of the last of the 1950s era motels on the Boulevard. It took forty-five minutes to reduce the fourteen-room building to an eight-foot pile of splinters and boards.

Even as Horry County Council approved six new housing developments, insurance reviewers said county fire service was lacking in manpower, equipment and fire stations. "Simply put, developers are putting up homes faster than the government can add firefighting crews and stations to ensure adequate fire protection," *The Sun News* reported.

On U.S. 17 Bypass, land was being cleared for an 800-seat seafood buffet restaurant on Burroughs & Chapin land. Residents around the site complained about the traffic the restaurant would bring. "There are children riding bikes and people jogging on those side streets," a resident said.

County police arrested six dancers at the Pure Titanium Club in Little River on public nudity charges and another black bear became road kill in Horry County. The S.C. Hospitality Association tallied up at least seventy-nine cancellations of events across the state as the NAACP boycott gained momentum. And Hurricane Lenny, the last major storm of the season, ripped through the Virgin Islands with 150 mile-per-hour winds.

In early November, *The Sun News* editorialized against Horry County Council giving second approval to B&C's business park until more details were known: "No action is deserved at this moment because the negotiations, rightly being played out in public, have yet to bear fruit. . . .

"Until the county and the company reach a final agreement, second or third reading on this complex proposal completely misses even the broadside of a barn. . . .

"Until the agreement is completed in public view and the public has its input on major changes, if any, no official approval by any government body should be granted."

On November 9, Horry County Council voted 7-3 to give second approval to B&C's thirty-year development agreement covering 7,200 acres. Under the agreement, Horry County Schools would receive 56.1

percent of money generated by the development agreement and business park, the same percentage they would receive without the business park in place. School officials indicated they would be satisfied with this arrangement.

"The bottom-line intention of this council has been to make the school board whole," Chairman Chad Prosser said. "I don't see us backing off that one bit. I don't see that being changed." The stage was set for the surreal county council meeting of November 29.

When council members entered the chamber and took their seats on the dais that evening, several found a folder with a five-page "script" explaining how council members should vote on five critical changes in the proposed B&C agreement. Most significantly, the script called for cutting back the schools' portion of business park funds to fifty percent. Four of the five scripted motions – including the cut in school funds – passed the council by large majorities. After his pledge to the school district, Chad Prosser voted to cut their funds to fifty percent.

Who provided the mysterious script and how had it gotten onto the council dais? Doug Wendel left the meeting before he could be asked about it. Pat Dowling denied any knowledge of the document. "Whoever put typewriter to paper, I don't know," he said.

A visibly troubled Chad Prosser was more forthcoming: "There was a folder [on the dais]," he told *The Sun News*. "Apparently, [B&C] must have deposited it before the meeting. . . . They're trying to bring this thing to a conclusion. We all are."

On December 2, a furious letter from Pat Dowling appeared in *The Sun News*, blaming that paper for the company's poor public image: ". . . each time Burroughs & Chapin moves to provide leadership and momentum so that the multicounty business park issue can be settled once and for all, *The Sun News* paints the company as being intrusive on the political process and somehow worthy of dark suspicion. . . .

"Parlaying the notion that B&C is driving the multicounty business park bus might help sell newspapers, but *The Sun News'* approach to the issue does a genuine injustice to the County Council members who decided to take this particular issue by the horns and wrestle it down."

In the letter, Dowling accused the school board of "selfishness" for wanting the full millage rate from property taxes that was due them.

At a meeting on the evening of December 2, the Horry County School Board announced once more that they wanted their full millage. "My goal is not to have to go to court," Chairwoman Helen Smith said. "That is our intent and our goal tonight."

"The schools have never asked for one penny more than what we normally get," board member Morris Williams said. "If there is greed here, it is someone other than the schools. . . . I feel the County Council is taking a big gamble with the future of this county and education."

On December 5, Bob Bestler struck back at Dowling for accusing the school board of "selfishness": "What is one to say of such an accusation? The school board members are not the ones who will get rich off the Mall of South Carolina and the million-dollar residences at Grande Dunes Resort. One could better argue the school board's chief interest is in protecting the system's tax base from greedy developers."

Of the county council he wrote: ". . . this council, as well-intentioned as it may be, is a limited bunch at best. It is certainly no match for an all-out Burroughs & Chapin blitzkrieg. It is not reassuring that so far the council has sided with the developer in most every vote. . . .

"I watch from a distance, but in my view Burroughs and Chapin and Horry County Council have never been held in such low esteem as they are today."

December 7: The day started with a special meeting of Myrtle Beach City Council, in the conference room at City Hall. The meeting was marked by rancorous debate over the city budget, in which Councilwoman Judy Rodman famously told off the mayor and walked out.

That was the warm-up for the long day to come. That evening, Horry County Council was scheduled to give third and final approval to B&C's multicounty business park.

As the meeting neared, furious letters continued to appear in *The Sun News*: "Burroughs & Chapin Co. Inc. has played Chairman Chad Prosser and most of the Horry County Council like a banjo," said one.

"Burroughs & Chapin seems to be asking the county to fill a busted flush with Horry County Schools' dollars," said another. "I ask County Council to not interfere with local economic conditions. Allow Burroughs & Chapin to play on a level economic field or fold its hand and get out of the game."

In preparation for the meeting, county employees worked into the night copying the council's agenda – including the muticounty business park agreement. Under the weight of making twenty-seven copies of the 300-page agenda, one copier broke down and another "was on life support," *The Sun News* reported.

I was the first person in the council chamber at 4:45 p.m. for the 6:00 meeting. Wendel and Dowling arrived and took their seats in the front row at 5:10. Within minutes the place began to fill with surly, murmuring citizens, school district employees, TV lights and cameras and talking heads, all spilling out into the hall. By 5:40, the place was packed and there was a scent of blood in the air, the kind of atmosphere one expects before a heavyweight fight.

Council members took their seats around the dais at 6:00, barely looking at one another. After the perfunctory prayer and Pledge of Allegiance, the meeting opened for public comment on the business park. School board Chairman Helen Smith began the hearing with a prepared statement, reiterating the board's position and stating that B&C's numbers would not work. She closed by wishing the council a Merry Christmas.

Angry residents took turns standing up to denounce county council, B&C and the business park. James Millwood opened his remarks by asking the council cheerily, "Does everyone have his script?" There were hoots and chuckles from the gallery, but Chairman Prosser and council members only glared.

Another speaker denounced "corporate welfare" and said B&C was only bringing more low-wage jobs to Horry County. Brian Voyce of We the People accused council members of bad ethics, poor leadership and ignoring their own paid consultants. He said council members – and he singled out Chad Prosser – had violated their oaths not to sell their office.

Myrtle Beach Primary School teacher Robert Rorrer spoke passionately of his work teaching young children with learning and emotional disabilities. He drew hearty applause when he denounced Pat Dowling for allegedly describing opponents of the business park as "bugs on our windshield."

"I'm not a bug on a windshield," he said. "I've been working twelve hours a day for four years for your children. I don't want anything extra, but I don't want you to take something else from us when it's hard enough to meet the objectives we have been assigned."

Two of eleven citizens spoke in favor of the park.

Councilman John Kost looked at Wendel and told him bluntly that the business park would not work. The whole scheme was a corruption of the business park concept and he could not support it. Wendel, who had sat stone-faced for the first hour of the meeting, spoke tensely to consultant Michael Ey, sitting at his right. Ey took the podium and dueled with Kost and Councilwoman Liz Gilland, who tried to pin him down on whether the agreement maintained current land-use regulations or rolled back regulations. Wendel squirmed and tried to look pugnacious from his chair as his lawyers and consultants scrapped with Kost for an hour over seven proposed amendments to the agreement. An exasperated Wendel finally took the podium from his embattled aides and addressed council and throng in soothing, palliative tones.

The ploy worked. At 9:00 p.m. the council voted on the first item of business, approving a thirty-year development agreement with B&C. The vote was 7-3 in favor, with one abstention.

Then it was on to the discussion of the multicounty business park. Council members Terry Cooper and Liz Gilland got into a snotty exchange, accusing one another of smirking and making snide comments. "Mr. Cooper, if you want to leave and don't want to listen, you can leave," Gilland said.

Cooper shot back, "Ms. Gilland, you smirk and make faces more than anyone I've ever seen on this council and everyone knows that. Then you sit here like a big baby."

Gilland and Prosser snapped at one another, Prosser saying she was speaking too many times. Gilland then accused Councilman Ray Brown of talking to Wendel during an executive session a couple of weeks before, when the B&C proposal was being debated: "Doors have been shut, meetings have been closed, deals have been made in the back room, scripts have been handed out, council members have maneuvered in and out of our back room to talk with Mr. Wendel. I didn't know that until there was a picture in the paper and it showed Mr. Brown talking with Mr. Wendel."

Brown angrily denied any impropriety: "How dare you sit over there, who had probably never worked a day in your life and saying people are taking money. . . . I don't like your accusations, Ms. Gilland. You go all over town accusing this and accusing that! . . . I want to look you in the eye tonight and tell you I'm sick of people like you. . . ."

Cooper claimed that he had been harassed and threatened at his home by opponents of the business park. Councilman Chandler Brigham said, "We've been ostracized, criticized, cussed and threatened by the opposing side and I'll bet you if you really knew the truth, ninety-nine percent of those people have a vendetta against Burroughs and Chapin."

Brigham then attacked Gilland for questioning the integrity of the council. When she tried to interrupt, he snarled, "You just can't keep your mouth shut, can you?"

In an air of weary submission, Gilland told Wendel, "I have no objection to your development, but why can't you use your own money to do it?" She said the Burroughs and Chapin families had lost a lot of credibility in the community.

"I understand I have been out-voted and out-maneuvered on this issue," she said. When some of the audience applauded her remarks, Prosser told them to restrain themselves.

Councilman Ulysses DeWitt made a motion that the business park be put in an advisory referendum, allowing the public to vote on it. "It would give us an idea what the citizens of this county want," he said. The motion was defeated, 4-6.

Councilman John Shelley pressed to use part of the business park funds to pave some of the county's many dirt roads. "That way the western part of the county will get something out of this," he said. That effort also failed, by the same 4 to 6 votes.

The normally quiet Shelley then asked to see the "no" votes raise their hands again. "These are the people willing to take from the dirt roads and put in the multicounty park," he said.

Before the final vote, Chairman Prosser lectured council members on their behavior. Liz Gilland sat motionless, her fist clenched against her lips, a devastated, far-away look in her eye.

The vote on the business park came at 10:00 p.m. and was fore-known: the same six who had defended the park against DeWitt's and Shelley's proposed amendments now voted to approve the monstrous project. Gilland, Kost, DeWitt and Shelley voted against. B&C employee Marvin Heyd abstained. There were howls and jeers from the crowd when the vote was taken, but the deed was done.

"Overall, I think we got a document that made an effort to address all the issues raised," said a very satisfied Doug Wendel, when the vote was in. "This was the major step."

Two days after the bitter vote, *The Sun News* reported that B&C had put the full 2,500 acres – including the Mall of South Carolina – back on the table and resumed negotiating with the City of Myrtle Beach for a grand annexation. Pat Dowling made it clear, though, that the company required further "inducements" to allow annexation to go forward. Neither company nor city officials would divulge what those inducements were. Rumors continued to float that the annexation was tied to the city allowing a 3,000-foot separation for a new runway at the airport.

The last days of this miserable year saw more old beachfront motels cleared away, as a federal judge handed down a sentence of three years' probation to former state senator Bud Long for his conviction under Operation Lost Trust.

With the South Carolina Republican presidential primary rising on the national radar screen, a large sign appeared in front of Robber's Roost Golf Course in North Myrtle Beach: "Let's Save America – Bush – 2000." The next day, Steve Forbes was campaigning at Myrtle Square Mall. He surely saw Bush's campaign headquarters, where a Christmas tree stood in the front window, decorated with balls and candy canes and Bush bumper stickers. A straw poll at the Horry County Republican Party convention revealed seventy percent support for Bush, twenty-six percent for John McCain and four percent for Forbes.

Rachel Broadhurst went to court in Conway to appeal the election runoff. A few days later, Judge J. Stanton Cross ruled that Dunes I precinct must vote again. The judge declared Michael Chestnut had won his council seat, but Broadhurst and Wilson Cain would have to face another runoff in Dunes I to decide who would get the last seat.

I got my car back from the body shop. It looked and ran like new, with the entire left side replaced. The uninsured kid, who smashed me up on November 19, made a down payment toward the cost of the repair, but when it came time to pay the balance, he skipped town.

With the spirit of the season warming cold hearts, city council and county council compromised on a 2,000-foot separation for the new airport runway. City council and B&C moved forward on annexation and approval of the business park and development agreement.

At the December 28 meeting, city council voted to annex the first 909-acre parcel of B&C land – the largest annexation in Myrtle Beach history. To get the remaining 1,600 acres, the city and the company would have to negotiate a few more sticking points.

Fireworks sales boomed in preparation for New Year's Eve, as did prophecies of doom and damnation. The Y2K bug was about to be unleashed on the world – or so a lot of kooks and crackpots proclaimed. Church signs declared it wasn't too late to repent. Hardware and gun dealers declared it wasn't too late to buy a generator or an AK-47.

Bars, clubs and restaurants advertised their New Year's Eve party packages. Around my apartment there were several premature fireworks outbursts in the days before December 31. I eschewed a couple of party invitations to do a nostalgic, solo bar crawl along the Boulevard and uptown to some of my favorite saloons. I hit them all – Bummz, Michael's, Marvin's, Gypsy's, Blues Alley. For several hours I exchanged toasts, greetings, kisses and handshakes with bartenders and barflies.

The clock struck midnight while I was at Michael's. The world did not end. In fact, it felt like it had just begun. There was an explosion of cheers. I found myself wearing a party hat and dancing with a fat lady in a black sweater and Spandex pants.

About 12:20 a.m., I broke out of Michael's and made my way down the crowded Boulevard sidewalk toward my apartment. Fireworks exploded on the beach and streaked across the sky. Crowds sang and wassailed in their finery. A bevy of six drop-dead beautiful babes in black velvet dresses, leather and lamé swept along the street, drawing hoots and whistles.

A less joyful couple had an intense "discussion" of how to spend the rest of the evening. "I'm not going back there with those ass holes," she was saying.

"So you want to stand here and be a bitch all night?" her beau replied.

The marquee on the front of the Pavilion Arcade carried Doug Wendel's holiday message to the world:

MERRY CHRISTMAS
HOLIDAY SPECIAL PAVILION SEASON PASS 39.95
3 PARK PASS 99.95   INCLUDES PAVILION
NASCAR SPEEDPARK AND MYRTLE WAVES

At the arcade, I turned down the alley and walked toward the beach, which was smoky with fireworks. Waves broke on the cold, dark sand. Voices rang shrill and happy through the crisp air. I stood watching the surf for several minutes. The seagulls, which usually roosted in this sand, were nowhere to be seen.

Strolling north on the boardwalk, I heard the cracked strains of "I Fall to Pieces" wafting from the door of Boardwalk Bill's, where karaoke reigned without shame. It was almost too dreadful to listen to and the badly made-up, middle-aged blond who was strangling the Patsy Cline classic was too grotesque to look at. I stepped in the door just long enough to take it all in – a joyous crowd, with more balloons, streamers and hats than I had seen all night. It was too late to linger and I had a lot of work to do. As I turned to leave, something poked me in the ribs. It was Kevin, pointing his pool cue at me and taunting, "C'mon, Will, wanna play?"

Maybe next time, I told him.

"Aw, c'mon. I won't beatcha too bad."

At a nearby table sat his mother with another woman and three bearded, tattooed creatures. I walked over to exchange greetings. Like the rest of her friends, Margaret was drunk. She barely looked up at me as she clutched a Budweiser in one hand, a Doral in the other. There were a dozen empty beer cans on the table and a large ashtray full of butts. Margaret always was a barrel of fun. The cigarette smoke was stifling. "Patsy Cline" wailed away.

I made my way back toward the door. Kevin stopped me again, begging me to play a game of pool. The *karaoke* was driving me crazy. I wanted to get away from the sight of Margaret.

"Where you going?" he asked.

"Home," I said. Then, anticipating his next question, I reached in my pocket and handed him a dollar for a rack of balls.

"Hey, thanks, Will."

"See you in a few days," I said. And I knew I would.

I walked back out on the boardwalk and down to the beach. Only an hour old and the new century was beginning to feel as complicated and troubling as the last.

Epilogue

A few weeks after that New Year's Eve encounter, Kevin was accused by school authorities of threatening another boy. The incident was minor and no one was harmed. But because he already had a history of trouble with school officials and local police, Kevin was expelled from school, taken into custody by the state Department of Social Services and sent to a supervised residence for boys near Columbia. His mother abandoned him, leaving South Carolina without notice. I was told by one of my sources that she was in Florida, working with a traveling carnival. I kept in touch with Kevin by phone and mail, until I was ordered by a DSS caseworker to have no further contact with him.

The economic slowdown of 2000 spelled the end of the Grand Strand golf course boom. The dream of opening ten courses a year over the next decade was a bitter memory. Only ten courses opened since 1999.

Doug Wendel kept the Pavilion Amusement Park on Ocean Boulevard and sealed the deal with a spectacular new roller coaster, called the Hurricane, which opened in the spring of 2000.

In 2002, the Myrtle Beach International Wax Museum, the Castaways Motel and adjoining oceanfront buildings were demolished to make way for a park. The Bon Villa Motel, which was condemned in 1999, was demolished in April 2003.

The Conway Bypass opened in 2000 and was officially christened the Veterans Highway. Long before the first section of the Carolina Bays Parkway opened in December 2002, developers were lobbying the Department of Transportation for more off-ramps, thus assuring the expressway it would soon be choked with traffic and the interior of the county would be opened to a new wave of development.

On February 19, 2000, the Horry County Republican Party temporarily moved its headquarters into Shamrock's Sports Bar to count votes in the South Carolina Republican presidential primary. George W. Bush defeated John McCain and Alan Keyes, launching himself on his way to the White House. McCain carried Horry, Georgetown and several other coastal counties.

In preparation for the June state primary, Horry County Republican Party issued a pledge supporting "proper business incentives" in future state economic legislation, which GOP candidates were required to sign. The pledge was generally taken to be an endorsement of the B&C multicounty business park. In the primaries, three challengers refused to sign the pledge and were "excommunicated" from the county GOP. Phil Render, a candidate challenging Mark Kelly for his House seat, denounced the pledge as "McCarthyism."

"We don't need that kind of incentive in the sixth-fastest-growing county in the nation," Render said. "It appears to be giving special privilege to the few at the potential expense of the many." All three of the apostate challengers lost their races.

After months of acrimonious debate, the General Assembly agreed to remove the Confederate flag from the State House dome and place it at ground level in front of the State House. The ceremony to lower the flag took place on July 1, in a confrontational atmosphere amid thousands of pro-flag and anti-flag demonstrators. The NAACP still maintains a boycott against the state until the flag is completely removed from the State House grounds. On that same day, video gambling became illegal in South Carolina. Within three months of closing down video gambling, the number of active Gamblers Anonymous groups in South Carolina dropped from 32 to 16.

In February 2000, Horry County Schools sued Horry County and the City of Myrtle Beach to stop the multicounty business park, arguing that money intended for schools cannot be used for other purposes. The Mall of South Carolina was put on hold, pending the outcome of the school district's lawsuit. Grande Dunes, Plantation Pointe Shopping Center and other B&C projects moved ahead without the business park in place.

A state circuit court judge upheld the business park law in July, finding in favor of the city and county. The school district appealed to the state Supreme Court. In November, Myrtle Beach annexed a further parcel of B&C property, including 1,000 acres west of the

Intracoastal Waterway. The next month Myrtle Beach, Horry County and B&C signed the final annexation and business park agreements. In January 2001, the Supreme Court heard Horry County Schools' appeal on the business park decision.

On September 4, 2001 – two and a half years after B&C publicly proposed the multicounty business park – the state Supreme Court upheld the circuit court in a 5-0 decision. The business park would stand and the way was clear for B&C's development plans, including the Mall of South Carolina. B&C paid the county's and city's legal bills throughout the protracted litigation.

However, in ruling that the multicounty business park law was constitutional, the Supreme Court wrote this: "We can scarcely believe the General Assembly intended, in authorizing the creation of the [multicounty business parks], to allow wealthy counties – like Horry County – to spuriously impoverish themselves at the expense of truly poor school districts. Nevertheless, the statute permits this result."

The business park law "allows the county to determine unilaterally what percentage of revenue derived from the fee in lieu to allocate to schools," the opinion stated. "Certainly nothing in the ballot question authorizing the constitutional amendment alerted voters that this result was possible."

In March 2000, the S.C. School Boards Association delivered a fifty-page report blasting economic incentives laws, which take money from public education. Using fee-in-lieu-of-taxes and special source revenue bonds within a business park "pose the greatest threat to a school district's tax base," the study said.

"The Horry County case offers a good illustration of how the current laws allow a county government to unilaterally decide how the total property tax revenues are to be distributed and ultimately to divert school funds from school purposes and keep the schools from receiving their prorated share of taxes," the report stated. Laws should be changed "so that school districts will be better protected from the involuntary loss of revenues."

A Democratic-led attempt to amend the state business park law to protect school funding died in House committee in April 2000.

On November 9, 2001, B&C received final stormwater permit from the Office of Ocean and Coastal Resource Management to begin moving earth on its 170-acre mall site. B&C broke ground on the massive project on April 3, 2003. Contrary to the dire warnings of company officials, the mall lost no tenants or partners in the protracted dispute.

Chamber of Commerce Chief Ashby Ward was at the groundbreaking for the mall, just as he had been at the groundbreaking for the Ashby Ward Official Myrtle Beach/Grand Strand Welcome Center in January. On April 13, 2003, Ward died suddenly in his home. He was 66. Twelve days later, former state Senator J.M. "Bud" Long, caught in the Operation Lost Trust corruption sting, also died. He was 76.

The FBI investigation into Horry County government and its relationship to developers produced no indictments.

Things went along much as they had at City Hall. On May 23, 2000, Mayor McBride launched into a tirade against Councilman Chuck Martino, pounding his gavel for more than a minute, until council members got up and adjourned in the middle of their agenda. "You're out of order, Mr. Martino," McBride said.

"No, sir, you are," Martino responded.

McBride gave up his weekly column in the *Myrtle Beach Herald* and began holding weekly news conferences on the sidewalk in front of City Hall. In a new attack against the staff, he charged the city manager and others were overpaid, despite figures from the Municipal Association of South Carolina that Myrtle Beach salaries were in line with comparable positions around the state. In other sidewalk announcements, the Mayor accused the council of illegally going into executive session and the city staff of illegally awarding contracts. The state Ethics Commission and Municipal Association defended the council's actions.

On August 20, 2000, *The Sun News* editorially called for Mark McBride to resign as mayor: "This city has much too much on its plate to allow further the constant bickering, nitpicking and backbiting in which the mayor has engaged, almost since the moment he was elected. . . ." the editorial said.

"[The city's] needs . . . cannot be easily resolved as long as almost each meeting becomes a 6-1 vote on most major issues against the mayor and his churlish behavior in office. The mayor fails to understand he is not always correct. The mayor fails to learn the manly art of compromise and consensus-building," wrote *The Sun News*.

"McBride can and should resign. . . . He has treated this city with little or no respect. . . . He no longer deserves to be held in voters' respect as mayor."

Rachel Broadhurst pursued her election bid to the state Supreme Court, which ruled in August 2000 that the botched city council runoff election must be held again in a citywide vote, with Broadhurst again facing Wilson Cain and Michael Chestnut. The new runoff election was set for November 7, 2000. In the interim, Broadhurst retained her council seat and Chestnut continued to attend all council meetings as an unofficial, non-voting member.

McBride put his machine to work for Chestnut. On November 7, the machine ran flawlessly. Chestnut and Cain overwhelmed Broadhurst at the polls. Broadhurst had been the leading critic on city council of B&C's multicounty business park and of Mark McBride. Her departure was a huge victory for the company and the mayor.

In 2000, Mark McBride, returned to the restaurant business, taking over a Calabash seafood house on U.S. 17. In his new restaurant venture, McBride found himself once again a tenant of the Burroughs & Chapin Co. The development company, which lost $26,000 in unpaid rent to McBride in 1996, apparently had no qualms about renting the mayor a building for this new venture.

In early 2001, 65-year-old businessman and civic leader Vernie Dove announced he would challenge Mayor McBride in the November election. Within days, McBride produced a police report showing that Dove had been arrested on a DUI charge six years earlier. Dove had beaten the charge in court, convincing a judge that he was under the influence of a medication that caused the Breathalyzer to register intoxication. Nevertheless, this first taste of mayoral politics caused Dove to fold his campaign before it had even begun.

Councilman Wayne Gray next stepped up to challenge McBride. After exchanging pledges to run a clean campaign, things turned ugly. In shades of the mysterious newspaper ad in the 1997 mayoral race, a mysterious four-page flyer appeared in thousands of Myrtle Beach mailboxes, two weeks before the election, from a group calling itself Citizens for A More Reasonable City Government. The flyer attacked Gray and council members Chuck Martino and Judy Rodman with copies of old newspaper stories. It stated the salaries of key city employees and whether those employees lived within the city limits, two of McBride's hot issues. According to *The Sun News*, there were several inaccuracies in the flyer, which endorsed McBride and a slate of candidates supported by his machine. Furthermore, the flyer violated state ethics laws, because it gave no contact name.

"The law is designed so the public will know who is making these particular statements so they can attach some validity," said Herbert Hayden, executive director of the State Ethics Commission.

McBride and other candidates endorsed by the flyer denied any knowledge of it, despite the fact that it cost thousands of dollars to print and mail.

On November 6, 2001, Mayor Mark McBride was reelected, defeating Wayne Gray with fifty-four percent of the vote. Other candidates on his slate were all defeated.

In 2002, Wayne Gray was a candidate for Horry County Council. In the days before the November election, a mysterious mailing went out to a number of residents in Gray's district, resurrecting the old charge of his misconduct with a city staff member, and included a copy of the alleged police report. No one has ever claimed responsibility for the mailing. Gray lost the election.

In January 2003, McBride announced himself a candidate for the United States Senate in 2004. Three weeks later, County Council Chairman Chad Prosser was named director of the state Department of Parks, Recreation and Tourism, in the new Mark Sanford Administration.

In May 2003, the Conway branch of the NAACP filed federal discrimination suits against Myrtle Beach, Horry County and a hotel for alleged discrimination against black bikers during the Atlantic Beach Memorial Day Bike Festival.

There came a time when I had to take the advice I had offered to so many young waitresses and bartenders. I had to leave Myrtle Beach, for my peace of mind and perhaps for Myrtle Beach's. As with any worthwhile quest, I did not find what I expected when I set out. And this is certainly not the book I thought I would write when I moved to Myrtle Beach, looking for some evidence of my youth. Events – political and personal – overwhelmed me and I fashioned what I could from the messy details of life.

I have found Charleston, South Carolina, to be more to my liking, more civil, more cultured, more cosmopolitan; not a great metropolis, by any means, but not the mining camp culture of the Grand Strand.

Still, Myrtle Beach beckons, as it always has, and I occasionally respond, driving two hours up the coast for a weekend. It is not the fountain of youth I had once hoped to find, but it is a splash of therapy at the end of a long week. Even the most reserved and cerebral among us need a little Myrtle Beach, in one form or another. It is nothing to be feared; it is nothing to be ashamed of. The trick is to know when the weekend is over.

Because we are human, we will always return to Myrtle Beach. And Myrtle Beach will always be there.

Acknowledgments

The writing of this book was a three-year undertaking, which could not have been consummated without the help of many friends and acquaintances and even a few antagonists. Many of the interviews that went into Banana Republic were as brief as a five-minute phone call. Others were lengthy, long-planned, scheduled, postponed, rescheduled, postponed and scheduled again. I have tried to mention all who shared their time and knowledge with me in formal interviews.

Aside from them, there were dozens of others who asked not to be identified. Before I cleaned out my files, their words filled scores of cocktail napkins and corners of newspapers; words that were recorded in barely legible scrawl in dimly lit venues where I would never want my mother to know I had been. I have used fictitious names to protect these folks when necessary. Most of them are guilty of nothing worse than following their dreams down the wrong path.

There were others, whose names I never learned in our brief encounters in bars and restaurants, supermarkets and parking lots, but their observations added depth and color to this narrative. To them, too, I am grateful for being in the right place at the right moment.

And to Pat Dowling, faithful gatekeeper and spinmeister for the Burroughs & Chapin Company, who never allowed me to interview a single B&C officer, I just want to say, "No hard feelings, guy."

Long before I turned my eye to Myrtle Beach, *The Sun News* was there to record life and politics along the Grand Strand. I have drawn heavily on that record and commend the scribes – past and present – for their years of hard work. Columnist Bob Bestler gets special plaudits for both his style and insight – though I did take him to task for one faux pas. Others who deserve special attention are business editor David Wrenn; Mike Sorghan, Craig Lovelace and Kevin Wiatrowski, who covered the intersection of politics, road building and the environment; Mary-Kathryn Kraft who covered the intersection of county council and the multicounty business park and Steven Jones, who covered the county council and the business park. Chandra McLean reported on North Myrtle Beach, Tanya Root covered cops and courts and Zane Wilson kept an eye on the State House crowd in Columbia.

A revolving door of reporters wrote about Myrtle Beach City Hall. They included Katie Merx, Charbonne La Belle, Kent Bernhard, Anitra Brown, Stan Choe and David Klepper. Other Sun News reporters whose bylines I got to know intimately were Isaac Bailey, Clay Barbour, Colin Burch, Natalie Burrowes, Dawn Bryant, Kathleen Dayton, Greg Fields, Elaine Gaston, Yolanda Jones, Bob Kudelka, Lenore McKenzie Morris, Helene Oliviero, Melissa Huff Salvatore, John C. Stevenson and Garrison Wells.

Research for this book began on Ocean Boulevard and so shall this alphabetical list, starting with beachwear proprietor Max Alon. Other beachwear dealers, body piercers, artists and entrepreneurs include Angie Baird, Yael Benzaken, A.V. Blake, Ed Friend, Nate Fogel, Scot Freeman, David Hallman, Brandy McKinnon, Tommy and Jackie Michaels, Kyle and Karon Mitchell, George and Sandi Parag, Gyo Park, Mark Paskuly, Buzz Plyler, Richard Rugg, Richard Russell, Victor Schama, Eddie Shasko, Fred, Eric and Michael Straube, William Tomlinson, Eddie Wilkins and Josh Woolbright. Also on the Boulevard were Rich Hair, Mike Holt and Alan Kanter of Pavilion Amusement Park and Donnie Sipes of Family Kingdom Amusement Park.

Others who were generous with their time and assistance include Robin Akel, B.J. and Wendy Bellamy, Martin Bernstein, George Bessent, Betty Bibbey, Larry Bragg, John and Shirley Brown, James Bryan III, Jimmy Chandler, Harry Charles, Harold Clardy, Beverly and Steve Clark, Terry and Michelle Coffey, Carroll Craig, Jimmy D'Angelo, Marion Joe Davis, Ed de Rhodes, Vernie Dove, Donna Dewitt, Clyde Doyle, Gene Euchler, Wallace and Charlotte Evans, Mike Fling, Al Ford, Tom Fowler, Marion Foxworth III, Curtis Fredericks, Margaret Frierson, Isla Mae Gaffney, Zola Gerald, Archie Gilchrist, Emery Gore, Ted Gragg, Sam Gray, J.P. "Beaver" Greenway, Randy Hardee, Terri Hooks, Sally Howard, Reuben Hyman, Olge Valeryevich Isayev, John Jenrette, Deborah Boggs Johnson, Vance and Helen Kinlaw, Harry Love, Bill Nagel, Kathi Patrick, Deborah Pittman-Page, Anton Poster, Linda Robertson, Steve Sadler, Tom Salvatore, Eleanor Schiller, Doc Sealy, Robert Siegel, John Skeeters, Ernie Stallworth, Myra Starnes, Barry Thigpen, Mike Todd, Henry Thompson, Jack Thompson, George Trakas, Rayford Vereen, Jeff Weathers, Randall Wells and Randolph Wilson.

Among Myrtle Beach city employees to be recognized and thanked are the staff of Chapin Memorial Library, with very special thanks to Lee Oates and Kathy Wiggins; the elected officials of Myrtle Beach, including Mayor Mark McBride and council members Rachel Broadhurst, Wayne Gray, Susan Grissom Means, Michael Chestnut and Randal Wallace; Chief Warren Gall, Lt. Jay Holder, Cpl. Mike Hull and Cpl. Brenda Christie of the police department; the staff of the City of Myrtle Beach, including manager Tom Leath, public information officer Mark Kruea, planning director Jack Walker, and planning staff David Fuller, Diane Moskow-McKenzie, Kelly Mezzapelli and Allan Blum, attorney Joe Wettlin, clerk Joan Grove; zoning director Mandy Todd; public works director James Ewing III and director of Myrtle Beach Convention Center, Steve Jones.

In North Myrtle Beach: Mayor Phil Tilghman and former Mayor Bryan Floyd; city engineer Kevin Blayton. Also, Briarcliffe Acres Mayor Dot Herron.

A number of other public and semi-public officials must also be singled out. They include the staff of the Myrtle Beach office of Ocean and Coastal Resource Management; Mark Bara and Jamie Dozier at the S.C. Department of Natural Resources; Stephen Greene and Fred Hunter of the Myrtle Beach Area Chamber of Commerce; Horry County public information officers Cheryl Henry and Lisa Hammersley Bouricer, former county administrator Linda Angus, county councilman Ray Brown, county emergency planning director Paul Whitten; county planner Danny Taylor; chief of building inspections David Jacobs; and county auditor Lois Eargle.

Also Stewart Pabst and James D'Angina of Horry County Museum; Eddie Lott of the S.C. Children's Museum; Pat Creswell of Burroughs & Chapin Art Museum; Margie Willis and Michael Burgess of Community Coalition of Horry County; Diane Scroggins of the Theater of the Republic; Mickey McCamish and Deborah Hesla of Golf Holiday and Terri Causey of Entertainment Holiday; Martha Hunn of the Myrtle Beach Area Hospitality Association; and state Representative Vida Miller.

Also Mary Ann Jacobs and Mort Kohn of Time Warner Cable;

Barbara Pavilack of Wings Stores; Diane Slotnick of Waccamaw Factory Shoppes and Deb Bramlett of Myrtle Beach Factory Stores; Samantha Burns and Kristin Wilkins of Algonquin Coffee House; Frances Hartdige and Michael Carlos at Street Reach Ministry; Coleman Turner, James Hewitt and other members of Jericho March; Ann Conlon and Barbara Plews of the Meher Baba Center, with special apologies to Ms. Plews for forgetting to remove my sandals on my first visit to Saraja Reading Room.

At Coastal Carolina University: Peter Barr, Tom Secrest, Michael Gilbert, Susan Libes, Dan Abel, Jack Riley, Andy Hedrick and Anne Monk. At Duke University: Orrin Pilkey and Linda George.

For editing, proofreading, design and other assistance I wish to thank Beth Littlejohn, Julie Burnett and Laura Ingram; for the use of her beautiful art on the jacket, Lorna Effler Savizpour; for photography, Jack Thompson and Nancy Santos; for logistical support, Diane Schroeder; for moral support and marketing advice, Karen Sundstrom; for building and maintaining the Frontline Press Web site, Lynn Berry Bernstein, for building my office internals, Jim Miller..

To those I forgot to mention – and I'm sure there are some – you know who you are and you know how much you meant to this project. Thanks to one and all.

Selected Bibliography

Barnes, Jay, *North Carolina's Hurricane History*, University of North Carolina Press, 1995.

Brady, John, *Bad Boy – The Life and Politics of Lee Atwater*, Addison Wesley Publishing Co., Inc., Reading, Mass., 1996.

Burroughs, Franklin G., "Returning Home to Rivertown," *Preservation Magazine*, September-October, 2000, pp. 26-33.

Carter, Dan T., *The Politics of Rage – George Wallace, The Origins of the New Conservatism and the Transformation of American Politics*, Simon & Schuster, New York, N.Y., 1995.

Carter, W. Horace, *Jimmy D'Angelo and Myrtle Beach Golf*, Atlantic Publishing Co. Tabor City, N.C., 1991.

Carter, W. Horace, *Virus of Fear*, Atlantic Publishing Co., Tabor City, N.C., 1991.

Cash, W.J., The *Mind of the South*, Alfred A. Knopf, Inc., New York, N.Y., 1941.

Dean, Cornelia, *Against the Tide – The Battle for America's Beaches*, Columbia University Press, New York, N.Y., 1999.

Edgar, Walter, *South Carolina – A History*, University of South Carolina Press, Columbia, S.C., 1998.

Egerton, John, *Speak Now Against the Day – The Generation Before the Civil Rights Movement in the South*, University of North Carolina Press, Chapel Hill, N.C., 1994.

Floyd, Blanche W., *Tales Along the Grand Strand of South Carolina*, Bandit Books, Winston-Salem, N.C. 1996.

Floyd, Blanche W., *Tales Along the Kings Highway of South Carolina*, Bandit Books, Winston-Salem, N.C., 1999.

Gragg, Rod, *The Illustrated History of Horry County*, Burroughs & Chapin Co., Myrtle Beach, S.C., 1994.

Gragg, Rod, *Planters, Pirates and Patriots*, Rutledge Hill Press, Nashville, Tenn., 1985.

Harwell, Richard B., *The Confederate Reader*, Dorset Press, New York, N.Y., 1992.

Hopkinson, Tom and Dorothy, *Much Silence: The Life and Work of Meher Baba*, Meher House Publications, Bombay, 1982.

Jones, Lewis Pinckney, *Stormy Petrel*, University of South Carolina Press, Columbia, S.C., 1973.

Lancek, Lena and Gideon Bosker, *The Beach – The History of Paradise on Earth*, Viking Press, New York, N.Y., 1998.

Lennon, Gerred, et. al., *Living with the South Carolina Coast*, Duke University Press, Durham, N.C., 1996.

Lewis, Catherine, *Horry County, South Carolina – 1730-1992*, University of South Carolina Press, Columbia, S.C., 1998.

Marscher, Bill and Fran, *The Great Sea Island Storm of 1893*, Authors Choice Press, San Jose, Cal., 2001.

Mileti, Dennis, *Disasters by Design – A Reassessment of Natural Hazards in the United States*, Joseph Henry Press, Washington, D.C., 1999.

Oliphant, Mary C. Simms, *The History of South Carolina*, Laidlaw Brothers, Publishers, River Forest, Ill., 1964.

Phillips, Kevin, *The Emerging Republican Majority*, Arlington House, New Rochelle, N.Y., 1969.

Plotz, David, "Busted Flush: South Carolina's Video-Poker Operators Run A Political Machine," *Harper's Magazine*, August, 1999, pp. 63-72.

Tomsen, Stephen, Homel, R. and Thommeny, J., 1991, "The Causes of Public Violence: Situational 'versus' Other Factors in Drinking Related Assaults," in *Australian Violence: Contemporary Perspectives*, eds. D. Chapell, P. Grabosky and H. Strang, Australian Institute of Criminology, Canberra, 177-193.

Wilson, Charles Wilson and William Ferris (Editors), *Encyclopedia of Southern Culture*, University of North Carolina Press, Chapel Hill, N.C., 1989.

Woodward, C. Vann, *Origins of the New South – 1877-1913*, Louisiana State University Press, Baton Rouge, La., 1951.

Index